MACQUARIE AUSTRALIAN SLANG DICTIONARY

COMPLETE & UNABRIDGED

MACQUARIE

cack 1. excrement. An old word going back to medieval times. A charming Aussie insult is the classic, *Go dip your eye in hot cocky cack!* 2. to defecate; to soil with excrement. *The baby cacked its nappy.* To **c[illegible]k the corduroys** is to be sca[illegible]les. 3. a person or thing tha[illegible] funny; something tha[illegible] cack yourself laughi[illegible]sly good time. As, *That [illegible]ack* or *This movie's a c[illegible]*

good sort 1. a spunky woman. Aussie blokes have been referring to delectable sheilas as good sorts since at least the 1940s. In recent years the term has been adopted by women to refer to spunky men. 2. a reliable and likeable bloke; [illegible] decent chap. This meaning is [illegible] the wane nowadays.

bike 1. a derogat[illegible] woman who sleep[illegible] is, everyone 'ride[illegible] Us[illegible] restricted to a ce[illegible] sphere[illegible] operations, as t[illegible] **office bike** [illegible] the **town bike**. Aussie slang since the 1940s. 2. If you say to someone **On your bike!** you are telling them to leave. However, to **get off your bike** is to become furious, to really lose control.

c[illegible] [illegible]ussie slang this is a real littl[illegible] word with many uses. Y[illegible]our occupation or job: *W[illegible] caper are you in?* Or, it can refer t[illegible]ehaviour: *There was singing an[illegible]lancing and all that kind of cape[illegible]* Finally, caper can merely refer to whatever is going [illegible]n: *What's the caper?*

AUSTRALIAN SLANG DICTIONARY

COMPLETE & UNABRIDGED

GENERAL EDITOR
JAMES LAMBERT

Published by The Macquarie Library Pty Ltd
The Macquarie Dictionary, Macquarie University, NSW 2109 Australia

First published 2004

Cover design: Jeremy Nicholson
Typeset by Macmillan India Ltd, Bangalore-25

Printed in Australia by McPherson's Printing Group

National Library of Australia Cataloguing-in-Publication Data

Macquarie Australian slang dictionary.

ISBN 1 876429 52 6.

1. English language – Australia – Slang – Dictionaries.
I. Lambert, James, 1965– .

427.99403

CONTENTS

FOREWORD

Susan Butler
Publisher
Macquarie Dictionary

The first edition of the *Macquarie Dictionary*, published in 1981, set out the aims of the dictionary – 'to present a set of entries for a comprehensive word list in which all the pronunciations, all the spellings, and all the definitions of meaning are taken from the use of English in Australia'. This was its initial brief and this is what the dictionary has continued to do through three major editions and a number of subsidiary dictionaries.

The *Macquarie Australian Slang Dictionary* provides an opportunity to focus on the colloquial aspects of Australian English, encompassing everything from the mildly informal to the downright obscene. The value of the dictionary as a descriptive tool is dependent on its accuracy, so this dictionary has trawled through the jargons of different occupations and activities, the slang of different age groups and different communities, and the expressions that currently find favour with today's fashions. So much of slang is to do with setting a certain tone, capturing a style, and indicating one's position in the scheme of things.

This collection is a nice balance of the old with the new, of words and phrases that we regard as Australiana along with the newest additions to the slang lexicon. There is much to amuse, as well as shock. What matters is that this lively selection offers a convincing self-image of who we are as a community today, of what our interests and attitudes are. At that point a book that is a source of entertainment is also functioning as a cultural text.

This latest addition to the Macquarie stable of dictionaries carries on the Macquarie tradition of faithfully recording our language so that we might better know ourselves.

INTRODUCTION

James Lambert
General Editor
Macquarie Australian Slang Dictionary

The words *Aussie* and *slang* go together like *swagman* and *billy*, like *bloke* and *sheila*, like *fair dinkum* and *true blue*. Call it Strine, call it Ocker, call it whatever you like, but the way we speak is at the very heart of our national identity. We are a relaxed country with a healthy dismissiveness of authority and formality, so it stands to reason that the informality of slang has burgeoned here like nowhere else. In fact, you'd have to be bloody un-Australian to not use slang, to not like slang, to not love slang. This book is a celebration of all that is bonzer in the Australian idiom, from the quaint to the hair-curlingly vulgar (so be warned – these pages contain some terms that may be pretty offensive).

But before we start, let's have a bit of a look at just what Australian slang really is.

Beginnings

Australian slang has one of the longest traditions of any variety of English. It is fair to say that Aussie slang began the very day the ships of the First Fleet left the docks of the Old Dart and set out on the arduous journey Down Under.

The convicts, settlers, soldiers and sailors aboard spoke a mish-mash of differing dialects and versions of British working class slang – all of which were mixed together in a unique medley during the long voyage to the remote shores of distant New Holland.

Words spoken on that trip would have included the familiar and enduring *bloke* and *booze*, the obsolescent *chiack* 'to tease', *rum* meaning 'bad' (which survives in the Tasmanian colloquialism *rum'un* 'a character'), probably *conk* 'the nose', and most definitely the ubiquitous Great Australian Adjective *bloody*.

Much is made of our convict beginnings, especially by those who wish to denigrate us, and it is well established that members of the criminal fraternity did continue their former habits in their new land. One word which began in the shadows of life is the quintessential Australianism *bludger*. This is a shortening of the term *bludgeoner* which referred to a prostitute's pimp who carried a bludgeon to keep his women in line, and no doubt to assist in enforcing payment, or else to out-and-out rob mug clients. The bludgeoner was a cowardly bastard who *bludged* off women and the modern word *bludger* still carries the vitriol of its original application. Other words of convict or underworld origin are *cove*, *nark* 'an informer', *beak* 'a judge', and *dunny*, the modern descendant of the earlier *dunnekin*.

Dialect Influence

Throughout 19th-century Britain – before the days of telecommunications – language changed strikingly from region to region and it was possible to detect where a person came from by the way they spoke English. These different versions of the language are known as regional dialects. During the colonial period large numbers of dialect speakers migrated to Australia, each bringing with them a store of words, phrases and expressions from their own locality – and it is to these that a number of modern Australian slang words owe their origin. Examples include *fair dinkum*, *chook*, *dag*, *billy*, *burl*, *fossick*, *larrikin*, *skerrick* and *tacker*.

Irish English is of course just another British dialect and Australia saw no small number of immigrants from the Emerald Isle, which fact can be seen today in the words *barrack*, *gob*, *shenanigans* and the very Australian second person plural pronoun *youse* – a variation of the typical Irish *yez*, which owes its existence to the fact that Gaelic had separate forms for the singular and the plural second person pronoun.

Aboriginal Influence

When the first white settlers arrived there were over 300 separate languages spoken by the traditional owners of this country. Sadly most of these languages are now extinct. Naturally the colonists borrowed many words from Aboriginal languages, especially for unfamiliar flora and fauna – *budgerigar, dingo, kangaroo, koala, bindi-eye and yabby* – and for items of traditional Aboriginal culture – *boomerang, humpy*, etc. In terms of slang, a number of Aboriginal words were taken and then given slightly different meanings. Thus the *dilly* which was a traditional Aboriginal bag made from native grass twine, in slang becomes a general term for any small bag for bits and bobs. *Gibber* was an Aboriginal word for stone and but became kids' slang for a pebble or rock for chucking at other kids. Other notable examples are *bogey* 'a swimming hole', *bung* 'no good', *cooee*, *yakka* 'hard work' and *yabber* 'to talk', and from Aboriginal pidgin English we get *the big smoke* and possibly also *jumbuck*.

Native-born Slang

As change is a natural and inevitable part of language, so Australian English continued to develop on its own and in its own way – a new shoot cut off, as it were, from its parent plant a world away in the northern hemisphere. Part of this natural growth was the creation of new slang terms. Unique Australian coinages are legion, such as *battler, beaut, bonzer, bottler, chunder, digger, dill, drongo, footy, franger, G'day, grouse, hoon, joey, middy, norks, ocker, perv, ropeable, rort, sanger, schooner, sheila, skite, spruik* and *wowser*, just to name a few. There are also countless slang phrases, many of which demonstrate the Aussie love of humour, such as *a shingle short, happy little Vegemite, London to a brick, map of Tassie, no flies on you, not much chop, no worries, like a shag on a rock, shoot through like a Bondi tram, dry as a dead dingo's donger* and *I hope your chooks turn into emus and kick your dunny down.*

Cockney and Rhyming Slang

Cockney is the name for the dialect peculiar to the East End of London and is sometimes incorrectly regarded as the precursor to Australian English. In fact, the amount of Aussie slang that can be directly attributed to Cockney is next to nothing. Still, it was in London's East End that rhyming slang first appeared, way back in the 1840s. This new slang phenomenon swept through Britain and within the space of a few decades had made its way to Australia. Very few of the original Cockney rhyming slang terms are still in existence, two notable exceptions being *plates of meat* 'feet' and *elephants* (short for *elephant's trunk*) 'drunk'.

In Australia, the inherent humour of rhyming slang caused it to take off and very soon Aussies were coining their own rhyming slang terms. These include *babbling brook* 'cook', *bag of fruit* 'suit', *billy lid* 'kid', *butcher's hook* 'crook', *Captain Cook* 'look', *Dad 'n' Dave* 'shave', *Reg Grundies* 'undies', *horse's hoof* 'poof', *Joe Blake* 'snake', *Noah's ark* 'shark', *optic nerve* 'perv', *septic tank* 'yank', *trey bits* 'tits', *Warwick Farms* 'arms' and *woolly woofter* 'poofter'.

Part of the fun of rhyming slang is to try it out on unsuspecting people and see if they can work out the rhyme. The guessing game is further enhanced by the dropping of the rhyme word – thus calling a shark a *Noah* requires a knowledge of the full form *Noah's ark*. This contrivance has led to the interesting situation where some words have lost their rhyme word entirely and are commonly used by the general public in complete ignorance of the fact that they are using rhyming slang.

How many people know that the word *jack* meaning 'a venereal disease' is short for *jack in the box* – rhyming slang for 'pox'? Similarly, when someone sticks their tongue out and blows a *raspberry*, do they understand that *raspberry tart* is rhyming slang for 'fart'? Other examples are *chunder*, short for *Chunder Loo* (an old cartoon character) which is rhyming slang for 'spew', and *Pommy*, short for *pomegranate*, rhyming slang for 'immigrant'. To these might be added the phrase *to give someone the flick*, which is short for *flick pass*, rhyming slang for 'arse' – that is, to give someone the arse. And if people knew the missing rhyme to the terms *berk* and *dropkick*, well, they may not be so keen to use those words! (You can look them up in this dictionary!)

Regionalisms

A regionalism is a word that is used only in a restricted area, and there are quite a few of them in Australia. In 2001, Macquarie Dictionary, in conjunction with the ABC, established a website – Australian Word Map (www.abc.net.au/wordmap) – devoted to collecting and preserving regionalisms from around the country.

As websites go, Australian Word Map has been an enormous success. It was by far the most extensive survey of Australian regional English ever undertaken, resulting in around 3500 words recorded from thousands of correspondents from around the country. It uncovered for the first time untold numbers of Aussie words and phrases that had never been recorded by any other dictionary writer or glossarist in the history of Australian lexicography – from 1812 to the present. It has a mind-bogglingly stunning array of fascinating material, contributed from fair dinkum, ridgy-didge Aussies, the country over. Naturally, Australian Word Map was a rich source of material for the *Macquarie Australian Slang Dictionary*.

US Influence

Perhaps one of the greatest concerns for lovers of Australian slang is the seemingly endless encroachment by American slang. At any given point in time there are a number of piquant examples, generally adopted by the younger generations, that make the blood of all ridgy-didge blokes and sheilas boil. In the 1960s it was *cool* and *groovy*, and in the 1980s it was *rad* and *humungous*, and, at present it's terms like *sick* meaning 'excellent' and *skanky ho* 'a disreputable woman'. But it is not as bad as some people like to make out.

The influence of American slang has been felt since the days of the gold rush, way back in the 1860s. In fact, the term *bushwhacker* – which virtually screams 'Australian' – is in origin an Americanism! Further words from the US were picked up during both World Wars, and then, with the advent of rock'n'roll, TV, and finally the internet, the floodgates of cultural imperialism have been irrevocably opened.

Still, despite all this, all is not lost – Australian English is in no real danger of being overtaken by American English. The basic reason is that once an American word is adopted into Australian speech it immediately becomes naturalised. Take for instance the terms *ciggie* 'cigarette', *clobber* 'to hit', *dough* 'money', *floozy* 'a loose woman', *jerk* 'a fool', *knock back* 'to refuse', *mole* 'a spy', *on the blink* 'malfunctioning', *ripsnorter* 'amazing thing', *shack up* 'to live together', *suds* 'beer', *wino* 'a drunkard' and *worrywart* 'an inveterate worrier' – who would dare to question the place of these in Aussie slang? Yet each and every one of these began life in the US!

Even the recently adopted word *sick*, meaning 'excellent', has been Australianised. In the US teenagers say *way sick*, but Aussie kids say *fully sick*. The use of *fully* – as an intensifier – is a uniquely Australian invention.

In just which country a certain slang term was invented is an esoteric fact known only to specialists in the field of etymology. Who would guess that *get a wriggle on* is Australian, but *get a wiggle on* is American? How is one to know that *fag* meaning 'homosexual' is originally US slang, but *fag* meaning 'cigarette' is British? Most people think that *Al Capone*, rhyming slang for 'phone', is American, when actually it is an Australianism! In fact, when people are asked to say whether a certain slang term is originally British, American or Australian they tend to get it right about 33% of the time. In other words, people generally have no idea. So before slagging off at some term as a hideous Americanism one might do well to make sure it really is one! Of course, in the new *Macquarie Australian Slang Dictionary* great attention has been paid to this area and the ultimate origin of many slang terms has been indicated – especially those terms that seem to be quintessentially Australian.

But leaving the question of origins aside, people should not forget that new Australian slang is being coined every day – and this more than anything else is what keeps the American influx at bay. Recent additions to the Australian slang vocabulary include *doof* 'dance music', *feral* 'New Agey conservationist', *filth(y)* 'excellent, wonderful', *bowlo* 'a bowling club', *pov* 'poor' and, as a counterfoil to the term *wog*, the 'wogs' themselves now call Aussies *Anglos* or *skips*.

Another area in which Aussies have been particularly productive is in slang names for those tight, revealing, men's swimmers. Witness *budgie smugglers* – no one but an Aussie would have come up with that one! But they also get called *cock jocks, dick daks, sluggos* and *toolies* – just to name a few (the full set of synonyms can be found within the body of the dictionary).

Basically, Aussies can't help themselves. They just have to come up with new slang terms – it's the Australian way – bugger the Yanks and Poms.

Further solace might also be gained from the fact that some Australianisms are making their way to America! The irrepressible Steve Irwin has taught them all to say *Crikey!* And there are reports that phrases such as *no worries, it's my shout, onya* and *fair dinkum*, are now being used in downtown USA. How long will it be before they'll be saying *root your boot, silly as a two-bob watch* and *don't come the raw prawn with me*? Don't hold your breath, I suspect.

The Future

The *Macquarie Australian Slang Dictionary* is an up-to-date account of Australian slang, warts and all. But what of the future? Where are we heading? Well, dear readers, those are questions that only you can answer! It is entirely up to Aussies how their language will develop. What about those dinky-di Aussie words that are dying out? Well, if you are unhappy that you never hear *cobber* and *bonzer* any more – then get out there and start saying it. If you do, others will follow. If you don't give a rats – then so be it. You can't control language by legislation, education, or by whingeing about it – language is what you say, on a day-to-day basis. Speak and ye shall preserve!

Acknowledgements

I would like to thank David Downie, Chris Harrison, Tom Dalzell, Jesse Sheidlower, my co-workers at Macquarie Dictionary, all the contributors to Australian Word Map, and my beautiful partner in all things, Jane McGettigan.

A

ABC **1.** an Australian-born Chinese. In the US it stands for an American-born Chinese. **2.** a derogatory term for a white Australian. Standing for *Aboriginal Bum Cleaner*.

Abo a racist term for an Australian Aboriginal. Been around since the 1900s. Formerly in common use by whites but now taboo, at least by non-racists.

Aboriginal suitcase a racist term for a cask of wine. Also called an **Aboriginal briefcase**.

acca a university academic. Aussie slang since the 1970s. Also spelt **acker**.

Acca Dacca a nickname for the undisputed kings of Aussie rock, AC/DC.

AC/DC bisexual.

ace **1.** excellent, outstanding, terrific. *The kids think he's ace. That's the acest haircut.* **2.** to do something with ease. *He aced the exam.* **3.** in golf, to get a hole in one. *She aced the third hole.*

acid **1.** the drug LSD, which was a big hit with the hippies in the 60s but now is popular among the trendy clubbing and dance set. One doesn't 'take' acid, one 'drops' it. **2.** a different sort of acid this – if you **put the acid on** someone you are trying to pressure them into doing something they are reluctant to do, especially to come across with sexual favours.

acid head a habitual user of LSD.

ack emma the morning. From military signals code for *a.m.*

acker **1.** a pimple. Derived from that bane of teenage life – the dreaded *acne*. **2.** a playing marble. **3.** a testicle. *Got kicked in the ackers.* **4.** an academic.

acre the backside – so called because it is an expanse. *He was six axe handles across the acre.* Aussie slang since the 1960s. Also spelt **acher**.

action potentially sexually available people. Or by extension, what they have to offer. A bit of a wank word generally used by someone talking things up rather than actually getting any.

act the goat to behave foolishly.

Adam famous first man of the Bible. Used in the slang expressions **to not know someone from Adam**, that is, to not know them at all, and **since Adam was a pup**, from time immemorial.

Adrian Quist Aussie rhyming slang for 'pissed', that is, drunk. The Adrian so immortalised was a famous Australian doubles tennis player.

aerial ping-pong a derogatory term for Australian Rules football used by followers of the Rugby codes. Used derisively since the 1960s.

aesthetically challenged a mincing way of saying 'Ugly!'

affluence of inkahol the deleterious effects of alcohol on the cognitive processes.

Afghani cricket a cross between cricket and baseball played by detainees at the Woomera detention centre.

after dark rhyming slang for 'shark'.

after grog bog a particularly noisome excrement produced the morning after the night before. Abbreviated to **AGB**. Also called the **post grog bog** (or **PGB**), the **beer grog**, the **grog bog**, or simply the **groggy**. Keep away!

afternoon delight sexual intercourse in the afternoon.

aftie a variant of **arvo**, the afternoon.

agate **1.** a playing marble. **2.** a testicle. Also spelt **aggot**.

AGB an **after grog bog** (see entry).

aggers aggressive. *She was aggers to the max.*

aggie **1.** a playing marble. Also known as an **aggle**. **2.** a student studying agriculture. **3.** agricultural pipe. **4.** an agapanthus.

aggro the Australian way of saying 'aggressive' or 'aggression'. Actually, also the British way of saying it, and, it's even starting to be picked up by the Yanks. First appeared in the 1980s.

agricultural shot in cricket, a wild slog of the ball, usually over square leg or mid wicket. So called as it is the sort of shot a farmer might make.

A-grouper in Broken Hill this means the locals, as opposed to the **B-groupers**.

air **1.** in skating, basketball, and the like, the amount of height gained when getting airborne, usually in a complimentary phrase like *Great air!* To **get air** is to become well airborne. **2.** in surfing, a controlled manoeuvre in which the rider and board become airborne.

air guitar the pretence of playing an imaginary guitar: *He was alone in his room playing air guitar.* Originally only a thing done by kids who couldn't afford guitars (or were too lazy to learn how to play), but now well in the domain of adults as evidenced by that prize celebration of geekhood – the **air guitar competition**.

air head an empty-headed, brainless person.

air kiss a formalised kiss in which the cheeks sometimes touch but never the lips.

air quotes the twitching of the upheld index and middle fingers of both hands to mark out a spoken word as a quotation or otherwise distance oneself from the word. Greatly reviled by many people.

AJ some jerk who's in the army. The initials stand for *Army Jerk*. Generally used by civvies living around army bases.

Albany doctor in wheat-belt areas of WA, a southerly sea breeze that blows after a hot day.

Al Capone rhyming slang for 'phone'. Interestingly, Aussie slang – not American.

alibi a cryptolanguage used by schoolchildren in which normal words are modified by adding into each syllable the sounds 'ullab'; thus *hug* becomes *hullabug*; *You are a pig* becomes *Yullaboo ullabar ullaba pullabig*. Also called **nullabat**. Similar secret languages are **arpie-darpie**, **aygo-paygo**, **obo language**, **pig Latin** and **rechtub kelat**.

the Alice Alice Springs, the capital of the Red Centre.

alko a heavy drinker; an alcoholic. Also, **alkie**. One of the few words that has both an *-o* and an *-ie* form.

all alone like a country dunny on your lonesome; totally alone.

all behind like Barney's bull having a fat arse.

alley **1.** a playing marble. Probably derived from *alabaster*. Allies are carried by schoolkids in an **alley bag**. To **make your alley good** is to redeem yourself or otherwise improve your situation. To **toss in your alley** is to die or give up. **2.** a two-up school. **3.** a horse's position at the barrier. *He went to the front from a wide alley.*

alley oop an exclamation of encouragement when giving someone a leg-up. From French *allez hop!*

all over bar the shouting finished with, for all intents and purposes. Aussie slang since the 1950s.

all over the place like a madwoman's breakfast in complete confusion and disarray. Some would have it that it should be **all over the place like a madwoman's custard**, still other's say **knitting**, or **lunchbox**, or **washing**, or even **piss**. Which shows an amazing versatility in your average madwoman.

all over the shop confused; in disarray; not knowing whether you are coming or going.

all piss and wind wordy but insincere; all talk but no action. A fuller version is **all piss and wind like the barber's cat**.

all prick and ribs skinny, emaciated. A fuller version is **all prick and ribs like a drover's dog**.

all yack and no yakka all talk but no action.

also-ran in horseracing, an unplaced horse in a race. Hence, a dud or nonentity.

alterna- a prefix meaning alternative, that is, unconventional in a good way, not an ordinary or run-of-the-mill example of something. Such as *alternababe, alternateens, alternadom, alternarock.*

amber fluid a beer lover's word for beer. Also called **amber liquid**, **amber nectar** or just simply **amber**.

ambo an ambulance or an ambulance officer. Aussie slang since the 1990s.

American a china playing marble with red, white and blue colouring. Sometimes called a **good American**, as opposed to an **ordinary American**, a glass marble. Aussie kids' slang common in the 1950s and 60s.

American screwdriver a hammer!

ammo ammunition. If you have a really low opinion of someone you can say **I wouldn't use you for ammo at a shit fight**.

amp to be excited, thrilled or energetically enthusiastic. *Keep amping!*

amyl the chemical amyl nitrite, used as a sexual stimulant.

anal **1.** obsessively concerned with neatness and order. *Don't be so anal – just whack 'em in the box.* This is Sigmund Freud's great contribution to the vocabulary of slang. In psychoanalysis the 'anal stage' is one in which infants learn to control bowel movement. According to the theory, an 'anal personality' develops because of frustration with toilet training. **2.** anal sex. *She enjoys a bit of anal.*

anal floss G-strings or other items of skimpy underwear that ride up the bum cleft. Also called **bum floss**.

anally retentive excessively meticulous and rigid about minor details that everyone else thinks are unimportant. A person so afflicted is known as an **anal retent**, or simply a **retent**. See the entry for **anal** for an explanation of these terms.

anal probe **1.** a mythical piece of alien technology used to probe the anal passages of abductees. **2.** a type of dildo for the anus.

anchors the brakes, as in *hit the anchors* or *throw the anchors out.*

and that et cetera; a common yobbish Aussie shorthand for 'and stuff like that'. *We were just hangin' around an' that.* Been around at least since the 1930s.

angel dust the illegal drug phencyclidine – originally used as a human and veterinary anaesthetic, but discontinued due to overwhelming negative side effects. However, now used recreationally.

angel gear a vehicle's neutral gear when used in the dangerous practice of coasting. So called because of the high likelihood of your becoming an angel.

Anglo a derogatory term for an Australian of Anglo-Saxon or Anglo-Celtic descent used by Australians of other ethnic backgrounds. First coming to prominence in the 1980s, this word, along with **skip**, was coined as a counterfoil to **wog**.

angst out to suffer an anxiety attack; to really worry.

angsty anxious.

animal **1.** a vulgar, disgusting person. **2.** a highly-sexed person; a real goer. **3.** among used car dealers, a very dirty car.

ankle a loathsomely crass term for someone you don't like – the explanation being that 'an ankle is three feet lower than a cunt.'

ankle biter a young child. Generally thought to be Australian, but recorded from as early as 1963 in the US, so it's probably an Americanism. Similar to the **rug rat**.

anothery another drink of beer or other alcoholic drink. Aussie slang since the 1960s.

any Wee Georgie Wood? rhyming slang for 'Any good?' From the name of a famous midget who stood a staggering 4ft 9in (145 cm) tall.

Anzac **1.** a soldier from Australia or New Zealand. Originally referred only to Gallipoli campaigners, (the Australian and New Zealand Army Corps), then to all World War I soldiers, and later extended to any Aussie or Kiwi soldiers. It is interesting to note that at the time the word first came about (1915) acronyms were very scarce things. It just wasn't common practice to make words out of the initial letters of a phrase.

It was the telegraphers who first started to use the shorthand ANZAC – saving themselves many dots and dashes, and no doubt valuable time. The troops quickly picked the term up and started using it to refer to themselves and to coin names for things in their immediate surrounds, as the **Anzac button**, a bent nail used as a button substitute, **Anzac soup**, a shell hole polluted by a corpse, **Anzac stew**, boiled water with a single bacon rind, and **Anzac wafer**, a hard biscuit issued instead of bread – 'one of the most durable materials used in the war'. A sadly telling collection of slang phrases if ever there was one. On a more positive note we have the term **Anzac spirit** or the **spirit of Anzac**, in other words, courage, tenacity and sacrifice. **2.** an Anzac biscuit, an Australian culinary treat beyond compare. *I took a few Anzacs for morning tea.*

aorta Strine for 'they ought to'. If you don't know what Strine is, you can look it up at the entry for **Strine**.

APC a quick perfunctory wash from a bucket of water (often cold). From the phrase *Arm Pits and Crotch*, punning on the brand name of a once popular headache powder.

ape **1.** a large, uncouth, boorish man. **2.** to **go ape over** something is to go crazy about it. Also, **go apeshit**.

ape hangers the handlebars of a bike or motorbike that rise above the level of the rider's shoulders.

the Apple Isle Tasmania, famed for its apple orchards. A Tasmanian is an **Apple Islander**.

apples okay, all right. When you say **she's apples** or **she'll be apples** you mean all is well or all will come out well. Aussie slang since the 1940s. It has been suggested that this is from rhyming slang *apples and spice* 'nice' – but this explanation seems a bit weak. When you say 'she'll be apples', you're not trying to say 'she'll be nice' – that just doesn't make sense.

apples and pears rhyming slang for 'stairs'. Originally British.

apple sauce rhyming slang for 'horse'.

apricots the testicles.

aqua bog **1.** a bogan who surfs, or who visits the beach. **2.** an excrement done while swimming in the ocean.

arc up **1.** to become upset; to bridle or become livid with anger; to 'flare up' – like a welder's torch. **2.** to light a cigarette.

arfie-darfie a cryptolanguage used by schoolchildren. For an explanation see **arpie-darpie**.

Argie an Argentinian.

argue the toss to dispute a decision or command. Originally British, but common in Australian since the 1950s.

argy-bargy argument. *Right, that's enough argy-bargy from you two!*

aristotle rhyming slang for 'bottle'. From Cockney. Hence, in Australia, through a convoluted process, also rhyming slang for 'arse'. The logic goes: aristotle = bottle; bottle and glass = arse; so, aristotle = arse! Sometimes shortened to **aris** or **aras**.

arks an Aussie working-class way of saying 'ask'. *I arksed him to do it tomorrow.*

arpie-darpie a cryptolanguage used by schoolchildren in which normal words are modified by adding into each syllable the sound 'arp'; thus *hug* becomes *harpug*; *You are a pig* becomes *Yarpu arpar arpa parpig*. Kids have been diligent in coming up with lots of alternative names for this secret language, including **arfie-darfie**, **arpie-garpie**, **arple-darple**, **arp language**, or, simply, **arp**. It was also curiously called **kerosene language**. For other similar secret languages, see **alibi**, **aygo-paygo**, **obo language**, **pig Latin** and **rechtub kelat**.

arple-darple another name for **arpie-darpie**.

arse **1.** the rump, bottom, buttocks, posterior. What the Americans call an **ass** – the asses! Actually, *arse* is one of the true and original Anglo-Saxon four-letter words, though in Anglo-Saxon, spoken over a thousand years ago, it was only three letters *ærs* or *ars*. In the US the traditional spelling *arse* is used as a euphemism. To **sit on your arse** is to laze around doing nothing when there is work to do. If you want to do some work, then you need to **get off your arse**. And if you get stuck into it, you'll be **working your arse off**. If you crawl to the boss then you are **up his arse**, but if you get jack of him, you might say something like, 'You can bloody well shove the job **up your arse!**' If the **arse drops out of** something, then it has failed dismally. **2.** a contemptible person; a fool or jerk. Aussie slang since the 1940s. **3.** your body or person; yourself. *Move your arse out of here*. Originally British slang of the 17th century. **4.** impudence or hide. *What arse!* Aussie slang since the 1950s. Hence, good luck, as opposed to skill. *Can you believe the arse of him?* **5.** dismissal from work; rejection. *She's given me the arse*. Aussie slang since the 1950s.

arse about in reverse or illogical order. *He did the exercise completely arse about.*

arse around to act like a fool; to waste time.

arse bandit a homophobe's term for a gay man, clearly arising from subconscious fear of male rape. See **dung puncher** for a bunch of synonyms.

arse end the tail end; the base.

arse end of the world a thoroughly hideous place; a hole. Even worse is the **arse end of the universe**.

arse-fuck to sodomise. Hence, **arse-fucker**, a sodomite.

arsehole **1.** the anus. If you've got something **coming out your arsehole**, then you have a superabundance of it. **2.** a contemptible person, especially a male; a prick or jerk. **3.** to remove a person from a place quickly and without ceremony; to throw someone out. **4.** to dismiss from work. *I got arseholed for sleeping on the job.*

arsehole about to fool around; to waste time.

arse licker a no-holds-barred term for a sycophant or bum crawler.

arse-licking **1.** sycophantic; crawling. **2.** extremely good. *On this record you'll find the most arse-licking bass of all time.*

arse over tit head-over-heels, generally used of a heavy fall. Euphemised to **A over T**. Other variants are **arse over head** and **arse over tea kettle**.

arse sucker a sycophant; an arse licker.

arse up to spoil, wreck or ruin. *You've really arsed that up.*

arse-up wrong side up; topsy-turvy; incorrect.

arse wipe the Aussie version of the US *ass wipe*, in other words, a dickhead.

arsy someone who has a *tin arse* is *arsy* – in other words, lucky. Aussie slang since the 1950s.

Arthur Murray world famous dance teacher who pioneered selling step-by-step dance lessons by mail. Has gone down in rhyming slang history for 'curry' and 'hurry', both of which are used in Australia. Of local coinage is the phrase **no Arthur Murrays**, which of course means 'no worries'.

artist a person notorious for a specified aspect of their behaviour. Such as a *booze artist*, a *bullshit artist*, and the like.

arvo the afternoon. A classic Australian shortening using the *-o* suffix. Been around since the 1920s. You can also use the *-ie* suffix and say **arvie** or **aftie**.

Ashgrove boots women's knee-high boots. So called because they are 'half way to the Gap'. The Brisbane suburbs of Ashgrove and the Gap are next to one another. Similar is the **Ashgrove skirt** – very short.

aspro **1.** a homosexual man. From *ass* 'arse' and *pro* 'professional'. Originally Aussie prison slang of the 1950s. **2.** an associate professor. Both terms punning on the brand name of a painkiller.

ass the American spelling and pronunciation of 'arse'. There is some evidence that this Americanism is being used by the younger generation of Aussies, but it will probably never get a firm hold here. Even when we borrow an American phrase, like *kick ass*, we automatically change it to *kick arse*. Traditionally Aussies have used the word **ass** to mean a donkey and hence a foolish person (though, of course, this *ass* is of a totally different origin, coming ultimately from Latin).

as the crow flies in a direct route. Originally British slang, but used here since the 19th century.

Athens of the South **1.** Adelaide – because of its sunny climate. **2.** Melbourne – because it has the second largest Greek population of any city in the world, after Athens!

at it **1.** engaged in sexual intercourse. **2.** arguing.

attitude a hostile or assertive attitude. *They have heaps of attitude.* US slang from the 1960s, picked up in Australia in the 1980s.

aunty **1.** an affectionate moniker for the Australian Broadcasting Corporation. **2.** an effeminate or homosexual older male.

aunty arms the arms of an overweight or matronly woman, having flabby triceps.

Aussie **1.** Australian, as in *Aussie beer, Aussie know-how, Aussie English* or *Aussie tucker*. You probably won't believe this, but this word was recorded earliest in New Zealand. Yep, **Aussie** is Kiwi! It is recorded there since 1910, and the earliest Australian source so far uncovered is from 1914. But let's not get too carried away with details. Of course the word is more Australian than anything else, no matter who first said it. Travellers to America will be amused to hear the Yanks pronounce it *ossy* (rhyming with *bossy*) – which means that they have more often seen the word in print than actually heard it. It is sometimes spelt **Ozzie**, and, even more uncommonly, **Ossie**.

2. an Australian. *There were a couple of Aussies at the bar.* In its widest sense this refers to any citizen of this highly multicultural land, however, contextually it is also commonly used to refer to your typical Anglo-Australian, as opposed to Aboriginals, Asians, Islanders or other ethnic Australians. For instance, you might hear someone say *Spot the Aussie!* – and sure enough, there'll be one fair dinkum ocker standing out like dogs balls in a crowd of fair dinkum multicultural Aussies. In this use it is mildly derogatory. **3.** Australia. *I can hardly wait to get back to Aussie.* **4.** in the money market it means the Australian dollar. *The Aussie fell against the greenback today.* **5.** a type of pizza or hamburger with bacon and eggs.

Aussie battler a typical member of the Australian working class who has to struggle hard to make a decent living. Also affectionately known as the **little Aussie battler**.

Aussie cheer the now traditional sporting cheer for Australian sporting heroes. For the record: 'Aussie, Aussie, Aussie, Oy, Oy, Oy! Aussie, Aussie, Aussie, Oy, Oy, Oy! Aussie, Oy! Aussie, Oy! Aussie, Aussie, Aussie, Oy, Oy, Oy!' Popularised and brought to the rest of the culturally-starved world during the 2000 Olympics.

Aussie crawl the Australian-invented swimming stroke now used the world over.

Aussieland this wide brown land; God's own country; a land girt by sea; Australia by any other name.

Aussie Rules Australian Rules football; the national game.

Australian as a kangaroo true blue, dinky-di, ridgy-didge, fair dinkum Aussie.

Australian kiss just like a French kiss – only Down Under.

Australian salute the movement of the hand and arm to brush away flies from your face. Also called the **Barcoo salute**.

average pretty bad. *I'm feeling pretty average after last night.* Typical Aussie understatement.

avoid list a list of people one wishes not to socialise with; in other words, a list of geeks.

awake up fully aware of what's going down; wise to. *I didn't see it at first, but I'm awake up now. We're awake up to your little scheme.*

away with the fairies daydreaming; mentally unsound or eccentric; not in touch with reality. You can also be **away with the pixies**, which is the same thing.

awesome extremely impressive; of high quality; totally excellent. One of those blatant Americanisms that was adopted in the 1980s and has now pretty much become totally naturalised, especially among the youth of this wide brown land – much to the chagrin of older Aussies. *You missed an awesome gig last night.*

axe **1.** among jazz musos an **axe** is just about any instrument, but among rock 'n' rollers it only refers to an electric guitar, which makes a bit more sense as at least a guitar somewhat resembles an axe. But despite this, it was those groovy hepcat jazzbos that came up with the word in the first place. **2.** to **get the axe** is to be dismissed from work.

axe handle a rough unit of measurement mostly used by country folk. *It was about six axe handles wide. She was a couple of axe handles across the beam.*

axe man a man who plays guitar.

axe mark a rather indelicate synonym for the vagina generally used by laddish, male chauvinist pigs who are intimidated by women but don't know it.

axe woman a woman who plays guitar.

ay caramba an exclamation of dismay. Originally adopted into US English from Spanish in the 19th century, and brought to Australia via cartoon shows in the 70s. The recent resurgence can be blamed on the television show *The Simpsons*.

ay chihuahua another exclamation of surprise brought by US cartoon shows. Never very popular here.

aygo-paygo a cryptolanguage used by schoolchildren in which normal words are modified by adding into each syllable the sound 'ug'; thus *hug* becomes *hu-gug*; *You are a pig* becomes *Yu-goo ugar uga pugig*. Also called **aygo-paygo**. For similar secret languages see **alibi**, **arpie-darpie**, **obo language**, **pig Latin** and **rechtub kelat**.

B

b a euphemism for *bastard*, especially back in the days when this was a taboo word. *He was a right b.*

babbling brook rhyming slang for 'cook'. Often shortened to **babbler**, or even just **bab**. Venerable Aussie slang, dating back to 1905.

babe **1.** a familiar term of address to a woman. *Hey, babe. How've you been?* **2.** a sexually attractive female. *Babes find me irresistible* (Yeah, right). An Americanism dating back to the beginning of the 20th century, and long considered sexist and offensive. Still, in recent years a reversal of fortune has happened with this word and it is now not uncommonly used by women to refer to an attractive man.

babe alert a cry informing others of the opportunity to have a perve.

babefest a place or event at which there are many sexually attractive females or males. Generally used by the eager but unattached.

babelicious absolutely gorgeous; incredibly attractive. Popularised by the Mike Myers movie *Wayne's World* (1992).

babe slayer a man women find irresistibly attractive.

Babewatch a nickname for the television show *Baywatch*.

-baby a diminutive element added to the end of a name, or a familiar shortening of a name, in order to make it more informal and colloquial. *Chuck-baby*; *Gorby-baby*.

baby blues blue eyes.

baby-poo brown a yucky brown colour, reminiscent of a baby's faeces. Also called **baby-cack brown**.

Bacchus Marsh See the entry for **Ballarat** for an explanation of this term.

baccy an old slang word for tobacco, little heard nowadays. Also, **bacca**.

bach of a man, to keep house for himself. A shortening of the word *bachelor*. Very common in Australia (since the 1880s) and New Zealand (since the 1890s), but recorded first in America (since the 1860s) and it is still used there. Nowadays can also be used of a young woman living out of home. *She was baching with a friend at North Sydney.* Also spelt **batch**.

backblocks **1.** remote, sparsely inhabited inland country; the sticks. Aussie slang since the 1860s. **2.** the outer suburbs of a city.

backchat insolent answering back. Hence, as a verb, to answer back insolently. Originally British military slang and picked up by Aussie soldiers in World War I.

backdoor **1.** anal intercourse. **2.** to have anal intercourse with.

backdoor bandit a male homosexual. An alliterative variation of **arse bandit**. See **dung puncher** for a host of synonyms.

backhander **1.** a bribe. *He slipped the witness a backhander.* **2.** a blow to the face with the back of the hand.

back o' beyond the far outback; anywhere remote. Aussie slang since the 1870s.

back of Bourke any remote outback area; the backblocks. Recorded since 1896. Bourke is a town in north-west NSW.

back off the map If you **back** a racehorse or greyhound **off the map** you wager heavily on it and thus reduce its odds.

backseat bogan in WA, a person sitting up the back of the bus – the traditional seating choice of the bogan. In Brisbane, they are called **backseat bevans** or **backseat bevs**.

backslang a cryptolanguage in which words are pronounced backwards. It originated with costermongers in London in the early 19th century and has had a modest impact on the general slang vocabulary by supplying the word *yobbo*. Backslang for *boy* is *yob*, and *yobbo* is an extension of this. Compare **rechtub kelat**.

backstop a second or support in a fight. Aussie slang since the 1940s. Also called a **back-up**.

backs to the wall! a homophobic catchphrase used to warn men that a gay man is in the vicinity.

back the card to bet on every race at a meeting.

back up for to come back for a second portion.

bad 1. good. This ironic reversal of meaning comes from US English. In Oz it is generally only used by teenagers going through their 'rap' stage. **2.** an error or mistake, especially one made while playing a team sport: *Sorry everyone, my bad.* A more recent adoption from US English.

bad call a really poor decision.

badger 1. in Tasmania, used to refer to a wombat. A quaint survival of a usage dating way back to colonial times. **2.** among schoolkids a somewhat less quaint usage of the word is recorded. In order to avoid being punched after farting (according to the universal unwritten law of kids), all you need to do is to exclaim **Badger!** and then whistle. Those of the offended nose are able to punch the farter before they say badger – just so long as they are quick enough.

bad hair day a day in which you cannot get your hair to look good. By extension, a day in which you're in a bad mood and nothing goes right. The opposite is a **good hair day**.

bad lot dishonest people. Can also be used in the singular for a crooked person. *He's a bad lot, he is.*

badmouth to speak unfavourably of; to criticise with malice.

bad trot a run of bad luck. Aussie slang dating from at least the 1940s.

bag 1. an ugly woman. *My blind date was an absolute bag.* **2.** in cricket a bag is a good haul of wickets obtained by a bowler. However, when someone calls out **get a bag!** it is not at all complimentary, rather it is an expression of extreme contumely directed at some useless sod who's dropped a sitter. **3.** a bookmaker's satchel into which the takings go (and out of which the losses come). Hence, to **swing the bag** is to work as a bookie. If a horse or jockey is **in the bag**, it means that they are going to go all-out to 'look' like they are trying to win while making damn sure they do not. In other words, the money bet on the horse is already *in the bag* and isn't going anywhere. **4.** a measure of marijuana, heroin, or other drug. **5.** the breathalyser. **6.** to criticise harshly; to knock. *Me mates all bagged me for buying the wrong beer.*

baggy green the Australian Test Cricket cap. To **don the baggy green** is to represent Australia at Test cricket.

bag it to drive a car at speed.

bagman 1. historically, a swagman, tramp or travelling pedlar. Such men were said to belong to the **Bagman's Union**. **2.** a bookmaker. **3.** a bookmaker's clerk. **4.** a person who collects bribe money.

bag of fruit Aussie rhyming slang for 'suit' – dating back to the 1920s.

bag of tricks a trademan's tool box; a miscellaneous collection of things.

bag of yeast Aussie rhyming slang for 'priest'.

bag out to criticise harshly; to knock.

bags a cry by which you establish a right by the mere virtue of having made the first claim, as in *Bags I have first ride* or *Bags the window seat*. As a verb, to reserve by making the first claim. *It's not fair, I bagsed it first!* Generally used by kids. In Queensland you find the term **bar** is also used in this way. The original form appears to have been *bag*, as found in Mary Grant Bruce's *Billabong's Daughter* (1924): 'It's quite enough for you two to own him, so I bagged telling the story'. Clearly this term is an extension of *bag*, to kill game and hence claim it as your own, literally, to add it to your bag.

bag swinger a bookmaker's clerk.

bail 1. to depart, leave. *Come on, let's bail.* **2.** to withdraw in a cowardly manner; to pike out. **3.** to **bail on** someone is to abandon them.

bail up! 1. Stick 'em up! Stand and deliver! The cry of the Australian bushranger on pay day. Recorded first in the 1840s. It is curious to note that this aggressive term which struck fear into the hearts of law-abiding citizens of the day actually has its origins in dairy farming. A *bail* is a frame used to secure a cow's head for milking, and thus, to *bail up* is to place a cow's head into a bail for milking. **2.** to corner someone, usually in order to have a go at them, or to bore the pants off them.

bald as a bandicoot totally bald. Bit of a weird one this, as bandicoots are manifestly furry – not bald.

bald monkey the penis.

baldy **1.** a bald person. **2.** a coin with Edward VII on the obverse, traditionally used in the game two-up. **3.** a tyre with no tread to speak of. **4.** a Hereford, a breed of beef cattle with a white face or head. **5.** the white-headed pigeon.

Bali belly diarrhoea, as suffered by travellers to South-East Asia.

ball **1.** a testicle. *He got hit right on the left ball.* A usage dating back as far as the 1300s. Generally used in the plural (see **balls**). **2.** of a man, to have sex with someone.

ball and chain the wife. Used in a jocular way. Sounds like a convict metaphor, but it is originally US Black English, from the 1920s.

Ballarat **1.** rhyming slang for 'cat'. **2.** rhyming slang for 'fat', as in an erection. A **Bacchus Marsh** is used for a semi-erection – Bacchus Marsh is halfway to Ballarat from Melbourne.

ball bag the scrotum.

ball huggers speedos. For a full set of synonyms see **sluggos**.

ballistic If you **go ballistic**, you explode with anger.

ball of muscle a fit, strong and healthy person.

balloons large, round breasts.

balls **1.** the testicles. To **have someone by the balls** is to have them in your complete power. And, if a man **does his balls on** someone, it means he is totally infatuated with them. When something **stands out like dogs balls**... well, surely the meaning of this stands out like dogs balls! **2.** courage, moral strength. *He hasn't got the balls to ask for a raise.* **3.** an exclamation equivalent to *bullshit!*

balls and all aggressively and enthusiastically.

balls-out without restraint. *He went balls-out down the slope.*

balls up to make a mess of; to bungle. Hence, a **balls-up** is a mistake or blunder; a complete mess; a fiasco.

ballsy **1.** showing great courage. **2.** aggressively masculine.

ball tearer **1.** an aggressive woman. **2.** something extremely good. *This is a ball tearer of a book.*

Balmain basketweaver a wealthy inner-city trendy with pretensions to an alternative lifestyle. Also called a **basket weaver from Balmain**. Balmain is a yuppified Sydney suburb.

Balmain bulldozer Sydney slang, a derogatory term for a city-only 4WD. See **Toorak tractor** for a host of synonyms.

Balmain kiss a headbutt. An Aussie equivalent to the British **Liverpool kiss**. The now-refined Sydney suburb of Balmain was formerly the abode of wharfies and assorted rough working-class men.

Balmaniac an inhabitant of the Sydney suburb of Balmain.

Balmoral bulldozer Sydney slang, a derogatory term for a city-only 4WD. See **Toorak tractor** for a host of synonyms.

baloney nonsense or waffle. US slang from the 1920s. Also spelt **boloney**.

Balt an immigrant from the Baltic region, though applied indiscriminately to all European migrants. A derogatory term used principally in the 1940s and 50s.

banana **1.** a fifty dollar note. From its colour. **2.** a jump into water with one leg tucked under your arms and hugged into the chest and the other extended straight out. Also called a **can opener**, **horsey** or **peg leg**. **3.** a type of 'nimby' in extremis. Stands for *Build Absolutely Nothing Anywhere Near Anybody.*

banana balancer the steward of a naval officer.

banana bender a derisive term for a Queenslander. See **Cornstalk** for similar terms of derision for people from other states.

bandicoot **1.** a small marsupial formerly much more common than it is today and the inspiration for a number of metaphors which still survive where the animal does not. The most common are **bald as a bandicoot**, completely bald, **miserable as a bandicoot on a burnt ridge**, pathetically miserable, and **barmy as a bandicoot**, off your rocker. **2.** as a verb, to **bandicoot** is to dig up potatoes while leaving the top of the plant undisturbed. Long a common practice, done either to get a few of the larger spuds while leaving the plant in situ so that the smaller ones can grow, or in order to steal spuds from someone else's garden without letting them know it is happening.

band moll a female groupie who sleeps with the men in a rock group.

B and S a bachelor and spinster ball; a dance held for young people in country areas. Held in a woolshed or out in the open, patrons dress in formal clothing, drink copious amounts of alcohol, and generally end up sleeping outdoors for the night. Circle work – the creation of circular patterns on the ground with the back wheels of the patrons' utes or cars – is an obligatory end of the dance ritual.

bandy diminutive shortening of 'bandicoot'.

Bandywallop an imaginary remote town. Aussie slang since the 1950s.

bang **1.** an act of sexual intercourse. **2.** a person rated according to their sexual ability. *She's a great bang.* **3.** to have sexual intercourse. A red-hot lover is said to **bang like a dunny door in a gale**.

banger **1.** a sausage, as in *bangers and mash.* If you are **a couple of bangers short of a barbie**, then you're not very intelligent. **2.** a beat-up old car, one that might best be used as a paddock basher.

banjo old slang for a shovel. Aussie slang since the 1910s. Especially used by miners and diggers, and also used for a fireman's shovel on a locomotive. To **swing the banjo** is to shovel material or dig.

bank an amount of money used for betting when out gambling. Aussie slang since the 1910s.

banker When a river **runs a banker** it is completely full, right up to the top of the banks.

bap a laddish word for a woman's breast, named after a type of soft bread roll.

Bappo a Baptist. Aussie slang since the 1950s.

bar **1.** in children's chasing games if you are **bar** it means you are not able to be tagged, tipped, or otherwise caught. Similarly, a designated place can be bar, as in *All the trees are bar, except the last one* – which means you are safe from being caught if you are touching any tree but the last. More forceful expressions are **B.A.R. bar** and **barred for life!** This is the common term in Qld, NSW and ACT. To remove the injunction in order to carry on the game, all you have to do is say **unbar**, or, if you have become barred for life, **unbarred for life!** **2.** If you **won't have a bar of** something, it means you can't take it, you won't put up with it. Aussie slang since the 1930s. **3.** among kids, to reserve something by making the first claim on it. Especially common in Qld. Similar to **bags** (see entry). **4.** to carry as a second passenger on a horse, bicycle, or motorcycle. Chiefly used in coastal areas of southern Qld and northern NSW. For a full set of regionalisms see **dink**.

the Bar the WA township of Marble Bar. *Spent two years out at the Bar.*

barbed wire Castlemaine XXXX beer. Queensland slang for a Queensland beer.

barber Aussie underworld slang for a thief who steals from hotel rooms. Hence, as a verb, to rob hotel guests.

barbie a barbecue, both the cooking apparatus and the social event. First recorded back in the 1970s.

Barcoo a river in south-western Qld, well represented in Australian slang. The most common term being the **Barcoo rot**, a type of scurvy caused by drought, hard living, and bad water in which the skin breaks out in sores, scabs, and suppurating eruptions, and often accompanied by vomiting, nausea, and digestive problems. Then there is the **Barcoo spews**, a distinctive illness once prevalent in the outback, characterised by nausea and vomiting at the sight of food, probably due to cyanobacteria. A **Barcoo lawyer** is the same as a **bush lawyer** (see entry). The **Barcoo salute** is equivalent to the **Australian salute**, the brushing away of flies.

bare-bellied joe a ewe that has been shorn. The 'joe' part of this phrase is actually a variant of the word **yoe** (see entry). Kept alive only in the song 'Click Go The Shears'.

barf to vomit or spew. Originally US slang from the 1940s.

barf bag a paper bag for the travel sick, provided to passengers on an aeroplane or coach.

bargain! excellent! terrific!

barie in NSW, to carry as a second passenger on a horse, bicycle, or motorcycle. For a full set of regionalisms, see **dink**.

barker's egg a piece of dog excrement, especially when annoyingly in the way, as on the lawn or footpath. A great big pile of dog turd is called a **barker's nest**.

barley a cry used by kids to gain immunity from being caught in a game of chasings, usually when they are having a break from the game. Chiefly used in Victoria. Originally used in British dialect and thought to be from French *parlez* 'to talk'. In WA and SA the word **barleys** is used instead.

barmy crazy. If you're really crazy, you might be called **barmy as a bandicoot**. In other words, hopping mad. Also spelt **balmy**.

Barmy Army the English cricket supporters.

barney an argument or fight. Also found in British dialect, and probably from there, even though it is recorded earliest in Australia. Also used as a verb meaning to argue or fight.

Barossa Deutsch a variety of German spoken in the Barossa Valley in SA which was settled in the early 1840s mainly by refugees from Silesia and Prussia. Also used for the German settlers themselves, or their descendents.

barouche in SA, an operating theatre trolley.

barra the fish barramundi.

barrack **1.** to shout encouragement for a player or team; to support, as in *I barrack for St George – Up the mighty Dragons!* Can also be used outside of sporting contexts, as in *I barracked for Whitlam back in '72.* This dead-set Australianism dates back to the 1890s. There has been a lot of discussion about the origin of this term, and many fabled origins have been put forward, generally having something to do with soldiers from army barracks supporting a certain team at a certain place. None of these theories have anything going for them other than that they are nice stories. An alternative theory suggests a connection with the dialect of Northern Ireland which had *barrack* meaning to boast or brag. Since barracking for a team often involves elaborate boasting about their prowess, this seems a more likely explanation. **2.** For the language historians – it should be noted that **barrack** was formerly used to mean to jeer at someone or ridicule them. This meaning dates back to the 1870s and was common in Australia in the late 19th and early 20th centuries. Today it is as scarce as hen's teeth, if it is around at all.

barrel **1.** to knock over by running into or striking hard. *I'll barrel the bastard.* **2.** among surfies, the hollow tube of a wave. Hence, as a verb, to ride inside the tube of a wave.

Barrier Reef rhyming slang for 'teeth'.

barrier rogue a horse that is difficult to manage in the starting barriers.

barro embarrassing. *It was heaps barro.*

barry **1.** a terrible blunder, mistake or poor performance. Shortened form of **Barry Crocker**, rhyming slang for 'shocker', Barry Crocker being the Australian popular entertainer who took the title role in the *Barry McKenzie* films of the 1970s. Also known as a **bazza**. **2.** a westie, bogan or bevan. **3.** an unpopular person; a nerd, dag or geek. Same as a **Neville** or **Nigel**.

bars a cry indicating that you are safe during a chasing game. A variant of the usual **bar** and especially common in Adelaide and Canberra.

Barwell's bull a railcar run by South Australian Railways, mainly servicing country lines from the 1920s to the 1950s, and noted for its bellowing horn. Named after Sir Henry Barwell, SA premier 1920–24. Also called a **Brill car**.

base over apex upside down; head over heels; arse over tit.

base wallah a derogatory term for any serviceman stationed at the base, as opposed to at the front. Also called a **base bludger**.

bash **1.** a party. *I'm having a big birthday bash.* Originally British slang. **2.** an attempt or try. *Go on, give it a bash.* Also originally British, but used in Oz since the 1950s. **3.** a dent put into a slouch hat to make it look better. **4.** an act of sexual intercourse. Hence, a person judged on their sexual performance. *He's not such a bad bash.*

bash the spine to sleep. Great Aussie layabout slang since the 1940s – trying to make sleeping sound like hard work.

basin cut a poor haircut, which appears as though the barber merely placed an inverted bowl on the head and trimmed the hair that hung below the rim. Also called a **bowl cut**.

basket a euphemism for *bastard.*

basket case a person suffering badly from stress so that they can no longer function properly. Borrowed from America. Originally it was a US military term relating to widely circulating rumours about quadruple amputees – who couldn't be carried on a stretcher but had to be kept in baskets.

baso a basin cut.

bastard **1.** Originally a person born of unmarried parents, but now used generally to mean an unpleasant or despicable person. As in *Don't let the bastards grind you down.* A term well-loved in Australia since colonisation and still enjoying great popularity. In fact, the overuse of the word here has led to it being used to refer to any person – whether they are a bastard or not. So a bloke might come up to a bunch of friends and say 'What have you bastards been up to?' You can even use it affectionately, as in 'Poor bastard, wasn't his fault'. **2.** When not applied to a person, a **bastard** is anything that causes difficulty or aggravation, as in 'This engine's a bastard', or 'What a bastard of a day, it's 45 in the shade'. If it is raining heavily, then it is 'raining like a bastard'. You can even use it adjectivally, as in 'That was a bastard thing to do'.

bastard from the bush a stereotype of a male from the bush who is crude, mean, stingy, lazy, cruel, dishonest, etc., the very epitome of every vice. Supposedly from a crude poem 'The Captain of the Push', attributed to Henry Lawson.

bastardisation debasing initiation rituals performed at some Australian institutions.

Bastille the police station; the cop shop.

bat **1.** the piece of wood used to toss the coins in two-up; the kip. **2.** an ugly woman.

bat for the other team from a heterosexual perspective, to be homosexual, or, from a homosexual perspective, to be heterosexual.

bath dodger a Pom.

bat pad in cricket, a close-in fielder.

battery an illegal device which delivers an electric shock to a racehorse when racing in order to make it run faster. If a horse is said to be **battery-trained**, then it has been trained with a battery device used continually on a certain part of the body, so that during a race a smart smack in that area will make it go like the billyo. Highly illegal of course.

battle to struggle courageously to make ends meet in the face of adversity. A great Australian pastime.

battleaxe a crabby old unfriendly woman; a harridan.

Battle of the Wazzir a riot in which Anzac soldiers attacked and 'scoured' the red-light district of Cairo. The troops were tired of the high prices, watered down drinks, and swindling that went on there, not to mention, the venereal infections they picked up. They looted the buildings and burnt the furnishings in the street. An official inquiry was held but little came of it. Celebrated in a poem by C.J. Dennis at the time, but his verse was supressed by the censors.

battler **1.** a decent and fair person who struggles continually and persistently against heavy odds; a doer; a typical member of the Australian working class. Also known as the **little Aussie battler**. **2.** in the horseracing game it also refers to a small-time punter who tries to live on their winnings, or a small-time owner/trainer who is always struggling to make a living. **3.** formerly, was also used for a prostitute.

Bauple nut a macadamia nut. See **bopple nut**.

the Bay Long Bay jail.

bazoomas a woman's breasts. A delightfully silly piece of 1950s British slang.

BDs in WA and Tas, desert boots. A type of suede leather shoe commonly associated with bogans.

beak a judge. Originally British slang and going back to 16th century thieves' cant. Ultimate origin unknown.

beam the backside: *She was pretty wide in the beam.* A person thus dimensioned is **beamy**.

beamer in cricket, a full toss which goes towards the head of the person batting. Also called a **beam ball** or **bean ball**.

beamie in Qld, a children's ball game played underneath a highset building. The thrower has to hit the beam to score a point and stay in. If they miss, the other player claims the ball.

bean counter an accountant. Originally US slang from the 1970s.

beanie brigade people who wear checked flannel shirts and beanies.

beano a bang-up meal; a real feast. Originally British slang of the 1880s, used by printers for their annual work dinner or 'bean feast'.

bean pole a tall, lanky person.

bear in homosexual slang, a large and hairy homosexual man.

bear-up an obsolete term for 'the approach amorous', that is, an attempt to pick a woman up. First recorded by Henry Lawson, but not heard of since the 1940s. A top Aussie term that has sadly died out.

beast **1.** a great big hulking car, like they used to make in the good old days, you know, hewn out of the living metal and guzzling gas like nobody's business. **2.** among surfies, it can be a big thick surfboard, or a very large wave.

beast with two backs two people having sex; a couple engaged in coupling. We can blame this one on that well-known Elizabethan bard, William Shakespeare.

beat **1.** a public area where a street prostitute solicits. **2.** a public place which homosexual men frequent to pick up casual sexual partners.

beat off to masturbate; to wank.

beat queen a male homosexual who frequents beats.

beat the bishop of a male, to masturbate.

beauj beaujolais wine. *Had a bottle of beauj with dinner the other night.*

beaut **1.** good, excellent, wonderful. *You've been beaut, thanks. It's a beaut car.* Aussie slang since the 1910s. Also used as an adverb. *She sings real beaut.* **2.** as a noun, an excellent person or thing. *It's an absolute beaut.* Aussie slang since the 1890s. Also common in the cry of praise **you beaut!** (see entry).

beautiful people a derogatory term for young, affluent, self-centred people with tickets on themselves.

beaut ute a competition where owners of utes show off their pride and joy.

beauty **1.** a cry of joy. Dating back to the 1960s. A shortening of **you beauty!** **2.** something of excellent quality. Aussie slang since the 1850s. Also spelt **bewdy**, to represent the dinkum Aussie pronunciation.

beaver borrowed from the US, this term for the vagina is now well ensconced Down Under. Sadly replacing the Aussie terms *fanny* and *micky*. A **beaver shot** is a pornographic, often almost gynaecological, photo of a woman spreading her legs. Such images are known collectively as **split beaver**.

bed flute the penis.

bediddle to continuously spin a frisbee on the point of your finger.

bedlam a common schoolyard chasings game, which is usually banned by teachers. This term is used in Qld only. For the full set of regionalisms, see **British bulldog**.

Bedourie shower a dust storm.

Beecham's pill old Aussie rhyming slang for 'dill'. From the name of a brand of laxative that was formerly promoted as a wonder remedy for just about any ailment.

bee cocky an apiarist.

beef **1.** body weight; muscle and/or fat. *He's got plenty of beef on him.* **2.** a complaint, or, as a verb, to complain or grumble, as in *What are you beefing about?* Originally US slang from the late 19th century.

beef bayonet an erect penis. Occasionally called the **beef bugle**.

beef curtains a crude metaphor for the vaginal lips. To **part the beef curtains** is for a male to have sex with a woman.

beer the Australian national drink. In Vic, WA and Qld, if you go into a pub and order *a beer*, you will get a seven fluid ounce glass of beer. If you try this in other states you will most probably be asked 'What size?' See **glass** for other names of a seven ounce glass.

beer bog a particularly noisome excrement produced the morning after a night of heavy drinking. See **after grog bog** for more synonyms.

beer coat the ability to endure icy cold weather gained from getting so tanked you can barely feel anything.

beer goggles a distorted view of things gained from getting drunk on beer, especially the drunken attraction to less than attractive people.

beer map a map drawn in beer spilt on the bar top.

beer o'clock time for a beer. Generally after work, but it depends on the individual.

beer wench a woman who goes and gets beers for a bunch of blokes drinking.

bees and honey rhyming slang for 'money'.

bee's dick an extremely small amount. *Just move it to the left a bee's dick.* More politely called a **bee's whisker**.

beetle crushers heavy shoes. Sometimes used to refer to the feet. Originally 19th century British slang.

beg, beg, grovel, grovel a jocular way of pleading your cause.

be in it to be actively involved. Aussie slang since the 1920s. *You've got to be in it to win it.*

bell a telephone call. *Give me a bell tomorrow.*

Bellambi handbag in Wollongong, a cask of cheap wine. From the name of a suburb. Same thing as a **Dapto briefcase**.

Bello the township of Bellingen in northern NSW.

belly buster a dive in which your stomach hits the water with a resounding slap and contingent excruciating pain. Also called a **belly flop**, a **belly flopper** or a **belly whacker**.

bench warmer in sport, a reserve who does not get many games, if any.

bender a drinking spree. *They were out on a bender.*

bend the elbow to drink beer.

Bennie in Tasmania, a simpleton.

benny a benzedrine pill.

bent **1.** corrupt, like a cop or politician. **2.** whacked out on drugs.

berk a detestable person; a jerk or prat. Originally used in 19th century Britain where it was short for *Berkeley Hunt*, which was rhyming slang for 'cunt'. A little tidbit of information unknown to most people. It is interesting to see just how much this term's impact has softened over the years for it is nowhere near as rude as its origin. In Australia it is often assumed to be an application of the town name of *Bourke*, just as *Dubbo* is used to mean a jerk.

berko berserk. *He's gone absolutely berko.* Thought by some to derive from 'Birko', a brand of electric kettle, with the idea that boiling water is like a person going berserk. A derivation that doesn't have the ring of truth.

berly bait thrown into the water to attract fish. A uniquely Aussie term dating back to the 1870s, but of unknown origin.

the Berrimah Line the imaginary line which separates the privileged Darwin from the unprivileged rest of the Territory. Berrimah is a small township south of Dariwn. The joking allusion is to the Brisbane Line, a notional division of Australia during World War II into that part of the country that would be defended, that is, from Brisbane down, and that part which would be left to the Japanese to overrun, that is, from Brisbane to Cape York.

bestest a superlative of the superlative *best*; even better than best, like *He's my bestest, bestest friend.* A kid's word mostly, or otherwise used when being a bit of a dag.

best friend the penis.

betcha bet you. *Betcha she'll win.*

bet like the Watsons to bet heavily at the races. Who the Watsons were is lost in time.

better half a complimentary appellation for your wife. Less commonly used by women of their husbands. Also used by unmarried people of their 'significant others'.

betting with rubber bands desperation betting with the very last of your money after a day of nothing but losses. The rubber bands are the ones that held your massive wad at the beginning of the day.

Betty an attractive young woman.

bev an alcoholic drink; a refreshing beverage. Also called a **bevvie**.

bevan the Queensland term for a flannie-clad, mullet-sporting, unrefined, ill-educated yobbo. Same as a *westie* in NSW, or a *bogan* in WA, a *chigger* in Tasmania, and so on and so forth. Not a complimentary term. Apparently from the name *Bevan*, seen as typical of this type, though of course women can be bevans too. To create compound words, bevan is reduced to the simple **bev**, so you get **bev-curls**, the long trailing locks of their mullets, and **bev-cars**, the type of mean street machine favoured by male bevans. Female bevans are sometimes referrred to as **bev-chicks**. And to **bev out** is to idle away time sitting around doing nothing much.

bevan heaven a Queensland Seven Eleven store.

bewdy the normal Aussie slang way of saying **beauty!**

B-grouper in Broken Hill this means the outsiders, as opposed to the locals or **A-groupers**.

bhang marijuana. From the Hindi word for the same. In Rajasthan you can get **bhang lassis**, yoghurt drinks laced with marijuana – which are semi-legal and popular with youthful tourists. On menus of cafes catering to westerners, they are often listed as *special lassis*.

bi a bisexual person. Also used as an adjective to describe someone of bisexual orientation.

Bible basher a nark of a person who tries to shove Christianity down other people's throats.

bickie a biscuit. If you are **a few bites short of a bickie**, then you are not very smart. If you have **big bickies**, then half your luck, you are rich.

biddy a fussy old woman.

the Bidgee the mighty Murrumbidgee River.

biff **1.** a blow or punch, *I gave him a biff*, or the act of fighting, *There was a bit of a biff at the pub.* Also, as a verb, to punch. *I biffed him in the earhole.* To **go the biff** is to get into a fight. All of which come from the onomatopoeic sound of a punch – just like in superhero cartoons – Pow! Bam! Biff! **2.** intentional rough play in sport. *The visitors turned on the biff.*

biffo fighting. *He got into a bit of biffo.*

big A the arse, as in the sack. *Got the big A from the boss yesterday.*

big ask a request or expectation that is difficult to fulfil; a major imposition on your generosity.

big balooga enormously big. *I want one of those big balooga 4WDs.*

big bickies lots of money.

big bucks a great expense; lots of money.

big C cancer.

big call a contentious statement; a gutsy prediction.

big day your wedding.

the Big Donger local nickname for the large observation tower situated in Newcastle, NSW. Famed for its phallicity.

Big Dub the colloquial way of saying Big W.

big eye in the Antarctic, insomnia caused by the effect of extra long days or nights upon the body's normal internal clock.

big fellow upstairs God.

bigger than Uluru Aussie version of **bigger than Ben Hur**.

biggie **1.** something large. **2.** an adult, as opposed to a *littlie*. **3.** if something is **no biggie**, then it is no big deal.

big girl's blouse a wussy, effeminate bloke; a great big sissy.

big gun **1.** a powerful or influential person. **2.** a long surfboard for big waves.

big hair hair teased out to add as much volume as possible. Popular with rock stars in the 80s, and with Effie-type ethnic women.

the Big Island a typically Tasmanian way of referring to mainland Australia.

big jobs a word for defecation, used when speaking to ankle biters.

big mob a large number or quantity of things.

big-note to boast; to exaggerate your own importance. One who makes a habit of this is known as a **big-noter**. Which, in the racing game, is also slang for a racecourse tipster or urger.

big O orgasm.

big one **1.** a thousand dollars. Also jokingly used to refer to one dollar. **2.** in Aussie Rules, the **big ones** are the goal posts.

bigs in pool, striped balls.

big sick an Aboriginal term for leprosy, from which Aboriginals suffered greatly in former times, especially in WA and NT.

big smoke the city, or any built-up area, as opposed to the countryside. Originally a word used in Aboriginal pidgin English. Dating from the 1840s.

big spit vomit. *He went for the big spit.*

big sticks in Aussie Rules, the goal posts. Also called the **big white sticks**. *He's dobbed it through the big sticks.*

the Big Stoush World War I. See entry at **stoush** for more information.

big swinging dick an aggressively powerful businessman.

big swing, no ding in cricket, a taunting phrase said to someone who makes a glorious swipe at the ball but misses it entirely.

big time to a great degree, always used after the verb. *You owe me big time.*

big trip a trip to Britain and Europe. Formerly it was traditional for Aussies to take such a trip just once in a lifetime, and not like it much over there, almost as though it was something to be endured with a 'Can't wait to get back to Godzone' attitude. Such trips are now commonplace and no longer seen as such an onerous task.

Big Wet the monsoon season in the tropical north.

big whoop! so what! Spoken with a heavily sarcastic tone. Also in the forms **big whoopee**, **big whoops** and **big whoopsie**.

bike **1.** a derogatory word for a woman who sleeps around. That is, everyone 'rides' her. Usually restricted to a certain sphere of operations, as the **office bike** or the **town bike**. Aussie slang since the 1940s. **2.** If you say to someone **On your bike!** you are telling them to leave. However, to **get off your bike** is to become furious, to really lose control.

bikie a member of a gang of motorcycle riders. In the US they are called **bikers**. In Australia *biker* is often used to refer to motorcycle riders who aren't part of a bikie gang.

bilk to cheat or swindle; to rip off; to evade payment of a debt. Venerable slang dating back to the 17th century.

billabong an Australianism for a branch of a river that fills in flood time only, or a lake formed by a river branch that has been cut off. To most Aussies primarily known as an excellent place for sheep-thieving swagmen to camp beside. The word is from Wiradjuri, a nearly extinct Aboriginal language of central NSW.

billy **1.** a quintessential item of camping in the Australian outback, a tin with a lid and a wire handle used for boiling water, making tea, etc., over an open fire. The origin of this term is a bit of a mystery. Conjectured by some to be from French and by others from the Australian Aboriginal language Wiradjuri. However, the most likely source is Scottish English which had a cooking utensil known as a *billy pot*. To **boil the billy** is to have a break from work or a journey for some tea or other refreshments. In fact, you don't even have to boil a billy to 'boil the billy'. To **swing the billy** originally meant to swing the billy from a stick over a fire, but more recently has come to mean to take a billy full of tea and swing it around in a great circle at arm's length, done in order to help settle the leaves. **2.** a bong for smoking marijuana or hash. A nice piece of word play this. It stems partly from the pun *billy bong* (that is, billabong), and partly from the fact that is a small receptacle containing water, just like a traditional billy. **3.** shortening of rhyming slang *billy lid* for 'kid'.

billy boulder a large rock.

billy can a billy.

billy cart a small four-wheeled cart, usually homemade, consisting essentially of a box on a board and steered by ropes attached to its movable front axle. Originally these were a more elaborate affair and were drawn by billy goats – hence the name. Also called a **go-cart**, or in WA, a **hill trolley**, or in WA and SA, a **soap box**.

billyful as much as a billy will hold.

billy grips metal tongs for lifting a hot billy off the fire. Also called **billy lifters** and **billy tongs**. See also **spondonicles**.

billy lid rhyming slang for 'kid'.

billyo originally a euphemism for the 'devil' or 'hell' when used in various phrases and imprecations. Thus, to **run like billyo** is the same as *to run like the devil*, or, to **go to billyo** is to *go to hell*, in other words, get lost! If something is **off to billyo** it is far away, or a long way off course.

billy tea tea made in the traditional bush way – in a billy.

bimbo an attractive but empty-headed woman. The female version of the **himbo**. From the Italian word for a baby, *bambino*.

bin **1.** a pocket. *Stick that in your bin.* **2.** to throw into a bin or otherwise discard. *What should I do with these papers? Bin 'em?*

bindi-eye a dreaded lawn weed, the bane of barefooted summers. This annoying addition to Australia's flora comes from South America and was introduced in the early part of the 20th century. **Bindi-eye** is the name of the plant, and also the spiky seeds which stick painfully into your feet. It is commonly shortened to **bindi**. The word itself comes from Kamilaroi, a nearly extinct Aboriginal language of central and northern NSW, though it referred to another plant entirely, a spiny native plant of the genus *Calotis*. In the Newcastle region, a bindi-eye is called a **joey**, and in WA they are termed **jo-jos**.

bingle **1.** a minor dent, as in a car or surfboard. **2.** a minor car accident involving slight damage to the car and no injury to the occupants.

bingo wings the flabby triceps of an overweight or matronly woman.

Binjour bear a supposed bear living wild on the Binjour Plateau, near Gayndah in south-western Qld. Some think it to be an escaped circus bear. Some cryptozoologists would have it that is a type of reclusive native creature like a yowie.

binny the stomach.

bint a demeaning word for a young woman. Originally military slang used in the Middle East during both World Wars. It is a borrowing of the Arabic word for a girl.

bird **1.** a derogatory word for a woman. **2.** a word for a man. Not very common any more, except in the phrase 'He's a queer bird'. **3.** airforce slang, a plane. **4.** in horseracing, a certainty. A shortening of the older term *dead* *bird.* **5.** a prison sentence. Short for *birdlime*, rhyming slang for 'time'.

birdcage **1.** an enclosure at a racecourse where jockeys mount and dismount. So called because it is often surrounded with a wire mesh fence. **2.** a child's glass playing marble with an internal net pattern; a Shirley Temple.

birdo an ornithologist, birdwatcher or bird enthusiast.

birdwatcher a male who perves at women.

birthday suit what you were wearing when you were born, that is, nothing but naked flesh.

bit sexual intercourse, as in *Fancy a bit?* A **bit on the side** is the same thing, only indulged in outside of a marriage or monogamous relationship.

bitch **1.** a disagreeable or malicious woman. The most common abusive label applied to women. Used by both men and women. **2.** since the 1990s, there has been some use among Aussie teenagers of the US slang sense of bitch meaning any woman, whether they are malicious in nature or not, as in *There'll be plenty of bitches at the party.* Also as a kind of male bravado word for a woman who is supposedly 'owned' by a man. This has reached our shores via the medium of rap music – along with the similarly opprobrious word **ho** (see entry). **3.** although primarily used of women **bitch** can also be directed at men, though generally in a joking way. Thus a guy that makes a bitchy comment can be called a bitch. Or, on a sporting field, you can sledge another player by saying *You're my bitch.* But it's hardly serious. In a more insulting way, a man who is a bit of a sissy can be called a bitch. **4.** any annoying thing that really ticks you off. *The bitch of a thing won't start.* **5.** a complaint or gripe. *I was just having a bitch about it.* **6.** to complain. *Oh, stop your bitching.*

bitch fight a fight between women.

bitchin' excellent, terrific, great. From the US, and given impetus by Bart Simpson.

bitch tits the flabby boob-like contours of the overweight male's chest. Also called **man boobs**.

bitchy **1.** inclined to make snide comments. *There's no need to be so bitchy.* **2.** of a comment, cruelly cutting; malicious.

bite **1.** to borrow money from someone. To **put the bite on** someone is to cadge off them. **2.** a person borrowed off, or whom you wish to borrow off. *He's not a bad bite.* **3.** the money you have borrowed, if you're lucky.

bite your bum! piss off!

a bit more choke and you would have started said to someone who has just let out one of those short sharp farts that sound like a struggling starter motor.

a bit of all right a sexually attractive person.

a bit of arse a person considered as a sex object.

a bit of how's your father sexual intercourse.

bit of skirt a woman seen as a sex object. In misogynous use since the 1890s.

bitser a dog of mixed breed. From the phrase *bits of this, and bits of that.* Also spelt **bitzer**.

bitumen sealed road, as opposed to dirt road.

bitumen blonde an Aboriginal woman.

bizzo **1.** business, as in *politics, and all that bizzo.* **2.** a businessman's club. *It's on at Caringbah bizzo.*

black **1.** formerly, a common term for an Aboriginal. Now little used except by racists. **2.** Toohey's Old. *A schooner of black, please.*

black and tan a drink of half beer and half stout, or half old and half new.

black as dog's guts totally black.

black aspro a cola soft drink, used as a curative for a hangover. Also called the **black doctor**.

black boy the grass tree or xanthorrhoea. From the supposed resemblance to a grass-skirted, dark-skinned figure bearing a spear.

black budgie a blowfly.

blackfellow an Aboriginal man. Used since colonial times by European Australians and thence adopted by Aboriginals. For most of its history very racist in its application. A common joke answer to a question regarding a woman's whereabouts used to be 'She's run off with a blackfellow'. Nowadays, **blackfellow** is used among Aboriginals to refer to themselves, but is still offensive when used by non-Aboriginals. Also commonly spelt **blackfeller** or **blackfella** in order to capture the usual pronunciation. Compare **whitefellow**.

black guts a crass way of referring to the stomach of a human being. A cheery encouragement to eat is *Get that into your black guts.*

Blackheathen a person from the Blue Mountains township of Blackheath.

blackie **1.** an old racist term for an Aboriginal person. Not heard so much nowadays. **2.** a black snake. **3.** a Pacific black duck (which are more brown than black, so what's the deal with that?) **4.** a black bream. **5.** a black yabby.

black maria a police van for the conveyance of those in custody.

black over Bill's mother's a heavy rainstorm is approaching.

black peter a punishment cell in a prison devoid of light and furniture.

black prince a species of black cicada.

black rat a can of Bundy and cola.

blacks a full driving licence, obtained after having a provisional licence. *I'm on me blacks after this week.*

black snake a crowbar.

black snow the ashes that fall after burning off a sugarcane field.

black stump a putative remote region in the far outback. As in *It's out beyond the black stump*, or *He is the biggest drongo this side of the black stump.*

Blacktown by the Sea **1.** a nickname for the Central Coast region of NSW, alluding to the low socio-economic status of its population, similar to that of the Sydney suburb of Blacktown. **2.** a nickname for the Sydney suburb of Dee Why.

black tracker an Aboriginal tracker traditionally employed by police due to their exceptional skill.

black velvet **1.** Aboriginal or any other dark-skinned women viewed as sex objects. **2.** sexual relations with an Aboriginal or other dark-skinned woman.

bladder a football.

blast a shot of an intravenous drug. Hence, as a verb, to take a drug intravenously.

Bleak City a disparaging nickname for the less-than-sunny city of Melbourne.

bleeding dog's eye a meat pie with tomato sauce.

Blighty **1.** England. Originally British military slang from India. The word ultimately comes from the Hindi word for a foreigner. **2.** in World War I, a wound sufficiently bad enough for repatriation to England. Generally seen as a good thing to get. Similar to the World War II **homer**.

blimey an exclamation expressing surprise or amazement. Shortened form of *gorblimey*, from *God blind me*. Originally late 19th century British slang, but used in Oz since the early 1900s. An Australian variation is **blimey Charlie!**

blind drunk, to the point of barely being able to see.

blinder something incredibly amazing. *She had a blinder of a game.*

blind Freddy could see that that's obvious.

blind mullet a tube of excrement floating in the water you are swimming in. Also called a **blind trout** or a **brown trout** or a **pollywaffle**. In Sydney these also go by the name of **Bondi cigar** or **Bondi shark**, and in Victoria you will find, if you're unlucky, the **Werribee trout** or the **King River prawn**.

bling bling flashy, shiny jewellery and other ostentatious displays of wealth – the sort of diamond-encrusted bijoux favoured by hip-hop artists. Coined by New Orleans rap family Cash Money Millionaires in the late 1990s and popularised by the song 'Bling Bling' by Cash Money artist BG.

Blinky Bill **1.** rhyming slang for 'dill'. After the well-known koala character created by Australian children's author Dorothy Wall in 1933. **2.** railway slang for an end-of-train marker, the flashing light attached to the rear of a freight train.

blister **1.** a parking infringement attached to a car window. **2.** Aussie rhyming slang for 'sister'.

blitz wagon a type of military vehicle.

blob **1.** in cricket, a score of nought. *The captain was out for a blob.* **2.** a fat person.

block the head, used only in the phrases **lose** or **do your block**, to lose your temper, and **knock someone's block off**, to thump them mightily in the head.

block bombing a Tassie term for driving around the block over and over again, as a form of youth entertainment.

blockhead a stupid or slow person. Venerable slang from the 16th century.

blockie a rural land-owner of a small property, as opposed to a large-scale farm. Also called a **blocker**.

blockies in Qld, Vic and Tas, circuits of a street block in a car for the purpose of entertainment. *We spent a few hours doing blockies.* Compare **bog laps**, **lappies**.

bloke **1.** general slang word for a man, especially a man's man, a down-to-earth man without pretensions. In Australia, a **good bloke** is one of the highest accolades that can be bestowed. Slightly lower on the scale is a bloke who is **not a bad bloke**. Funnily enough, there isn't any such thing as a 'bad bloke', per se, only 'not a bad bloke'. A real bad bloke is a 'bastard'. Originally British slang from as early as the 1820s. Perhaps derived from Shelta, a secret language used by tinkers in Ireland and parts of England. 'Bloke' was common in the US in the late 19th century but now is obsolete there. **2.** a boyfriend. *Come and meet me new bloke.* **3.** also used as an affectionate term for a male animal. *That pony is a nuggety little bloke.* **4.** in olden days **the bloke** was the boss. An Australianism now obsolete.

bloke of... a man by the name of... Thus, 'I'm looking for bloke of Smith' = 'I'm looking for Mr Smith.' Particularly used in rural NSW.

blokette a woman who can hold her own with the blokes. *Champion blokes and blokettes dropped their daks for some naked bungee jumping.*

blokey crassly masculine. A newish word first appearing in the 1990s.

blonde stupid. Especially used by women in self-admonishment, as *I'm having a blonde day.* From the standard image of the *dumb blonde.*

blood and blister Aussie rhyming slang for 'sister'. Also in the form **blood blister**.

bloodhouse a really rough pub.

bloodnose bleeding from the nose, usually from having been punched. Also called a **nosebleed**. Both terms are equally common throughout the entire country.

blood nut a redhead.

bloody a word used to add emphasis in signifying approval, as in *bloody beauty*, or disapproval, as in *bloody bastard.* It can also be inserted in the middle of words, as in *abso-bloody-lutely*, or *vege-bloody-mite.* Formerly the iconic Australian swearword, so prevalent that it was known as the *great Australian adjective.* There have even been poems written to it. Used to be considered extremely taboo and never to be used in polite society, and accordingly gave rise to many euphemisms as *blooming, bleeding, blinking, flaming, plurry* and *ruddy.* Nowadays it has lost its former glory. A weary, worn-out, aging prize fighter, no longer packing a punch. Lost its championship belt to the upstart *fucking* back in the 1960s.

bloody oath! too bloody right! my word! no two ways about it! Also heard as **blood oath!**

bloody well the usually adverbial form of the intensifier **bloody**, as in *You bloody well do owe me fifty bucks.* It has gone the same way as *bloody* under increasing competition from *fucking well.*

bloomers women's sports briefs worn over underwear and under a skirt. Chiefly used in Qld, NSW and WA. See **scungies** for the full set of regionalisms.

blooming a euphemism for *bloody.* As an adverb, **blooming well**. Still heard, but becoming rare.

blot the anus; the backside. *Just sitting around on my blot, doing nuthin'.*

blotting paper food eaten when out on a drinking binge.

blotto very drunk; pissed as a parrot.

blouse a sissy. More commonly found in the fuller form **big girl's blouse**.

blow **1.** a rest from work. An Australian usage dating back to the 1910s. **2.** a furious wind or big storm. Also Australian, since the 1930s. **3.** to brag or boast. Used in Australia since the 1850s, but not exclusively Aussie. **4.** to abscond, decamp or flee. Aussie since the 1950s. **5.** to ejaculate; experience orgasm. Generally used of a male. Australian, since the 1950s. **6.** to fellate. Finally we get to some US borrowings. This dates back to the 1930s in the States but only reached Australian shores in the 1980s. **7.** to fail; to spoil, ruin or wreck. *He really blew that exam.* **8.** cocaine. **9.** an old euphemism for 'damn'. As in, *Well I'll be blowed!* or *Blow that!* Originally British slang from the 18th century. Formerly very common in Australia.

blow away to amaze or astound.

blow chunks to vomit explosively.

blower **1.** a supercharger in an engine. **2.** the telephone. This one seems very American, but was first recorded in England back in the 1920s.

blowie **1.** a blowfly. **2.** a blowfish. **3.** a blow job.

blow in to make an unexpected visit; to drop in. Originally US, from the 1880s.

blow-in a derogatory term for a visitor or newcomer, especially one who is not going to stay. Aussie slang of the Great Depression, during which itinerants were looked upon unfavourably by locals who were already having trouble scraping by without the added burden of newcomers.

blow it out your arse! an exclamation of contempt.

blow job an act of fellatio.

blown out amazed, astounded. Also in the form **blown away**.

blow off **1.** to ejaculate or orgasm. Generally used of a male. **2.** to fart.

blow out **1.** to amaze someone. **2.** of odds, to lengthen. Aussie racing slang since the 1910s. *Hyperno Boy has really blown out in the betting.*

blow the gaff an old slang term for disclosing a secret. Originally convict slang recorded back in 1812.

blow through to leave or depart; to go. Aussie slang since the 1950s.

blow up **1.** to lose your temper. **2.** to scold vehemently. *He blew me up for being late.*

blubber among fishos, jellyfish.

bludge **1.** to waste time when you should be doing something; what the Americans call loafing. Long a classic piece of Australiana, bludge originally meant to live off the earnings of a prostitute, which was the occupation of the pimp or **bludger**, of which the verb is a backformation. **2.** to cadge, as in *Can I bludge a ciggy off you?* To be **on the bludge** is to be actively engaged in bludging. **3.** to **bludge on** someone is to impose on them or live off their hospitality. Strange to say, **bludge off** has exactly the same meaning. **4.** any job which requires next to no work. *This class is an absolute bludge.*

bludger **1.** someone who imposes on others, evades responsibilities, or does not do their fair share of work. It originally meant a low scoundrel living on the earnings of a prostitute, in other words, a pimp. This, in turn, is derived from the obsolete term *bludgeoner* 'a thug who uses a *bludgeon*'. In days of yore a bludgeon was a common weapon used by cowardly pimps for robbing clients and doing over their women. **2.** a detestable person. *Let him go, you filthy, rotten bludger!* **3.** any person (without any negative sense). *What are you bludgers up to? The poor bludger doesn't know any better.*

blue **1.** a fight, dispute or row. You can **bung on a blue**, **stack on a blue** or **turn on a blue**. Hence, as a verb, to fight or argue, as in *There's no sense bluing over it.* Been around since the 1940s. **2.** an error. Also around since the 1940s. **3.** a nickname for a bloke with red hair. Typical Aussie irony. A little earlier, since the 1930s. **4.** a blue flyer kangaroo.

blue a cheque to squander your entire salary, as on grog. Formerly a common practice among seasonal workers, such as shearers.

blue balls a painful, temporary condition of the testicles following a long period of unrelieved sexual arousal. Also called **lover's balls**.

blue bird in SA, any of various railcars servicing country areas from 1954 onwards which were painted blue and named after various birds. Compare this with **red hen**.

blue blazes an intensifier; a euphemism for 'hell'. *What in the blue blazes are you doing?*

blue bomber a parking inspector. See **brown bomber** for the full set of regionalisms.

blue bottle a large noisy blue-black blowfly.

blue can a can of Fosters beer. As opposed to a **green**, **red**, **white** or **yellow can** (see entries).

blue duck a failure or flop. First appearing in the 1890s, and seen as late as the 1950s, but now a thing of the past. A bit of a blue duck itself.

blue-flame to ignite a burst of flatulence.

blue flyer the adult female of the red kangaroo, noted for her exceptional speed.

blue heeler a purebred dog with black or red face and ears and dark blue body speckled with lighter blues, developed in Australia for work with cattle by crossing the blue merle Scotch collie with the dingo, then crossing the result with the Dalmatian and the black-and-tan kelpie. Formally recognised as a breed in Australia in 1897.

blue mouldy a delightful and sadly out-moded slang term meaning out of sorts or stale. *A bloke goes blue mouldy in a place like this.*

blue movie a pornographic film.

Blue Orchid in World War II, a member of the RAAF.

blue swimmer a ten dollar note, the colour of which resembles the well-known crab.

blue tongue **1.** a rural worker engaged upon menial or easy tasks. A reference to the well-known blue-tongued lizard, noted for its slowness. **2.** a child, because they are low to the ground.

bluey **1.** historically, a rolled blanket, originally blue, containing the possessions carried by a traveller through the bush; in other words, a swag. Hence, to **hump the bluey** was to lead the life of a swagman. **2.** in Tasmania, a large grey-blue woollen coat or jacket used in cold, wet weather. **3.** hospital slang, a blue plastic bedsheet for patients with incontinence. **4.** a summons issued for a traffic or parking offence. Dating back to the 1900s, and now especially common in NSW, SA and Tas. **5.** a blue cattle dog. **6.** a blue-tongued lizard. **7.** a blue swimmer crab. **8.** a blue yabby. **9.** a nickname for a red-headed person, in use since the early 1900s.

Blunnies a pair of leather boots of the *Blundstone* brand, very popular in Tasmania, where the company originated in 1870.

blurter the anus.

boardies boardshorts. Favoured by surfies, who would never be seen dead wearing **clubbies** (see entry).

boasters speedos – alluding to their revealing nature. For a full set of synonyms see **sluggos**.

boatie a boating enthusiast.

boatrace **1.** rhyming slang for 'face'. **2.** a competition between teams of beer drinkers to see which team can drink its beer the fastest. The teams line up on either side of a long table, facing one another, and the drinking starts at one end and progresses to the other, the rule being that you are not allowed to begin drinking until the teammate next to you has finished.

bob old slang term for one shilling. Transferred to ten cents after the introduction of decimal currency in 1966. From 18th century British slang, of unknown origin. Pluralised (like *sheep*) by the addition of nothing, thus *one bob, two bob, ten bob*. Used also to mean money in general, as in *That'll cost a few bob*, or *They aren't short of a bob*. The Boy Scouts Association used to run a fundraising **bob-a-job** day, in which Scouts would do menial tasks for payment of a bob. In the old days when a bob was actually worth something, a subscription to a common fund was commonly a **bob in**. If someone was a bit light on in the brains department they were said to be only **eighteen bob in the pound**, or **fifteen**, or even **ten**, depending on how stupid you thought they were.

bobby-dazzler an excellent person or thing. From Yorkshire and Lancashire dialect of the 19th century. Still used in Britain as well as here.

Bob Hope **1.** rhyming slang for 'dope', as in marijuana. **2.** rhyming slang for 'soap'.

Bob's your uncle everything is okay. Used in both Australia and Britain, but who the original uncle Bob was remains a mystery.

bocka **1.** a Victorian term for a type of short haircut. **2.** among schoolkids, a sharp punch on the arm with a knuckle, inflicted as punishment for some misdemeanour like farting. Also spelt **bocker** or **bokka**.

bod **1.** a person. *What an odd bod.* **2.** a body. *He's got a cute bod!*

bodacious remarkable; outstanding. From US slang, from British dialect, *boldacious*, a blend of *bold* and *audacious*. Made its way to Australia in the 1980s.

bodacious ta-tas stunning breasts. A US slang term that took off after its use in the Mike Myers movie *Wayne's World* (1992). Its popularity in Oz was partially helped along by Sydney morning radio show host Doug Mulray. In August 2000, a pornographic website carrying this name had its registration cancelled as a result of a complaint by Tata Sons Limited, a large Indian company well-known there for vehicle manufacture.

bodge **1.** to do or make something in a sloppy manner. *I bodged together a few examples.* **2.** to ruin or wreck. *Now you've really bodged it.* **3.** no good; hopeless. *It was a totally bodge movie.*

bodgie **1.** of poor quality, second-rate, as in a *a bodgie repair job*. The earlier expression was *bodger*, and it no doubt has its origins in the

British dialect word *bodge* 'to mend clumsily', a close relative of the general English word *botch*. **2.** false; phoney; fake. *She gave the cop a bodgie name.* **3.** In the 1950s and 60s, a **bodgie** was a type of young hooligan or lout that was the terror of refined society. Their girlfriends were **widgies**, and together they were known as **bodgies and widgies** – a term that struck fear into the hearts and minds of the rest of the population. Basically, they were disaffected youths who rejected the stodgy morality and world view of the time, slept around a lot, drove motorbikes and fast cars, got pissed and fought, and indulged in petty crime. Clothes-wise they were influenced by American fashions of the day, wearing long draping, waistless, leather jackets, and stovepipe jeans or pants. They later morphed into **sharpies** – which was the same thing, but with a different name. **4.** a large playing marble.

bodgie up to mock up or fake. *The photos had been bodgied up.*

bodice ripper a paperback romance novel with a pictorial cover featuring a muscular hero and big-breasted heroine in a steamy pose.

boff to have sexual intercourse. Originally American slang of the 1930s, and surfacing in Oz the 1980s.

bog **1.** an act of defecation. As in *going for a bog* or *hanging a bog*. Hence, as a verb, to defecate – which the Oxford English Dictionary of 1885 exquisitely defined as 'to exonerate the bowels'. In Britain, the **bog** is the toilet, and this usage has some currency in Australia, but is not as common as our usual *dunny*, *loo* or *toot*. **2.** a mining term from WA meaning to work shovelling ore underground. **3.** also in WA a **bog** is a bogan, especially a really rough one. See **bogan**. **4.** a putty-like material for patching dents in vehicle bodies. Hence, to fill in dents with bog. *Bog it and flog it!*

bog a duck descriptive of extremely boggy land. Used by Ned Kelly in his famous Jerilderie Letter of 1879, and still in use today. Apart from the adjectival use as in *a bog-a-duck track*, you can also come across it used verbally – *You could bog a duck in that paddock, come the wet.*

bogan **1.** especially among schoolkids, a fool or idiot. Popular in the 1980s. Perhaps from the *Bogan* River in NSW, as a place from which unsophisticated country bumpkins hail. **2.** in WA, a lout or hooligan, especially of a particular social group noted for wearing flannos, black jeans and DBs; equivalent to the NSW *westie* or the Qld *bevan*. **3.** in Tasmania, a rough lout or hooligan; in Hobart, equivalent to a **chigger**.

Bogan gate a gate made from barbed wire and stakes found in the bush.

bogan juice iced coffee.

bogan navy bogans who visit the beach.

bogart a joint to smoke more than your fair share of a joint. Very poor manners among the dope-smoking fraternity. Alluding to Humphrey Bogart who played various cigarette-smoking, tough guys in 1940s movies.

bogey **1.** a swim or bath in a creek, waterhole, dam, etc. The word is from the Australian Aboriginal language Dharug, formerly spoken in the Sydney district. After a hard day's slog rural workers often grab a bogey. Working dogs know that upon the command 'Go bogey' they can have a refreshing dip in a nearby waterhole. Hence, as a verb, to take a bath or swim in a **bogey hole** (see entry). **2.** The first definition is not to be confused with **bogey** meaning a piece of nasal mucus, either dried, moist or semi-dried, as in *You got a bogey on your chin.* Also used as a verb, meaning to expel snot from the nose, as in *Don't bogey on it, you filthy bastard!* This is a variation of **boogie** and **booger**.

bogey hole a naturally occurring pool in which you can swim.

bogger **1.** in WA, a person employed to bog soil from a mine Also, piece of machinery, a bit like a front-end loader, used for the same job. **2.** a toilet. *I'm off to the bogger.*

bog house a dunny. Venerable slang, dating back to the 17th century.

bog in to tuck into a meal. A bit of genuine Aussie English from as early as 1917.

bog it in to win easily or perform a task easily.

bog laps in WA, circuits of a street block in a car for the purpose of entertainment. *Those kids are out there doing bog laps again.* Compare **blockies**, **lappies**.

bog locks in WA, long locks of hair as worn by bogs.

bog standard not containing any special features. *It's a bog standard interface.* Also, **bog stock**.

bogus 1. very bad; unfair; no good. *That was a bogus stunt you pulled.* 2. in a bizarre reversal of lexical fortunes, **bogus** can also mean excellent, brilliant, terrific. The idea being that it is so-o-o good that it is unbelievable. *That was absolutely bogus, dude!*

boiler an uncomplimentary title for an elderly woman. From the normal sense 'an old chicken that is only good for boiling', in other words, a tough old bird.

boilover a win by a long-priced entrant in horse or greyhound race.

boil-up in prison, an illegal brewing of tea or coffee in your cell.

boko old slang for the nose. Origin unknown.

bollocks 1. the testicles. A classic Anglo-Saxon word, though this time more than the usual four letters. Also spelt **ballocks** or **bollicks**. 2. rubbish or nonsense, as in *What a load of bollocks.* Also used as an exclamation decrying the verity of another's statement.

bollocky used to refer to a state of complete nakedness, as in *stark bollocky naked.* If you are **in the bollocky**, you are in the nude. Aussie slang since the 1950s. Also, **bollicky**, or shortened to **bols**.

boloney nonsense; insincere or idle talk; waffle. Also spelt **baloney**.

bolt to escape from custody; to run away from authorities. Genuine Australian convict slang.

bolt in to win easily. Originally horseracing slang. Also, **bolt it in** and **bolt home**.

bomb 1. an old, crappy car; a car that has been flogged to death. An original and genuine Australianism. Now also used in the UK and the US. 2. a stimulant drug given to a racehorse or greyhound. Hence, to administer such a drug. Highly illegal. 3. in sapphire areas, a lump of black corundum of no value. 4. a jump into water with the knees tucked into the chest and the arms clasped about the knees so as to make an enormous splash and annoy nearby swimmers. As a verb, to jump into the water in this manner. Generally banned but not illegal. 5. to fail a test, exam, or the like; to perform badly; to dud out or flop. 6. among graffiti artists, to cover with graffiti. *We bombed six carriages last night.* 7. lately teenagers have adopted the American usage **You're the bomb**, or more correctly, **You're da bomb**, from US television and rap music. In Aussie it means 'You're bonzer!'

bombie a bomb into a swimming pool, etc.

bombo an old word for low-quality liquor. Stuff that bombs you out. Australian since the 1940s.

bombshell 1. a sudden or devastating action. *His resignation was a bombshell.* 2. an amazingly sexy woman.

bommie a bombora.

bommy knocker 1. the spiny seed pod of the liquidambar tree. 2. a large object used as a club by children. Both named after the spiky-headed club in the children's book *The Hungry Giant*, by Joy Cowley, 1980.

Bondi chest the puny chest of a weakling. Because Bondi is 'far from Manly'.

Bondi cigar a floating piece of human excrement in the ocean. So called because a major Sydney effluent outlet was located near Bondi beach. Also called a **Bondi shark**. See **blind mullet** for a swag of synonyms.

Bondi tram the tram line out to Bondi beach from Sydney was notoriously fast, and hence became used as a metaphor for speedy departure. *He shot through like a Bondi tram.* Sydney's trams were discontinued in 1961, but the term remains.

Bondi whistler a painful tweaking of another's nipple.

bone 1. If you **jump on someone's bones**, you have sex with them. Half your luck. 2. If you **make old bones**, you reach a ripe old age. Half your luck again. 3. If someone **points the bone** at someone, they wish them bad luck, or they indicate that they are guilty of something. This alludes to the traditional Aboriginal custom of pointing the bone. 4. Among schoolkids and blokey blokes, a **bone** is an erect penis. Also known as a **boner**.

bonecrusher in rugby, a heavy tackle.

bonehead a stupid, obstinate person; a blockhead.

boner 1. a foolish mistake; a gross blunder. *You made a boner that time.* 2. a difficult question. 3. an erect penis.

boneshaker an ancient and rickety bicycle; any vehicle with crap suspension.

bong 1. an apparatus for smoking marijuana or hashish consisting of a container, partially filled with water, with a pipe passing into it. The drug is packed into the cone – a conical receptacle attached to the pipe. The container is often improvised out of a plastic fruit juice bottle. The harsh smoke is made smoother as it passes through the water. The same principle as a hookah but not as elaborate. The word itself comes from the Thai language. **2.** an instance of smoking through a bong; or as much marijuana as contained in a bong. *Had a few too many bongs with me mates last night*. **3.** as a verb, to smoke marijuana or hashish through a bong.

bong on to take part in a dope smoking session; to smoke dope. A phrase often seen proudly emblazoned in graffiti as a credo of the dope-smoker.

bonk **1.** to hit smartly but not too forcefully on the head. *She bonked her little brother on the head.* **2.** to have sex. A choice bit of British slang that swept the world back in the mid 1980s. Hence, an act of sexual intercourse, or a person considered in light of their sexual prowess, as in *He's not a bad bonk.*

bonkable attractive enough to have sex with.

bonker a large marble.

bonkers crazy, insane, out of control. *He's gone bonkers.* Originally British slang.

bonk song a song played while having sex in order to enhance the experience. *One of the greatest bonk songs of all time.*

bontosher obsolete term equivalent to **bonzer** (see entry).

bonus! great! excellent! tops!

bonzer great, excellent, terrific. A bonzer bit of Aussie slang, of mystifying origin. The word dates back to the early 1900s where it was one of a set of similar sounding words, namely *bontosher*, *bonster*, *boshter*, and *bosker*, all with the same meaning and now all obsolete except for *bonzer*. Some have suggested that it is a variant of British dialect *bouncer* meaning something remarkable – but this doesn't explain the other forms. It is most probably influenced by or otherwise connected with the French word *bon* meaning good. Occasionally spelt **bonza**.

boob **1.** a woman's breast. Occasionally in the diminutive form **boobie**. Originally an Americanism from the 1920s. **2.** prison. A shortening of *booby hatch.* Also originally an Americanism, though slightly earlier, dating back to the 1900s. In Australian prisons, it has taken on an adjectival role where it refers to any item that is jail issue, and hence is of poor quality. As in *boob tea* or *boob tobacco.*

boob happy suffering from a form of neurosis brought about by the strain of jail routine, stir crazy.

boob head a privileged prisoner; a prisoner with great influence among the inmates.

boob job any cosmetic surgery done to the breasts.

boob tube **1.** a television set. **2.** a woman's strapless, tubular, elasticised upper garment primarily covering the breasts; a bandeau top.

boofhead an idiot; a stupid fellow with an oversized head; a fathead. Been around since the 1940s where it was popularised by the cartoon character *Boofhead* appearing in the Sydney *Daily Mirror* from 1941. The most likely origin is that it is a variant of earlier *bufflehead*, which had the same meaning, but which literally means 'buffalo head'. Naturally, anyone with a boofhead is described adjectivally as **boofheaded**.

boofy **1.** of men, brawny but a bit thick. *I'm sick of all the boofy boys in the gym.* **2.** of the hair, having lots of volume. **3.** puffed out. *The blouse had big boofy sleeves.*

booger **1.** a surfie's derogatory word for a boogie boarder. **2.** a piece of nasal mucus. An Americanism which dates back to the 1890s.

boogie a piece of nasal mucus, especially one that has come out into the world, as in *Hey drongo, you got a boogie on your chin.* Hence, as a verb, to expel snot from the nose, as in *Don't boogie on it!* A variant pronunciation of **bogey**. Recorded in the US since the 1890s. Origin unknown, but it is interesting to note that the British dialect of Yorkshire and Lincolnshire had *boggle* and *boggart* for the same thing. Not to be confused with the musical term *boogie.*

bookie a bookmaker. Also, simply a **book**.

bookie's runner a bookmaker's assistant engaged in collecting prices, laying off bets with other bookies, and like duties.

boomer **1.** something impressive; a great success; a bumper. Dating back to the 19th century in Australia, the US and in British dialect. No one can decide who owns the term originally. **2.** a large, crashing wave. **3.** a large, mature kangaroo. Originally a Tasmanian term, dating back to the 1830s; from the same source as the other senses, but influenced by the *booming* sound of the kangaroo's hop. **4.** a male quokka. **5.** an exclamation of joy. **6.** a hoon in a hotted-up car with a booming sound system. **7.** the Australian bittern (*Botaurus poiciloptilus*), which makes a loud booming noise.

boomerang the traditional throwing stick of the Australian Aborigines, especially the well-known returning type. This word comes from Dharug, the Australian Aboriginal language formerly spoken in the Sydney district. Used in slang for various things that return or are returned like the following: **1.** a small fish that is thrown back into the water. **2.** a borrowed item that the lender stipulates must be returned. *Yes, you can borrow my copy, but remember – it's a boomerang.* **3.** as a verb, to return or recoil upon the originator. *The argument boomeranged.*

boomerang bender a teller of tall stories.

boondie in WA **1.** a lump of yellow sand that explodes on impact used as missiles by children at war. **2.** a medium to large rock. Used in the mining industry to mean a large rock, a rock that won't go through the crusher, or a smaller rock on a haul road that is a nuisance and could cause tyre damage. See **coondie**. **3.** a small stone suitable for throwing, equivalent to a yonnie, brinnie or gibber. See **yonnie** for the full set of regionalisms. **4.** an excrement or turd. This one is not restricted to WA, and probably has a different origin.

boondocks any remote region; the sticks. Borrowed from the US, this term originally was used by the US military in the Philippines to refer to the mountains or jungle. It is actually the Tagalog word for mountain. Also called the **boonies**.

booner the Canberra term for a westie, bevan or bogan. A yobbo from the boondocks. Also called a **boonie**.

boong a derogatory and racist term for an Australian Aboriginal. Also used for the natives of Papua and New Guinea, especially during World War II. Occasionally used to refer to black people of any race or nationality. The word first appears in the 1920s and is from the Aboriginal language Wembawemba of central Victoria. There is a common story that it derives from the sound of an Aboriginal bouncing off the bumper of a car – which gives you an idea about the type of people who use this word.

boonger **1.** a racist term for an Aboriginal person. **2.** a dilapidated old car used for crashing around the farm or in the bush; a paddock basher. Also spelt **boonga**.

boonted messed up or broken.

booshit very good; excellent, as in *booshit surf.* A variant of the word *bullshit.*

boost to shoplift. Originally US underworld slang.

boosy a breast.

boot **1.** a kick, as in *Watch yourself or you'll get a swift boot up the khyber.* To **put the boot in** is to attack unmercifully. This phrase is a genuine Australianism from the 1910s. **2.** rejection or ejection; dismissal from employment. *I got the boot after donging the boss.* **3.** to kick; to expel with a kick or as with a kick. *He was booted out of the club.* **4.** In Australia and Britain cars have boots for storing luggage and the like; in the US they have *trunks.*

boot home **1.** to ride to win, kicking the horse to greater speed. **2.** to emphasise strongly.

bootlace If you are **not someone's bootlace**, it means you are no good at doing what that person does. *You're not a jockey's bootlace.*

bootlicker an arrant flatterer; a bloody crawler.

boots and all completely; with all your strength or resources. Australian slang since the 1950s. *Go in boots and all.*

booty the buttocks or rump; the arse, as in *Get your booty shakin'.* A borrowing from the US where it has been in use in Black English since the 1920s. It is merely a pronunciation variant of the word *body.* Also in the form **boody**.

booyah! all right! okay! excellent! Also commonly in the form **booyeah!**

booze **1.** alcoholic drink. Not originally Australian, but a much-loved word here. Actually dates back, in one form or another, to the 14th century, where it was borrowed from the Dutch language. If you are **on the booze**, you are drinking heavily. **2.** as a verb, to drink immoderately. *We've been boozing all day long.*

booze artist a heavy drinker.

booze bus a mobile police unit used for random breath tests.

booze cruise an outing on a boat which stops at various wharves while the participants patronise a local pub; a pub crawl via water.

boozer **1.** one who drinks booze, especially immoderately; a booze artist; a pisspot. **2.** a hotel.

booze-up a drinking session.

boozing mate a drinking partner. Aussie slang since the early 1900s. Also called a **boozing buddy**.

bo-peep a peek. Aussie slang since the 1940s. *Have a bo-peep at that!*

bopple nut a macadamia nut. More correctly a **Bauple nut**, from Mt Bauple near Maryborough, Qld. Also called a **Queensland nut**.

borak To **poke borak at** someone is to ridicule them. Formerly quite common, but scarcely heard any more. Earlier on, **borak** meant nonsense and in origin comes from the Aboriginal language Wathawurung, from the Geelong area.

bore it up to give someone heaps. Dinkum Aussie this one, since the 1950s. *He was boring it up me about being ten minutes late.*

borket a Brisbane slang word equivalent to a bevan.

born-again a Christian who has been 'born again', especially a zealous or evangelical one. A derogatory term used by accursed heathens.

born loser an unsuccessful person; someone who seems destined to misfortune and failure.

borrie a turd. Aussie slang, more prevalent in Vic than elsewhere.

boshter obsolete term equivalent to **bonzer** (see entry).

bosie in cricket, a delivery bowled by a wrist-spinner which looks as if it will break one way but in fact goes the other; a googly or wrong'un. From B.J.T. *Bos*anquet, English cricketer renowned as the inventor of this bowl. Also spelt **bosey**.

bosker obsolete term equivalent to **bonzer** (see entry).

boss **1.** the male owner of a rural property or station. Traditionally having jurisdiction over the running of the property outside of the homestead, which is run by the **missus**. **2.** the principal of a school. **3.** in the military, a commanding officer. **4.** in prison, a polite and ingratiating form of address to a warder. **5.** an Aboriginal term for any whitefella, whether they were an employer or not. A demonstration of the traditional power imbalance between black and white. Formerly in common use, but now no longer heard.

boss cocky **1.** the top bloke in an organisation; the person running the joint. In rural areas, a station owner or manager. **2.** also used in a negative way for an upstart who lords it over others; a little authoritarian git.

bot **1.** a parasitic insect larva. **2.** an inveterate borrower or cadger. Hence, to cadge or borrow: *Can I bot a ciggy from you?* Someone who is botting is said to be **on the bot**. **3.** short for the bottom, as in your rump. **4.** short for **bottle-oh**, the marble (see entry).

bottle **1.** to knock over someone as though they were a bottle. *Bottle 'im!* **2.** If you are **on the bottle**, it means you are on a drinking binge. To **hit the bottle** is to start drinking.

bottle blonde a person with dyed blonde hair.

bottle-oh **1.** a person whose job was to collect used bottles for cleaning and re-sale; a bottle collector. **2.** a type of glass marble. Also known as a **bottley**. In the olden days there used to be a type of soft drink bottle with an internal marble stopper. The pressure from the carbonated drink kept the stopper in place. To obtain these marbles you needed to smash the bottle, the fervent smashing of which has led to these bottles now being very scarce collectables.

bottler something absolutely brilliant. *You little bottler!* Dating back as early as 1855, the origin of this classic Australianism is lost in time.

bottlo a bottle shop.

bottom **1.** the passive partner in homosexual anal sex. As opposed to the **top**. **2.** an exclamation of mild disappointment; blast! drat!

botty the bottom; the buttocks. A child's word, used by adults.

bouncy-bouncy sexual intercourse.

bovver boot any large, tough, lace-up boots, as army boots.

bovver boy an aggressive skinhead of the type commonly found in Britain. From the Cockney pronunciation of the word *bother*.

bower bird an avid collector of things.

bowl cut a poor haircut, which appears as though the barber merely placed an inverted bowl on the head and trimmed the hair that hung below the rim. Also called a **basin cut**.

bowlo a bowling club. Chiefly an eastern states word.

box **1.** a television set. **2.** the vagina or vulva. **3.** If something is **out of the box**, then it is strikingly remarkable, an outstanding example. If on the other hand it is decidedly not remarkable, then it is **nothing out of the box**. **4.** In the racing game, to **box** a bet is to make it so that one receives a return whether the horse or dog wins or runs a place.

boxer one who runs a two-up school and receives a set proportion, usually twenty per cent, of the spinner's earnings; the ringie.

boxhead one who has a large, squarish head; a bullethead.

box monster a cask of wine. *I had a big night on the box monster*. Also shortened to **boxie**.

box seat the premier or best position. The original box seat was the seat on a horse-drawn buggy next to the driver, the best place to see the world go by.

boy **1.** an adult man, as in *the boys down the pub*. Often in the encouraging phrase *That's the boy*, and the classic Aussie compliment *I like the boy*. This phrase almost landed Bert Newton in deep strife when he used it to refer to Mohammed Ali who was helping him present an award at the Logies. Ali bristled, thinking of the US racist usage of *boy* for a black man. Historically, the same racist usage was of course applied to Aboriginal men over the years, but seems to no longer be very common. **2.** a boyfriend.

boyf a teenage girl's boyfriend.

boy in the boat the clitoris. Sometimes called the **man in the boat**.

boy of... a boy by the name of... Thus, 'Boy of Smith, come here!' means 'Young Master Smith, come here!' Particularly used in rural NSW.

boy's germs among children, a supposed contagion of boyness avoided by girls. Compare **girl's germs**.

boys in blue the police force.

boy wonder any man of marvellous attributes, though, generally used ironically. *We were doing fine until boy wonder showed up*.

bozo a fool or buffoon. US slang from 1910s, perhaps from Spanish *bozal* 'stupid', or Italian *bozzo* 'bastard'.

the Bra the Sydney suburb of Maroubra. The Bra Boys is a gang of youths of some notoriety.

brace and bits rhyming slang for 'tits'. Originally US, from the 1920s.

Brahms and Liszt rhyming slang for 'pissed', that is, drunk out of your brain. Commonly shortened to **Brahms**.

brain **1.** to hit someone hard on the head. *If you do that again, I'll brain you!* **2.** a narky, scoffing term for a highly intelligent person.

brain dead **1.** stupid; moronic; without two brain cells to rub together. **2.** mentally exhausted.

brain explosion a momentary fit of madness, especially common on the sporting field.

brain-fried having your mental abilities seriously impaired by too much drug-taking.

brainiac a highly intelligent person. From *Brainiac*, arch-criminal of *Superman* cartoons.

brains trust a group of people deferred to for intelligence.

brandings a common schoolyard game in which a tennis ball is thrown at the other players by the person who is 'in'. The person hit is then 'in'. **Brandings** is the common term in NSW, ACT and Tasmania. In the other states it is usually known as **brandy**. The idea is to throw the ball hard enough to *brand* the person hit – in other words, to leave a glowing red mark. Ouch! For some reason, it's banned by school teachers the country over.

brasco a toilet. Recorded first in 1955, defined as 'the dunny at a showground'. Some have conjectured that it arose from from a toilet manufacturer named *Brass Co.* – but there is no confirmation that such a company existed. At any rate, it is pronounced with a short 'a', not the long 'a' of 'brass'.

brass **1.** money. **2.** underworld slang, to con someone out of their money. **3.** high ranking military officers. Also called **brass hats**.

brass monkey weather extremely cold weather – in other words, weather that is **cold enough to freeze the balls off a brass monkey**. The monkey referred to here is, of course, a brass statue of a monkey, and the balls are his testes. The widely-held theory that this originally referred to a type of nautical artillery piece that would liberate cannonballs in extremely cold weather is nothing but an urban myth. In other words, it is wrong, Wrong, WRONG! So all those people going around spreading this story can just stop. I mean, let's just think about it for a second. Firstly, you can't have cannonballs rolling around the ship, that's just not on, for obvious reasons. Secondly, ships on the high seas are inevitably destined to be tossed around violently in bad weather. Thus, an apparatus built to hold shipboard cannonballs must of necessity be made to prevent cannonball escape. Now, if cannonballs are falling off these supposed monkeys due to the infinitessimal metal shrinkage caused by cold weather, then surely they'd be rolling off in high seas also. You see, it just doesn't make sense. Anyhow, logic aside, the lexical evidence is totally against this theory. The earliest examples of the phrase (from the US in the mid 19th century) refer to other parts of the monkey's anatomy. It wasn't *balls* that were frozen off, but rather *tails, legs, noses* and *ears.*

brass razoo a supposed coin of negligible value. *I haven't got a brass razoo.* See **razoo** for more information.

Brazilian a full waxing of the pubic region, or one where a 'landing strip' is left at the front. Hence, a pubic region so waxed. So called since G-string bikini bottoms are all the go in Brazil, requiring the removal of much more hair than a normal bikini wax. Introduced to the west in 1987 at the J. Sisters International Salon, Manhattan.

bread money; earnings. Originally US underworld slang of the 1930s.

bread and duck under the table an answer to the question 'What's for dinner?'

break eggs with a big stick to do something in an over-the-top manner, well beyond what was required.

break it down **1.** calm down; be reasonable. **2.** stop it.

bred a person from a small town or remote place. Short for *inbred*, incest being a common slur directed at such people.

breeder among homosexuals, a derogatory term for a heterosexual.

brekkie breakfast.

breville a toasted sandwich made in a sandwich toaster – the electric equivalent of the older **jaffle iron**. Originally from the popular brand name Breville, but came to be used generically, irrespective of which brand of sandwich toaster you were using.

brew **1.** a pot or cup of tea or coffee. **2.** in prison, alcoholic beverage illicitly made by prisoners.

brewer's droop alcohol-induced sexual impotence in men. Aussie slang since the 1970s.

brick **1.** a good, reliable person; a staunch friend; someone who is 'solid'. **2.** in olden days, £10 or a £10 note. So called from the colour of the note. After decimal currency in 1966, this was transferred to $10, but has now died out. **3.** underworld slang, a prison sentence of ten years' duration. **4.** to falsify evidence.

Brickfielder formerly, an unpleasant southerly buster in Sydney which brought dust from the brickworks at Brickfield Hill. Now obsolete.

brickie a bricklayer. Has been around for yonks and was recorded as early as 1900.

bricking the falsification of evidence against someone in order to substantiate a criminal charge.

a brick short of a load mentally wanting. For similar comparisons see the entry for **short of**.

brick venereal disease the dreaded spread of brick veneer housing.

bridge to accidentally display underwear when wearing a skirt.

Bridgewater jerry a fog bank that rolls down the Derwent River from Bridgewater to Hobart.

brief **1.** a barrister or judge. **2.** any ticket, as a betting ticket, bus ticket, etc.

brill a colloquial shortening of the word 'brilliant'. Sometimes extended to **brillo**.

Brill car a railcar run by South Australian Railways, mainly servicing country lines from the 1920s to the 1950s. After J.G. Brill Company, the US manufacturers. Also called **Barwell's bull**.

the Brindies local slang for the Brindabella Ranges near Canberra.

bring a plate a common request found on invitations to social functions where guests are asked to contribute some food. Clear as a bell to all Aussies, but famed for confusing foreigners, who have on many occasions unhappily interpreted the phrase literally and so turned up at a party, dressed to the nines, and carrying a plate – an empty plate!

brinnie a small stone suitable for throwing. Used chiefly in Vic and south-east Qld. See **yonnie** for the full set of regionalisms.

Brisso **1.** Brisbane. **2.** an inhabitant of Brisbane. Generally a derogatory term used by Sunshine and Gold Coast residents. Also spelt **Brizzo**.

Brissy Brisbane. Also spelt **Brizzy**.

Bristols breasts. From rhyming slang *Bristol City* (the British soccer team) for 'titty'.

Bris-Vegas Brisbane. Partly with ironic reference to Brisbane's lack of showy opulence (for which Las Vegas is famous), and partly because Brisbane was the first Qld city to have a casino. Also shortened to the simple **Vegas**. Inhabitants of this fair town are, of course, **Bris-Vegans**.

Brit a mildly derogatory term for a British person.

British bulldog a schoolyard game in which a group of children run repeatedly through an area guarded by other children. Those who are caught each time join forces with their catchers until only one child remains uncaught and is the winner. It is often banned by teachers as too dangerous. This is the most common term. The next in frequency is **red rover**, which is particularly common in Qld, NSW and SA. Also known as **red rover cross over**. In NSW it is generally called **cockylora** or **cockylora 1,2,3**. The term **bullrush** is found in NSW, the ACT and Qld. And the term **bedlam** is unique to Qld.

Britney a glass of beer. From rhyming slang *Britney Spears* for 'beers'.

bro a brother; a close male friend; a member of your gang. Also used as a cool greeting: *Sup, bro?* A 1980s adoption from US English, mostly used by today's youth.

broadie a sideways skid of a pushbike. The same thing as a **broggie**.

Broadmeadows briefcase **1.** a cask of cheap wine. **2.** one of those cheap red, white and blue striped bags purchased at $2 shops.

Broadmeadows wedding shoes rubber-soled moccasins.

Broady the Melbourne suburb of Broadmeadows. A tough suburb. Home to a gang of street toughs known as the **Broady Boys**, who have been terrorising unfortunates for many a decade. Used to fight the **Sandy boys** from the nearby suburb of Sandringham.

broggie in WA and SA, a sideways skid of a pushbike. The same thing as a **broadie**.

broke to the wide out of money; bankrupt.

brolly an umbrella. Originally 19th century British slang.

Bronte buggy Sydney slang for a 4WD that never sees off-road driving.

bronze the anus. Aussie slang since the 1950s. An extended use of the now obsolete slang term *bronze* 'a one penny coin'. Also called a **bronza** or a **bronzo**.

bronzed sun-tanned in that iconic Australian way.

brothel a room or house that is a frigging mess that you should be ashamed of.

brothel creepers sandshoes or sneakers. Also called **brothel boots**.

brother a close male friend, especially a member of a gang. Not used too much except by youngsters consciously imitating US usage. The shortening **bro** is more common.

brown baker a type of brown cicada.

brown bomber a parking inspector. Chiefly used in NSW and SA, but now dying out as the uniform has changed. In SA you can find the term **sticker licker**. Vic has **grey meanie**, and the **grey ghost**, the latter also found in NSW and WA. In any area where the uniforms are blue the term has become **blue bomber**.

browneye an obscene gesture of contempt in which one bends over and presents the bared anus.

brownie point an imaginary point scored to your credit or in your favour.

brownnose to flatter servilely; to crawl.

brown noser a sycophantic crawler.

brown sandwich a bottle of beer. Common slang term in Qld.

Brownsville a nickname for Townsville, Qld, alluding to lack of greenery. For the same reason called **Mount Isa by the Sea**.

brown trout faecal matter floating in your swimming water. See **blind mullet** for a swag of synonyms.

Bruce **1.** a name used to mock the typical Australian bloke: *G'day Bruce.* It has its origins in a Monty Python sketch. **2.** a name used for a bloke who has done something deemed effeminate or lacking in appropriate masculinity, with the imputation that they are homosexual. Spoken with a camp accent. Also, the twee diminutive **Brucie** is used in this manner.

bruiser a glass of beer, half old and half new.

brumby a wild horse, especially one descended from runaway stock. The story goes that this is named after one Captain (or Major) Brumby, a noted horsebreeder in colonial times. It should be remembered however, that this tale first appears in the 1930s, some 50 years after the word was first recorded. Another possibility is that it comes from the Irish word for a colt.

brush-off a rejection of romantic advances. Aussie slang since the 1940s.

bub **1.** a baby. **2.** a child in their first years of school, as in kindergarten or infants. Hence, **the bubs** is kindergarten. **3.** used as an affectionate name for a girlfriend, wife or daughter.

bubble and squeak rhyming slang for 'Greek'. Originally British World War I slang.

bubbler a small water tap attached to a basin in a public place for the refreshment of the thirsty. This word is especially common in NSW, the ACT and Qld. The most common term for the rest of the states is **drinking fountain**. In Vic the same item is also called a **bubble tap**. The terms **drink tap** and **drinking tap** are common in Qld and Vic. Just plain **fountain** is common to all states and territories. The last term in the set is **water fountain**, which is especially common in Qld, Tas, SA and WA. Territorians seem to use the lot. That about sums it up, except to say that none of these synonyms are exclusive to any state or territory, so don't get too precious about it.

bubble tap a chiefly Victorian term for a drinking fountain. See **bubbler** for the full set of regionalisms.

buck **1.** a dollar. Originally an Americanism dating back to the mid-19th century where it was short for *buckskin*, the skin of a buck or deer, formerly an accepted form of exchange on the US frontier. **2.** historically used in Australia as a racist term for a male Aboriginal. A usage that has thankfully died out. **3.** any man; now only in the collocation **young buck**. **4.** the groom-to-be when out on his buck's night. **5.** to have sex in a vigorous manner. Yee-haa!

buckboard in SA, a utility truck. Older slang, dying out now.

bucket **1.** to criticise strongly; to denigrate. In other words, to **tip the bucket on** someone. The bucket in question is, of course, a full sanitary can. Thus equivalent to 'put shit on'. **2.** short for bucket bong. *Had a few buckets after work.*

bucket bong a type of bong for smoking marijuana in which a bottomless plastic soft drink bottle is sunk partially into a bucket of water, the chamber is filled with smoke and then consumed all at once with the release of air pressure.

Buckley's chance no chance at all. Possibly referring to a famous escaped convict William Buckley, although, the said Buckley did manage to elude the authorities for some 32 years by living with Aboriginals before giving himself up, so it seems that he had a pretty fair chance after all. Sometimes the phrase is expressed as **You've got two chances – Buckley's and none**. This is a pun on a well-known Melbourne department store *Buckley and Nunn*.

bucko a term of address used in a mildly confrontational manner, as in *You just mind your language, bucko.* From US English, probably from the Irish Gaelic word *buachaill* 'boy'.

buck's night an exclusively male get-together, held before the wedding for the bridegroom by his mates. The male counterpart of the **hen's night**. Traditionally marked by such things as lots of drinking, obscene pranks, strippers, copious vomiting, loutish behaviour and the like. Also, **buck's ding**, **buck's party**, or **buck's turn**.

bud the budding heads of the marijuana plant prepared for smoking.

buddha marijuana.

buddy a friend, mate or cobber. Also shortened to **bud**. Obviously an Americanism, but used quite commonly here since World War II, though with much less frequency than the traditional *mate*. It was originally a Black English word, and is a pronunciation variant of *brother*. Aussies don't use it as a term of address to a unknown person.

budget in WA and SA, a booklet containing information about the week's round of AFL games. Called the **record** in Vic and Tas.

budgie a budgerigar, the small green outback parrot commonly incarcerated as a cagebird. Originally from an Aboriginal language. The Aboriginal name was ignorantly supposed to mean 'good bird' or 'good eating', and this pseudo-fact is still commonly bandied about though it has long been proved incorrect.

budgie smugglers speedos; sometimes used to mean male underwear. Occasionally also called **budgie huggers**. For a full set of synonyms see **sluggos**.

budjo cheap and hence of poor quality.

Bug a Volkswagen Beetle.

bugger **1.** originally, a person taking part in anal sex or bestiality, or as a verb, to perform anal sex, to sodomise, or to have sex with an animal. In origin it is from French and is ultimately derived from the Latin word *Bulgarus* meaning Bulgarian, referring to a medieval heretical sect who were accused of buggery. Formerly a word of high taboo, as was the practice, which for centuries was a felony punishable by hanging. Over the years, the word's impact has been greatly reduced, especially in its slang senses. It is hardly ever used in its original signification any longer. **2.** a contemptible or despicable person; now more generally a merely annoying person as in *little buggers* or *stupid bugger*. **3.** to **play silly buggers** is to muck around. **4.** any person. *Come on, you old bugger*. **5.** a nuisance; a difficulty; something unpleasant or nasty as in *That recipe is a real bugger* or *It's a bugger of a day*. **6.** damn! blast! As in *Bugger him, I'm going home*. **7.** to ruin or wreck, as in *That's buggered it!* Or to 'stuff' or 'fuck', as in *Well, that buggers me!* Or that common expression of personal ignorance *Buggered if I know!*

bugger about to mess around; to fiddle-fart about. Also, **bugger around**.

bugger-all very little; nothing. *He's done bugger-all all day*.

buggered **1.** tired out; exhausted. **2.** broken; wrecked. **3.** damned. *I'm buggered if I'll do that*.

buggerise around to waste time fiddling about instead of doing something constructive or useful.

buggerlugs a mock abusive term, used affectionately.

bugger me! damn me! well I'll be damned! Also, more forcefully, **bugger me dead!**

bugger off to decamp; to leave in a hurry.

bugger up to ruin, wreck or root.

buggery used as an intensifier this is equivalent to 'hell'. *It hurts like buggery*.

bug house a picture theatre, especially if old and decrepit.

bugle the nose. When something's **on the bugle**, it stinks like hell.

bug rake a hair comb.

Bugs Bunny **1.** rhyming slang for 'money'. **2.** in Canberra, a derisive name for the American war memorial at Blamey Square, Russell Hill.

builder's crack bum cleavage appearing above the top of the pants. Also called the **builder's smile**.

build-up in the tropical north, the approach of the Wet. You will experience a gradual increase in heat and humidity causing extreme tension and irritability. Also called the **suicide season**, and sometimes leading to **mango madness**.

built **1.** of a woman, curvaceous and large-breasted. **2.** of a bloke, solid and thick-set. More poetically, **built like a tank** or **built like a brick shithouse**.

bukakke a genre of pornography, emerging in Japan in the 1980s, portraying ejaculation onto the face. From a Japanese word meaning to splash.

bulbing the inhalation of nitrous oxide gas from bulbs for a soda siphon.

bulk **1.** a great many; a great amount. *We've got bulk people staying at our place*. **2.** great, terrific, excellent. *That was bulk fun*.

bull nonsense; boasting; crapping on. A euphemistic shortening of **bullshit**. As a verb, to exaggerate or boast. Also commonly used as an exclamation to reject what someone else has said.

Bullamakanka an imaginary remote town; any remote place.

bull artist a person who habitually speaks crap. A euphemism for the more explicit term **bullshit artist**.

bulldust **1.** a fine mineral dust which is a vehicle hazard in the outback. **2.** a euphemism for *bullshit*.

bull dyke a butch lesbian. Also called a **diesel dyke**.

bullet-head **1.** a person with a large, squarish head. **2.** an obstinate or stupid person.

bullfuck an expression of disgust, disbelief, etc.; a stronger form of *bullshit!*

bull head a term for a three-corner jack or doublegee, chiefly found in coastal Qld. See **doublegee** for the complete set of regionalisms.

bullie a bull terrier.

bullrush a common schoolyard chasings game, which is usually banned by teachers. This term is found in Qld, NSW and ACT. For the full set of regionalisms, see **British bulldog**.

bulls! nonsense! rubbish!

bullshit **1.** nonsense, rubbish, crap; hence, as a verb, to lie. Originally an Americanism from at least the 1910s. Politely shortened to **bull**, or sometimes **bullsh**. **2.** something totally amazing or excellent; something so excellent as to be almost unbelievable. *This movie is complete bullshit – well worth seeing.*

bullshit artist a person who craps on, speaking bullshit all the time. Also called a **bull artist**.

bullswool **1.** fibrous bark used for kindling a fire. **2.** a euphemism for *bullshit*. This is a deadset Australianism.

bum **1.** the rump or backside. Formerly classed among the taboo words – back in the 1950s a female radio announcer was sacked for saying this terrifying word on air. Nowadays it is barely considered rude, except by little kids, who often use it as an insult to one another, as in *Leave him alone, ya big bum!* Adults can talk with impunity about **bums on seats** (audience numbers), and can affectionately described things as being **as smooth as a baby's bum**. Still, bum is ruder than *bottom* or *backside*, and not as rude as *arse*. In fact, it is used as a euphemism for *arse*, especially in the phrase **pigs bum!** When mildly annoyed, people often exclaim *bum!* **2.** a homeless person living on the street. An Americanism from the 19th century. **3.** to cadge as in *to bum a cigarette* or *to bum a ride*. **4.** to move about idly. *He spent his youth bumming up and down the coast surfing.* **5.** among schoolboys, to sodomise. **6.** of poor, wretched, or miserable quality; bad. *a bum deal.* **7.** if something fails completely, it is said to have **died in the bum**.

bum around to hang around doing nothing in particular.

bum chum one of a gay male couple; a homosexual. A homophobic term much favoured by schoolboys. See **dung puncher** for a swag of synonyms.

bum-crawl to be servile and fawning. To act the part of a **bum crawler** or arselicker.

bum floss G-strings or other items of skimpy underwear that ride up the anal cleft. Also called **anal floss**.

bumfluff light hair growing on the face of an adolescent male.

bum-fuck to sodomise; to perform sodomy.

bummer a bad outcome; a big disappointment, as in *Couldn't get tickets for Friday. Major bummer.* An Americanism wholeheartedly adopted in Oz in the late 1970s, early '80s. Formerly in Australian English a **bummer** was a swagman, a usage long forgotten.

bummers women's sports briefs worn over underwear and under a skirt. Chiefly used in Qld. See **scungies** for the full set of regionalisms.

bum nut **1.** a chook's egg. **2.** a dag hanging off the behind of a pet animal.

bump in television and radio, to drop a performer or segment in favour of another. *I'm furious – they bumped me for the bloody cricket report.*

bump and grind sexual intercourse.

bumper **1.** something large or successful; a boomer. Now virtually Standard English. Originally 18th century British slang and dialect (Yorkshire and Lancashire). **2.** a cigarette butt. An Australianism from the 1890s. Origin unknown. Something of little value is **not worth a bumper**. Searching the ground for discarded cigarette butts is called **bumpering**.

bump off to kill.

bump uglies to have sex.

bum rap **1.** an unjust or false conviction. Originally American underworld slang. **2.** an unfair assessment or review.

bum-root to perform anal intercourse.

bum shorts women's sports briefs worn over underwear and under a skirt. Chiefly used in Qld. See **scungies** for the full set of regionalisms.

bum sniffer a derogatory term used by Aussie Rules people for Rugby people – referring to the packing of scrums.

bum's rush the bodily removal of an unwanted person, or the abrupt rejection of an idea or proposal. From US slang of the 1910s, originally referring to a rough type of frog-marching in which a person was kicked along in the bum.

bum steer incorrect information or advice.

bun **1.** a woman who has sex with a group of men in quick succession. In sexual slang is also known as a *buttered bun*, a term dating back as far as the 17th century! **2.** to sodomise. A blokey, homophobic word.

bunch of fives the fist.

Bundaberg snow the ashes that fall after burning off a sugarcane field.

Bundy **1.** the Qld town of Bundaberg. **2.** Bundaberg rum. **3.** a trademark term for a time clock used to record the arrival and departure times of employees. Thus, in slang, to **punch the bundy** or **bundy on** is to begin work, whether you use a *Bundy* clock or not. To finish work is to **bundy off**.

bung **1.** not in good working order; busted; injured. Borrowed from the Australian Aboriginal language Yagara of the Brisbane region. To **go bung** originally meant to die, but now means to break down, fail, become bankrupt, that kind of thing. **2.** in the railways a **bung** was an official 'please explain' regarding a misdemeanor, error, or the like. **3.** to put or place, especially hastily or carelessly. *Bung it in the cupboard*, *Bung a few records on*. **4.** to toss or throw. *She bunged it out the window.*

bunger **1.** a large, exploding firecracker. **2.** a cigarette.

bunghole cheese. First used by Aussie soldiers in World War I.

bung it on to behave temperamentally; to put on a display of bad behaviour. Also, to put on airs and graces.

bung on to put on a party or event. *We're bunging on a barbie for our eldest.*

bung on an act to make an appallingly big fuss over nothing.

bung on side to behave in a pompous and overbearing manner.

bun in the oven a baby in utero.

the Bunker Parliament House, Canberra.

bunnies to that! a phrase equivalent to 'No way José!' or 'Bugger that!'

bunny **1.** a fool or dupe; a gullible person; an easy victim. **2.** a person who accepts the responsibility for a situation. **3.** in cricket, a poor batsman. Also called a **rabbit**. Neither of which are as bad as being the **ferret** (see entry). **4.** to **shoot a bunny** is to fart.

bunny boiler a woman whose obsession with a partner verges on the psychotic. So called after the character played by Glenn Close in the 1987 hit movie *Fatal Attraction*. Also called a **rabbit cooker**.

bunny-hop to release the clutch of a car unevenly so that the car moves forward in a series of jerks. The same as **kangaroo-hop**.

buns the buttocks.

bunyip a mythical Australian beast of amphibious nature inhabiting rivers and deep, dark pools, and retreating to underwater caverns known as **bunyip holes**. So shy or stealthy are they that one has never yet been caught. The word for this animal is from the Aboriginal language Wembawemba of Victoria and southern NSW. Not to be confused with the **yowie**.

bunyip aristocracy a derogatory term for what passes for peerage in Australia.

'burbs the suburbs.

Burdekin duck in Qld, corned beef or fritters of corned beef.

Burdekin snow the same as **Bundaberg snow**.

the Burgh the Sydney suburb of Helensburgh.

burl **1.** an attempt. *I'll give it a burl*. From British dialect *birl* 'to spin'. **2.** to move quickly. *To burl along.*

burn **1.** to drive at a high speed. Also, such a drive as habitually taken by revheads. **2.** to successfully outplay an opponent; to torch. **3.** an older slang term for a cigarette.

burn off to drive off at speed from the traffic lights in order to beat someone else and thereby show how fab you are because you've got a fast car.

burnout a car stunt in which the back tyres are made to spin on the spot at very high speed and thus cause as much smoke as possible.

Burnside warrior Adelaide slang, a derogatory term for a city-only 4WD. Also called a **Burnside bus**. See **Toorak tractor** for a host of synonyms.

burnt offering overcooked food, especially proffered at backyard barbies.

burr up to become livid with anger. This is a term more common in the Top End and Far North Qld.

burst a blood vessel to become agitated or overly excited.

bury the bishop of a male, to have sex.

bus **1.** a motor car, especially when giving a lift to someone. *C'mon, the bus is leaving right away.* **2.** a large police or prison van used to transport prisoners.

bush **1.** the great Australian native vegetation. The soul of this highly urbanised nation. Hence, uncultivated or unsettled country; the country as opposed to the city. Thus, to **go bush** is to visit the country, either for a short while, or more permanently, to turn your back on civilisation. **2.** to camp out in the bush as in *bushing it under the stars.* **3.** the pubic hair.

bush banana a turd.

bush bashing the same as **scrub bashing** (see entry).

bush bellows a hat used to fan a camp fire.

bush blow the ejection of snot through one nostril while closing the other off with a finger. Also called the **bushman's hanky**.

the Bush Capital Canberra.

bush carpenter a rough carpenter.

bush chook **1.** the emu. **2.** in Tasmania, the endemic flightless native hen. Also called a **narkie**.

bushed **1.** lost in the bush, a very dangerous situation to find yourself in – often times lethal, especially if you are without water. Also, completely lost anywhere, even in the city. **2.** exhausted, tuckered out. In origin, an Americanism.

bushfire blonde a redhead.

bush hat **1.** any wide-brimmed hat as commonly worn in the bush. **2.** in the army, a giggle hat.

bushie **1.** a person who lives in or comes from the country. A person wise to the ways of the bush; a person adept at living in the bush; a person having exceptional bushcraft. Some city slickers view bushies as unsophisicated country bumpkins, but what would they know? **2.** a member of a volunteer bush fire brigade.

bush lawyer a person without legal qualifications but who has a good knowledge of the law and is crafty in applying it.

bushman **1.** a man from the bush; a male bushie. **2.** in Tassie, a chainsaw operator in a team of loggers.

bushman's breakfast a piss and a good look round; that is, no breakfast at all. Sometimes called a **dingo's breakfast**.

bushman's hanky the act of blowing nasal mucus through one nostril while closing the other off with a finger. Also called a **bush hanky**.

bush mechanic a person skilled in keeping busted old bombs going in the outback, through lateral thinking and crafty ingenuity.

bush oyster the product of a bush blow.

bush pig a term of extreme contempt directed at a girl or woman. The implication is that they are ugly, unpleasant, oversized and rough as guts.

bushranger **1.** Australian for highwayman. The Dick Turpin of Down Under. One of a bunch of enterprising young men who thought they could make a living holding up coaches and travellers and decamping into the bush. Noted for yelling 'Bail up!' and 'Stand and deliver!' Most of them came to sticky ends. Terrors of the colonial countryside and the stuff of legends. **2.** any unscrupulous bastard who rips you off.

bushranging the traditional Australian art and science of holding up coaches and wayfarers in colonial times.

bush telegraph the outback rumour mill. Also, called the **bush wire** or **bush wireless**. A message sent via this system is a **bush telegram**.

bush telly a campfire, or the stars – in other words, what you watch for entertainment at night in the bush.

bush tucker **1.** simple fare, as eaten by one living in the bush – damper, tea, kangaroo-tail soup, that sort of thing. **2.** food gathered from nature in the bush, as traditional Aboriginal foods.

Bush Week a fictitious week when country people come to town. Used only in the phrase *What do you think this is – Bush Week?* In other words 'What do you take me for – a fool?'

bushwhacker a person living in the bush; a bushie; often viewed as unsophisticated. Not that you'll like to hear this, but this term originated in the US. Yep, way back in 1809, Washington Irving wrote about bushwhackers, some 80 years before the word first appears in Australia. It is obsolete in the US now, having been replaced by *backwoodsman.*

bushwoman a woman from the bush; a female bushie.

business end the dangerous part of something. *Don't get near the business end of that snake.*

bust **1.** to catch someone doing something illegal; to cop. *We were busted smoking behind the dunnies.* **2.** to raid an illegal establishment. **3.** a police raid. **4.** underworld slang, a break and enter. **5.** an arrest.

bust a gut to work relentlessly; to give it your all.

buster **1.** a bad fall from a horse, hence, any heavy fall. Often in the phrase **come a buster**. **2.** a strong wind, especially one coming at the end of the day.

bustitute the substitution of buses for a section of track when trains are not running.

busy as a one-armed paper-hanger in a gale extremely busy; too busy to spit.

but the usual English conjunction, which in Australian (and New Zealand) English can often to be found dangling around at the end of sentences. Like, *I didn't do it, but!*

butch **1.** of a woman, especially a lesbian, overtly masculine, unfeminine. The opposite of **femme** (see entry). From *Butch*, used as a nickname for a tough young man, originally a shortening of the word *butcher.* **2.** a lesbian who has strong masculine characteristics. Also used of a gay man who plays the masculine role in a relationship.

butcher a small beer glass found in SA. Either six or seven fluid ounces (170 or 200 ml) depending on who you ask. The origin is a bit of a mystery. Some say it refers to abattoir workers in North Terrace, Adelaide, who used to nick over to the Newmarket Hotel opposite for a quick drink in their lunch break. They could only have a small glass as they didn't have much time. Could be true, but there is no hard evidence to back the story up. In fact, an early description from 1908 says that a butcher holds over a pint! Others would have that it is from the German word *Becher*, but the German pronunciation makes this just as dubious as the previous suggestion. See entry for **glass** for other names of seven ounce glasses.

butcher's canary a blowfly.

butcher's hook **1.** rhyming slang for 'look'. Commonly shortened to **butchers**, as in *Give us a butchers at that.* **2.** rhyming slang for 'crook', as in ill, unwell. Also shortened to **butchers** as in *I'm feeling a bit butchers today.* **3.** Can also be used for 'crook' meaning angry, especially in the phrase **go butcher's hook at**. The short form **butchers** is seen in expressions like *No need to go butchers at me.*

butt the rump; the buttocks; the arse. Seen as archetypically American now, but in origin British English of the 18th century. Commonly used in Australia in phrases adopted from US slang, as *kick butt*. Sometimes used as a euphemism for 'arse'.

butterfly in two-up, to toss the coins so that they do not spin properly but appear to do so. A very tricky skill, and highly illegal in the game – you don't want to be caught doing it.

buttface an extremely ugly or irritating person.

butt-fuck to sodomise; to perform sodomy.

butthead a stupid person; a blockhead. A recent adoption from US television and cinema. It's been around in the States since the 1970s.

butthole the anus.

butthole surfer a homosexual man.

buttinski a stickybeak; a person who habitually butts in. A mock Russian name formed from *butt in* 'to interrupt', and the Russian name element *-ski.*

butt plug a smooth tapering plug with a flat base inserted into the anus for erotic purposes.

buy **1.** a bargain. *That was the buy of the century.* **2.** a purchase of goods. *I was out on a buy this morning.* **3.** a turn to shout. *I'm glad you arrived, it's your buy.*

buy-up in prison, the purchasing of necessities, as groceries and toiletries.

buzz **1.** a telephone call. *I'll give you a buzz tomorrow.* Hence, as a verb, to call someone on the phone. **2.** a feeling of exhilaration or pleasure. *It was such a buzz.* **3.** a euphoric sensation induced by various recreational drugs.

buzz box a derogatory term for a cheap little car that has been hotted up.

buzz off to depart; leave. Often used as a command.

buzzy **1.** in Tasmania, the burr of the bidgee widgee plant, or the plant itself. Can also be used to refer to any burr that sticks to your clothing. **2.** of a drug, giving a good buzz.

bye nows the flabby triceps of an overweight or matronly woman. They wobble when saying goodbye.

by jingo an iceblock, as termed in Qld and the north coast of NSW.

by jings a variant of the exclamation 'by jingo'. Originally Scottish, but now common in Australia. Also **by the jings**.

BYO **1.** bring your own. A great Aussie entertaining tradition. *We're having a barbie next Saturday, but it's BYO meat and drinks.* **2.** a restaurant which allows clients to bring their own booze.

by the living Harry By God!

C

cabaret a dance at which alcoholic drink is available.

Cabbage Garden an old derisive nickname for Victoria, sneering at its smallness. New South Welshmen reckoned you could put the whole of Victoria inside the backyard of a New South Wales sheep-station. Also sometimes called the **Cabbage Patch** or **Cabbage State**. A Victorian was a **Cabbage Gardener**, **Patcher** or **Stater**. See **Cornstalk** for similar terms of derision for people from other states.

cab sav cabernet sauvignon wine.

cack **1.** excrement. An old word going back to medieval times. A charming Aussie insult is the classic, *Go dip your eye in hot cocky cack!* **2.** to defecate; to soil with excrement. *The baby cacked its nappy.* To **cack the corduroys** is to be scared shitless. **3.** a person or thing that is extremely funny; something that makes you cack yourself laughing; a hilariously good time. As, *That guy's such a cack* or *This movie's a cack.* **4.** to laugh uncontrollably. *We were cacking ourselves!*

cacker in WA, an undersized crayfish, too small to be harvested. Probably from Italian *cacca* 'shit'.

cack-handed left-handed. Also **cacky-handed**.

cackle berry a chook's egg.

cactus ruined, kaput. *We aren't going anywhere, the engine's cactus.* Someone in trouble is said to be **in the cactus**. No doubt referring to the dreaded prickly pear which once covered so much of the country, at least, before being eaten holus bolus by the **cacto**, the wondrous *Cactoblastis cactorum* moth, introduced as a biological control.

Cadbury a person who can't handle their drink. That is, they only need a glass and a half to get drunk.

cake-eater an effeminate or effete male; a sissy.

cakehole the mouth.

call **1.** a decision to say or do something or act in a certain way. *He swore at the pack of footballers drinking at the bar – a dodgy call in anyone's books.* Calls generally fall into one three categories. The **bad call** (like the example above), the **good call** (such as deciding to buy up big before a property boom), and the **big call** (where you go out on a limb with a prediction). **2.** as a verb, to make a decision about. *I couldn't tell if he was joking or not. It was hard to call.* **3.** in two-up, the **call** is the nomination of either heads or tails to win the toss.

call a spade a fucking shovel the typically direct Aussie way of calling a spade a spade.

call God on the big white telephone to vomit into a toilet bowl, especially from having drunk too much alcohol.

call of nature the need to urinate or defecate.

call the shots to be in charge.

calorie-attack a session of over-eating.

camel bite a sharp painful blow to the skin, usually someone else's bare legs, with a cupped hand. In use by schoolkids in WA, whereas the rest of the country prefer the term **horse bite**.

camel driver in horseracing, an unsuccessful jockey.

camel jockey a racist term for a person of Middle Eastern origin.

camel's piss really crap beer.

camel toe the fashion no-no resulting from a pair of lycra pants that are too tight and thus reveal the shape of the female genitalia.

camo in military use, camouflage.

camp **1.** of a man, effeminately homosexual, especially in an exaggerated or ostentatious way. Hence, exaggeratedly effeminate behaviour. Started life as a slang word but is now Standard English in these senses. Probably from the French *se camper* 'to assume a proud or provocative pose', *camp* first makes its appearance in English street slang of the 1900s. The explanation that it is an acronym from *Known As a Male Prostitute*, is a load of codswallop. **2.** in Australia, the sense of effeminacy was weakened, and **camp** came to mean homosexual, whether effeminate or not. Since the 1970s replaced by *gay*. **3.** a male homosexual. Formerly common in Aussie slang, now little heard. **4.** as a verb, to act in a camp manner. Especially in the phrase to **camp it up**. **5.** on a different tack altogether, to **camp** at someone's place is to stay there for a brief time. As in, *You can camp at my place until you find somewhere to rent*. This Australianism comes straight from the outback.

camp as a row of tents exaggeratedly camp. When this metaphor won't suffice you can crank it up by saying **camp as a row of pink tents**.

can **1.** jail. **2.** the toilet or dunny. **3.** dismissal from a job; the sack. All three borrowed from US English. **4.** a measure of driving distance equivalent to the distance travelled while consuming one bottle or can of beer. *It'll be a three-can trip*. Aussie slang this one!

canary **1.** in colonial times, a convict. So called from the colour of their prison uniforms. Also called a **canary bird**. **2.** the punishment of one hundred lashes meted out to convicts. **3.** in modern times, a yellow defect notice stuck to a car window. Chiefly Victorian slang. Also called a **yellow sticker**, both in Vic and the rest of the country.

Canberra Crimes in the ACT, a derisive name for the *Canberra Times* newspaper.

cancer stick a cigarette.

cane **1.** to beat severely in a competition or game. **2.** to treat harshly or roughly. **3.** to drive a vehicle furiously; to flog it. **4.** to be extremely painful; to hurt deeply. *It really canes that she called me a liar*.

caned intoxicated or under the influence of drugs, especially marijuana.

cane toad a player for the Queensland state team in the Rugby League State of Origin football competition. Hence, any Queenslander. As opposed to a **cockroach**.

canned drunk.

can opener a jump into water with one leg tucked under your arms and hugged into the chest and the other extended straight out. Also called a **banana**, **horsey** or **peg leg**.

cans headphones – the type with large earpieces.

cant a secret language or jargon formerly used by vagabonds, beggars and the criminal class in England so that they could speak about criminal activities without being understood if overheard. The precise origins of the words used in cant have been lost in time, many of them were either new coinages or perverted words from different languages and dialects. A number of current slang terms owe their origins to cant – notable examples being **beak**, **prat** and **quod** (see entries).

can you keep one down? Do you want a beer? A question on the lips of Aussie drinkers since the 1910s.

cap coffee shop slang for a cappuccino.

caper In Aussie slang this is a real little doer of a word with many uses. Your **caper** is your occupation or job: *What caper are you in?* Or, it can refer to behaviour: *There was singing and dancing and all that kind of caper*. Finally, **caper** can merely refer to whatever is going on: *What's the caper?*

captain a person buying the drinks. Dating from the 1950s.

Captain Cook Aussie rhyming slang for 'look'. Also shortened to **Captain**. Dating from the 1930s.

Captain Coordination an ironic name for a clumsy, uncoordinated person.

carbie a carburettor.

carcass your body or yourself. When directing a guest to a chair it is the height of ocker decorum to say: *Park your carcass, mate!*

card-carrying certified. *A complete and utter card-carrying ratbag*.

cardie a cardigan.

cardies electronic poker machines which display playing cards.

cark to die. This word has been around since the 1970s but no-one seems to know exactly where it came from. Some will have it that it is from *carcass*, and others that it is from the *carking* of crows.

cark it to die; to collapse; (of a machine) to fail or break down.

carn a sporting barracker's cry. *Carn the Blues!* The phonetic descendant of 'Come on!'

carnie **1.** an agricultural show amusement stall or fun ride operator; a showie. **2.** a carnation – either the flower or the plant.

carpie a carpenter.

Carrara Koalas a derogatory term for the former Brisbane Bears AFL team (now the Brisbane Lions) – referring to their humble beginnings and poor performances at Carrara football stadium.

Carringbush a fictitious suburb created by Frank Hardy in his novel *Power Without Glory* (1950) to talk about the Melbourne suburb of Collingwood. The disguise was deliberately thin. Quickly became used in slang to refer to the Collingwood football team. Also used in the names of businesses, such as the *Carringbush Hotel.*

carrot top a red-headed person.

carry the can bear the responsibility; take the blame. With reference to carrying a sanitary can, that is, to do the dirty work.

carve to make a wake with a surfboard along the wall of a wave, or, to slice a track in snow with a snowboard. Hence, to surf or snowboard exceptionally well.

case **1.** a severe drug addict. **2.** a weirdo; a nut case. **3.** an out-moded bloke's term for a raving nymphomaniac. *She's a bit of a case, ain't she?*

caser **1.** an obsolete term for a five shilling coin. Originally British slang, from Yiddish. **2.** prison slang, a five year sentence.

Casey's cartwheel coin collector's slang for the whopping big 1937 five shilling coin commemorating the coronation of King George VI. Named after the then Federal Treasurer, Richard (later Lord) Casey.

cashed-up having ready money. A good old Australianism dating from the 1930s.

cashie a cash-in-hand job.

Cashies a Cash Converters store.

cash in your chips to die.

casting couch a supposed couch in a film or stage director's office for the seduction of those auditioning.

castle in cricket, the stumps.

castor **1.** obsolete slang for a hat. Originally a hat made from beaver-skin, from the Latin and Greek word for a beaver. **2.** good, excellent, all right, okay, satisfactory. *She'll be castor* or *Don't worry, everything's castor.* Dating from the 1940s, and referring to a tick-tack code in which the brim of the hat was touched to signify that all was okay.

cat **1.** prison slang, an inmate who, while usually heterosexual outside of prison, submits to the passive role in homosexual sex when inside. Opposed to a **hock**. It has been suggested that this is a shortening of *catamite* (an archaic word for a boy kept for homosexual activities), but this hardly seems likely. First recorded in 1950. **2.** in more general slang use, a gay man. **3.** if someone tells you that you **look like something the cat dragged in**, then you've probably looked better. **4.** if you are prone to **too much of what the cat licks itself with**, then you are very talkative (too much tongue).

catch and kiss **1.** a derisive term for soccer, used by aficionados of the other football codes. **2.** a schoolyard game in the style of Georgie Porgie.

catch me, fuck me a derisive name for Rugby League.

cat fight a fight between two women.

cathedral underpants very tight undies. Because they have no ball room.

Catho a Roman Catholic.

cat's eye **1.** in NSW, a term for a three-corner jack or doublegee. Also called **cat head**. See **doublegee** for the full set of regionalisms. **2.** a type of playing marble resembling a cat's eye.

cat's pyjamas something excellent; the bee's knees.

cattle dog Aussie rhyming slang for 'catalogue'.

cattle duffing the thieving of cattle, generally involving the alteration of brands. One who does this is a **cattle duffer**, what the Americans call a cattle rustler. Australian since the 19th century and still going on.

cattle tick Aussie derogatory rhyming slang for 'Catholic'.

caught short in dire need of a toilet.

celeb a celebrity.

cellar dwellers the team at the bottom of the competition table.

Centralia the inland region of continental Australia.

centre in two-up, the person who holds all bets made by the spinner. Also, the amount of money bet by the spinner which must be covered before any side bets can be made.

the Centre the arid inland parts of Australia.

cert anything regarded as certain to happen; a certainty. *She was a cert to win.* In the language of the turf there are always certs, and yet, if you ask anyone what a cert is, they'll tell you 'There's no such thing.' If a cert is more certain than an ordinary certainty, then it is called a **dead cert**.

Chaddy the Melbourne suburb of Chadstone.

chaff money.

chalkie a schoolteacher. Since the 1940s.

champ **1.** a champion. **2.** an absolutely cool person; a legend. **3.** a form of address among males.

champers champagne.

champy feeling like a champion; in good spirits.

chances! you wish! in your dreams! *You want a back rub? Chances!*

Changa a racist schoolyard term for a Chinese person. Also called a **Chonga**.

chap a bloke or fellow. More associated with British English, but has always been quite common in Australia. Also in the diminutive form **chappie**.

chardie chardonnay.

chardonnay socialist a yuppie who espouses socialism.

charge **1.** a thrill; a kick. **2.** a blast of an alcoholic drink. Aussie English since the 1960s. Hence, to **charge up** is to get drunk. And **on the charge** means drunk. **3.** in surfing, to surf extremely well.

Charlene the female counterpart of the male westie, bevan or bogan; a bev-chick. Sometimes called a **Charmaine**.

charlie a girl or woman. From rhyming slang *Charlie Wheeler* for 'sheila'. Aussie slang since the 1940s. Charles Wheeler was an artist who painted nudes.

Charlie in the Vietnam War, a Viet Cong soldier, or the Viet Cong in general. Hence, any Asian person. Used disparagingly. From military signals code (*Victor*) *Charlie* for 'VC'.

charlies breasts. Old British slang from the 1870s. Not very common in Oz.

Charlie's Trousers a nickname for the Qld town of Charters Towers.

Charnie **1.** the Canberra suburb of Charnwood. **2.** a Canberra term for a westie, bogan or bevan, seen as typical of this suburb. Also called a **Charnie bum**. The more common term in the ACT is **booner**.

chase the dragon to inhale the smoke of heated heroin.

chase up a cow to find a dry spot outdoors, usually with sexual intentions.

chasey the well-known schoolyard game, known by this name in all states, though it is the favoured term in Vic, SA and WA. Also called **tag** in all states, though this is the commonest term in ACT. In NSW and Tas it is more commonly called **chasings**. In NSW it can also be called **tip** or **tips**. Victorians commonly use the term **tiggy**, which is the most common term in Qld, where the shortened form **tig** is also found.

chat **1.** convict slang for a louse. Now obsolete. **2.** in prison, a filthy prisoner; hence, a derelict.

chateau cardboard cask wine. Also called **chateau d'cardboard**.

chat's yard in prison, a section where drunks and derros are held.

chatterbox **1.** a talkative person. **2.** a children's origami fortune-telling device which is manipulated by the thumb and index finger of each hand to reveal prophetic messages written therein; a chimper-chomper.

chatty rough, dirty, in poor condition. Since the 1940s. Originally convict slang meaning infected with lice. Interestingly this follows the same evolution as the word *lousy*.

chat up to woo someone with glib conversation.

cheap as chips extremely cheap.

cheap at half the price an ironic expression meaning not very cheap.

Cheap Charlie in the Vietnam War, a soldier who was stingy. Used by bar girls as an insult.

cheapie a cheap product.

cheapies cheap thrills. *He gets his cheapies looking at lingerie ads.*

cheapo cheap, inexpensive; hence, crappy.

cheats originally a programmer's shortcuts employed in designing a computer game. Now any information helpful for getting through a computer game without actually playing through all the levels you are supposed to.

cheat stick a pool rest.

checkout chick a woman, especially a young woman, serving at a checkout or cash counter in a supermarket.

check you later a supposedly 'cool' way of saying *See you later!*

cheerio a cocktail frankfurt in Qld and northern NSW.

cheers, big ears a jocular toast, made irrespective of the size of the ears.

cheese and kisses rhyming slang for 'missus', that is, the wife. Aussie slang since the 1890s.

cheesed off irritated, annoyed.

cheese off to upset or annoy.

cheesy **1.** daggy but sophisticated; cool, but only because it is so uncool. *She likes cheesy lounge music.* **2.** smelly, as *cheesy socks* or *cheesy undies.* **3.** in WA, a snack of cheese on bread toasted under a grill.

cheesy grin an exaggerated smile. Referring to the usual photographer's request to say 'cheese' to the camera.

Chellyblook a racist nickname for the Sydney suburb of Cherrybrook – noted for its preponderance of Asian Australians.

chemo laconic Aussie form of 'chemotherapy'.

chequed-up newly supplied with a pay cheque.

cherabin a large freshwater prawn found in northern Australia. Also called a **cherub**. From the Aboriginal language Walmajarri of the Fitzroy Crossing region of WA.

cherry **1.** virginity; the hymen; a virgin. All these are US in origin. **2.** a cricket ball, especially a new one. **3.** in cricket, the red mark made on the bat by hitting a new ball or by a vigorous stroke.

cherrynose a species of black cicada with a red nose.

Chevvie a Chevrolet motor car. Also called a **Chev**.

chewie **1.** chewing gum. Since the 1920s. **2.** in WA, a piece of chewing gum. *Would you like a chewie?*

chewie on your boot! a cry intended to disconcert a footy player taking a kick.

chew-'n'-spew a fast-food joint.

chew out to scold or upbraid.

chew someone's ear to talk to someone insistently and at length; to earbash.

chew the fat to gossip. Also, **chew the rag**.

chew the rag **1.** to discuss; to chew over something. **2.** to grumble about something.

chiack **1.** to taunt or tease; to stir. Also spelt **chiak** or **chyack**. In origin, from *chi-hike*, British costermonger's slang of the 19th century, where it was used as a friendly hurrah. **2.** teasing or taunting; cheek. No longer common as a noun.

chiack the nanny old slang meaning to muck around.

chick a young woman. These days not the sort of thing most women like to be called. Originally American slang, dating back to the 1890s. Common in Australia since the 1960s. To **pull a chick** is to successfully woo her into bed.

chicken a coward. Hence, as an adjective, cowardly. American slang from the 1930s.

chickenfeed a meagre or insignificant sum of money. American slang of the 1830s.

chickenhawk a pederastic homosexual man.

chicken out to opt out in a cowardly way.

chicken scratch scrappy handwriting.

chickenshit **1.** something worthless or pathetic. Used adjectivally, contemptible, lousy, shithouse. **2.** a coward. Hence, cowardly.

chick flick a movie that appeals to women more than men.

chick magnet a man who is attractive to many women.

chick thing something that only females are concerned with or know about. The opposite to a **guy thing**.

chicky babe **1.** a term of familiar address from a male to a young woman. Not PC, but most often used in a joking way. **2.** an attractive young woman.

chief cook and bottle-washer the person in charge and doing every bloody thing as well.

chigger the Hobart term for a westie, bogan or bevan. From the suburb of Chigwell. Also spelt **chigga**.

chill **1.** to relax; to chill out. US slang from the 1970s. In Australia used since the 1990s. **2.** a chill-out room at a dance party or rave. *He spent most of the night in the chill.* **3.** a relaxing time. *A great chill after a hard night.*

chill out to relax; to calm down. US slang of the early 1980s, adopted in Australia by the late 1980s.

chill-out room an area at a dance party where people can rest and cool down from the exertions of dancing.

chimper-chomper a children's origami fortune-telling device which is manipulated by the thumb and index finger of each hand to reveal prophetic messages written therein; a chatterbox.

china a mate. From rhyming slang *china plate*. Originally Cockney, from the 1880s.

Chinaman **1.** a now outdated term for a Chinese man. Formerly in common use in Australia. If you had some bad luck it was common to say that you **must have killed a Chinaman**. **2.** in cricket, a left-hand bowler's googly. Some suppose this originally referred to Ellis Achong, a former Trinidadian cricketer of Chinese descent. Others, that it is so called because the ball 'slants' away, and yet others because it is 'inscrutable'.

Chinese burn a sort of torture among schoolchildren consisting of grabbing someone's wrist with both hands and twisting the skin in opposite directions.

Chinese cut in cricket, an inside edge wide of leg stump. Also called a **French cut**.

Chinese safety boots a pair of thongs. Also called **Japanese safety boots**.

Ching a racist schoolyard term for a Chinese person. Given to much melodic embellishment, as **Ching-chong**, **Ching-chong-changa**, **Ching-chong-chonkie**, and so on.

Chink a Chinese person. A dinky-di Aussie contribution to the vocabulary of racism. Dating back to the 1880s.

chinky apple a Qld slang term for the Chinese apple or lilly pilly tree. Also called **chonky apple**.

chinless wonder a feeble, pathetic male.

chip **1.** to reprimand. *He chipped me for being late*. **2.** to **cash in your chips** is to die. A gambling metaphor. **3.** if you have **had your chips** you are finished. **4.** to **spit chips** is to voice considerable anger.

chip on the shoulder a grudge. An American phrase from the 1830s. This idiom relates to the strange practice of a man placing a chip of wood on his shoulder and daring his antagonist to knock it off. If the chip was knocked off, then the fight would begin in earnest. A bit like drawing a line on the ground and daring another to step over it – which gives us the phrase *to step over the line*. Boys will be boys.

chippie **1.** a carpenter. **2.** a childish term for a potato chip or potato crisp.

chiro a chiropractor. Typical laconic Aussie abbreviation.

chisel **1.** an old, paper five-dollar note. A slangy version of **Chisholm** (see entry). **2.** to cheat or swindle; to get by cheating or trickery.

chiseller a swindler.

Chisholm an old, paper five-dollar note. Because it sported a picture of Caroline Chisholm, famous Australian women's welfare worker.

chiv a knife. Classic underworld slang dating back to the 17th century. From the Gypsy word for a blade.

choad the penis. From US slang of the 1960s. Commonly used in pornography and on the alt.tasteless newsgroup. Sometimes jokingly defined as 'a penis that is wider than it is long'. Origin unknown, but definitely not related to the Hindi word *chodna* 'to have sex'.

choc-attack an acute desire to eat a great deal of chocolate.

chock-a-block of a male, fully lodged in sexual embrace. *I was caught chock-a-block up her*. Crass Aussie bloke slang from the 1960s.

chocker completely full; packed or overcrowded. *The hall was chocker*. Hence, replete with food; stuffed. Aussie slang since at least the 1970s. In British slang this dates back to the 1940s, but means fed up with. Also commonly in the form **chockers**. Both are short for *chock-a-block* which was originally a nautical phrase referring to a block and tackle that was hoisted to its utmost limit.

chockie a chocolate.

chocko **1.** a person of Mediterranean or Middle Eastern extraction, or of similar complexion and appearance. Can cause offence, but, now widely adopted in the ethnic community to refer to themselves. Partially 'reclaimed' in the same way that the word **wog** has been. Commonly used as an adjective, as in *chocko food*, *a big chocko dinner*. Can be lengthened to **chocky** or shortened to **chock**. In origin, short for **chocolate frog**, and used in World War II to refer to any of the peoples of North Africa or the Middle East. **2.** any language spoken by such people. *My parents make me speak chocko at home*. **3.** in military slang, short for **chocolate soldier**.

chocoholic a person suffering chocolate addiction.

chocolate frog **1.** rhyming slang for 'wog', that is, a person of Mediterranean background.

See **wog** for more information. **2.** in prison, rhyming slang for 'dog', that is, an informer.

chocolate soldier **1.** in World War I, a member of the AIF's 8th Infantry Brigade, also known as *Tivey's chocolate soldiers*, or *Tivey's chocs*, after Major General Edwin Tivey. Originally a derisive name, but after this brigade saw action, the title was conferred with honour. **2.** in World War II, a term of contempt for a member of the Australian Military Force, which was a national militia whose purpose was the defence of Australian territory, and thus did not fight overseas.

choice among teenagers, fantastic, wonderful, excellent. *What a choice dress.*

choke **1.** to bomb out from lack of nerve; to snatch defeat from the jaws of victory. *Norman choked on the last day of play.* **2.** the act of choking. *What a choke!*

choke a brown dog of food, to be disgustingly repulsive.

choke a darkie to defecate. Since the 1970s.

choker a sports player who gives in to pressure.

choko the pear-shaped, light-green, fruit of a South American vine, often grown in backyards and eaten as a vegetable. The choko vine was once ubiquitous to Australian backyards. They were especially widespread during the Depression as they took little, if any, looking after (except perhaps for cutting back) and thus provided a cheap source of food. Tenacious and fast-growing, the plant commonly spread from its source over and along fences, trellises, sheds and carports. Outside dunnies proved a particularly popular location. Someone who is totally useless **couldn't train a choko vine to grow up a dunny wall**.

choko pie a derogatory term for a McDonald's hot apple pie, based on the mistaken belief that they are made with apple-flavoured choko rather than real apple.

chompers **1.** the teeth. **2.** in the Australian Antarctic Territory, a snack or meal.

Chonga a racist schoolyard term for a Chinese person. Also called a **Changa**.

chonk a term for a lolly, restricted to the Gippsland area of Vic.

chonky apple a Qld slang term for the Chinese apple or lilly pilly tree. Also called **chinky apple**.

choof to smoke marijuana.

choofer an inveterate marijuana smoker.

choof off to depart.

chook **1.** a domesticated chicken. *The chooks got out last night and it took me half an hour to round them all up again.* Classic Australianism, first recorded in 1900. In earlier use it was *chooky* or *chuckey*, from British dialect, ultimately imitative of the cackling of chickens. In fact, to call chickens you shout *Chook! Chook! Chook!* A formerly common greeting was **How are your mother's chooks?** It didn't require an answer. To **run around like a headless chook** is to behave in an erratic manner. To wish ill luck upon someone you need merely utter **I hope your chooks turn into emus and kick your dunny down**. **2.** a chicken slaughtered for eating. *frozen chooks, a barbecued chook.* **3.** chicken meat. *It's chook for dinner tonight.* **4.** a woman. *She's a nice old chook.* **5.** a common nickname for boys or men. **6.** a silly person; a fool. **7.** a cowardly person. *I'm a bit of a chook when it comes to swimming in the surf.*

chook chaser a derogatory term for a trail bike or other small road motorcycle, or for a person who rides such a bike.

chookers all right; excellent. *Everything is going chookers.*

chookery **1.** a chicken pen. **2.** chook-like behaviour; foolishness. **3.** womenkind.

chookie **1.** a chook. **2.** a person who drives around the block multiple times for an evening's entertainment. Such laps are called **chookie laps**. **3.** a chook chaser.

chook raffle a fund-raising raffle in which the prize is a chook.

choom a derisive term for an Englishman, representing their pronunciation of *chum*. Originally used in World War I to refer to English soldiers. Dying out since the 1970s.

chop **1.** a share or cut, as in *Get in for your chop.* World War I slang. **2.** the sack; dismissal. *I got the chop yesterday.* **3.** if something is **not much chop**, then it is no good.

chop chop! Hurry up! From Chinese pidgin English.

chop-chop loose-leaf tobacco that is sold illegally, thus avoiding the payment of government excise.

chopper **1.** a helicopter. **2.** a large, powerful, customised motorcycle with wide handlebars. **3.** a push-bike popular in the 70s with wide handlebars and having the front wheel smaller than the back. **4.** an old cow sold expressly to be chopped up for dog food. **5.** among fishos, a small tailor. Also called **chopper tailor**. **6.** the penis.

choppers the teeth.

chop picnic formerly, a picnic at which chops were cooked over a camp fire. Especially common in SA and Broken Hill. The term has been on the wane since the 1960s.

chop shop a panelbeater's.

chow food. Originally nautical slang of South-East Asia, from Chinese pidgin English.

Chow a racist term for a Chinese person. Used in Oz and NZ since the 1870s.

chow down to begin eating with gusto; hoe into.

Chrissie Christmas. At least since the 1960s. Hence, **Chrissie prezzie**, a Christmas present.

Christ bird the comb-crested jacana or lily-trotter. So called because it 'walks on water'. Also called the **Jesus bird**.

christen to use something for the first time. *He christened the new bathroom.*

Christmas overly commercialised religious season. Used in various slang expressions, such as **regular as Christmas**, very regular; **done up like a Christmas tree**, gaudily over-dressed; and to **think you're Christmas**, to have a very high opinion of yourself. If you have extremely good fortune then **all your Christmases have come at once**. Lastly, the phrase **What else did you get for Christmas?** is a derisive retort to someone showing off.

Christmas hold a grasping of another's testicles, in other words, 'a handful of nuts.' Compare **squirrel grip**.

chrome dome a bald person.

chromo an old Aussie slang term for a female prostitute. In the 19th century *chromo* was short for *chromolithograph*, a type of coloured lithograph, and thus the slang term refers to painted faces of prostitutes.

chronic **1.** absolutely terrible; chronically bad. *He was a chronic driver.* From British slang, but in Australia since the 1930s. **2.** good quality, strong marijuana.

chub change change in the form of silver coins; shrapnel.

chuck **1.** to do or perform right away. In Australia certain things are 'chucked' rather than 'done' or 'taken'. For instance, when driving you almost invariably *chuck a U-ie*, or *chuck a left or right*. If you jump into a pool in order to make an enormous splash then you *chuck a bombie*. Also, *mentals, wobblies, spazzes, nanas, mickeys* and *willies* are all chucked. **2.** to vomit. *He chucked on my new carpet*. Hence, as a noun, vomit, as in *I made him clean his chuck off my new carpet*. Aussie slang since the 1950s. **3.** to stop; be rid of. *I smoked for years before I decided to chuck it*. **4.** older slang meaning to reject or spurn. *She's chucked me for another bloke.*

chuck a lap to drive around the block as a form of entertainment. *The hoons spent Saturday night chucking laps and screaming out at chicks.* Since this is nearly always done off the main street it is also called **chucking a mainy**. In Whyalla, a hoon around the beach is **chucking a beachie**.

chuck a micky to throw a tantrum; to bung on a show. Truth be known, Aussies don't really approve of people losing their temper – it is seen as overreacting and this phrase is meant to belittle the behaviour. In fact, there is a veritable plethora of putdowns on this same theme, including **chuck a mental**, **chuck a nana**, **chuck a spaz**, **chuck a willy** and **chuck a wobbly**.

chuck a spread of a woman, to spread her legs in a sexual way.

chucker in cricket, a person who throws the ball instead of bowling it; technically, one who bends the arm during bowling.

chucker-out a bouncer. Originally 19th century British slang. Also called a **chucker-outer**.

chuck in to finish with; to resign from; to give up on. *I chucked in my job on Friday.*

chuckle to vomit. Aussie slang since the 1960s.

chuck off at to have a go at; to denigrate, ridicule or scold. Aussie slang since the 1900s. A bit out-moded nowadays.

chug a draught of a drink.

chug-a-lug a bout of drinking; a booze-up.

chum a mate or friend. British slang from the 17th century.

chump **1.** a blockhead or dolt. **2.** the head.

chum up with to befriend.

chunder **1.** to vomit. First appearing in the 1950s. From rhyming slang *Chunder Loo* 'spew', referring to the cartoon character drawn by Norman Lindsay in a series of advertisements. The fanciful notion that it is a clipping of the nautical cry *Watch under!* used to warn the lower decks when someone from the upper decks was vomiting over the side, is nothing but a silly story. **2.** the act of vomiting. *She ducked into the bathroom for a quick chunder.* **3.** the substance vomited. *There was chunder all over the carpet.* **4.** among surfies, to be roughly battered about by a wave. *I got chundered by a massive wave.*

chunder daks someone with their pants pulled right up.

chunderer an inveterate spewer, especially one who drinks to the point of vomiting on a regular basis. Also, **chunder guts**.

chunderish nauseous; likely to vomit.

chunderous revolting, unpleasant.

chutty chewing gum. Also, **chuddy**.

ciao goodbye. Common Italian farewell used here.

cigar a long piece of excrement. **Bondi cigar**.

cigarette swag during the Depression, a swag rolled into a long, thin shape like a cigarette.

ciggie a cigarette. Actually, this is recorded earliest in US slang, from 1915. The home-grown abbreviation is **cigger**, which has been around since the 1920s, but is not as popular as the US import.

cinch something certain or easy.

cinchy easy to do; no problem; a snack.

circle work the creation of circular skid marks with the tyres of a motor vehicle. A rural male ritual entertainment.

circs circumstances.

City of Churches Adelaide, from the prevalence of such edifices.

city slicker a person living the slick, fast-moving lifestyle of a large city.

civvies any clothing other than a uniform. From *civilian clothing*.

CJs speedos. Standing for **cock jocks**. For a full set of synonyms see **sluggos**.

clacker **1.** the backside or anus. Probably referring to the sound of farting. The idea that it is an alteration of *cloaca* is ludicrous. Aussie slang since the 1960s. **2.** the vagina.

clackers false teeth.

clams money.

clancy in the petrol industry, an overflow or spillage of petrol, as when filling a tanker. From the Banjo Paterson poem *Clancy of the Overflow*.

clap gonorrhoea, or any other venereal disease. *Got a dose of the clap from a prostitute.* Dating back to the 16th century, where it probably came from French.

clapped-out **1.** exhausted, weary. **2.** broken, in a state of disrepair.

claret blood. A metaphor common in sporting parlance.

clarrie the menstrual period. *I've just got clarrie.*

classic **1.** excellent, brilliant, unreal. *That joke was classic.* **2.** used to express great appreciation of something. *I just won $40. Classic!*

Clayton's false, existing in name only, as in a *Clayton's choice*, or a *Clayton's pay increase*. This word had a great vogue in the 1980s, when there was a long-running TV ad campaign for Clayton's, an alcohol-free drink which was advertised as 'the drink you have when you're not having a drink'.

clean **1.** free from addiction to drugs. **2.** free from sexually transmitted diseases. **3.** not carrying concealed weapons.

cleaner-upper the person responsible for cleaning or tidying up. Also known as a **cleaner-upperer**.

cleanskin **1.** an unbranded animal. Around since the 19th century. **2.** a novice at something. Since the 1900s. **3.** underworld slang, a person without a police record. Since the 1940s.

clever dick a smug show-off.

click a kilometre. Also spelt **klick**.

clifty military slang, to steal. Used principally during the World Wars. From the Greek *klephtes* 'a thief'.

clinah old slang for a young woman or girlfriend. From the German *kleine* 'little'.

clink prison, jail. Old British slang from the 18th century, referring to Clink Prison in Southwark, London.

clip joint an establishment that overcharges or rips off customers.

clit a small tuft of facial hair under the bottom lip on an otherwise clean-shaven face. Also called a **fanny tickler**.

clitty litter **1.** feminine hygiene products. **2.** any stray vaginal secretions found on women's underwear.

clobber **1.** clothes or gear, as in *your best clobber*. Borrowed from British slang. **2.** to batter severely. *Say that again and I'll clobber you.* Borrowed from US slang.

clock a speedometer or odometer. *100km/h on the clock*. Hence to **clock it** is to drive a car until its odometer has returned to the initial position reading of all zeros. Equally, you **clock it** if on pinball machines or computer games, you make the digital read-out of the scoreboard return to the initial position of zeros in a single game of continuous play.

clocker a person who frequents the racetrack in the early morning when horses are being trained, and times the runs in order to get betting information. Since the 1890s.

clock-watcher a worker who thinks they are employed to anticipate the end of the working day.

clodhoppers large, ungainly boots. Hence, **clodhopper**, a country bumpkin who wears such boots.

close, but no cigar a phrase indicating that someone has made a good, but nevertheless incorrect, guess. If they guess correctly then you can say **give the man** (or **woman**) **a cigar**.

close out of a wave, to break simultaneously along the entire length, thus offering no practical surface for surfing.

cloud suck in hang-gliding, the increase of lift often found at the base of a cloud, sometimes strong enough to cause a glider to unavoidably enter the cloud. Compare **pub suck**.

clubber a nightclub aficionado.

clubbie a member of an organised surf-lifesaving club.

clubbies speedos. Favoured by surf lifesavers, as opposed to surfies, who wear boardies. For a full set of synonyms see **sluggos**.

clucky desiring children of your own; feeling the biological urge to procreate.

clued-up well-informed.

clueless patently stupid; ignorant. Actually recorded in British English since the 1940s. Given a new lease of life after the popular 1995 Hollywood movie of the same name.

cluey smart, shrewd, well-informed. Aussie slang since the 1960s.

clumsy as a duck in a ploughed paddock extremely clumsy.

clunky **1.** not running smoothly, as *a clunky engine*. **2.** unsophisticated or unpolished; not smooth. *He delivered some really clunky lines.*

cluster busters speedos. For a full set of synonyms see **sluggos**.

clusterfuck **1.** an orgy. US slang from the 1960s. **2.** an unholy mess.

coalie a wharfie employed to load or unload coal.

coals to Newcastle an expression meaning that something is entirely useless – like taking coals to Newcastle, where coal is mined. Actually this phrase dates back to the 17th century in Britain, where it referred to Newcastle-upon-Tyne. In Australia, it just so happens that Newcastle in NSW is also a coal-mining region, and so the phrase still makes sense locally.

the Coathanger the Sydney Harbour Bridge. A quaint metaphor in use since the 1940s.

cobber **1.** a mate, friend, pal or buddy. Began life in Australia in the 1890s. Formerly in wide and common use. Today still quite common as a form of address in Tasmania. Also shortened to **cob** (since the 1960s). Most likely to come from the Suffolk dialect word *cob* 'to take a liking to'. Others have suggested origins in Yiddish and Aboriginal languages, but these seem less likely. **2.** a lolly consisting of a block of thick caramel coated in milk chocolate.

cobber dobber a person who informs on a mate.

cobber up to unite as mates; to form a friendship.

cobbler in WA, an eel-tailed catfish. Hence, **cobbler wobbler**, a stick for whacking the sting out of a cobbler.

cobblers **1.** the testicles. From British rhyming slang *cobbler's awls* for 'balls'. **2.** nonsense. Generally in the phrase **a load of old cobblers**.

cock **1.** the penis. One of the Anglo-Saxon four-lettered words, though this meaning isn't recorded in the scant Anglo-Saxon texts left to us today. The earliest examples do however date back to the 15th century. It is a metaphorical extension of *cock* meaning rooster. It is interesting to note that German *Hahn* means both rooster and, in slang, penis. **2.** a despicable male. An application of the former meaning, identical in meaning and use to *dick* and *prick*. **3.** in Tasmania, a term of friendly address. It's true! In Tasmania, if you're a bloke, a complete stranger might say to you 'G'day, cock.' And mean it in a perfectly friendly way. No pun or double entendre, and certainly no malice, is intended. Has flummoxed many a Mainlander visiting the Apple Isle over the years.

cockatoo a lookout who keeps watch for an illegal activity, as a two-up game. Hence, as a verb, to act as lookout. So called in reference to the sulphur-crested cockatoo which is known for its habit of posting 'sentries' to noisily warn the feeding flock of any approaching danger. Classic Aussie slang dating as far back as 1827.

cockatoo farmer a small-scale farmer. More commonly called a cocky.

cock breath a contemptible person. Implying that one has performed fellatio, and thus similar in metaphor to **cocksucker**.

cock chokers speedos. For a full set of synonyms see **sluggos**.

cockeyed bob in WA and NT, a particularly violent storm or squall. Different to a **willy-willy** (see entry) which is a dry wind and generally less powerful and destructive.

cock head a despicable person; a ratbag.

cockie a cockroach.

cock jocks speedos. Politely abbreviated to **CJs**. For a full set of synonyms see **sluggos**.

Cockney the dialect of the people from the East End of London (or more precisely, those born within the sound of Bow Bells). Although Cockney is commonly believed to be a strong influence upon Australian slang (you even hear people go so far as to say that Australian slang is derived from Cockney) this is not entirely true. In fact, it isn't true in the slightest. The truth is that the original convicts sent to Australia would have spoken the working class slang prevalent in whichever region of Britain they came from. They were hardly all East Enders. Today, the terms we use that are from Cockney slang are few and far between. A few of the ones that have survived to the present are *china plate* = mate, *elephant's trunk* = drunk, and the adjective *lairy*, from which we have developed the Aussie slang term *lair*. And as for pronunciation, well, Australians don't say *bruvver*, *larf*, *mouf*, *loverly*, *puffick* (perfect), nor *sparrer*. And, we don't drop initial aitches, as *'oo* (who), *'elp* (help) and the famous *I'll 'ave 'arf.*

cockroach **1.** a player for the New South Wales team in the Rugby League State of Origin football competition. Hence, any person from NSW. As opposed to a **cane toad**. **2.** a hard, dark lump of brown sugar. Recorded since the early 1900s. Such lumps used to be commonly found even up until the 1970s, but the now refining process has obviously improved and they do not occur very often, if at all.

cock rock aggressive, masculine rock music.

cocksucker **1.** literally, a fellator or fellatrix; one who goes down. Despite its appearance of modernity, this was originally British sexual slang of the Victorian era. **2.** a contemptible person. In this sense, recorded first in the 1910s in America. It has always been a popular term in the States. In fact, in World War I the US troops used the term so much they were known by Aussies soldiers as *carksuccers*.

cocksucking dreadful, shithouse, awful; used as an intensifier: *You cocksucking arsehole.*

cockteaser a woman who leads a man on but doesn't come across. Can also be used of a gay man who behaves in the same way. Also called a **prickteaser**.

cock up to mess up.

cocky **1.** a cockatoo, or other parrot. After a big night out you invariably wake with a **mouth like the bottom of a cocky's cage**. **2.** a small-scale farmer. **3.** a lock of hair sticking up, looking like a cockatoo's crest.

cockylora a common schoolyard chasings game, which is usually banned by teachers. This term is used in NSW. Also called **cockylora 1,2,3**. For the full set of regionalisms, see **British bulldog**.

cocky on the biscuit tin the Arnott's Biscuits logo consisting of a rosella-like parrot eating a cracker, which has appeared on the sides of tins of Arnott's biscuits since the early 20th century. Used metaphorically to denote being ostracised or left out, that is, being on the outside looking in.

cocky's delight treacle, golden syrup or molasses. Also, **cocky's joy**.

coconut a derisive term for an Aboriginal who has adopted the values of white Australia.

code brown a signal given by swimming pool staff when a toddler does number twos in the pool. *Jimmy, there's a code brown at the shallow end, better get the scoop net.*

COD gate a gate found in the bush made from barbed wire and stakes. Standing for Carry Or Drag.

codger an old man. *He's a lovable old codger.*

cod jocks speedos. For a full set of synonyms see **sluggos**.

cods the testicles.

codswallop if something is **a load of old codswallop** then it is rubbish or nonsense. British slang dating back only to the 1960s. It is claimed that this originally referred to a type of drink bottle with an internal marble stopper invented by Hiram *Cobb. Wallop* is British (and Aussie) slang for beer. Thus *Codd's wallop* would be beer bottled in this type of bottle. It's a nice story, but lacks supporting evidence.

coffin nail a cigarette.

Coffs the typically efficient Australian way of saying Coffs Harbour.

cog 1. a hoon who likes driving noisily around the block multiple times for entertainment. A term in use in the Hunter Valley region of NSW and also in Tasmania. Also called a **cogger** or **cog head**. **2.** as a verb, to drive around a block of the main street in a town; to chuck laps. *We were out cogging the other night.*

coin slot bum cleavage appearing above the top of the pants.

coit 1. the anus. A respelling of the word *quoit*, obviously referring to the shape. **2.** an annoying or obnoxious person.

coke cocaine. *He's quick with a smoke or to line up your coke.*

Coke bottle glasses spectacles with thick, thick lenses. Also called **Coke bottom glasses**.

coldie a nice cold glass, bottle or can of beer. Been around since the 1950s.

cold one the same as a coldie. *Let's have a few cold ones before going home.*

collect in the racing game, a winning bet. *I got a nice collect on race two.* Also, as a verb, to win a bet. *The lucky bastard collected on a 100-1 winner.*

Collins Street cocky in Victoria, a person who owns a country property, often for purposes of tax avoidance, but who lives and works in Melbourne. See **Pitt Street farmer**, **Queen Street bushie**.

collywobbles 1. queasiness in the stomach. 19th century British slang. Possibly an alteration of *cholera morbus*, a dysenteric disease. **2.** an ailment affecting the Collingwood AFL team which causes them to lose premiership matches. Post World War II the Pies have only won in 1953, 1958 and 1990. During that time they were runners-up 11 times. **3.** aquatic insect larvae; wrigglers.

combo 1. any combination of things. Originally US slang from the 1920s. **2.** a derisive term for a white man who lives with an Aboriginal woman. Hence the phrase **go combo**, to start such a relationship.

come 1. to orgasm. Venerable slang from as early as the 17th century. Common in Aussie slang since at least the 1960s. Also spelt **cum**. **2.** as a noun, semen. Recorded first in America in the 1920s.

come a cropper 1. to fall heavily, especially from a horse. **2.** to fail, collapse, or be struck by misfortune.

come across 1. to pay up. **2.** of a woman, to grant sexual favours.

come a gutser 1. to suffer a heavy fall, as from a horse. Aussie slang since the 1910s. **2.** to fail badly; to flop.

come down to come off a drug.

comedown the flooding of a dry creek after a big rain storm.

come-fuck-me sexually alluring. *Give me your best come-fuck-me look.*

come-fuck-me boots a longer way of saying **fuck-me boots**. Also called **come-fuck-me's**.

come in on the grouter to arrive after the work's finished, either through luck or contrivance. Hence, to be lucky, to have things fall your way.

come in, spinner! 1. in two-up, a call made to signify that all the bets are laid and it is time to spin the coins. **2.** a phrase used to inform someone that they have just been successfully duped.

come off it! be reasonable!

come on to to attempt to seduce.

come out to openly admit your homosexuality or queerness.

come the raw prawn See the entry for **don't come the raw prawn**.

come up and see my etchings a stock excuse to invite a person back to your place in order to seduce them. Never worked of course.

come your guts to confess.

Comical Railways old nickname for the Commonwealth Railways used in the outback – referring to the regular lateness of services due to washaways, derailments, and other such mishaps.

comic cuts rhyming slang for 'guts'. Traditional Aussie slang since the 1940s.

Commie a Communist or Leftist sympathiser. Formerly the bugbear of all that was right and true. Has lost a lot of its impact now that the Communist threat has died.

Commo **1.** a Communist or Leftist sympathiser. **2.** now generally used in to malign namby-pamby, non-right-wing types. *I can't stand bloody poofo, Commo, pinko, nancy-boys!*

compo **1.** workers' compensation. **2.** in cricket, a ball made from a composite of cork and rubber.

con **1.** a prisoner or ex-prisoner. Shortened form of *convict*. **2.** a shortened form of *confidence trick*. Hence, as a verb, to swindle someone.

con artist a swindler; a confidence trickster.

conchie **1.** a conscientious objector. **2.** an overly conscientious school student. Also shortened to **conch**.

cone **1.** the conical attachment to a bong or pipe in which the drug to be smoked is placed. **2.** a cone's worth of marijuana. *I like to have a few cones after work.*

cone head a dope addict.

cone on to partake in the smoking of cones.

congrats congratulations!

coning the smoking of marijuana.

con job a practised confidence trick; a swindle.

conk the nose. Also spelt **konk**. First recorded in a glossary of Australian convict slang back in 1812. Common in British and American English in the 19th century, but no longer used in either.

conk out **1.** to break down: *The engine's conked out again.* **2.** to collapse from exhaustion or the like.

conky a gum nut.

con man a man who swindles by gaining the victim's confidence. Also called a **con artist**.

connie **1.** a tram conductor or conductress. Formerly an institution of Melbourne's tramways, and sadly mourned when dispensed with for some newfangled automatic system. **2.** a small stone suitable for throwing. Used chiefly in Qld, NSW and Vic. Possibly from an Aboriginal language. See **yonnie** for the full set of regionalisms. **3.** a playing marble. Perhaps an alteration of the word *cornelian*. **4.** a condom.

connie agate a marble made from agate. The most prized type of marble in any alley bag. A term most common in NSW. Recorded as far back as 1916.

continental a fete or the like held as a fund-raiser and usually having an evening dinner and dance. Especially common in rural SA and NSW.

control freak a person who needs to assert their control over every detail.

convict a derogatory term for an Australian – used by Yanks, Kiwis, Poms and the like. Referring to our penal beginnings.

convo a conversation.

coodies head lice. Typical Aussie pronunciation of **cooties**, recently adopted here from American television shows. First appears in World War I where it was in common use by the troops. The suggestion that it comes from Malay *kutu* 'biting louse' seems unlikely.

coods the testicles. Perhaps a variant of *cods*.

cooee the great Australian bush contact cry. Adopted by the first European colonists from the Sydney Aboriginals. To not answer the call of cooooo-eeee is un-Australian. That's of course if you are **within cooee**. Metaphorically, if you are close to achieving a goal you are **within cooee**, and on the other hand, if you are far from an achievement, you are **not within cooee**.

cook **1.** to be going along well. *Her career is really cooking.* **2.** to chemically prepare amphetamines for recreational drug use.

cooking with gas to be doing superlatively well.

Cook's piss in Canberra, a derisive name for the Captain Cook Memorial Jet in Lake Burley Griffin.

cook up **1.** to concoct or fabricate. **2.** to prepare heroin for injection.

cool **1.** suave and sophisticated; up-to-date and in fashion; stylish. The opposite of *daggy*. 20th century American slang that was especially used in the jazz and blues music worlds, before becoming widely popular in the 1960s. **2.** excellent! radical! unreal! *You'll meet me there? Cool!* **3.** all right; okay. *Don't worry, it's cool.* **4.** composed; under control. *Stay cool.* **5.** composure. *He lost his cool.* **6.** sophistication and stylishness. *It was the very essence of cool.*

cool as a cucumber astoundingly calm; unruffled. British slang dating back to the 18th century.

cool bananas! okay! alright! groovy!

cool drink carbonated soft drink. Especially used in SA and WA. Also used in other states, but not as common.

cooler prison.

cool hand a person who is aloof and calmly calculating.

Coolie the Qld township of Coolangatta.

cool it! stop it! take it easy! settle down!

coolite a type of surfboard made of a foam substance. Generic use of a trademark term.

coon a racist term for an Aboriginal person. Local use of the American racist's term for an African American. Derived from *raccoon*. Introduced by a minstrel song, *Zip Coon*, published in 1835.

coon and goon night a wine and cheese night. From *Coon*, a brand of cheese.

coondie in WA, a rock. The first vowel is short, as in *book*. Some use it to mean a large rock, one that is too large to move. Others remember it as a small rock you could pick up and throw. In general terms it is harder than a boondie. See **yonnie** for the full set of regionalisms.

co-ord a clumsy, uncoordinated person. Short for *co-ordinated*, used ironically. Also called a **co-ordie** or a **co-ort**.

coot **1.** a silly bloke or fellow, as in *Ya silly coot.* **2.** a man, especially an old one. *Leave the poor old coot alone.*

cop **1.** a police officer. A shortening of *copper*. First recorded in the US in the 1850s, and in Australia since at least the 1880s. **2.** to catch someone out doing something illegal; to bust. *We were copped jigging school.* **3.** to get or receive. As in, *She copped more than her fair share* or *He copped a $200 fine.* To **cop a feel** is to be allowed some sexual fondling by a partner. The phrase *Cop this!* is a polite Ockerism uttered before jobbing someone unmercifully. To **cop a gong** is to be awarded a medal. Cop can also mean to accept resignedly, put up with or take, as in *He could dish it out but he couldn't cop it* and *You wouldn't find me copping a deal like that.* **4.** to steal. **5.** to look at. As in *Will ya cop the red-head by the bar!* **6.** as a noun, a **cop** can be a profit, as in *He could sell it now and make a cop out of it.* It can also be a job, especially when not difficult, commonly called a **sweet cop** or an **easy cop**. A **sure cop** is a certainty.

cop a load to contract an venereal disease.

cop it **1.** to receive punishment. **2.** military slang, to get hit with enemy fire; hence, to be killed in action.

cop it sweet to endure or put up with.

cop out to opt out in gutless way, as by giving some feeble justification.

cop-out a craven way out of an unpleasant situation. *Her going overseas was a bit of a cop-out.*

copper a police officer. Recorded from the 1840s in both Britain and the US, and since the 1880s in Australia. Probably from the old verb *cop*, to steal.

copper's nark a police informer.

cop shop a police station. Aussie slang since the 1940s. Now used in America and Britain. A fine Aussie export.

copspeak police jargon.

copter a helicopter.

cop the lot to bear the brunt of some misfortune; to suffer multiple misfortunes at once.

cop you later a way of saying 'See you later'. With a feeble pun on the word *copulator*, or the phrase *copulate her*.

cop your wallop to get your drift.

corby in Tasmania, a grub which causes damage to grass by burrowing into the roots.

cordial in Tasmania this is used to refer to carbonated soft drink, such as lemonade, cola, lemon squash, etc., and not the concentrated liquid mixed with water, which is how the rest of the country uses the term. The concentrated cordial is sometimes called **mixup** in Tassie.

cordie **1.** a derisive term for a cadet from in Royal Military College Duntroon in Canberra. From *kordies*, the zombie-like servants of the evil Baron Kord, of the *Mandrake the Magician* comic strip, which appeared in the *Australian Women's Weekly* in the 1940s. **2.** cordial. Hence, any alcoholic drink. *He had a few too many cordies last night.*

cords corduroy trousers.

corker something superlatively good. Originally British slang of the 19th century.

corky a corked thigh.

Corner Country the region where the borders of Qld, SA, and NSW meet. Also, called **the Corner**.

Cornstalk **1.** a obsolete term for a native-born white Australia male. A popular 19th century stereotype: six feet two inches tall, dressed in corduroy pants, a red shirt, a cabbage-tree hat, high boots, and stock-whip wound in graceful loops on his arm. Supposed to be generally taller and thinner than the English immigrant. **2.** a derisive nickname for a person from New South Wales. Similar derisive nicknames for inhabitants of other states are **Banana bender** – Queenslander, **Cabbage Gardener** or **Gumsucker** – Victorian, **Crow-eater** – South Australian, and **Sandgroper** or merely **Groper** – West Australian.

corroboree a traditional Aboriginal ceremony. Formerly used in whitefella slang to refer to any gathering, party or dance. Little heard these days as it is not considered PC.

cossie a swimming costume. Aussie slang since the 1920s. Chiefly used in NSW. Also spelt **cozzie**.

cot bed. *Time to hit the cot.*

cot case someone who is exhausted, drunk, or in some way incapacitated, and fit only for bed. In use since the 1930s.

couch potato a dull and inactive person, generally found plonked in front of the telly.

cough up a lung to have a severe coughing fit.

could crack a flea on it said of your stomach after having gorged on epicurean delights.

could eat the crotch out of a low-flying duck said of someone starving hungry. Other similar expressions are **could eat a horse and chase the rider** and **could eat a horse if you took its shoes off**.

couldn't fight your way out of a wet paper bag extremely weak or puny. Another version is **couldn't spread marge on a Sao**.

couldn't organise sex in a brothel a phrase descriptive of someone who is totally useless. A cruder version is **couldn't get a fuck in a brothel**. Other similar metaphors are **couldn't get a kick in a stable**, **couldn't pick a winner in a two-horse race**, **couldn't catch a fly in a country dunny**, **couldn't pour water from a boot**, **couldn't train a choko vine to grow up a dunny wall**, **couldn't organise a piss-up in a brewery**, and **couldn't find his dick with both hands**.

counterjumper a salesperson at a counter.

the country any part of a sports ground which is far from the main area of activity, as the outfield in cricket, or the part of the course away from the stands in horseracing.

country dunny a traditional rural toilet, consisting of a small shed furnished with a lavatory seat placed over a sanitary can, or a pit, located a decent distance from the house. Hence, to be **all alone like a country dunny** is to be totally alone. An extremely incompetent person **couldn't catch a fly in a country dunny**.

country mile if you win **by a country mile**, then you've won by a great extent. Estimates of distance in the country never do justice to the actual distance to be travelled.

County Coogee the beachside suburb of Coogee, Sydney, heavily populated by British tourists.

a couple of lamingtons short of a CWA meeting stupid; lacking a full complement of intelligence. For similar comparisons see the entry for **short of**.

couta a barracouta.

couth civilised, well-mannered. A joking backformation from the Standard English term *uncouth*.

cove a man, as in *He was a rum sort of cove*, or *I'm looking for a cove with a red shirt.* Formerly extremely common, but dying out from the 1960s and little heard today.

cover your arse to protect yourself.

cow **1.** a contemptible person. Aussie slang since the 1890s. *You miserable cow.* **2.** a bad-tempered woman. *She was a mean old cow.* **3.**

something unpleasant or annoying. *That's a cow of a thing to say. I've had a cow of a day.*

cowabunga! yippee! excellent! A fanciful coinage used in the US television show *Howdy Doody*, from where it made its way into the slang of both US and Australia surfies in the 1960s. In the 1980s it had a short vogue among schoolchildren under the influence of the *Teenage Mutant Ninja Turtles* phenomenon.

coward's castle parliament, when used as an arena in which to vilify and abuse others while under parliamentary privilege.

cowboy **1.** in rural areas, a man employed to milk cows. Quite different to the American cowboy. **2.** an unreliable and poor worker; one who cuts corners and does a sloppy job. **3.** an entrepreneur or business executive who similarly cuts corners.

cow cocky a small-scale cattle farmer.

cow confetti a euphemism for bullshit.

cow corner in cricket, the area of the field over mid wicket. So called because it was such a remote fielding location that the cows could graze there.

cow juice milk.

cow-pat lotto a form of lottery in which a cow is placed in a pristine paddock which has been divided into squares which are numbered and raffled off. The winner is decided by the fall of the first cow-pat.

cow shot in cricket, a stroke made without style or discrimination.

cozzie another spelling of **cossie**.

crack **1.** to obtain. *Did you crack an invite?* **2.** to break into a safe. **3.** to gain unauthorised access to a computer; to break the security code on a piece of software; to break an encryption code. **4.** to win a free game on a pinball machine. **5.** the anal cleft; the anus. **6.** the vagina or vulva. **7.** a highly-addictive form of cocaine prepared for smoking.

crack a fat to get an erection.

crack a lay to divulge information. Old slang dating from the 1940s, not heard much any more.

crack a tinnie to open a can of beer.

crack a wave in surfing, to catch a wave and ride it. In use since the 1940s.

cracker **1.** a firework. Hence, **cracker night**, a night upon which fireworks were let off around the country in celebration of the Queen's birthday. Dispensed with in recent years when the authorities decided there were just too many nongs blowing their hands off, blinding their kids, and generally making a nuisance of themselves. **2.** someone who breaks a computer security system. **3.** excellent. *They scored a cracker try in the first half.* **4.** used to refer to money in the expressions, **to not have a cracker**, to be penniless, and **not worth a cracker**, utterly worthless.

crack hardy to endure hard times courageously. Good old Aussie slang since the 1900s.

crack head an addict of the drug crack cocaine.

crack it **1.** to be successful, as in *I cracked it for an invite to the wedding.* Since the 1930s. **2.** to be successful is obtaining sexual favours. Also Aussie, since the 1940s. **3.** to work as a prostitute. Also of 1940s vintage.

crack on to to woo into bed. An Australian original this, dating from the 1950s.

cradle snatcher a person dating a much younger person.

Craft's disease forgetfulness brought on by old age. Standing for *Can't Remember A Fucking Thing!*

cranking excellent, hot, firing. *The surf's really cranking.*

crank out to sing or perform forcefully; to play music loudly.

crank up to stir into action; to rev up.

crap **1.** excrement, or a piece of excrement. Hence, an act of defecation, and, as a verb, to defecate. Not an original Anglo-Saxon four-letter word as it only dates back to the 1840s. Related to the English dialect word *crap* 'a scrap', and the medieval *crappe* 'chaff', and ultimately from either Dutch or French. **2.** nonsense; rubbish. **3.** junk; odds and ends. **4.** worthless; of poor quality; crappy: *a crap magazine.* **5.** to be mightily scared. *I was crapping myself at the thought of it.* **6.** used as an intensifier. *We beat the crap out of them.*

crap artist same as a bullshit artist.

crap off to annoy.

crap on to blab on at length; to talk nonsense.

crap out to fail or flop.

crapper a toilet. American slang from the 1920s. There is a story that toilets are called crappers in honour of Sir Thomas Crapper, the supposed inventor of the flush toilet. Unfortunately this story is a load of crap.

There was an English plumber by this name, and he even served as the royal sanitary engineer, though he was never knighted. He did not invent the flush toilet, though his company did make toilets which bore his name. Perhaps US soldiers in Britain in World War I associated the name Crapper with the word *crap*.

crappy **1.** of poor quality: *a crappy magazine*; *a crappy performance*. **2.** soiled: *a crappy nappy*.

craptastic hopeless, shithouse, crap.

crap wrap toilet paper.

crash **1.** to sneak into a party uninvited. **2.** to sleep over. *You can crash at my place*. **3.** to collapse or fall asleep, as from exhaustion.

crash and burn **1.** to collapse from exhaustion. **2.** to fail miserably; to flop.

crash-hot excellent.

crash out **1.** to suddenly fall deeply asleep. **2.** to be knocked out of a contest.

crate a run-down, dilapidated vehicle, be it a plane, a boat or an automobile.

crater face a person with an acne-scarred face.

crawbob a name for the yabby in Qld and NSW. Also called a **crawchie** in these states. See **yabby** for an explanation of the regional variants.

crawl to ingratiate yourself to others; to brownnose.

crawler an person who behaves ingratiatingly to another; a sycophant; an arselicker. In Australia, one of the worst epithets you can apply to a person. The word has been around at least since the 1820s.

cray **1.** a crayfish. **2.** a colloquial name for the yabby. See **yabby** for an explanation of the regional variants. **3.** a twenty dollar note.

craybob a name for the yabby in Qld and NSW. Also called a **craydab** in NSW. See **yabby** for an explanation of the regional variants.

craybobbing fishing for yabbies.

crayfish **1.** a twenty dollar note. From its colour. Compare **lobster**. **2.** in Tas, SA and NSW, the marine rock lobster. **3.** a colloquial name for the freshwater yabby. See **yabby** for an explanation of the regional variants. **4.** as a verb, an old Aussie slang term meaning to back down in a cowardly fashion. If you surprise a yabby out and about it will retreat backwards into its hole.

cream **1.** to beat up in a fight. **2.** to beat convincingly.

cream between chiefly in Vic and Tas, an ice-cream wafer.

cream your jeans **1.** to have an orgasm while dressed. **2.** to become overly excited, as in *Don't cream your jeans!*

cred the type of credibility that stops you from being a dag.

crescent in WA and Tas, a term for what the rest of the country calls a shifting spanner, or shifter.

crew **1.** a gang of youths; a posse. **2.** a group of surfies, skaters or snowboarders, from a certain area, as *the Newport crew*, *the Straddie crew*. **3.** a group of rap or hiphop musicians. *They're Melbourne's finest rap crew*.

crib **1.** especially among miners, steelworkers, construction workers, and the like, a lunch box or bag. Also called a **crib bag**, **crib box** or **crib tin**. Hence, a packed lunch, or, the lunch break, also known as **crib break** or **crib time**. A room set aside for lunch is known as a **crib cuddy**, **crib house** or **crib room**. This use of the word *crib* goes back to Cornish dialect, whence it most probably made its way into Australian mining communities, but the term was also in use in Scotland, Northampton and Devon. It is the same word as *crib* meaning (originally) a barred receptacle for fodder, a baby's bed, a cabin, a hovel, (in NZ) a beachside holiday house, a bin used in hop picking, and numerous other related items. **2.** the action of illegally moving your hand over the line when shooting in a game of marbles. Also called **cribs** or **cribbing**. See **fananny-whacking** for a full set of synonyms.

crikey! a euphemism for the blasphemous exclamation *Christ!* Not exclusively Australian, but taken on board by Aussie swearers with great gusto. The vociferous crocodile hunter Steve Irwin has recently brought this oath to the attention of Americans who now think we all go around saying *Crikey!* all day.

crim a criminal.

crime in military slang, to discipline a soldier for breaking regulations. Since World War I.

cripes! a euphemism for the blasphemous exclamation *Christ!* Not exclusively Australian, but recorded earliest here, way back in 1902.

cripple among surfers, a derisive term for a kneeboarder. Because they can't stand up.

critter an ugly or despised person.

croak to die. Used elsewhere but recorded earliest in Australia, back in 1812.

crock **1.** a load of nonsense. Short for a *crock of shit*. Borrowed from the US of A. **2.** in good old Aussie slang a **crock** was a worn-out, decrepit old person or someone laid-up by ill health. Not heard much any more. Derived from *crock*, an old ewe or horse.

crock of shit nonsense; lies; a load of rubbish. Originally US, dating back to the 1940s.

cronk dishonest, illegal, crooked. A bit out-of-date nowadays.

crook **1.** sick, *I'm feeling real crook*. Hence, injured, *Her crook leg is keeping her up at nights*. Genuine Aussie slang, dating from the 1900s. **2.** bad; inferior. *That food was crook, He did a pretty crook job*. **3.** a criminal; a thief or swindler. Originally US slang from the 1870s, now Standard English. Hence, as an adjective, dishonest or illegal; of an item, stolen. This second usage is an Australian original, and not used elsewhere except New Zealand. **4.** angry, annoyed, upset. To **go crook on** someone is to scold them. Used since the 1910s.

crook as Rookwood extremely ill. A bit of an exaggeration as it refers to Rookwood Cemetery in Sydney.

crooked dishonest, criminal, illegal. Commonly elaborated as in the slang phrases **as crooked as a dog's hind leg** and **so crooked you could hide behind a corkscrew.**

crooked on angry with. An Aussie original dating from the 1940s.

crool to ruin or spoil, as in *He's crooled his chance*. A respelling of the word *cruel*, much favoured by C.J. Dennis.

the Cross the Sydney suburb of Kings Cross, long noted for being a hotbed of vice. Now popular with backpackers and tourists, despite (or because of) being still very seedy.

cross-country ballet a derisive term for Australian Rules football. Not to be confused with **cross-country wrestling**, that is, Rugby League or Union.

crow **1.** any of various all-black birds of the corvid family, generally reviled by the European invaders of their country. Used in some slang phrases, such as **the land where the crow flies backwards**, meaning any remote outback place. **As the crow flies** relates to a measure of distance in a straight line, as opposed to taking the road. To **draw the crow** is to be given the worst job. And let's not forget that old Australian classic: **stone the crows!** (see entry). **2.** in older slang, a female prostitute. Also used as a derogatory term for a man's wife or girlfriend. A shortening of **chromo** (see entry).

crowd surf to be carried across the top of a crowd of moshing audience members.

Croweater a person from South Australia. A derisive epithet dating back to the 1880s. See **Cornstalk** for similar terms of derision for people from other states.

Crowie the Sydney suburb of Crows Nest.

crowl a stupid or clumsy person. Used by schoolkids in Sydney in the 1960s and 1970s. From Crowl Home, a centre caring for sufferers of cerebral palsy. Kids can be so cruel. See **minda** and **moonya**.

crown jewels the testicles. Also called the **family jewels**.

crow peck a sharp blow to the noggin with the knuckle of the bent index or middle finger. A kind of schoolyard bullying behaviour.

crud **1.** rubbish, nonsense, junk, crap, as in *Who scripted this crud?* **2.** a contemptible person. Also, **crud-face**.

cruddy inferior; unworthy.

cruel to ruin or spoil. To **cruel someone's pitch** is to ruin someone's chances. An Aussie original dating from the 1890s. Little heard today.

cruet the head. If you **do your cruet**, you lose your temper. Aussie slang since the 1940s.

cruets the testicles.

cruise **1.** to go about with a view to picking up a sexual partner. **2.** to wander about in a relaxed, cool way. **3.** to take it easy while doing something.

cruising for a bruising in imminent danger of receiving a beating.

crumb in Aussie Rules, a loose ball on the fringe of a pack. Hence, as a verb, to scoop up such a loose ball. *He crumbed well from a ball-up*. A player who is skilled at this is called a **crumber** or a **crumb gatherer**.

crumpet **1.** a woman considered as a sexual object, as in *What a nice bit of crumpet*. British slang of the 1930s. Now also used of attractive men. **2.** sexual intercourse with a woman. *Had any crumpet lately?* **3.** the head.

He's a bit soft in the crumpet. British slang from the 1890s. If you are **off your crumpet** you are crazy. **4.** if something is **not worth a crumpet**, then it is worthless.

crunch time the time for a critical decision to be made or for critical action to take place.

crusher 1. navy slang for a ship's corporal. **2.** in horseracing, a person who places multiple bets on a horse as its price shortens in the odds.

crust a living or livelihood. Common in the question *What do you do for a crust?* An Australian original dating back to the 1880s.

crusty 1. shabbily dressed and unwashed. **2.** hungover. **3.** a dirty person dressed in old clothes. **4.** a feral. **5.** dried semen on men's underwear.

cry Ruth to vomit. Also, **call for Ruth**.

crystal cylinder among surfies, the tube of a breaking wave. Ooh – very poetic!

crystally a derogatory term used to describe namby-pampy, woolly-headed, alternative types, who are into aura healing, chakra balancing, reiki, crystal power, and all that jazz.

the CT in the ACT, the *Canberra Times* newspaper.

cuddy a horse. An Aussie original. From British dialect where it was used to refer to donkeys, not horses. Used since the 1890s.

cum semen; also, to orgasm. Merely a respelling of the word *come*, commonly used in pornography.

Cunnamulla portmanteau old slang for a sugar bag used to hold your belongings. From Cunnamulla, a town in outback Qld which was once a regular stop for swagmen on the wallaby track

Cunnamulla tune-up a prank tune-up in which spark-plug leads are randomly swapped around. Not recommended by ten out of ten car mechanics.

cunning as a shithouse rat extremely cunning. This little Aussie gem has been around since the 1940s.

cunning kick a secret pocket for hiding cash.

cunning linguist a jocular alteration of the word *cunnilinguist*, that is, someone who performs oral sex on a woman.

cunt 1. the vagina or vulva; a woman's external genitalia. The dreaded C-word. The crudest and rudest word in the language. Hated by many women, embraced by others. Not used by all men, but unabashedly so by those that do, though strictly avoided in polite conversation. Its appropriateness depends on the context in which it is used and which particular sense is intended. One of the traditional Anglo-Saxon four-letter words. Recorded since the 13th century, where it appears in a London street name, *Gropecuntelane*, that is, 'Grope Cunt Lane', presumably in a red-light district. Also, from 1246, we find one Mr John Fillecunte (=fill cunt), presumably well-hung, or else, a braggart. Other medieval surnames include Cleavecunt, Crushcunt and Twitchcunt. All of which points to the fact that in medieval times there was less of a taboo on the word than there is nowadays. In other Germanic languages we find Old Norse *kunta* and Old Frisian *kunte*. The Standard English term *vagina*, a borrowing from Latin, doesn't make an appearance until the 17th century.
2. crudely used to refer to women considered as sexual objects. *There'll be plenty of cunt at the party*. **3.** a contemptible man; a bastard; a fucker. Used in America since the 1860s. In Australia, no doubt since World War I. Sometimes applied to women, but not commonly. In the US it is much more common to use this word to refer to women, especially to mean a contemptible woman, a 'bitch', but also merely a woman. This usage is absent from Australia. **4.** in a weakened sense, any person, as in *He's a lucky cunt*. Generally used of men. **5.** sexual intercourse with a woman. As in *Got any cunt lately?* British slang since the 17th century. **6.** something that is annoying or frustrating. *I can't get this cunt of an engine to run*.

cunt hair a very small fraction of the smallest graduation on a scale, as in *Move it another 5.2 mm and a cunt hair*. US slang from the 1950s.

cunt head a contemptible person. Another US adoption, this time since the 1970s.

cunt-lapping despicable or objectionable, as in *I hate those cunt-lapping bastards*. Once again, American, from as early as the 1920s.

cunt off a mega-crude way of saying *piss off!*

cunt starver a prisoner serving time for defaulting on maintenance payments. Also called a **wife starver**. Aussie slang since the 1950s.

cunt-struck infatuated with women. British slang from the 1870s.

the Cup the Melbourne Cup horserace, held annually on the first Tuesday in November. The race which stops the entire country (except for wowsers). An Australian institution since Archer won it back in 1861. If you want to refer to a great length of time in Aussie lingo, you say **since Archer won the Cup**. The day on which the race is run is **Cup Day**, and the night before is **Cup Eve**, and the week in which it falls is **Cup Week**. And, come each November, millions of Aussies are struck with **Cup fever**.

cup of cheeno a cappuccino. Used by many people as a joke, but also used seriously by people who don't know any better.

a cup of tea, a Bex, and a good lie down a method of relaxation once popular among Australian housewives. The phrase was originally a 1950s advertising line for the pain-killer *Bex*. Unfortunately at the time Bex was an APC, that is, a compound drug containing Aspirin, Phenacetin, and Caffeine, which turned out to be highly addictive and the abuse of it led inexorably to renal disease. Eventually legislation was passed to outlaw the use of phenacetin in analgesic compounds and the abuse of the drug subsided. But, happily, the harmless and charming phrase has stayed with us.

cuppa a cup of tea or coffee. *It's time for a cuppa!*

curl the mo! an old exclamation of surprised admiration. Evoking an image of a long moustache curling up on both sides. How this one died out is a mystery!

currency back in colonial days, Australian-born. Especially in the terms **currency lad** and **currency lass**. Used in opposition to sterling, British-born.

the 'Curry the north-west Qld mining town of Cloncurry.

curry muncher a racist term for an Indian or Pakistani.

the curse menstruation.

custard arm in cricket, a player who cannot throw the ball very far.

custard brains a stupid person.

custard chucker the penis. What a charmer of a word this is!

cut **1.** to dilute a drug with another substance. **2.** circumcised. As opposed to **uncut**. Used in personal ads, for those who have a preference.

cute sexually pleasing or attractive; gorgeous; used of both males and females, as *He/She is so cute I could die*. Also of specific bodily features, *What cute buns*. The widely-reported story that the dictionary defines cute as 'ugly but interesting', is nothing but a fable. No dictionary actually contains this definition.

cutie **1.** a sexy young woman. Now also used of men. **2.** a cute child.

cutie-pie **1.** a woman or girl who is cute. **2.** a term of endearment for such a woman or girl.

cut laps to drive around the block over and over again, as commonly done by bored youth.

a cut lunch and a water bag a measurement of how long something will take – especially used of a journey. *Brisbane is a bit more than a cut lunch and a water bag from Perth.*

cut-lunch commando a derisive military slang for a member of the Australian Army Reserve. Since the 1950s.

cut out **1.** to pay a debt with work, or with sexual favours, rather than with money. Done when you don't have the requisite funds to cover your debt, as in *Not having any money, they had to cut the fine out at the rate of five dollars an hour*. **2.** underworld slang, to serve time instead of paying a fine. **3.** to use up left over funds, as in *We'll cut out this grant cheque by buying special photographic paper*.

cuts corporal punishment with the cane. Formerly a practice beloved by sadistic schoolteachers. In the PC world of the present it is banned. This uniquely Aussie term for it dates back at least as far as the 1910s.

cut someone's grass to have sex with another's partner; to cuckold someone. Also, to **mow someone's lawn**.

cut someone's lunch to make a move on or steal someone else's girlfriend or wife.

cut the mustard to be up to the task.

cut your stick to be off; to begin a journey. Older slang, no longer common.

the C-word **1.** a euphemism for the word *cunt*. **2.** a euphemism for the word *commitment* in personal relationships, generally in reference to the fear thereof.

cyberbabe 1. a cool female user of the internet. Also called a **cyberchick** or a **cybergirl**. 2. a virtual 3D image of an uberbabe, such as Lara Croft.

cyberbludging wasting time at work using the employers computer resources.

cyberchondriac a hypochondriac who habitually visits internet medical sites in order to practise self-diagnosis.

cyberdude a cool male user of the internet. Also called a **cyberboy**.

cybersex sexual interaction via the internet; sex in cyberspace or virtual reality.

D

D **1.** a dozen long necks of beer. **2.** a detective or police officer. See **dee**.

da a pronunciation of the word 'the' which is now being used in Australia in some small way by youngsters who wish to sound like cool African Americans and rappers. Especially found in the phrases *You da man* and *You da bomb* (=you are great). You mostly see it in print rather than actually hear it. The question is, will it have legs?

dack to pull someone's pants down; to pants someone. *I was dacked in front of everyone.*

dacks another spelling of **daks**, that is, pants.

dadah illegal drugs. From Malay.

Dad'n'Dave Aussie rhyming slang for 'shave'. Sometimes used to mean 'grave'. After the two comical characters created by Steele Rudd in the late 19th century.

daff to have sex. From *Daffy Duck*, rhyming slang for 'fuck'.

dag **1.** a lump of excrement-matted wool on a sheep's rear. In use since the 1890s, coming originally from the British dialect of Kent. The more common British term was *daglock*, but this never made its way Down Under. In terms of animal husbandry, dags are terrible things as they can promote flystrike which is a real problem for the sheep. Thus the dags have to be removed. One employed to do this is a **dag-picker**. As a verb, to **dag** was to remove said dags. The command **rattle your dags!** means 'Move along!', evoking an image of a dag-laden sheep being given a hurry-up. **2.** a person who is neat in appearance, conservative in manners, and lacks style and sophistication; a person who is not cool. You know, like computer geeks and Yamaha guitar-toting, born-again Christians, or someone who continually makes bad puns, or wears socks and sandals. The Aussie species of the dweeb or nerd. This sense became common in the 1970s. Generally a direct insult, but of recent years there has been a movement for dags to 'reclaim' the word and be proud of their dagginess. This has had some partial success, so that calling someone a dag can now often be meant in an affectionate way. In origin perhaps partly derived from sense 3 below, but strongly influenced by sense 1 above. **3.** in earlier use, a **dag** was a something completely different. It used to refer to someone who was a bit of a character, someone who was an eccentric, but in an amusing way. It was vaguely negative, since it meant 'weirdo', but at the same time a bit complimentary, as it meant they were at least entertaining. Almost equivalent to a 'wag', but not as positive. This was in common use from the 1870s to the 1960s, but is now obsolete. In origin this sense perhaps comes from the British dialect sense of *dag* meaning 'a daring feat among boys'. One boy would do some daring act like dive from a great height, and then dare the others by saying 'There's a dag for you'.

dag bag a type of cotton bag slung over your shoulder.

dagdom the world of dags; the state of being a dag.

daggy **1.** uncool; conservative, lacking style and sophistication; dweebish, nerdy or geeky. Hence, **daggily**, in a daggy manner, and **dagginess**, the state of being daggy. **2.** of sheep's wool, befouled with dags. Hence, of a person, dirty or filthy, slovenly and unkempt. Of clothing, old and worn-out, scungy.

dago an old, old racist term for any person of Latin ethnic origin. It was originally a nautical slang word referring to Spanish and Portuguese, and comes from the common Spanish name *Diego*. In Australia it has been used since at least the 1890s, and post-World War II it is most commonly used to refer to Italians.

dags comfortable old clothes worn around the house.

dagwood dog a battered sav on a stick. Also called a **pluto pup**, or in SA, a **dippy dog**.

daisy chain **1.** a continuous chain of homosexual males engaged in having sex, each performing anal intercourse with the next. **2.** any group of people engaged in lovemaking forming some chain-like formation.

daisy-cutter in ball sports, a ball which, after being struck or kicked, skims along the ground.

dak-dak a Volkswagen Beetle. Imitative of the engine noise.

dakka marijuana. A borrowing from South African English, where it comes from Afrikaans, and ultimately from the native language Khoikhoi.

daks pants. Generic use of a trademark. Sometimes spelt **dacks**. In use since the 1960s. Also appears in the compounds *chunder daks, dick daks, underdaks* and *trackie daks.*

Dalkeith tractor Perth slang, a derogatory term for a city-only 4WD that never sees off-road driving. Also called a **Dalkeith diesel**. See **Toorak tractor** for a host of synonyms.

dam an artificially trapped body of water. This is a classic Australianism. In the rest of the world a dam only refers to the wall blocking off a river or stream.

damper a simple type of bread made with flour and water and cooked in a camp fire. Good Aussie tucker since the 1820s. So called since it dampens the appetite. Traditionally eaten when out bush, but nowadays available at local bread stores – but it's not the same thing.

damp squib **1.** a racehorse or greyhound that starts well but finishes terribly. **2.** a person who is a failure or dud. A *squib* is a firecracker, and a damp one won't go off.

D&M **1.** a deep and meaningful conversation about problems in your interpersonal relationship. Especially common among adolescents. **2.** as a verb, to have such a conversation. *They were D&M'ing all night.*

dandy in SA, a small container of ice-cream. Been around since the 1950s. In Vic and Tas called a **dixie**.

dangle the Dunlops of a plane, to lower its wheels for landing.

dangly bits the male genitalia. A recent Australianism, around since the 1990s.

Dapto briefcase in Wollongong, a cask of cheap wine. After Dapto, a small township in eastern NSW. Also called a **Bellambi handbag** or **goon box**.

Dapto dog Aussie rhyming slang for 'wog', a person of Mediterranean background (see **wog** for more info). The *Dapto dogs* is a greyhound racing meeting held at Dapto, NSW.

darbies in convict times, handcuffs. From 16th century cant where they were known as *Father Darbie's bands.*

darg an amount of work that has to be done in a certain time period. 1920s Australian slang, from British dialect. Seldom heard nowadays.

darkie **1.** a racist term for any dark-skinned person, in Australia used chiefly of Aboriginals. **2.** a turd, especially in the phrase **to choke a darkie**, to defecate. Classic Australiana, à la Bazza McKenzie, since the 1960s.

darl typical Aussie shortening of 'darling'. Been around since the 1930s. Also common in the form **darls**.

Darlo the Sydney suburb of Darlinghurst. Also called **Daaaaahlink Hurst**, due to its high camp population.

dart a cigarette.

Darwin rig the peculiar formal dress used in the Top End by men. Essentially there is no need for a jacket. After this you can replace the tie and collared shirt with an open-necked shirt, and long trousers can be replaced by shorts and long white socks. Thongs, stubbies and T-shirts are out. Also called **Territory rig**.

Darwin stubby a whopping bottle of beer, which at different times with different people, was anywhere from 40 to 80 fluid ounces (1.13 to 2.27 litres). Nowadays it is normally a 2.25 litre bottle and available widely in Darwin, especially for tourists.

the Dat the military base of Nui Dat, so called by Aussie soldiers in the Vietnam conflict.

date the anus, so called from the resemblance to the edible fruit, brown and puckered. Can also be used as a verb to mean to poke or prod between the buttocks. Very rarely **date** is used to refer to the vagina.

date packer a homophobic term for a gay man. See **dung puncher** for a swag of synonyms.

date roll toilet paper.

Datto a Datsun-make automobile. Also simply called a **Dat**.

day bug a day scholar at a boarding school. Also called a **day scrag**.

DDH among teenagers, an incredibly sexy person. Standing for Drop-Dead Honey.

dead **1.** completely, totally. Very common in Australian slang, as in *You're dead right*, or *That was dead stupid.* **2.** in horseracing, if a horse is **dead**, then it is not being run on its merits, that is, not being run to win.

deadbeat a person down on their luck; a jobless and homeless person; a derelict. An Aussie original since the 1890s.

dead bird in horseracing, a certainty. Metaphorically, a bird that has been shot and is in the bag. Old slang from the 1890s, and now shortened simply to **bird**.

dead cert an absolute certainty. *He's a dead cert to win.*

dead duck **1.** a failure or flop. **2.** if you **look like a dead duck in a thunderstorm**, then you look terrible.

dead fly biscuit a biscuit with dried fruit between two thin layers of sweet pastry; also called a **squashed fly biscuit** or a **fly cemetery**.

dead from the neck up lacking intelligence.

the Dead Heart the arid central regions of Australia. Here 'dead' is in the sense of lifeless and unarable. A rather dreary term clearly from a European perspective. The fabled Inland Sea never materialised and so the Great South Land turned out to be less of a paradise than some imagined. Of course, the Dead Heart is actually teeming with life, if you know where to look for it.

dead horse rhyming slang for 'tomato sauce'. Aussie slang since the 1940s.

dead-leg a cork of the thigh muscle. Also used as a verb. *He dead-legged me thigh in the first quarter.*

deadly **1.** excellent, fantastic, cool, as in *She was a deadly spunk in an even deadlier skirt.* Originally a word of Aboriginal English, at least since the 1980s. Recently has made some crossover into the speech of white adolescents, especially in the NT. **2.** also used as an adverb, as in *He sang deadly.*

deadly treadly classic Aussie slang for a bicycle. Generally, any bicycle could be a deadly treadly. Sometimes used to mean an excellent or fast bike. Other times used to mean a beat-up old bike. And other times used of one with a fixed wheel and no handbrakes, seen as unsafe. Has been around since the 1960s.

deadman's float the faking of a drowned person, effected by floating face down in the water. It's a thing kids do.

dead marine an empty bottle of beer, whisky, or the like.

dead meat ticket an identification tag used by the military. Aussie slang since the 1920s.

dead ringer an exact likeness; the spitting image. Aussie slang since the 1890s. *He was a dead ringer for the local policeman.* Also, **dead ring**, as in, *She was the dead ring of me mother.*

dead set **1.** as an adverb, completely, totally, as in *I'm dead set against it.* Aussie slang since the 1940s. **2.** as an adjective, total, utter, as in *He's a dead set prick. No doubt about it.*

dead set! honestly! fair dinkum!

deadshit a contemptible person. Australians can proudly claim this bonzer little insult as their own. Has been around since the 1960s.

dead spit the exact likeness; the spitting image. Originally 19th century British slang.

dead'un **1.** a dead person or animal. **2.** in horseracing, a horse that is deliberately run to lose; a horse not run on its merits.

deal **1.** a measured quantity of an illegal drug. **2.** a purchase of drugs.

deaner a variant spelling of **deener**.

death adders in your pocket stingy or miserly. Aussie slang since the 1940s.

death bag the bladder from inside a cask of cheap wine.

death seat **1.** the front passenger seat in a motor car. **2.** in a trotting race, a position on the outside of the leader, from which it is very hard to win.

debag to remove the trousers of someone as a prank.

deck **1.** to knock someone to the ground. **2.** in cricket, the deck is the wicket. **3.** among surfies, the top surface of a surfboard. **4.** among skaters, the top surface of a skateboard, or the skateboard itself.

deckie a deck hand.

decko a variant spelling of **dekko** (see entry).

dee a detective or police officer. Also simply spelt **D**. Australian and British slang since the 1870s.

deener until 1966, a shilling; the sum of twelve pence. After decimal currency was introduced, a ten cent piece or the sum of ten cents. Originally in British slang from the 1830s, and occurring in Oz since at least the

1880s. Perhaps from *dinar*, a coin of various Arab countries; less likely from Latin *denarius*, since that word forms the basis of the abbreviation 'd.' which was used for a penny not a shilling. Sadly, **deener** has not been heard very often since the 1970s and is all but dead now. Also commonly spelt **deaner**.

the Deep North Queensland, or rather, Far North Queensland, viewed as a region of backwardness and intolerance. By analogy with America's Deep South.

deep throat **1.** fellatio involving deep penetration and requiring the overcoming of the gag reflex. Derived from the title of a famous porn film that was all the rage in the early 1970s. **2.** an informer. From the name given to their anonymous source by the journalists investigating the Watergate affair.

def a word meaning cool or excellent, commonly heard in rap music, and hence picked up by Aussie adolescents since the 1980s. Apparently it comes from the pronunciation of the word 'death' in West Indian English.

dekko a look, as in *Have a dekko at that!* Originally British Army slang from India. It comes from the Hindi command *dekho!* look! Used in Australia at least since the 1950s. Sometimes shortened, as is the Aussie way, to **dek**.

Delhi belly severe diarrhoea suffered by travellers to India.

deli a delicatessen. A common abbreviation since the 1970s. Interestingly, in SA and WA a deli is actually a corner store, rather than a shop selling expensive smallgoods.

delish delicious.

delo a delegate. Aussie slang since the 1960s.

demo **1.** a public demonstration. Aussie slang since the 1900s. Also used in Britain and the US. **2.** a demonstration of a product, or, a demonstration model. **3.** among laddish blokes in the 1970s, the performance of the sex act in front of a bunch of other blokes.

demolish to eat or drink greedily.

demon a police officer or police detective. Originally prison slang, from the 1890s.

dent knocker a panelbeater.

depot duck Broken Hill slang for a crow or raven at a rubbish dump (known there as 'depots').

deppie in car sales, a deposit.

der a mocking exclamation indicating faked and exaggerated stupidity or bewilderment. Equivalent to 'You idiot!' or 'As if!' Meant to represent the natural exclamation of a brainless person when attempting to think. Been around since the 1970s, principally among schoolkids.

der brain a fool or idiot.

dermo the skin complaint dermatitis. So called since the 1940s.

derps underpants. Also, **underps**.

derro a dismissive term for a derelict. Unsympathetic Aussie slang since the 1970s.

Derwenter obsolete slang for an ex-convict from Tasmania. The original penal settlement was on the Derwent River.

desk wallah a derisive term for a desk worker, especially a government official or bureaucrat. We also use the US term **desk jockey**.

desperado a person, usually a male, who is desperate for sex.

despo a totally desperate person.

destructo a person who causes great havoc or destruction by being oafish or unrestrained.

devo (pronounced 'dee-vo') an absolute deviant. At least since the 1980s.

DFE absolutely easy; offering no challenge. Standing for *Dead Fucking Easy.*

DGs dark glasses, especially useful for hiding a hangover.

dhobi in the Navy, a bath or wash; the laundry. As a verb, to wash or do the washing. Old nautical slang, from Hindi.

dial the face. Hence if you are **off your dial** you are totally pissed, stoned or otherwise whacked out.

diamond duck in cricket, a dismissal without even having faced a ball, for example, being run out, or knocking the bails off while lining up the wicket, or some other similar catastrophe. The most ignominious of all dismissals. Worse than the **duck** and the **golden duck**. In the UK this term seems to be reserved for getting out on the first ball of an innings.

dice to throw away, reject. A nice bit of Aussie invention around since the 1940s.

dick **1.** the penis. From the male name. Not very rude as words for the penis go. With small children it can also refer to the female genitals, sometimes called the **girl's dick**. If something has **had the dick** then it is ruined. **2.**

an annoying or contemptible person; a dickhead. **3.** a detective. A different word this, from 19th century British underworld slang *to dick* 'to watch', which in turn comes from the Romani word *dik* 'to look', and ultimately from Hindi *dekho* – which, incidentally, happens also to be the origin of the word **dekko** (see entry). **4.** a dictionary. *Pass us the dick.*

dick around to fool about and waste time.

dick bathers men's speedos. For a full set of synonyms see **sluggos**.

dick brain a fool; idiot.

dick daks speedos. So called as they are daks that reveal the dick. For a full set of synonyms see **sluggos**.

dicken! really! honestly! fair dinkum! Used primarily in SA and the Broken Hill area. Also used as a question, meaning 'Is that true?'

dick eye an annoying, foolish person; a jerk. Referring to the meatus, or *eye*, of the penis.

dick face an annoying, foolish person; a dickhead. From US slang, as is **dick nose** and **dick wad**.

dick flop an annoying, foolish bloke; a jerk. Referring to a flaccid penis, and thus suggesting a lack of masculinity.

dickhead **1.** an idiot or fool; a jerk. *I couldn't care less what all the dickheads up the pub reckon.* **2.** as an adjective, stupid, foolish, befitting a dickhead. *It was a dickhead thing to do.*

Dickless Tracy a female police officer. Aussie slang since the 1970s. Based on the comic strip character *Dick Tracy*.

dick pointers speedos. Also called **dick pokers**. Politely abbreviated to **DPs**. For a full set of synonyms see **sluggos**.

dick rash an annoying person; a jerk. Comparing them to a sexually transmitted disease.

dick shit a contemptible person. A cruder version of dickhead.

dick-shitty despicable.

dick stickers yet another term for men's speedos. Chiefly used in NSW. For a full set of synonyms see **sluggos**.

dick togs the same as dick stickers, but this time the preferred term in Qld. Politely abbreviated to **DTs**. For a full set of synonyms see **sluggos**.

dickwhacker in Perth, a fool or idiot. Literally, a masturbator or wanker. Also, **dicky whacker**.

dickwit an annoying, foolish person; a jerk. A blend of *dick* and *fuckwit*.

dicky **1.** stupid and annoying; characteristic of a dickhead. Australian and NZ slang. *That was a dicky thing to do.* **2.** of a body part, in poor condition, as in *She's got a dicky knee.* Also used to mean difficult, as in *a dicky position.* Not related to the previous definition and seemingly not related to the word *dick* meaning penis. It first appears in the 18th century in the phrase 'It's all dicky with him' meaning 'it's all over with him'. Which is a long time before dick meaning penis was first recorded. Further, it has never been rude. Origin remains a mystery.

diddle **1.** to cheat or swindle. Originally British slang. **2.** to have sex with someone; to root or screw. **3.** to sexually stimulate a woman manually. **4.** a child's word for the penis. Variant of **doodle**.

diddly-squat absolutely nothing; none. Australians have picked up this term from US television shows.

diddums an exclamation indicating that someone is being childish and petulant. Spoken with a mock concern. From baby-talk *did 'ems* = did they?

diddy the toilet. Australian slang since the 1950s. Origin unknown. Sometimes shortened to **did**.

didgeridoo the well-known Aboriginal wind instrument. Often thought to be an Aboriginal word, it is more likely to have come from European efforts to imitate the sound. Early references to the instrument do not use this word. Nowadays colloquially shortened to **didj**.

die in the bum to fail completely.

diesel dyke a butch lesbian. Also called a **diesel dyke**.

dieso in the Australian Antarctic Territory, a diesel mechanic.

diff **1.** difference. *What's the diff?* Originally 19th century American slang. **2.** an engine differential, as in *Me car needs a new diff.* This one is Aussie, since the 1940s.

dig **1.** an Australian soldier, especially an Anzac. Short for **digger**. **2.** hence, a form of casual address among men, especially to older men. **3.** in cricket, an innings. **4.** to comprehend; to 'get'; to pay attention to; to find to your taste. *I can dig that*. Clearly unrelated to the previous senses, this word comes from US Black English and was originally used among jazz musicians. Many suggestions as to the origin have been put forward but no overwhelmingly convincing ones.

digerati the elite of the IT world. A blend of *digital* and *literati*.

digger **1.** a miner during the Australian gold rush. Recorded as early as 1849. Now only historical. **2.** in World War I, an Australian infantryman, used originally only of the lower ranks, not the officers. (Not used at Gallipoli, as it was first recorded in 1916.) Partly an application of the goldmining sense, and partly because the soldiers were required to dig trenches. Later became generalised to refer to any Anzac, no matter what the rank, and thence, in World War II and later conflicts, any Australian soldier. A term of great respect and pride. **3.** a form of friendly address among men. Equivalent to *cobber* or *mate*. Now mostly used only when addressing elderly men. All three senses have an almost identical existence in New Zealand English.

digger hat an Australian Army slouch hat.

dill a fool; an incompetent; an absolute nong. Sometimes elaborated to **dill brain** or **dill pot**. Been around since the 1940s. In origin a backformation from **dilly** (see entry).

dill-brained completely stupid; idiotic.

dilly foolish, stupid. Great Aussie slang term dating back to 1905. From Somersetshire dialect, perhaps a blend of *daft* and *silly*.

dilly bag a small traditional, hand-woven bag used by Aborigines. From the Aboriginal language Yagara, from the Brisbane region. Hence, applied to a toiletries bag, or to any small bag for various commodities.

dimmie a Victorian colloquialism for dim sim. An Australian-Chinese deep-fried culinary treat.

dine at the Y to engage in cunnilingus.

ding **1.** to dent; to hit lightly, causing minor damage. Hence, a dent, especially in a car panel or surfboard. **2.** a racist term for an Italian, sometimes used for a Greek or any other person of Mediterranean background. An Aussie slang original from the 1940s. Nowadays restricted to WA. Origin unknown, perhaps an abbreviation of *dingbat*. **3.** a party. Perhaps short for *wing ding*. Aussie slang since the 1950s. **4.** the penis. From US slang, 1960s. **5.** short for **dinger**, the backside or anus.

ding-a-ling a foolish person; a nong. Originally American slang from the 1930s.

dingbat an eccentric, peculiar, or stupid person. A mild insult. Used in Oz since the 1910s, but in the US since the 1870s.

dingbats **1.** the delusions brought on by the DTs. **2.** hence, as an adjective, crazy. *He's gone dingbats*.

ding-dong **1.** of a fight, strenuously contested. A good fight is described as a *ding-dong go*. Aussie slang since the 1920s. **2.** powerful. *I've got a ding-dong headache*. **3.** complete and utter. *He's a ding-dong, friggin' maniac*. **4.** as a noun, a simpleton. *Don't be a ding-dong*.

dinger **1.** the arse or anus. 1940s Oz slang. Shortened to **ding**. **2.** a shanghai or catapult. **3.** a condom.

dingleberry **1.** a piece of excrement clinging to the anal hairs. From US slang, itself a variant of British slang *dillberry*. **2.** a stupid or annoying person.

dingo **1.** a no-good, pathetic coward. Aussie slang since the 1860s. After the native Australian dog, universally detested by early European settlers, and still held in great disrespect by many. Of course, the real dingo wasn't any more cowardly than any other dog. The name comes from Dharug, the extinct Aboriginal language of the Sydney region, in which it meant a 'domesticated dingo', as opposed to a wild one (see **warrigal**). The dingo is now in real danger of disappearing for good due to cross-breeding with the feral domestic dog population. **2.** as a verb, to act in a cowardly manner; to back out ignominiously; to shirk or evade. **3.** to **turn dingo** on someone is to betray them.

dingo fence any of various fences built around pastoral country to exclude dingos. Also called the **dog fence**.

dingo fucker a derogatory term for an Australian. A similar racist slur is **roo fucker**.

dingo's breakfast a piss and a good look round; that is, no breakfast at all. Also called a **bushman's breakfast**.

dink **1.** to carry a second person on a horse, bicycle or motorcycle. Hence, such a ride: *I gave her a dink home*. Aussie slang since the 1930s. Used all over, but especially common in Vic, WA, ACT and Tas. There is a host of

regional slang terms for this practice. There are three base words, **bar** (referring to the top metal bar of the bicycle frame), **dink** (perhaps from the British dialect word *dink* 'to dandle a baby') and the more obvious **double**. In Qld and NSW we find **bar** and **barie**. 'Bar' is especially common in south coast Qld and north coast NSW, and 'barie' is restricted to NSW only. Also especially common in Qld and NSW is the term **double**, which can be colloquially shortened to **dub**, or suffixed with *-er* to form **doubler**, which is also common in the ACT. Dink has provided us also with **dinky**, which is especially common in WA and SA. A combination of two of the base words, has given us **double-dink** (especially WA, Victoria and Tasmania) and **dinky-double** (chiefly NSW and ACT). South Australia has gone out on its own with the term **donkey**. Which is partly from the name of the animal and partly an alteration of *dinky*.
2. a strongly racist term for an Asian, especially common in the military, and widely used by soldiers in the Vietnam War to refer to a Vietnamese. An Australianism of unknown origin, borrowed by US soldiers and thus making its way to the States where it is now quite common. One of the few true Aussie words that have infiltrated America – though perhaps not one to brag about. **3.** one of a couple, married or unmarried, who have separate incomes and no children. An acronym from *Double Income, No Kids*. One of the few survivors of the rash of acronyms for various sociological types during the 1980s. **4.** an abbreviation of **dinkum**. *Are you dink?*

dinks abbreviation of *dinkum*. See **fair dinkum**, **true dinks**.

dinkum **1.** genuine. As in, *Are you dinkum about that?* or *She was a dinkum Queenslander all right*. It appears earliest in the phrase *fair dinkum*, (1890 in Australia, but 1881 in Britain), and not as a separate word until 1905. Comes from the British dialects of Derbyshire and Lincolnshire, where it meant 'work', or 'a due share of work'. So if you did your fair dinkum, it meant you did your fair share of the work. The claim that the word was brought to Australia by Chinese miners in the gold rush era (from Cantonese *din kum* 'real gold') cannot be true, unless there was a secret population of Chinese goldminers in the south of England that no one knows about. Seems a bit unlikely. Altered variously to **dink**, **dinks** and **dinky-di**. **2.** used as an adverb, really, genuinely. As in, *He's me mate, dinkum he is!*

dinkum Aussie a genuine Australian, exhibiting all those aspects of the Australian character that we like to believe Australians have, like honesty, courage, laconic sense of humour, willingness to work hard, and so on.

dinkum oil the truth; reliable information.

dinky **1.** of small size; dainty; little and cute. **2.** a small tricycle for toddlers. **3.** to carry as a second passenger on a horse, bicycle, or motorcycle. Chiefly used in WA and SA. For a full set of regionalisms see **dink**.

dinky-di a slangier version of **dinkum**. Used since the 1910s. *He's a dinky-di Aussie.*

dinnyhayser a knock-out punch. Supposedly after a boxer named *Dinny Hayes*.

dip underworld slang for a pickpocket. From 19th century US slang, made its way to Australia by the 1940s.

dip out to opt out or renege. Aussie slang since the 1950s.

dippy dog in SA, a battered sav on a stick. Also called a **dagwood dog** or **pluto pup**.

dipshit a contemptible person. From 1960s American slang.

dipso an alcoholic or drunkard. From 19th century British slang, short for *dipsomaniac*.

dipstick **1.** an idiot or jerk. From 1960s US slang, euphemistic for *dipshit*. **2.** the penis. Hence, **dipsticks**, men's speedos. For a full set of synonyms see **sluggos**.

dip your lid to lift your hat as a mark of respect. Hence, metaphorically, to show admiration. Commonly used in the ungrammatical phrase *I dips me lid*, in allusion to C.J. Dennis' Sentimental Bloke who dips his lid upon first meeting his lady love Doreen.

dip your wick of a man, to have sex.

dirt work **1.** motorcycle riding on dirt roads. **2.** the same as **circle work**.

dirty **1.** angry, seething, 'filthy'. *No need to get dirty about it*. Commonly in the phrase **dirty on** as in *He was dirty on me for not inviting him last Saturday*. An Aussie original from the 1960s. **2.** to **do the dirty on someone** is to betray or cheat them. This one from Britain, 1910s. **3.** used with 'big' or 'great' for emphasis. *I stepped on a dirty big black snake*, or *They brought in a dirty great chocolate cake*.

the Dirty Acre a 3/4 acre block in the middle of the Golden Mile near Kalgoorlie. It was sold for 12 bottles of champagne in the 1890s by Tom Brookman and Sam Pearce (the discoverers of the Golden Mile). The small block was quickly covered with 5 hotels, a brewery and numerous other shops. Miners used to tunnel up into the cellars of the hotels to sell stolen gold over the bar. The 'Sunday Sesh' at the Block was a riotous affair right up to the early 1990s when the last hotel was demolished to make way for mining operations.

Dirty Annie Resch's Dinner Ale. Old slang from the 1950s and 60s. Not heard any more.

dirty deed **1.** sexual intercourse. **2.** to **do the dirty deed** is to do something underhanded, mean or unfair.

the Dirty Half Mile that strip of the Sydney suburb of Kings Cross renowned for prostitution and vice. So called since the 1930s.

dirty water to **get the dirty water off your chest** was a particularly uncharming way of referring to finding sexual release after a long period of going without.

dis to criticise; to disparage; put down; show disrespect to. A 1980s import, via rap music. In origin probably extracted from *disrespect*.

disco dancer Aussie rhyming slang for 'cancer'.

discombobulate to upset or confuse. A mock-Latin formation based on *discompose* or *discomfort*. Originally 19th century US slang.

diseasel among steam train enthusiasts, a derogatory term for diesel engines.

dish an attractive young woman; now also used of an attractive young man.

dishlicker a racing greyhound. Also, can be used to refer to any dog. Aussie slang.

dishy physically attractive; sexy.

dit in Australian naval slang, a yarn or story, especially used in the phrase **spin a dit**, to tell a yarn. Been around since the 1940s. Origin unknown. A raconteur or teller of tall stories is known as a **dit-spinner**.

the Ditch **1.** the Tasman Sea. **2.** Bass Strait.

ditsy flighty or empty-headed, most commonly used of a woman. From 1970s US slang. Perhaps an alteration of *dizzy*. Hence, an empty-headed woman is known as a **dits**.

dive a filthy, rundown place, especially a restaurant, hotel, pub, or similar establishment. From 19th century US slang, originally a cellar or basement used as a drinking den.

dive-bomb to jump into the water with the knees tucked under the chin, in order to make a large splash; to bomb.

divvy **1.** services slang, an infantry division. Used by Aussies since World War I. **2.** in gambling slang, a dividend or payout; a collect. **3.** a portion of profits, especially when illegally gained. Hence, to **divvy up**, to share out.

divvy van a police van for the conveyance of those in custody. Used all over Australia, but especially common in Victoria. Sometimes spelt **divi-van**.

dixie **1.** in the army, a small tin for eating out of. Originally British army slang, from Hindi. **2.** especially in Vic and Tas, a small container of ice-cream. Been around since the 1940s. In SA called a **dandy**.

DNA dumpster a crass term for the vagina.

do **1.** a festivity or party. Aussie slang since the 1950s. *We're having a big do next week.* **2.** a hair-do. *She traded her long locks for a short do.* **3.** to injure. Aussie slang since the 1960s at least. *He did his ankle jumping from a train.* **4.** to spend all your money. *He did his dough at the races.* Great Australian pastime since the 1890s. **5.** to have sex with. Venerable slang from the 17th century. **6.** underworld slang, to serve a prison sentence. *She did six months for drugs.* **7.** to arrest or book someone. *I got done for speeding. the cops did me on the way home.* **8.** to drink. *I could really do a beer right about now.* Also used of food. Aussies have been doing this sort of doing since the 1850s. **9.** to take drugs. *He's been doing hard drugs for years.* **10.** to have a meal with someone as a social or business occasion. *Doing lunch* was all the rage in the 1980s. It's all a bit passé now. **11.** of a person, to be admirable. Used as a compliment or statement of praise. As in *You'll do, mate*, or *How about that fullback? He'll do me!*

do a Bradbury to win unexpectedly. In honour of speed skater Steven Bradbury's unexpected gold medal win in the 2002 Winter Olympics after the rest of the field stacked it.

do a bunk to run away; to take flight; to abscond.

do a Melba to make a habit of returning from retirement, in a number of 'farewell' performances. Alluding to the famous opera singer Dame Nellie *Melba*.

do a perish old Aussie slang for dying from thirst or suffering a lack of sustenance.

do a runner **1.** to escape by running; to abscond. **2.** to bolt from a restaurant without paying the bill.

dob **1.** to tell on someone; to report someone to the authorities. A cardinal sin in Australia. *I'll tell you if you promise not to dob.* You can dob *on* someone, or dob them *in*. Been around since the 1950s. If you **dob someone in**, you nominate them for an unpleasant task. **2.** in Aussie Rules, to make a swift accurate kick; to kick a goal. *He dobbed three in the last quarter.* Also as a noun, *A last-minute dob from the forward saved the match.* Also, a player who is an accurate kicker is known as a good **dob**. **3.** in Aussie slang, to **dob in** also has another meaning, namely, to contribute funds to a collection. This also dates back to the 1950s.

dobber an informer or telltale. A term of high opprobrium in Australia. An older variant was **dobber-in**, but this is not heard much any more. Both terms date back to the 1950s.

dockie a dock worker.

docking the sexual act of stretching the foreskin of the penis over the glans of another.

doco a documentary. Aussie slang since the 1980s.

doctor in WA, a fresh sea breeze that arises in the afternoon or evening during summer. See **Albany doctor**, **Esperance doctor** and **Fremantle doctor**.

dodger **1.** bread. Aussie slang dating from the 1890s. **2.** a flyer or advertising leaflet. Also Aussie slang, from the same era.

dodgy **1.** liable to be dishonest, suspect, as a *dodgy salesman*, or a *dodgy call*. **2.** not stable or reliable. *Those foundations look a bit dodgy. He's got a dodgy hamstring.*

doer a hard and keen worker; one who succeeds through hard, honest work. *He was a real little doer.* A term of respect. The opposite of a bludger. Has been part of Australian culture since at least the 1900s. A particularly hard worker was known as a **hard doer**.

dog **1.** a contemptible fellow. **2.** an ugly woman. **3.** in underworld slang, an informer. An Aussie original from the 1840s. Hence, to **turn dog**, to betray someone to the authorities. **4.** a prison warder or other prison authority. Another Aussie original, dating from the 1910s. **5.** a worthless racehorse. Hence to **run like a dog**, to run poorly. **6.** something that is absolutely hopeless. *That new movie is a total dog.* **7.** our four-legged friend used as a measurement of coldness when camping out in the open: *It was a three-dog night*, *four-dog night*, etc. Referring to how many dogs you need to snuggle around to keep warm. **8.** to suddenly end a relationship with someone; to drop someone. **9.** to attack verbally; to criticise.

dog and bone Aussie rhyming slang for 'telephone'.

dog box **1.** a type of small, cramped compartment that used to be found in railway carriages. **2.** any cramped quarters; a kennel-like room. **3.** a transportable classroom used in schools.

dog fence any of various fences built in pastoral country to exclude dingos. Also called the **dingo fence**.

dogger **1.** a dingo hunter. Formerly a common occupation of the outback. **2.** in SA, a derogatory term for Anglo-Saxon Australians, used by those of ethnic background. **3.** in the Australian Antarctic Territory, a dogsled driver.

doggie a dog watch or night shift.

doggy do excrement of a dog.

doggy style describing sexual intercourse in which the recipient is on all fours and entered (either vaginally or anally) from behind. Also called **doggy fashion**.

dog's breakfast a mess; a confused state of affairs. Also called a **dog's dinner**.

dog's eye Aussie rhyming slang for 'meat pie'. So called since the 1950s.

dog's eye and dead horse rhyming slang for 'meat pie and sauce'. Also known as **bleeding dog's eye**.

dog squad undercover police. Aussie slang since the 1960s.

dog's vomit horrible food.

dog tag an identity disc. Also called a **dead meat ticket** or a **meat tag**.

dog tied up an unpaid debt. An Aussie original dating back to 1905.

d'oh a self-reprimanding grunt used when one has done something stupid. Comes from Homer Simpson of *The Simpsons* cartoon.

do it to have sex. Ancient slang. People have been 'doing it' since the 17th century.

do it on your ear to accomplish something easily.

do it tough prison slang, to take prison life badly. Also **do it hard**. On the other hand to **do it easy** is to make the best of it while inside, also known as **doing it on your ear** or **doing it on your head**. A prisoner who is serving their time with a light heart might brag 'I can do it on my shit-tub without getting a ring around my arse.'

dole bludger a derisive term for an unemployed person living off social security payments without making proper attempts to find a job. The term first came to prominence in the 1970s. An earlier term was **doley**, which has been in use since the 1950s.

do like a dinner to vanquish. Aussie slang since the 1840s.

doll an attractive young woman. From American slang of the 19th century.

dollar Although Australia has officially had dollars only since the introduction of decimal currency in 1966, it may amaze you to know that the word was in use here since colonial days. It used to refer to the sum of five shillings.

doll up to dress up in finery. Also, **dolly up**. Originally British slang.

dolly to falsify evidence against someone. *The police dollied Joe.*

dolly catch in cricket, a simple catch.

the Don Sir Donald Bradman, Australia's greatest batsman, Test captain 1936–48.

donah an obsolete term for a young woman; a sweetheart or girlfriend. Specifically, donahs were the female counterparts of the larrikin or street thug of the 19th and early 20th centuries. Originally in British slang, used in Cockney dialect, and by circus folk. From Polari (old British gay slang) from Italian *donna* woman.

Donald Duck rhyming slang for 'fuck'. Old Walt must be turning in his grave at this little Aussie gem.

done up like a Christmas tree overdressed in a gaudy way.

dong **1.** to hit or punch. *I donged him on the head.* Hence, a heavy blow. The Aussie love of stoushing has produced this little beauty, dating back to the 1910s. **2.** the penis. From American slang of the 1900s.

donga **1.** a shallow gully or dried-out watercourse. This word was borrowed during the Boer War from South African English where it meant 'a gully formed by running water'. The Boers had taken the word from the African languages Zulu and Xhosa. **2.** the bush or outback. *He's been out in the donga too long.* **3.** a makeshift or temporary dwelling; hence, a demountable, especially in a mining area. How a word for a dried-out watercourse came to be applied to a building remains something of a mystery. **4.** in the Australian Antarctic Territory, sleeping quarters. **5.** to loaf; to bludge.

donger **1.** a bludgeon. **2.** the penis. As in the classic Australian metaphor *dry as a dead dingo's donger*.

donk **1.** a donkey. **2.** an engine. Short for donkey engine. **3.** the penis. **4.** short for **donkey**, meaning to carry as a second person on a horse, bicycle, or motorcycle.

donkey **1.** chiefly in SA, to carry as a second passenger on a horse, bicycle, or motorcycle. Partly after the animal and partly an alteration of 'dinky'. For a full set of regionalisms see **dink**. **2.** a backyard coal-burning furnace.

donkey dick an exceptionally well-hung man, or the penis itself. Also called a **donkey dong**.

donkey drop in cricket, a poor bowl, pitched extremely high in the air and coming down almost vertically.

donkey-lick to defeat with ease. Commonly used in horseracing. Aussie slang since the 1890s.

donnybrook a fight or argument; a brawl. Originally with reference to a fair held annually until 1855 at *Donnybrook*, Dublin, famous for rioting and dissipation.

don't come the raw prawn Do not try to deceive me. *Don't come the raw prawn with me! How can you say you can't stand 'em when you've never even touched one!* A 'prawn' is a fool, and a 'raw prawn' is a naive fool. Originally military slang from World War II. A jocular variant of this phrase is **don't come the uncooked crustacean**.

don't go there! Do not move onto that undesirable topic!

don't pick your nose or your head will cave in a phrase used to deride another's lack of intelligence.

doodad any device or gadget, the name of which is unknown or temporarily forgotten.

doodle the penis. Dating back to the 18th century.

doodlem-buck a sideshow game of the 1920s using a threepenny piece.

doof (pronounced to rhyme with *poof*) dance music. *He will only listen to doof – nothing else.* Echoic of the sound of the deep thumping bass.

doof-doof a car with a pumping sound system.

doofus a stupid, dull-headed person; a fool; a gumby. From US slang of the 1960s. Made its way to Oz in the 1980s.

doog (pronounced the same as *goog*) a playing marble. Hence, in the plural **doogs**, the game of marbles. Used in Australia since the 1950s. Now only common in WA. From Suffolk dialect.

dook a hand. Hence, as a verb, to hand over or give; to give as a bribe. To **dook it out** is to fight in order to resolve a dispute. Such a fight may begin with the exhortation '**Put up your dooks**'. From 19th century British slang, the Cockney pronunciation of *duke*, from rhyming slang *Duke of Yorks* for 'forks' = fingers. This seems a bit far-fetched, but John Camden Hotten, in whose *Slang Dictionary* of 1874 this explanation is given, says 'a long way round, but quite true'. And who are we to doubt him?

doona a quilted bedspread filled with down or synthetic padding. Originally a trademark, now used generically in Australia. Elsewhere in the world they are called 'duvets'.

doona day a kind of sanctioned sickie or 'mental health day' in which you slop about the house in pyjamas and snuggle up on the couch with your doona.

do over to assault; to beat up. In Australia since the 1940s, but in origin a Kiwi term dating back to the 1860s.

doover a doodad or thingummyjig. Also expanded to **dooverlackie**. Originally Australian military slang of World War II. A general utility term which could mean a manoeuvre, an exercise, a thing, a soldier, etc. Was commonly used to refer to a dugout or shelter. Said by some to be from *do for*, as in the phrase *that will do for now.* Others prefer a Yiddish origin.

dope **1.** marijuana or hashish. A modern narrowing, since the 1960s, of earlier use when it could mean any drug or narcotic. **2.** a drug illegally given to a racehorse to either improve or impair its performance. American slang from the 1870s, and the origin of the 'drug' sense of the word. Ultimately from the Dutch word *doop* 'sauce'. **3.** information. *Have you got the dope on that?* Originally used in horseracing contexts and thus a derivative of sense 2, that is, the information about which horses have been doped or not. 19th century US slang, used in Australia since at least the 1920s. **4.** a stupid person. Originally British slang, picked up by Aussie soldiers in World War I. **5.** very cool and sophisticated. *It is the dopest nightclub around.* A recent (1990s) borrowing from the US.

dope fiend a person addicted to marijuana.

do-ray-me money. Punning on *dough* = money.

dorba a stupid person, especially someone who is clumsy or socially inept. Also shortened to **dorb**.

dork a dag, dweeb or nerd. From US 1960s slang, but only appearing in Australia in the 1980s. The original sense is 'penis', which meaning has had some small use here in Oz.

dorky befitting a dork; dweeby.

Dorothy Dixer a pre-arranged question asked in parliament specifically to allow a propagandist reply by a minister. This term has been in use since the 1960s. From *Dorothy Dix*, the pseudonym of E.M. Gilmer, US writer of a famous advice column which ran from the 1890s to 1950 – Gilmer was rumoured to have made up many of the readers' letters herself.

dorry a gossip.

dose an infliction of a venereal disease; the clap. *I hope I don't pick up a dose.* US slang, in Australia since at least the 1940s.

dosh money. Origin unknown. Recorded from 1850s in the US, but now entirely obsolete there.

doss **1.** to sleep at a place. *Can I doss at your place tonight?* Originally underworld and criminal slang of Britain, transported to Australia with the convicts. Back then it was *dorse*, and thus probably comes from Latin *dorsum* 'the back'. **2.** as a noun, a place to sleep. *It was only an overnight doss.*

doss house a cheap lodging house, usually for men only; a flop house.

dot the anus. *I got a swift kick up the dot.* Aussie slang since the 1950s.

dot ball in cricket, a maiden ball. So called from being marked with a dot on the scoring sheet.

do the bolt to run away or abscond, especially when caught in the act.

do the deed to have sexual intercourse.

do the Harry to run away or leave promptly; make oneself scarce. In full **do the Harold Holt**, rhyming slang for 'bolt'. Referring to our erstwhile Prime Minister who disappeared while swimming without so much as saying hooroo.

double to carry or convey a second person on a horse, bicycle, or motorcycle. Common in Qld and NSW. For a full set of regionalisms, including **doubler** and **double-dink**, see **dink**.

double adaptor a male who both gives and receives anal sex, especially at the same time.

Double Bay tractor Sydney slang, a derogatory term for a city-only 4WD that never sees off-road driving. Also called a **Double Bay shopping trolley**. See **Toorak tractor** for a host of synonyms.

double drummer a type of large cicada which has a very strident call.

doublegee in WA, the vicious spiky seed of the introduced plant *Emex australia*. The spines are extremely hard and long, being able to puncture tyres and jab through the redoubtable Aussie thong with ease. Both the plant and this name for it were imported in the 19th century from South Africa. In NSW the seeds get called **cat heads**, **cat's eyes** or **goat's heads**, the last of which is also used in Qld. Along the Qld coast they are also called **bull heads**. The most widespread term is **three-corner jack**, which is the favoured term in SA.

Double Pay the ultra-affluent Sydney suburb of Double Bay.

double pluggers thongs with two plugs keeping the straps attached to the base.

double whammy a double blow; two bad things happening at once, or one right after the other. For more info see **whammy**.

douche bag a contemptible person. A borrowing from US slang that has attained some little currency down under. Has been around in the States since the 1940s.

dough money. Used in Oz since the 1920s, but originally US slang from the 1850s. The phrase to **do your dough**, however, meaning to lose all your money, is an Aussie original.

doughnut a circular pattern made on the ground by driving a car in a tight circle at high speed and causing the rear wheels to skid. *The hoons were out doing doughnuts last night. He was copped chucking doughnuts.* Also called a **doughie**.

doughy **1.** dull-witted; slow. **2.** no good; dreadful.

downer **1.** a depressing experience; a bummer. **2.** a depressant drug, as Valium. Both senses from the US, 1960s.

down the gurgler ruined; irretrievably lost or destroyed. The home-grown Aussie version of the usual 'down the drain' or 'down the plughole'. Been around since the 1970s.

down the track in Darwin, to travel south down the Stuart Highway towards Alice Springs.

Down Under Australia. Also used of New Zealand, and of Australia and NZ together. Originally from the British point of view – as though they were on top. Despite this slightly negative perspective the term has been embraced by us Antipodeans and has been in use since the 1880s.

downy a person with Down syndrome. Hence, a clumsy, uncoordinated person. Very non-PC.

doxy a young woman; a girlfriend or sweetheart. Now obsolete. Originally a female companion of a beggar, dating back to the 16th century.

DPs **1.** speedos. Standing for Dick Pointers or Dick Pokers. For a full set of synonyms see **sluggos**. **2.** a Displaced Person – a civilian who had moved from their native country to escape the ravages of war during World War II.

DQ **1.** a drama queen. **2.** a drag queen.

drack **1.** unpleasant; dreadful. *It was a drack party.* **2.** of a woman, unattractive. *She was a drack sort.* Probably the original sense. Said to be from *Drac*, short for *Dracula*. The notion that it derives from Yiddish *drek* 'crap', 'cheap or shoddy', perhaps has some merit to it. Dating back to the 1940s. **3.** hence, an ugly woman. Since the 1960s.

drag **1.** a prison sentence of three months or less duration. **2.** in Aussie Rules, to take a player off the field for poor play.

drag queen a male who dresses in drag.

drag the chain to lag behind. A metaphor from the chain gangs of convict days, but not recorded from that era, first making its appearance in the 1910s, where it seemed originally to be a phrase used in the shearing sheds for the slowest shearer.

drag up to raise a child in a rough way. *He was dragged up in a slum by a drunk.* An old expression dating back to the 18th century in Britain. Also found in the form to **drag up by the hair**.

drain the dragon of a male, to urinate; to syphon the python.

drain the lizard of a male, to urinate.

drama queen a person who overreacts regularly to minor problems.

draw the crabs **1.** in military slang, to come under enemy fire. From World War I, where a *crab* was an artillery shell. **2.** to attract unwanted attention.

draw the crow to get the worst job.

dreaded lurgy a cold or flu virus or germ. See **lurgy**.

dream prison slang, a period of imprisonment for six months.

dream on! You are being unrealistic!

dreck rubbish; crap; nonsense. *I've never heard such dreck.* From Yiddish.

dribble among surfies, pathetic surf, not worth getting wet for.

drill for vegemite to perform anal sex. A little Aussie charmer since the 1980s.

drinkies a social gathering, as at a pub after work, for the purpose of sharing a few drinks.

drinking fountain a small water tap attached to a basin. The most common term the country over except for NSW and ACT. See **bubbler** for the full set of regionalisms.

drinking tap a chiefly Vic and Qld term for a drinking fountain. See **bubbler** for the full set of regionalisms.

drink tap a drinking fountain, especially in Vic and Qld. See **bubbler** for the full set of regionalisms.

drink with the flies to drink alone when at a pub. Since 1910s.

drinky-poo an alcoholic drink.

drip a dull or boring person.

drive the porcelain bus to vomit into a toilet bowl.

drongo a slow-witted or stupid person; a fool. A great Australian insult. Originally it was an RAAF term for a raw recruit, and first appears in the early 1940s. From *Drongo*, the name of a racehorse in the early 1920s which was famed for its poor form and used as a character in the political cartoons of Sammy Wells appearing in the *Melbourne Herald*. Some have suggested that it refers to the spangled drongo, a tropical bird of north-east Australia, but there doesn't appear to be any obvious connection.

droob a loser; a dud or dag. Origin unknown. Has been used in Oz since the 1930s. Little heard nowadays.

drool value level of sexiness.

droolworthy exceedingly spunky; luscious. A similar term is **droolsome**.

droopy drawers a slovenly, apathetic person.

drop **1.** an attractive young woman, as viewed by a supposed connoisseur. *She's a tasty drop.* **2.** in cricket, the fall of a wicket. Hence, a place in the batting order. *I was promoted to second drop.* **3.** in underworld slang, death by hanging. Obsolete since the punishment became so. **4.** to give birth to a child. *Looks like Meg's going to drop another.* **5.** to let out a fart. *Ohhh! Who dropped one?* **6.** to take a drug, especially LSD, orally.

drop a bombshell to make a startling announcement.

drop a bumshell to fart.

drop bear a vicious breed of koala that supposedly leaps upon unsuspecting tourists and attacks with unmitigated fury. A tale told to frighten unwary foreigners since at least the 1960s.

drop dead gorgeous majorly attractive; stunning.

drop in in surfing, to cut across the path of another surfer who has priority.

drop-in **1.** a drop-in centre. **2.** a place visited casually. *It's a favourite drop-in of mine.*

dropkick a contemptible person. Short for *dropkick and punt*, which is rhyming slang for 'cunt'. I bet you didn't know you were being so rude!

drop off the twig to die.

dropsy a supposed disease the symptom of which is constantly dropping things.

drop test a wry attempt to fix a faulty piece of equipment, usually electronic, by dropping it.

drop the kids off at the pool to go to the toilet for number twos.

drop your bundle to give up in despair.

drop your guts to fart.

drop your lunch to fart.

drover's dog **1.** a person of little importance. **2.** a drudge. **3.** a skinny or emaciated person is said to be **all prick and ribs like a drover's dog**.

drown some worms to go fishing.

drug-fucked suffering over-indulgence in recreational drugs. A choice bit of Australian slang this, dating from the 1990s.

druggie a drug addict. Originally US slang from the 1960s. In Oz also called a **druggo**.

the Druitt the Sydney suburb of Mount Druitt.

drum **1.** a swag. So called from the shape. From the 1860s. Now only historical. To **hump the drum** was to carry a swag on the track looking for work. **2.** a brothel. 1870s Aussie slang. Obsolescent, if not already dead. **3.** reliable information; the good oil. Dates back to the 1910s. To **give someone the drum** is to give them a tip, or some good advice. If a racehorse **runs a drum**, then it performs as tipped, that is, it wins. However, this phrase is mostly to be found in the negative. *He couldn't run a drum in a field of goats.*

drunk as Chloe extremely drunk. The origin of this phrase is a mystery. It is not derived from the famous painting of *Chloe* in Young and Jackson's Hotel, Melbourne, as the expression appeared in Britain in the 1820s and the painting was not around till 1875. Apart from Chloe, it is common in Oz to be **drunk as a lord**, **drunk as a skunk**, **drunk as a pissant**, **drunk as a tick**, and even **drunk as Larry Dooley**, whoever he was.

the Dry the dry season in Australia's tropical north.

dry as a dead dingo's donger completely dry; parched; badly in need of a life-giving beer.

dry as a frog's tit in the middle of the desert dying of thirst.

dry as a nun's cunt parched. Also in the alliterative form, **dry as a nun's nasty** – this latter perhaps the invention of Barry Humphries. A crass and profane Australianism that has been around since the 1970s. A different simile, namely, *cold as a nun's cunt*, was recorded as Australian prison slang way back in 1955. The inclusion of this phrase in the *Macquarie Thesaurus* caused a nationwide fracas in 1994, and received much media coverage, which only had the unfortunate effect of spreading the phrase to millions who had never heard it before.

dry as a Pommy's towel exceedingly dry; parched. Alluding to the stereotype of the English **bath-dodger**.

dry-root **1.** to engage in sexual activities while fully clothed; to indulge in frottage. **2.** to insert and rub the penis between the thighs or breasts, but not ejaculate.

DTs in Qld, speedos. Standing for **dick togs**. For a full set of synonyms see **sluggos**.

dub to carry a second passenger on a horse, bicycle, or motorcycle. Chiefly used in Qld and NSW. Short for *double*. For a full set of regionalisms see **dink**.

Dub a Volkswagen of the type first produced.

dubbo in NSW, a fool or imbecile. From *Dubbo*, a town in rural NSW, viewed as a source of country bumpkins. Has been around since the 1970s.

dubs the toilet.

Dubya a disparaging nickname for American president George W. Bush. So called from the US pronunciation of his middle initial.

duchess to entertain someone grandly in order to improve your social or political standing.

duchesse a Qld word for a dressing table. Also known elsewhere, especially in Tasmania. The brush and comb set for a dressing table is called a **duchesse set**.

duck in cricket, a score of zero runs. Short for a *duck's egg*, which resembles an '0'. A duck is pretty bad, but not as humiliating as a **golden duck**, or, even worse, a **diamond duck** (see entries).

duckhouse an enclosure for ducks, used in the now obsolete slang expressions **that's one up against your duckhouse**, meaning, that beats you, and to **upset someone's duckhouse**, to upset their plans. Choice bits of Australiana that have sadly died out.

ducks and drakes Aussie rhyming slang for 'shakes', as caused by illness, a bad hangover, or the like. Dates back to the 1960s.

ducks and geese Aussie rhyming slang for 'police'.

duck's disease shortness of stature.

duck's guts the very best: *That meal was the duck's guts!* Also heard as the **duck's nuts**.

duckshove **1.** to evade a responsibility. **2.** to illegally move your hand over the line when shooting in a game of marbles. See **fananny-whacking** for a full set of synonyms.

duco the shiny paintwork of an automobile. A trademark term registered in 1927, but now used generically. Aussies are a bit fanatic about their duco.

dud **1.** a failure of a person; a loser. *That guy is an absolute dud.* **2.** to swindle or cheat. *I suddenly realised I had been dudded.*

dudder **1.** a swindler or cheat. **2.** among car salesmen, a customer with no credit standing.

dude a bloke or fellow. *Some dudes at the pub were selling raffle tickets.* Also used as a form as address, as in *Hey dude, what's happening?* Now also used in a very positive way to mean someone who is cool, as in *Jason is such a dude.* The original sense was actually negative, referring to a person who was ostentatiously overdressed, equivalent to a dandy. This was originally US slang, dating back to the 1870s. The origin of the term is wholly unknown. Has been used in Australia since the very beginning of the 20th century.

dudette a cool young female.

dudical incredibly cool; terrific; excellent. An adjective formed from *dude*.

dud root a straight-talking Aussie way of referring to a person who is a flop in bed. Also known as a **dud bash**.

duds trousers; pants. *Hang on while I get me duds on.* Aussie slang since the 1920s. Formerly used to refer to clothes in general.

duff **1.** old Aussie slang meaning to steal cattle. **2.** to mess up or fluff – the sort of thing a silly duffer does. *It was an easy putt, but he's duffed it.* **3.** If a woman is **up the duff**, then she is pregnant. This is probably from old slang *duff* = pudding, as in 'in the pudding club'.

duffer **1.** a cattle thief. Aussie slang dating from the 1840s, a specific application of older British slang term meaning a person selling fake goods. The Aussie cattle thieves would commonly alter the brands. **2.** a stupid or incompetent person; one who is socially and practically inept; commonly used as a mild remonstrance to someone who has done something silly or clumsy: *He's a bit of a duffer, but harmless at that.* Probably from Scottish English *duffar* 'a stupid fellow'.

the 'Dulla the sleepy coastal township of Ulladulla, NSW.

dumbcluck a fool; a dolt. Someone who is as stupid as a chook. Actually an American original, from the 1920s.

dumb down **1.** to act dumber than one is. *She dumbed down because she didn't want to seem a smart-arse.* **2.** to write down for a less intellectual audience. *She has to dumb down her speech.*

dumb fuck a foolish, ignorant person. US slang from the 1940s, but used in Oz at least since the 1970s. Became popular here in the 1990s.

dump **1.** a place, house, or town that is poorly kept up, and generally of wretched appearance. **2.** an act of defecation. *John's out the back taking a dump.* As a verb, to defecate. Hence, to **dump on** someone is to criticise or scold them, or to offload all your problems on them without a thought as to how it might make them feel. American slang from the 1940s. **3.** to end a relationship with someone. **4.** a round piece cut from the centre of a silver dollar, and used as a coin in the colony New South Wales in the early part of the 19th century. The coin with the hole left in it was called a **holey dollar**. To **not give a twopenny dump** is to not care at all.

dumper a wave which, in shallow water, instead of breaking evenly from the top, crashes violently down, throwing swimmers or surfers to the bottom. Great Aussie slang dating from the 1920s. Picked up by American surfers and now used in the US.

dump shit on to denigrate or criticise harshly.

dumpty the dunny. Aussie slang from the 1940s. Hasn't stood the test of time.

dunderklumpen a dolt. From German. Also spelt **dunderclumpen**.

dung puncher a crass term for a gay man. Also called a **dung pusher**. Australian homophobes seem to have been fixated with the 'horrors' of anal sex and thus have invented a litany of similar terms, such as *arse bandit, backdoor bandit, bum chum, bum puncher, date packer, freckle puncher, fudge packer, mattress muncher, poo denter, poo jabber, poo puncher, poo shooter, shirt lifter, shit packer, turd burglar, turd surfer*, and *turd trapper*.

dunlop overcoat a condom.

dunny **1.** (originally) an outside toilet, found in unsewered areas, usually at some distance from the house it serves and consisting of a small shed furnished with a lavatory seat placed over a sanitary can or pit. Iconic Australiana. First recorded in the 1930s, it is a shortening of *dunniken*, which had been around since the 1840s, but has now completely died out, being last seen in the 1960s. *Dunniken* itself dates back to the 18th century in Britain where it was common in dialect and cant, and seems to be a compound of *danna* 'excrement' (probably from the word *dung*) and *ken* 'a house'. For the most part, the days of the outside dunny are finished. However, toilet blocks, say at school, or in a caravan park, are still known as **the dunnies**. In schoolyards, 'behind the dunnies' is a common place for all sorts of activities not approved of by the teaching staff, such as cigarette smoking, fighting, and amorous liaisons. **2.** a sanitary can or toilet bowl. *Damn it, I dropped my watch in the dunny.* **3.** the toilet or bathroom. **4.** the ubiquity of the dunny in Australia has led to it being immortalised in a numer of slang phrases. To be **all alone like a country dunny** is to be completely alone or isolated. A highly-sexed woman is said to **bang like a dunny door in a gale** – absolutely charming metaphor that one. Someone who is brainless **couldn't train a choko vine to grow up a dunny wall**, and something useless is described as being **as useful as a glass door on a dunny**. If your luck is out you can exclaim **If it was raining palaces I'd be hit on the head by the dunny door**, or alternatively, **If it was raining virgins I'd be locked in the dunny with a poofter**. Finally, if someone's luck is in, and you wish that it would change for the worse, you may cry **I hope your chooks turn into emus and kick your dunny down!**

dunny budgie a blowfly.

dunny can in the days before sewerage, a removable can forming the receptacle of the toilet. The unsavoury job of emptying these cans was the occupation of the **dunny man**. A detailed account of the dunny man's art is to be found in Frank Hardy's novel *The Outcasts of Foolgarah* – if you're interested.

dunny cart a horse-drawn cart used by the dunny man, formerly a feature of the Australian landscape.

dunny documents toilet paper.

durry Aussie slang for a cigarette. Claimed to be from Bull *Dur*ham, a brand of tobacco, but this seems a little far-fetched. Been around since the 1940s.

dust bunny a mass of dust and fluff found under furniture or in the corner of a room.

dust devil a miniature whirlwind that picks up dust and rubbish, common in the outback.

Dutch oven a prank in which you hold another's head under the covers of a bed and fart in it.

dweeb a dag. Originally US slang of the 1960s which made its way to Oz in the 1980s.

dyke **1.** a lesbian. Originally US slang of the 1920s, which probably comes from earlier US slang (1850s) *dike* or *dike out* 'to dress up in finery', and perhaps referred to women who dressed up as men. Although originally a lesbian word, it was commonly used derogatorily by homophobes, and is still used so, despite being successfully reclaimed as a positive term by the lesbian community. **2.** a toilet. An entirely different word this, with an entirely different origin. This one was originally British slang from the 1920s and has its origins in Middle English *dike* and the Anglo-Saxon *dic* 'a ditch for water'.

dykefest **1.** an organised lesbian event, dinner, or the like. **2.** a derisive term used by gynophobes for any social gathering of women.

Dykehardt the Sydney suburb of Leichhardt, having a large lesbian population.

dykon a person who has achieved icon status among the lesbian community. Also spelt **dycon**.

E

e **1.** the drug ecstasy. Hence, a pill or tab of this. **2.** used in respelling of words to indicate that the drug ecstasy was being taken. *It was a groove-E nite. Have a happee birthday.*

the eagle has landed it's pay day. The word 'shit' can be substituted for 'land' – *Has the eagle shat on you today?*

earbash to talk insistently to someone; to chew someone's ear. Aussie slang since the 1940s. Someone who does this is an **earbasher**, an inveterate bore you want to avoid.

earhole the ear. *I gave him a quick clip across the earhole.*

earn an amount of money earned; money won on a race. *You can make a nice little earn from it*. A job or concern that earns you money is thus a nice little **earner**.

earwig prison slang, an eavesdropper.

Eastern Stater in WA, a usually disparaging term for a person who comes from any of the eastern states of Australia. Also used in SA.

Eastern Suburbs Holden a Sydney slang term for a Mercedes-Benz.

easy as falling off a log very simple.

easybeat a person who is easily beaten. In the plural it refers to a team you can wipe the floor with who are probably the cellar dwellers. Of course, this term owes its origin to the great 1960s Oz band *The Easybeats*.

easy mark underworld slang for a victim who is easily duped or conned.

easy-peasy extremely easy. Commonly used by kids. Also found in the extended rhyming phrases **easy-peasy Japanesey** and **easy-peasy lemon squeezie**.

easy touch a generous soul who readily lends money or does other favours; a soft touch.

eat to perform cunnilingus on a woman. Also **eat out**, or **eat carpet**.

eat dirt to lose in a race. To **eat someone's dirt** is to lose to them.

eat for breakfast to beat someone resoundingly in a contest. *I eat players like him for breakfast.*

eating irons eating utensils.

eat my shorts a phrase equivalent to *Get stuffed!* Made its way into Oz via the TV cartoon series *The Simpsons.*

eats food. *What's for eats?*

eat shit a harsh expression of abuse. Commonly used in triumph over a competitor. *Eat shit, motherfuckers!*

eccy ecstasy, a recreational drug based on MDMA. Also called **e**.

echo in SA, a small beer bottle that was able to be returned for a refund and was then washed and re-used. Nowadays glass bottles are recycled, but the term is still in use.

Edgar Britt Aussie rhyming slang for 'shit'. In the plural **Edgar Britts** it can refer to a bad mood or a bad case of diarrhoea. Dates from the 1960s. Edgar Britt was a well-known Australian jockey. Another version of this is the **Jimmy Brits** (see entry).

eelerspee an obsolete slang term for a con artist. It is actually the word **spieler** rendered in pig Latin.

eelie obsolete Aussie underworld slang for a confidence trick, or the ruse by which a swindle is effected. Probably extracted from **eelerspee**. Perhaps the original source of the first part of **illywhacker** (see entry).

effing a euphemism for *fucking*.

egg to pass wind; to fart.

egg flip Aussie rhyming slang for 'tip', as at the races. Dating from the 1960s.

egghead **1.** an intellectual or highbrow. **2.** a fool or idiot.

egg roll a stupid person; idiot.

eggshell blonde a bald person.

eggy-peggy a cryptolanguage used by schoolchildren in which normal words are modified by adding into each syllable the sound 'ug'; thus *hug* becomes *hugug*; *You are a pig* becomes *Yugoo ugar uga pugig*. Also called **aygo-paygo**. For similar secret languages see **alibi**, **arpie-darpie**, **obo language**, **pig Latin** and **rechtub kelat**.

eh a tag used at the end of a statement generally inviting assent, as in *Wasn't that lucky, eh?* or *Great fun, eh?* In Queensland and New Zealand, used repetitiously at the end of virtually every statement, without any sense of it being a question. *I was goin' down the shops, eh. And I ran into Johnno, eh. Hadn't seen him for weeks, eh.*

eighteen an eighteen-gallon beer keg, generally the size put on for a domestic party. First recorded in 1918. No longer in use.

the Ekka **1.** the Brisbane Exhibition showground. **2.** the Royal Queensland Show.

elastics a girls' schoolyard game in which a long loop of elastic is held, usually between two children, and a set of various trick manoeuvres with the legs is performed by a third. After the completion of a set without mistakes the elastic is moved up higher thus increasing the difficulty. Also called **elastic skippy**.

elastic sides boots similar to riding boots, with a piece of elastic inset into the sides. Also called **laughing-side boots**.

el cheapo a product, service or venue that is cheap and nasty. Mock Spanish from the US.

elephant bucks an enormous amount of money.

elephant gun a surfboard used for riding big waves.

elephant juice **1.** a narcotic analgesic used to immobilise large animals such as the elephant or the rhinoceros, but now used illegally in small doses to stimulate racehorses. **2.** in World War II, a rough alcoholic drink originally made by soldiers in New Guinea. **3.** any powerful and rough drink.

elephants short for *elephant's trunk*, rhyming slang for 'drunk'. One of the earliest recorded pieces of rhyming slang, dating from the 1850s. Originally Cockney.

elevator If someone tells you that your **elevator doesn't go to the top floor**, they are saying you are a right dill.

elevener the mid-morning break in primary school, or the snack eaten then. Formerly used in Qld, now uncommon or obsolete. Also called **elevenses**, or shortened to **levna**.

Elizabethan in Adelaide, a person from Elizabeth, to the north.

ellie in the Antarctic, an elephant seal.

Elvis Presley **1.** among car salesmen, a car with many dents in the body and scratches in the duco. That is, it has had many hits. **2.** among fishos, a leatherjacket.

Emerald City a nickname for Sydney – so called from its sunny splendour and jewel-like magnificence, its glorious harbour and stunning architecture, equal to the fabled city that was home to the Wizard of Oz.

Emma Chisit the question 'How much is it?' as rendered in Strine. The beginning point and probably the most famous piece of Strine ever. First heard (or rather, misheard) in the 1960s. If you don't know what Strine is, you can look it up at the entry for **Strine**.

emu-bob to bend down to pick up things, as timber, roots, or the like, in order to clear an area. Hence, **emu-bobber**, a person doing this. Specifically, a person who stacks up sticks after a burning-off job. Also, at the racecourse, a fossicker after discarded betting tickets.

emu parade originally, a military parade to clean an area of litter. Dating back to World War II. Hence, any similar collection of people collecting litter or other unwanted material from an area. Commonly schoolkids are seconded for this job. Also, a line of police combing an area for forensic evidence. It can also be called an **emu bob**, an **emu patrol**, or an **emu walk**, and in WA, an **emu stalk**.

Enzed New Zealand. Hence **Enzedder**, a New Zealander.

erky revolting. An Aussie cry of disgust since the 1950s. Also, in kid's speech, **erky perky**.

eskimo pie an ice-cream wafer or a cream between.

esky a portable icebox. Quintessential item of Australian living. A trademark term, from *eskimo*, but used generically.

esky lid a disparaging term used by surfies for a bodyboard. Hence, a bodyboarder is called an **esky lidder**.

Esperance doctor a strong, cool, southerly wind which blows through Kalgoorlie, usually in the late afternoon and evening in summer.

euchre **1.** to outwit; get the better of someone. **2.** to ruin or spoil. *That's euchred it.*

euchred beaten, defeated; down and out.

eugari in Qld, a pipi. From the Aboriginal language Yagara from the Brisbane region.

euky oil the oil of the eucalyptus, deadly poisonous, but a great help around the home, and bonzer to sniff when you've got a head cold.

evac an abbreviated way of saying 'evacuation' common in the military. Hence, time to leave. *How long till evac?*

everything that opens and shuts all possible embellishments; all bells and whistles.

the evil weed marijuana.

evo laconic Aussie way of saying 'evening'. *What're you doing tomorrow evo?*

exec an executive.

ex-govie in the ACT, a house built by the Commonwealth Government but now privately owned.

exo among teenagers, excellent.

ex-pug a retired boxer. Short for *ex-pugilist*.

extra-curricular of or pertaining to sexual activities outside of a relationship.

exy expensive. *The suit looks pretty exy*. Also spelt **exxy**.

eyeball to look at. *I eyeballed the room looking for her*.

eye candy a luscious babe; a spunky individual.

Eyetie a disparaging term for an Italian. Actually originally British slang from World War I. Also spelt **Itie**.

eyewash an old slang term for nonsense.

fabbo the peculiarly Australian way of saying *fab* with enthusiasm.

face ache a contemptible person.

face fungus facial hair, as a moustache, beard or bum fluff.

face like a... someone with an ugly face is said to have a **face like a smashed crab**. Other sad cases include a **face like the northbound end of a southbound cow**, and a **face like a half-eaten pastie**. Compare **head like a...**

face plant a heavy fall from a skateboard, snowboard, or skis, in which the face hits the ground front on.

fag **1.** a cigarette. A British slang term dating from the 19th century. Probably picked up by Aussie soldiers in World War I (the word, that is, not the thing). **2.** a male homosexual. Short for *faggot*. US slang dating from the 1920s, common in Australia since the 1970s.

faggot a derogatory term for a homosexual man. US slang since the 1910s. Originally a term of abuse for a shrewish, offensive woman.

fag hag a woman who socialises with male homosexuals.

fair absolute or complete, as in, *He's a fair bastard*. And as an adverb, totally, completely, as in, *That fair took it out of me*. A peculiar Australian idiom since the 19th century.

fair cop **1.** a just punishment or outcome. **2.** an unequivocal busting of someone red-handed.

fair cow something distinctly unpleasant. Aussie slang since the 1900s.

fair crack of the whip! an appeal for fairness.

fair dinkum **1.** true or genuine; real, as opposed to phoney. *It's the fair dinkum article all right*. One of the best-known, best-loved and most enduring of all Australian slang phrases. Found in Oz since the 1890s. Comes from north Lincolnshire dialect of England (recorded in 1881), where it meant 'fair play'. For more info on the origin, see **dinkum**. **2.** fair and equitable. *It was the only fair dinkum raffle run in the pub's history*. **3.** in earnest. As in *Are you fair dinkum?* meaning 'Are you serious?' **4.** showing typical Australian honesty, guts, directness and the like. *They were all fair dinkum blokes and sheilas*. **5.** well and truly. *He was fair dinkum pissing himself laughing*. **6.** really, honestly. As in, *It's true, mate, fair dinkum*. In this sense can be shortened to **fair dink** or **fair dinks**.

fair enough All right, I suppose that's fair. No worries. This laconic summation of a situation has been in common use since the 1940s.

fair go **1.** a fair or reasonable opportunity; just treatment. As in, *He never had a fair go*. This phrase has been around since the 1900s. Giving people a fair go is a quintessential aspect of the national character. **2.** an appeal for fairness or reason. Equivalent to 'Be fair!'. *Fair go, mate!*

fair suck of the sauce bottle! Be fair! Classic Australiana. Very 70s. Also heard as **fair suck of the sav**, and even **fair suck of the Siberian sandshoe!** Or, laconically shortened to the simple **fair suck!**

fairy **1.** a derogatory term for an effeminate male homosexual. Hence, used as a slur against any male displaying effeminacy. Originally US slang from the 1850s. **2.** to be **full as a fairy's phonebook** is to be completely full, especially of food or booze. Alluding to the stereotype of homosexual men being excessively fickle. **3.** the fluffy airborne seed of various plants, such as the moth vine or Scotch thistle. See **Santa Claus** for synonyms.

fairy floss the peculiar Australian moniker for the pink spun sugar you get at fetes and the like. What the Poms call candy floss, and the Yanks call cotton candy.

fairy nuff jocular way of writing 'fair enough'.

fakie in skateboarding and snowboarding, a backwards movement or a trick done moving backwards.

falcon in Rugby League, originally being hit in the face with the ball but now any accidental headbutt. So called in honour of a famous incident involving the face of Mario Fenech, nicknamed 'the Maltese Falcon', or simply, 'the Falcon', because of his Maltese background.

fall off the back of a truck to be obtained by questionable or illegal means.

fam family. *It's fun for the whole fam.*

family jewels the testicles. Also called the **crown jewels**.

fanannywhacking the action of illegally moving your hand over the line when shooting in a game of marbles. Someone who commits this crime is known by the opprobrious title of **fanannywhacker**. Australian schoolkids have been quite inventive when it comes to this crime, which is known around the country by the names **cribs**, **cribbing**, **duck-shoving**, **fnudging** (or **phernudging**), **fudging**, and **lagging**.

fang 1. to drive at great speed; to hoon. Aussie slang since the 1960s. Supposedly in honour of the famous Argentinian F1 racing driver Juan Fangio. Hence, a speedy drive or hoon. *I'm taking the Datto for a fang around the block.* **2.** a tooth. Hence, a bite, as in *I gave it an exploratory fang*. To be **good on the fang** is to be a hearty eater. To **go the fang** on something, or to **fang down** on it, is to hoe into it. As a verb, to **fang** is to crave food, as in *I'm fanging for a steak*, or to eat voraciously, as in *She sat there fanging away for all she was worth.* **3.** to **put the fangs into** someone is to attempt to borrow from them. To **fang** then can also be used as a verb, as in *I fanged him for a couple of bucks.*

fang artist a voracious eater.

fang carpenter a dentist. Also called a **fang farrier**.

fanny 1. the vagina or vulva; the external female genitalia. British slang since the 1840s. Used in Australia since at least World War II. Always a bit rude, but never crude. In origin it is merely a use of the formerly popular female name, perhaps influenced by the famous pornographic novel *Fanny Hill* (that is, John Cleland's *Memoirs of a Woman of Pleasure*, 1749). **2.** in the US, used to refer to the buttocks or 'ass'. Actually a polite form. Not used in Australia, but well-known here.

fanny fart an audible escape of wind from the vagina, as sometimes follows sexual intercourse.

fanny tickler a small tuft of facial hair under the bottom lip on an otherwise clean-shaven face. Also called a **clit tickler**.

fantabulous marvellous; wonderful.

fantasy a designer drug consisting of ecstasy mixed with GHB (gamma hydroxybutyric acid).

fark a representation of the Australian pronunciation of *fuck!* Comedian Graham Kennedy was suspended from live TV broadcasting in 1975 after doing his impression of a crow: 'Faaark, faaark, FAAARK'.

Farmer Giles Aussie rhyming slang for 'piles', as in haemorrhoids. Dates back to the 1960s.

farnarkeling activity which creates an appearance of productivity but which has no substance to it. Coined by comedian John Clarke for a fictitious team sport for which he acted as sports commentator in the 1980s television series *The Gillies Report*.

far out amazing, incredible. Now generally used as an exclamation of amazement. Also used as an exclamation of frustration, and as a partial euphemism for *fuck!*

fart an emission of wind from the anus, either audible or inaudible. Hence, as a verb, to emit such wind. One of the genuine Anglo-Saxon four-lettered words. In rhyming slang known as a **Royce Hart**. Old people are often disparagingly referred to as **old farts**. If you are extremely drunk you might be described as **full as a fart** or **pissed as a fart**. And, something very unpopular is said to be **as popular as a fart in a phonebox**.

fart-arse a contemptible person.

fart-arse around to waste time; to fiddle about or idle. Australian slang since the 1970s. Also, **fart around** or **fiddle-fart about**.

farter 1. a person who farts habitually. **2.** the anus.

fartface a mild insult directed at someone who is annoying you. From US slang of the 1930s. Similar to this is **fart head**.

fart fodder baked beans.

fartmobile a car which makes a muffler noise resembling that of farting.

fart sack a sleeping bag. Originally World War II military slang.

fart sparks to vent anger; to 'spit chips'.

fastie a deceitful practice; a cunning act.

fat 1. an erect penis. As in, *to crack a fat*. Aussie slang since the 1940s. **2.** a fattened cow or bull that is ready for market. An Australian original in use since the 1880s. **3.** in modern, cool speech **fat** is equivalent to excellent, groovy or cool. *This nightclub plays some of the fattest, funkiest soul about town.* A 1990s adoption from US slang. Often spelt **phat**, in order to differentiate it from other senses. **4.** a child's playing marble.

fat chance little or no chance.

fat day a day on which a woman feels fatter than normal.

fat farm a resort where people go to lose weight.

Father Christmas the fluffy airborne seed of various plants, such as the moth vine or Scotch thistle. See **Santa Claus** for synonyms.

a fat lot very little. *A fat lot of good that will do. A fat lot she cares.* Since the 1900s.

fatty-boom-bah a fat person; a taunting nickname for a fat person. Especially used by kids. Also in the forms **fatty-boom-sticks** and **fatty-boom-bah-sticks**.

fave favourite. *Spag bol is my absolute fave.*

faze to disturb or daunt. *Nothing fazes me.* Originally from the US. Has been used in Oz since at least the 1970s.

fazzo fabulous; wonderful.

-features a word element used to make insulting compounds: *dweeb-features*; *snot-features.*

feature with to have sexual intercourse with. Aussie slang dating from the 1960s – a favourite expression of the inimitable Bazza McKenzie.

Fed a federal police officer, or loosely, any police officer. *The Feds are after me.*

feeding time at the zoo a disorderly rabble commonly found when there is something for free on offer. Similar to the **shark feeding frenzy**.

feed the fishes to be seasick; occasionally used to refer to drowning.

feisty high-spirited and volatile. Originally a US dialect word from the late 19th century, from *feist* 'a silent fart', in this sense originally applied to a type of small dog known as a *fisting dog*, which was aggressive, and flatulent into the bargain.

felch to perform anilingus; to lick or suck a partner's anus, especially after anal intercourse in order to extract the deposited semen. A person who performs this activity is known as a **felcher**. The widely repellant nature of this activity has won this word great notoriety. Originally US homosexual slang of unknown origin it was first recorded in Bruce Rogers' *The Queen's Vernacular* (1972), where it is labelled 'jocular, late '60s'. This word has to a certain extent replaced *cunt* and *fuck* as the rudest words known to people. I was able to note that it was often the first word looked up by people upon getting hold of the first edition of this dictionary back in 1996. A jocular variant of the farewell *catch you later* is **felch you later**. No thanks!

feminazi a derogatory term for an extreme feminist; often used as a mere insult by anti-feminists to any woman expressing the mildest of feminist viewpoints.

femme of a homosexual woman or man, having strong feminine attributes. Hence, such a person. Opposed to **butch**.

femmo a feminist. Generally used disparagingly.

fennackapants a term of endearment to a child.

feral 1. a type of hippie environmentalist. There are the real ferals who live in the bush, fight loggers and generally try to make a difference, and then there are the faux inner-city ferals who look the part with their dreads and rainbow-coloured clothing, but live with as many of the mod cons as they so desire. **2.** a westie, bevan or bogan. **3.** among teenagers, disgusting or gross. **4.** wild or unrestrained in behaviour. *The kids have gone feral.*

ferret 1. in cricket, a player at the tail-end of the batting order. So called since they follow the *bunnies* or *rabbits* in. **2.** the penis, in such Bazza McKenzie inspired phrases as **give the ferret a run**, **exercise the ferret**, and **run the ferret up the drainpipe**, which mean to engage in sexual intercourse or to urinate.

'fess up to confess to something. A newish phrase that arrived on our fair shores in the 1990s. Has been is the US since the 1840s.

fester to waste time while you are meant to be studying or working; to bludge.

festy 1. dirty; grubby; unclean and smelly. **2.** extremely bad; awful; dreadful.

few in Australia if you are going to 'have a few' it has only one meaning – namely, a few ice-cold beers.

a few sardines short of a tin not having full intelligence; stupid; moronic. For similar comparisons see the entry for **short of**.

fezza a feral.

FHB a signal for the family to show some restraint at the dinner table as there are guests. Stands for *Family Hold Back!*

fibro typically laconic Aussie way of referring to fibrocement, a type of asbestos and cement compressed into sheets and used as a building material. For many a year the basic component of domestic architecture Australia-wide.

fiddle-fart to waste time in frivolous activity.

fiddley old slang for a one pound note, or the sum of £1. From rhyming slang **fiddley-did** for 'quid'. Aussie slang since the 1940s.

fiddy fifty. A recent adoption of US slang that is all the rage. Hence, a fifty dollar note or the sum of fifty dollars. Also, a fifty dollar bag of grass.

field to work as a bookmaker. *He's been fielding for three years now.*

fielder **1.** a bookmaker. Aussie slang since the 1930s. **2.** in the Australian Antarctic Territory, a rum ration taken on a field trip.

the fields the goldfields or other mining operations. *He's been on the fields for six years.*

fifty **1.** laconic Aussie abbreviation of **fifty-fifty**. **2.** military slang, a .50 calibre machine gun.

fifty-fifty **1.** a glass of beer, half old and half new. Also, called simply **fifty**. *I'll have a glass of fifty, love.* Aussie slang since the 1960s. **2.** a dance, usually held in a country or suburban hall, at which the dancing and music is half old-time and half modern.

figjam an extremely conceited person. An acronym from *Fuck I'm Good, Just Ask Me*. Aussie slang invention of the 1990s, especially common among schoolkids.

File-o-phile a fan of the television show *The X-Files.*

fill in to fill a woman in is to get her pregnant. Aussie slang of the 1950s, little heard nowadays.

fillum the ocker Aussie way of saying the word 'film'.

filly a condescending term for a sexy young woman. *She's a nice little filly.*

filth among adolescents, excellent, brilliant, wonderful. *The waves were absolute filth.* Aussie slang since the 1980s. Based on the same notion as 'wicked' meaning good.

filthy **1.** angry or enraged; ropeable. *I've never seen him so filthy.* This is an extension of the term **dirty** (see entry). **2.** among adolescents, excellent, brilliant, wonderful. *The talent was filthy, the babes were lush and the mosh pit was going off.* Can also be shortened to **filth**. *The waves were absolute filth.* Aussie slang from the 1980s.

fin **1.** old slang for a five pound note, or the sum of £5. An Australian use of mid-19th century British thieves' slang, from Yiddish *finef* 'five'. **2.** after decimal currency was introduced in 1966, used for ten dollars, but this didn't last very long.

finger **1.** to point out or accuse. *He fingered his mate for the bank job.* You can also say **put the finger on**. **2.** to sexually feel a woman's genitals; specifically to insert a finger, or fingers, into the vagina. Hence, **finger up**, to fondle a woman's genitalia. **3.** to **pull your finger out** is to get down to business after having been inactive. **4.** to **give someone the finger** is to make an obscene gesture by holding up the middle finger at them. A semaphore equivalent to 'get fucked' or 'bugger you'.

finishipper (when *The X-Files* was popular) a fan who wished to see Mulder and Scully get together romantically but only in the final episode. As opposed to a **noromo** or a **shipper** (see entries).

fire to go extremely well. *She was really firing in the second half.*

fire-ie a firefighter. Also spelt **firee** or **firey**. Recent Aussie slang, dating from the 1990s.

fire o'clock among firefighters, the time in the afternoon when school finishes in summer, after which kids light fires.

firing blanks of a male, experiencing orgasm but not ejaculating, or, ejaculating infertile sperm.

first cab off the rank the first person to do something.

First Fleeter a person whose lineage can be traced back to the occupants of the First Fleet in 1788. A cause for great pride in Australia since as early as 1826.

fish frighteners speedos. For a full set of synonyms see **sluggos**.

fisho **1.** a fisherman or woman. **2.** a fish and chip shop. **3.** formerly, a street vendor selling fish.

fist fucking an extreme sex act in which the hand is inserted into the vagina, or, especially among homosexual men, into the anus. Also known as **fisting**.

fit **1.** to secure a conviction against an innocent person. Now commonly to **fit up**. Great Aussie slang since the 1880s. *He was fitted up for the warehouse robbery.* **2.** the equipment used to prepare and inject drugs. In use among druggies since the 1960s in Australia. Actually a shortened form of 'outfit'.

fit as a mallee bull supremely fit and healthy.

five-dog night a bitterly cold night in the bush, even colder than a four-dog night. About the coldest night you can get. See **dog**, def. 7.

five-finger discount stealing, shoplifting.

five o'clock wave a fictitious wave passing down the Murrumbidgee River through Wagga Wagga each day, supposedly created by the release of water from an upriver dam. A tale told to unwary visitors. *If you get your surfboard and hurry down to Wagga Beach you can catch the five o'clock wave.*

fiver **1.** a five dollar note or the princely sum of $5. In the olden days it referred to five pounds, which was a much more substantial sum of money. **2.** among currency traders, $5 million.

fix among druggies, a shot of heroin or some other drug.

fizgig **1.** a police informer. Aussie slang dating from the 1890s. **2.** as a verb, to inform on criminals to the police. Also spelt **phizgig**.

fizzer **1.** a dud firecracker which fails to explode. **2.** a failure, fiasco or dud. Aussie slang since the 1950s. **3.** a fizgig.

fizzog **1.** a firecracker that fails to explode. **2.** a failure or dud. *The evening was a complete fizzog.*

fizzy cordial in Tasmania, carbonated soft drink.

fizzy drink carbonated soft drink. Unlike the previous entry this is used throughout the country and not restricted to one region.

flabbie a fat person.

flaming used to add emphasis to a statement, originally as a euphemism for *bloody*, though now usually taken to be a euphemism for *fucking*.

flaming fury a toilet constructed over a pit, the contents of which are periodically doused with oil and burnt.

flange the labia.

flannelette curtain the boundary of an area full of westies, bevans or bogans. *Oh no, we've crossed the flannelette curtain now.*

flannie a flannelette shirt with a coloured checked pattern. The emblematic dress of westies, bevans and bogans. Also called a **flanno**. One of the few words which has both an *-ie* and an *-o* form.

flap **1.** underworld slang, a blank cheque leaf. Hence a **flap man** is someone who passes dud cheques. **2.** If someone says **get your flaps off me!** it means they want to be left alone.

flaps a none-too-charming word for woman's labia. Even less charming is the variant **piss flaps**.

flash **1.** showy or ostentatious. Originally British slang from the 1700s. **2.** among druggies, a powerful hit from a drug.

flash as a rat with a gold tooth extremely showy or ostentatious.

flash for cash a police speed camera or radar trap.

flash language the specialised jargon of the criminal class spoken in colonial times. Also called **the flash**. This term originated in England in the 18th century and was brought to Australia by transported convicts. There are quite a number of flash terms still forming part of modern Australian slang, including **beak, blow the gaff, chatty, conk, croak, galoot, gammon, grey, lag** and **new chum** (see those entries for more information).

flat **1.** the centre area of a racecourse, used by spectators. Aussie turf slang dating from the 1840s. **2.** in prison, quality tobacco brought in from outside, as opposed to the jail issue muck.

flat chat at full speed. *He drove flat chat down the road.* Aussie slang since the 1970s. Also occasionally in the form **flat bickie** or **flat strap**.

flatfoot a police officer.

flatline If you **flatline**, your heart ceases to function as registered on an electrocardiograph.

flat out going at the fastest pace possible; working your hardest. In a famous parliamentary exchange back in 1985 Treasurer Keating said to Wilson Tuckey 'You boxhead you wouldn't know. You are flat out counting past ten'. Originally British slang, but found in Australia from the 1930s, and, since as early as the 1940s, in the wonderfully expressive phrase **flat out like a lizard drinking**.

flattie **1.** a flatmate. **2.** a woman's low-heeled shoe. **3.** a flat-bottomed dinghy. Aussie slang dating from the 1910s. **4.** among fishos, a flathead fish. **5.** a flat tyre.

fleabag **1.** a decrepit old dog. **2.** a sleeping bag.

flea pit a shabby, dirty room or building, especially a cinema. Also called a **flea house**.

fleas and itches Aussie rhyming slang for 'the pictures', that is, the cinema. Dating from the 1960s.

flick **1.** to **give someone the flick** is to dismiss them, sack them or send them packing. Aussie slang since at least the 1980s. Little known to most people is that this is actually from rhyming slang *flick pass* for 'arse' – thus, to give someone the flick pass is to give them the arse. As an alternative, some have suggested that the phrase derives from the advertising slogan of the Flick Pest Control company: 'One flick and they're gone'. **2.** a movie or film. Originally British slang from the 1920s. **3.** to turn back an odometer so it reads less than it should.

flicks a schoolyard game using collectible cards, in which the cards are flicked towards a wall, with certain conditions being applied to where or in what position they land.

flied lice a mocking Chinese pronunciation of 'fried rice'.

flip **1.** a giddy, irresponsible, silly person. **2.** to become enraged; to go crazy; to go off the rails. Also, **flip out** or **flip your lid**. **3.** a euphemism for the exclamation *fuck!*

flipe to fold a pair of socks by placing them flat upon the other with the toes and heels together and then folding the uppermost over the one underneath it, to make a ball shape.

flip-flops rubber thongs.

flip off of a male, to masturbate.

flipper **1.** the hand. **2.** in cricket, a delivery similar to a wrong'un, which pitches short like a long hop, but actually kicks forward upon striking the pitch, stays low and comes through quicker than, hopefully, the person batting expects.

flipping a euphemism for the word *fucking*, used as an intensifier. *I got something in my flipping eye.*

flip wreck a male who masturbates too much. Aussie slang since the 1950s.

flivver a child's scooter.

floater **1.** a meat pie served in pea soup. Recorded since 1915. An Aussie culinary treat. **2.** in two-up, a coin which, when tossed, fails to spin. Aussie slang from at least the 1940s. Compare **butterfly**. **3.** in prison, an item, such as a book or magazine, that is kept illegally by prisoners and smuggled from cell to cell. **4.** in wharfie slang, a worker not attached to a gang. **5.** a dead person found floating in the ocean, a river, or the like. **6.** a floating piece of excrement in a toilet – one that won't flush.

float your boat If something **floats your boat** then it gives you pleasure.

flog **1.** to steal. Aussie slang since the 1960s. **2.** to sell, especially something that you have obtained illegally. Originally British slang from the early 20th century. **3.** to drive a vehicle at top speed. Aussie slang since the 1950s. **4.** to beat mercilessly. **5.** to make land useless by overgrazing, overcropping or the like. **6.** of a male, to masturbate. Hence, an act of male masturbation.

flogger a short stick with a bunch of crepe paper streamers in team colours attached, used in barracking in Aussie Rules.

flogging a euphemism for the word *fucking*, used as an intensifier. *Starve the flogging crows!*

flog the lizard of a male, to have a wank.

flooze **1.** to sleep around. **2.** to flirt openly.

floozy a derogatory word for a promiscuous woman; now also used of a man. US slang from the 1900s.

flop house a doss house.

flopping a euphemism for the word *fucking*, used as an intensifier. *I'm sick of this flopping muck.*

floury baker a large species of cicada, dark with greyish markings.

fluff **1.** to break wind. Hence, a fart. **2.** to blunder; to fail to perform properly. *He's really fluffed it this time.* Hence, a blunder or error. **3.** a **bit of fluff** is a sexy young woman, or a man's female partner. A belittling term, originating in British slang from the 1900s.

fluffer a person whose job is to orally stimulate male porn stars prior to their appearing in a scene.

fluffy dice large, colourful cloth-covered dice hung from a car's rearview mirror as an accessory.

fluorescent ducks a non-existent sight worth seeing. Similar to **submarine races**. *I was a newcomer to Bendigo, so he said he'd drive me up Mickey Mouse Hill to see the fluorescent ducks.*

flute the penis.

flutter-by a butterfly. A deliberate Spoonerism.

fly **1.** an attempt. *I'll give it a fly.* Aussie slang dating from the 1910s. **2.** aware of what's what; awake. Old slang from the convict days. *He was too fly for them.* **3.** in recent use, cool and stylish. *She was wearing a pretty fly dress.* Adopted from US usage. A cool bloke is a **fly guy**, and a cool chick is a **fly girl**.

flyblown old slang meaning broke or penniless.

flybog jam. Because it will bog flies if they land in it. Great Aussie slang dating from the 1920s.

fly cemetery a biscuit with dried fruit sandwiched between two thin layers of sweet biscuit. Also called a **fly pie**.

fly country any part of the inland where the flies are particularly bad.

flyer **1.** a fast kangaroo. **2.** a female quokka. **3.** any of various fast trains, as the Newcastle Flyer or the Darwin Flyer. **4.** a fast shearer; the ringer of a shed.

flying axe handles diarrhoea.

flying cane toad a disparaging name for the much hated Indian myna, a feral bird introduced into Australia in the 1860s and now common around large cities and cane-growing areas along the eastern coast. In reality, they are nowhere near as bad as cane toads.

the Flying Doormat a nickname for 1970s Aussie Rules player Bruce Doull.

flying fox Aussie rhyming slang for 'pox'.

the Flying Peanut delightful moniker bestowed upon erstwhile Queensland premier Joh Bjelke-Petersen. He was an aviator and peanut farmer, among other things.

fly's eyes the childish male display of the testicles, performed by placing each one out through the corresponding leg hole of the underwear, and then prancing about. It bears a loose resemblance to the ocular processes of the fly.

FMBs an abbreviation for **fuck-me boots** (see entry). Also called **FM boots**.

fnudge to illegally move your hand over the line when shooting in a game of marbles. *Hey – no fnudging!* Also spelt **phernudge**. See **fanannywhacking** for a full set of synonyms.

foamie a miserable type of surfboard made from plastic foam.

fob a derogatory term for a new migrant to the country. Standing for *Fresh Off the Boat*. In Australia commonly used for migrants of Pacific Islander and Arabic background.

foil a saleable measure of marijuana wrapped in aluminium foil.

folding stuff banknotes; paper (now plastic) money.

folkie a folk music performer or enthusiast.

folks parents or relatives. *My folks are having a big bash tonight.*

follicularly challenged bald or balding.

follicularly enhanced having had hair replacement therapy.

f-one-j-one Fiji.

foodie a connoisseur of food.

foof to expand in all directions at once. *On wet days her hair foofs out all over the place.*

foofy excessively fluffy.

footbrawl a derogatory term for football – either Aussie Rules or the two Rugby codes.

foot falcon in northern Australia, the feet used as a mode of transport. The same as **Shanks's pony**.

Footscray Florsheims Melbourne slang for ugg boots, slippers or moccasins.

footsy a children's word for a foot. To **play footsies** is to touch feet in secret under a table, more the domain of adults.

footy **1.** football. Aussie slang since the 1900s. In WA, SA, Vic and Tas this, of course, means Aussie Rules. Whereas in NSW and Qld it pretty much means Rugby League or Union. In Britain it means soccer. **2.** a football. *Who kicked the footy over the fence?*

footy nicks shortie shorts as worn by Aussie Rules players.

Forest Fortnight a rejoinder to the question 'What do you think this is – Bush Week?' 'No – it's Forest Fortnight!'

for fuck's sake an extremely impolite way of saying 'For Christ's sake!'

fork out to pay up.

fork over to hand over.

form **1.** a person's luck, especially when viewed enviously. *He's won Lotto again. How's his rotten form?* Aussie slang dating from the 1960s. **2.** a person's character. *A lousy dobber. Yeah, that'd be his form.* Also Aussie, since the 1920s.

for openers to begin with; for starters. *Well, for openers, this guy doesn't drink beer.*

Fort Fumble the Defence Department HQ at Russell Hill in Canberra. In the US this is a nickname for the Pentagon.

fossick **1.** to search through mining refuse for gold. Aussie slang since the 1850s. From Cornish dialect. **2.** to rummage through in search of something. *She was fossicking through the cupboards looking for the brown sugar.*

fossil **1.** an old-fashioned person or thing. **2.** an immensely aged person.

foulie a foul mood. *Stay away, she's really in a foulie.*

fountain a drinking fountain. See **bubbler** for the full set of regionalisms.

fourby **1.** a piece of four-by-two. A dimension of timber Australians have taken to their hearts. *I got whacked on the scone with a great lump of fourby.* **2.** a four-wheel-drive.

four-by-two **1.** rhyming slang for 'Jew'. Originally in British use in World War I. **2.** a prison warder, rhyming slang for 'screw'.

four-dog night an extremely cold night, colder than a three-dog night, yet not as cold as a five-dog night. See **dog**, def. 7.

four-eyes a person who wears glasses.

four-legged lottery a horse race.

fourpenny dark a cheap red wine. From the 1950s. No longer around, at least, not under this moniker.

four-pointer two slices of bread with filling, cut diagonally. Different to the **six-pointer** (see entry).

four square a version of the schoolyard game **handball** (see entry).

fox to get or fetch. *He went to fox the ball from over the fence.*

foxie a fox terrier. An Aussie abbreviation since the 1900s.

foxy sexy and stylish; having both animal attraction and sophistication.

fracteur among miners, gelignite.

frang a sausage.

franger Aussie slang for a condom. Since the 1970s.

frank the penis. A shortening of *frankfurter*.

freaking a euphemism for the word *fucking*, when used as an intensifier.

freckle **1.** the blot, dot or ort. In other words, the anus. Aussie slang since the 1960s. **2.** a chocolate drop lolly with a topping of hundreds and thousands.

freckle puncher a gay man. Oz slang since the 1960s. See **dung puncher** for a swag of synonyms.

Fred **1.** any electronic gadget or device that one finds annoying. An acronym from *Fucking Ridiculous Electronic Device*. **2.** in the army, the name given to the small eating implement that is found in most army ration packs. An acronym from *Fucking Ridiculous Eating Device.*

Fred Astaire **1.** Aussie rhyming slang for 'chair'. Dates back to the 1940s. **2.** rhyming slang for 'hair'.

Fred Nerks an archetypal Aussie drongo. *There goes Fred Nerks taking up the whole road with his caravan.* Australian slang since the 1960s.

free a free kick.

freeballing wearing no underpants.

free beach a beach at which nude bathing is permitted.

free snake it to wear no underpants.

the Freezer the Antarctic or South Pole.

freeze your tits off to feel extremely cold.

Fremantle doctor a strong, cool, southerly wind which blows through Fremantle late in the evening on hot summer nights. Also called the **Freo doctor**.

French **1.** a humorous term for mild swear words. *Pardon my French.* **2.** oral sex.

French cut in cricket, an inside edge wide of leg stump. Aussie and New Zealand slang. Also called a **Chinese cut**.

French tickler a condom with an attachment on the end to give extra stimulation.

Frenchy a condom or French letter. Aussie slang since the 1970s.

Freo the city of Fremantle, WA.

freshie a freshwater crocodile.

fricking a euphemism for the word *fucking*, used as an intensifier.

fried egg a traffic dome or silent cop.

friend of Dorothy a homosexual man. Aussie slang since the 1980s. From Dorothy in *The Wizard of Oz*, played by Judy Garland, a gay icon.

friends a euphemism for menstruation.

frig **1.** to masturbate. The original meaning. Dates as far back as the 1500s, which isn't old enough to make it an Anglo-Saxon four-letter word. **2.** to have sexual intercourse. In this sense, from the 1600s. **3.** an exclamation of vexation, surprise, and the like, used as a euphemistic substitution for *fuck*.

frig about to waste time; to fiddle-fart about. In use since the 1700s in Britain.

frigging **1.** a euphemism for the word *fucking*, used as an intensifier. **2.** masturbating. **3.** having sex.

frigging in the rigging wasting time. From the lyrics of a dirty song in the form of a sea shanty in which the phrase referred to masturbation.

frig up to ruin or wreck.

frig-up a confusion, muddle or mess.

frillie a frill-necked lizard.

frisbee to throw something flat so that it spins about its centre. *Just frisbee it over here.*

Fritz a German or the Germans. A term of abuse common in both World Wars.

fro an Afro hair style. *He had an amazing fro.*

frog **1.** a disparaging term for a French person. Because the French are famed for eating frogs' legs. This has been used in Britain since the 18th century. **2.** an old slang term for a pound note or the sum of £1. Short for **frogskin**. Because the Australian pound note was green. **3.** a condom. From 'Frenchy'. Dating back to the 1950s.

frog and toad rhyming slang for 'road'. Originally British slang from the 1850s, but used in Australia since at least the 1900s.

from arsehole to breakfast time from beginning to end, or rather, from end to beginning.

from away in Broken Hill, and certain other rural areas, anyone not from the local area is said to be **from away**.

from go to whoa from beginning to end. This has been used in Oz since the 1970s, but appears in NZ from the 1950s. Looks like we borrowed this one from the Kiwis.

front bum the female genitalia. Hence, a highly disparaging term for a female.

frostie an ice-cold beer. Also called a **frosty chop**.

frot an act of sexual intercourse. A backformation from the term *frottage* 'sexual rubbing against another person while clothed'.

froth and bubble **1.** Aussie rhyming slang for 'double', at the racetrack, that is. Dates back to the 1960s. **2.** rhyming slang for 'trouble'.

frozen mitt an old Aussie slang term for the 'cold shoulder'. *She gave him the frozen mitt.* From the 1940s.

fruit **1.** a disparaging word for a male homosexual. Originally US slang from the 1900s. **2.** a weirdo.

fruit and veg the male genitalia.

fruitcake **1.** a nut case; a ratbag. **2.** a homosexual man.

fruit loop a loony; someone of unsound mind.

fruit salad military slang for a large collection of medal ribbons.

fruit tingles a euphemism for the exclamation *fuck!*

fruity **1.** homosexual. **2.** crazy, insane, weird. **3.** in SA, a fit of hysterics.

fuck **1.** to have sexual intercourse; to screw or root. The dreaded F-word. The rudest word in the English language next to the dreaded C-word. Often euphemised to *eff*, or sometimes **frig** (see entry). Has lost some of its impact in recent years, and is now allowed on Australian public television after 9.30 at night. Originally almost exclusively used by men and referring generally to men fucking women, but nowadays commonly used by women, and used from the woman's perspective. Also used of any sexual thrusting or rubbing with the genitalia, referring to not only to straight heterosexual vaginal sex, but equally to hetero- or homosexual anal sex, and a variety of other sexual acts, as oral sex, bestiality, the use of dildos, the fingers, and the like.

In origin one of the Anglo-Saxon four-letter words. The earliest record extant is from a text written in about 1450. The word obviously shares a common Germanic ancestor with Middle Dutch *fokken*, Norwegian dialect *fukka*, Swedish dialect *focka*, and Dutch *fokken* 'to breed animals' (hence the surname *Fokker*, literally, 'breeder'). The German slang word *ficken* is probably from the same source. Some would like to go further and link these with Latin *pungere* 'to prick', and Greek *pygmé* 'fist'. Others have suggested that it is related to the hypothetical Indo-European root *peig-* 'evil-minded, hostile', which would make it cognate with *fickle*, *foe*, *fey* and *feud*, words all Germanic in origin.

It is certainly NOT derived from an acronym such as *For Unlawful Carnal Knowledge*, or *Fornication Under the Consent of the King*.

These urban myths cannot be true (a) because it was originally spelt *fuc* and *fuk*, (b) because there was no such thing as an acronym in 1450, and (c) because the term 'carnal knowledge' did not exist in 1450 either. So all you people who go around spreading these stupid myths about the origin of the word *fuck* can just stop it right now.

2. metaphorically, to ruin, spoil or wreck. *All that drinking has fucked my liver.* Also, used to mean astound or amaze. *It fucks me how he can keep going on.* **3.** as a noun, an act of sexual intercourse. *I haven't had a fuck in months.* Or a person rated on their sexual performance, as in *a good fuck*, *a lousy fuck*, or *an alright fuck*. Also, a sexual partner, as in *He was my first fuck.* **4.** a contemptible person. *Leave me alone you stupid fuck*, or *Geez he's a useless fuck.* **5.** used as a swearword or word of abuse, it is a much stronger equivalent of *damn*. Thus *I don't give a fuck*, meaning 'I don't give a damn'. *Fuck them all*, meaning 'Damn them all'. Also, used as a substitute for 'god' in oaths, such as *What in fuck's name are you doing?* **6.** as an adjective, pertaining to sex. As in *fuck books* or a *fuck session*. **7.** as an exclamation, used to express disgust or extreme annoyance. The sort of thing said when you hit your thumb with a hammer. But can also serve to express amazement, wonder, or delight. **8.** to **not give a flying fuck** is to not care at all. Back in 18th century England a 'flying fuck' was a fuck taken whilst riding on horseback. Giddy up! **9.** a sexually desperate male **would fuck a hole in the ground if it smiled at him**.

fuckable sexually desirable.

fuck about 1. to engage in casual sex; to cheat on someone sexually. **2.** to waste time; to fiddle about. **3.** to **fuck someone about** is to treat them unfairly.

fuck a duck! holy cow! good lord! wow!

fuckalicious deliciously fuckable.

fuck-all very little; virtually nothing or virtually none.

fuck around 1. to engage in casual sex; to cheat on a partner. **2.** to waste time; to fiddle about. **3.** to **fuck someone around** is to treat them unfairly.

fuckathon a long bout of lovemaking.

fuck book a pornographic book or magazine.

fuck brains a stupid or annoying person.

fuck buddy a friend who you have sex with but without all the trappings of a committed relationship.

fucked 1. broken, ruined or wrecked. **2.** done for; in an impossible situation. **3.** exhausted. **4.** astounded. *Well I'll be fucked!* **5.** bothered. *I couldn't be fucked making the trip.* **6.** heavily pissed or stoned. **7.** extremely bad; deplorable. *He's got a really fucked attitude.*

fucked by the fickle finger of fate having suffered bad fortune.

fucked if I know a strong assertion of ignorance.

fucked in the head mad, insane, deranged.

fucked off extremely annoyed.

fucked out exhausted from sexual activity. A choice bit of British sexual slang originally from the Victorian era.

fucked up 1. emotionally or mentally wrecked. **2.** completely bad; in a state of total abnormality. *This whole town is fucked up.* **3.** severely affected by drugs or alcohol.

fuckee 1. the person taking a passive role in an act of sexual intercourse, as opposed to the 'fucker'. **2.** a pidgin English way of saying 'fuck'. Often coupled with the term *suckee* to refer to sex and/or oral sex.

fucken a variant spelling of *fucking*, common in Aussie English. *I can't stand those fucken bludgers.*

fucker 1. literally, one who fucks; one much given to fucking. **2.** a contemptible person. One of the great insults of the English language. In World War I Aussie soldiers used to refer to British soldiers as *fookers* – that is, *fucker* said with a Pommy accent. **3.** any person. *So the old fucker was right!* **4.** any thing. *I can't get the fucker started!*

fuckface a contemptible person.

fuckfest an event, party, or the like, at which there is much sexual coupling.

fuck film a porno movie. Also called a **fuck flick**.

fuck head a despicable person; a fuckwit.

fuck hole the vagina.

fucking 1. sexual intercourse, or an act of sexual intercourse. **2.** contemptible, goddamned. Used as an intensifier. First recorded in the US in the 1850s and in Britain in the 1890s, but probably older in both cases. This is one of the most powerful words in the language, and as a substitute it shat all over *bloody*, the word that previously fulfilled this role in English. However, nowadays *fucking* suffers a bit from overuse, and has *motherfucking* and *cocksucking* to contend with. Can be used in negative contexts, as *The fucking thing's broke* or *Leave me alone you fucking arsehole*, but also is equally at home in positive contexts, as *It's a fucking marvel* or *She's a fucking genius.* Used repetitively to express extreme anger, annoyance, disregard, or the like, but often merely in an attempt at giving the impression of toughness or 'coolness' through gratuitous swearing. Occasionally used repetitively for jocular effect. Can also be used adverbially, as *I didn't fucking do nothin'.* Commonly spelt **fuckin'** or, especially in Australia, **fucken**. Euphemistic forms include **flipping**, **flogging**, **freaking**, **fricking** and **frigging**. **3.** inserted between syllables to add emphasis, as *abso-fucking-lutely*, *Kings-fucking-Cross*, or *vege-fucking-mite*.

fucking A! you bet! yea verily! all right!

fucking oath! a stronger, cruder version of **bloody oath!**

fucking well totally, absolutely. Used as an intensifier. *You fucking well did run into me!*

fuck-knuckle a wanker. An Aussie original this, dating back to the 1980s. The implication is that they are fucking their hands – that is, masturbating.

fuckless literally, without sexual intercourse. *He went to bed fuckless and forlorn.* Also, used as an intensifier, as in *bored fuckless.*

fuck-load an awful lot. *They've got a fuck-load of problems.*

fuck me Well I'll be damned! An exclamation of great surprise. Also, more emphatically, **fuck me dead**, **fuck me drunk**, or **fuck me blind**.

fuck-me boots women's long-legged, sexually alluring boots. Also called **FM boots** or **FMBs**.

fuck nose a contemptible person; a dickhead.

fuck off **1.** to depart. *We fucked off down to the beach.* **2.** as a command, Piss off! Rack off! Go to hell! A harsh expression of rejection. **3.** an expression of disbelief. **4.** to annoy severely; to piss off. *His spitting all the time really fucks me off.*

fuck-off large and imposing. *He was wearing his big fuck-off boots.*

fuck over to take advantage of someone; to swindle or cheat someone.

fuck pig a sexually promiscuous person.

fuck silly to have sex with someone energetically; to fuck to the point of sexual exhaustion. There are many variants on this theme, such as **fuck senseless**, **fuck the brains out of**, **fuck the head off**, or **fuck the legs off**.

fucks me it beats me. *Fucks me why they would want to spend their money that way.* Also, as an answer to a question, **Fucks me, Skip.** Referring to that macropodian Australian icon, Skippy the Bush Kangaroo.

fuck stick **1.** the penis. **2.** a stupid or annoying person.

fuck truck a panel van fitted out in the back with mattress and curtains as a retreat for sexual liaisons. This is an Australian original, dating back to the 1970s. Synonyms are **root ute**, **shaggin' wagon**, and **sin bin**.

fuck up **1.** to blunder. **2.** to ruin or wreck.

fuck-up **1.** a miscalculation; a bad mistake. **2.** a person who is mentally or emotionally unstable.

fuck up and die a harsh expression of rebuke.

fuckwit an incredibly stupid person. It can also be used to mean a despicable or detestable person. A uniquely Aussie blending of *fuck* and *nitwit*. It has been around since the 1960s, and has recently taken a Qantas flight to the UK where the Poms are finding it a very useful addition to their store of insults. Now, that's cultural imperialism.

fuck with to meddle with.

fuckwitted foolish, stupid. *That was a fuckwitted suggestion.*

fuck you damn you!

fudge to illegally move your hand over the line when shooting in a game of marbles. See **fanannywhacking** for a full set of synonyms.

fudge packer a homosexual man. See **dung puncher** for synonyms.

fugly **1.** extremely unattractive. An uncomplimentary blend of *fucking* and *ugly*. Aussie slang since the 1970s – now also used in the US. **2.** an extremely unattractive person.

full completely intoxicated; pissed as a newt. This word has given rise to numerous similes, such as **full as a boot** or **full as a goog**, which can mean (a) drunk, (b) satiated after a meal, or (c) overcrowded. Apart from boots and googs, you can be **full as a bull, a bull's bum, a butcher's pup, an egg, a family jerry** or **po, a Catholic school, a State school, a State school hat rack, a fart, a tick, a fairy's phone book, a Pommy complaint box, a fat lady's sock** (or

bra/knickers/undies, etc.), or **a seaside shit-house on Boxing Day**.

full bore to the maximum; all out.

full bottle an expert. *She was the full bottle on horse breeding.*

full hand an infection of both gonorrhoea and syphilis simultaneously. Also called a **full house**.

full monty everything; the lot; the whole kit and caboodle. To **go the full monty** is to go the whole way, to go all out, and when talking about a striptease act it means to get completely naked, to take it all off. This phrase no doubt owes its popularity to the 1997 movie *The Full Monty* which centred around men doing a striptease.

full of it talking nonsense. A euphemism for **full of shit**.

full of yourself conceited; up yourself.

full-on **1.** enthusiastic; full of energy; unrestrained. **2.** requiring complete involvement or total commitment. *This new course I've started is pretty full-on.* **3.** totally. *It's full-on relaxing, all the time.* **4.** as fast, strong, committed, as possible.

full up to dolly's wax satiated after a fine meal; replete with food; stonkered. *I couldn't eat another crumb, I'm full up to dolly's wax.* Referring to an old type of child's doll which had a cloth body and a head made of wax. You can also be **full up to pussy's bow** or **ribbon**.

fully completely; without reservation. Used as an intensifier. *It fully reminds me of my visit to London.* Aussie youth slang since the 1990s.

fun bags a blokey word for breasts.

fundie **1.** a derisive word for a fundamentalist Christian, or any fundamentalist for that matter. Also **fundo**. **2.** a fund manager.

fungus face a person with a beard or other facial hair.

funny farm a lunatic asylum; a psychiatric hospital.

funny money **1.** money made by dubious or dishonest means. **2.** counterfeit money.

furburger **1.** cunnilingus. **2.** the female genitals.

furgle to have sexual intercourse. Borrowed from US slang, from German slang *vogeln*.

furniture in cricket, the stumps.

furphy a rumour. From the name of a brand of watercart manufactured by J. Furphy and Sons, which, during World War I, were natural centres of gossip.

FURTB well-fed. Standing for *Full Up Ready To Burst*.

fuzz the police. Originally US underworld slang from the 1920s. Origin unknown.

Fuzzy Wuzzy Angels during World War II, a term used for the native Papua New Guineans who gave great assistance to Australian soldiers.

fwooar! a variant spelling of **phwoar**.

the F-word a euphemism for the word *fuck*.

the Gabba the internationally known Woolloongabba Cricket Ground in Brisbane.

gaddiyah a variation of the word **kartiya** (see entry).

gagging for immensely desirous of.

gaggle among hang-gliders, a collective noun for a group of airborne hang-gliders.

galah iconic Australian pink and grey cockatoo. The word is borrowed from the Aboriginal language Yuwaalarraay, from up Lightning Ridge way. The galah is noted for its erratically noisy behaviour which seems pretty bizarre to humans (no doubt it all makes sense to the galahs), and hence in slang **galah** means 'fool'. *Get out of it, you great bloody galah.* Someone acting the fool is described as **mad as a gumtree full of galahs.**

galah session a time set aside for the people of isolated outback areas to converse with one another by radio.

gallop the lizard of a male, to have a wank.

galoot an awkward, silly fellow. A great clumsy oaf. The origin of this one is a bit of a mystery. It was originally used by sailors to refer to soldiers or marines, and is first recorded in a glossary of Australian convict slang back in 1812. Its history before this is unknown.

galvo galvanised iron, a quintessential building material for a wide brown land.

gamarouche oral sex, or to perform oral sex. A bit of 19th century British sexual slang that had some small survival in Aussie English. Sometimes shortened to **gam, gamma**, or **gamo**. Ultimately from French.

game 1. typically Aussie way of referring to a business or profession, as in *Andrew is in the building game now.* However to be **on the game** refers only to the business of prostitution. **2.** to **give the game away** is to abandon whatever it is you're doing.

game as Ned Kelly imbued with the fighting spirit of Australia's national hero; plucky; resolute. You can also be as **game as Phar Lap**, Australia's other great national hero.

gammon 1. to lie or tell fibs; to pretend or kid; to tease. *I'm just gammoning.* Originally slang used by the criminal class, first recorded back in 1812. This word has survived over the years largely as a part of Aboriginal English, from where it has now been re-adopted into the speech of white people, especially in areas where they have contact with Aboriginal communities (as northern Australia). **2.** construed as a present participle (an *-ing* form), as though the verb is 'to gam'. *I think he's gammon us.* **3.** as a noun, a lie or fib; nonsense or rubbish; a fake; something no good. *I don't believe you. That's gammon!* Also used as an exclamation of disbelief. **4.** as an adjective, untrue; fake or phoney; no good. *What a gammon idea.*

gander a look. *Give us a gander at it.*

gang bang an occasion on which a number of males have sex with one female. Also called a **gangie** by aficionados. Also used of any sexual orgy involving multiple partners. Can be used in a homosexual context as well.

ganja marijuana. A word borrowed from Hindi.

gank to steal or shoplift.

garage door if someone's fly is open you can politely inform them that their **garage door is open**.

garbage bird the much despised Indian myna, a brown and black bird introduced into Australia in the 1860s and now common around large cities and cane-growing areas along the eastern coast.

garbage guts a person who eats to excess or will eat any food.

garbo 1. a garbage collector. Aussie slang since the 1950s. **2.** a garbage bin. *Chuck it in the garbo.*

garbologist a garbage collector. Aussie slang since the 1970s.

Gareth's Gazebo in the ACT, a derisive name for the Department of Foreign Affairs and Trade building. After Gareth Evans, former foreign affairs minister.

gargle **1.** an alcoholic drink. *Care for a gargle?* Aussie slang since the 1930s. **2.** alcohol, booze. *Had a big night on the gargle.*

gargle junket to suck off.

Garmahal in the ACT, the High Court building, commissioned by former Chief Justice Sir Garfield Barwick. A blend of *Bar*wick and Taj *Mahal*. Also called **Gar's Bar**.

garn go on! *Garn, there's stack of room.* A typical Aussie contraction (similar to **carn**) which has been around since the 1910s. In England it is common in Cockney speech.

Gar's Bar in the ACT, the High Court building, commissioned by Sir Garfield Barwick. Also called the **Garmahal**.

gasbag an empty, voluble talker; a windbag. Hence, to talk volubly; chatter. Originally US slang from the 1860s.

gas guzzler a car which consumes an inordinate amount of fuel.

gash a crass term for the vagina or vulva. Also used to refer to women in general, viewed as sex objects. *There'll be plenty of gash at the party.* Believe it or not, this term was common British sexual slang in the Victorian era – and you thought they were all prudes!

gasper a cigarette.

gastro a bout of gastroenteritis; a tummy wog.

gat a pistol; any gun. Originally US slang of the 1890s. An abbreviation of *Gatling gun*.

Gawler Place Adelaide rhyming slang for 'face'.

gay **1.** homosexual, originally and still principally of men, though it can be used to refer to lesbians. Hence, a homosexual man. First appears in the US in the 1920s. Originally a word used by gays themselves, it later spread to the wider community and was converted to a homophobic term of abuse. Reclaimed in the 1970s by the gay community as a positive word, and now no longer slang, but part of Standard English. **2.** among Aussie schoolkids and adolescents **gay** means uncool, daggy, socially unacceptable. As in, *What a gay haircut*, or *That band is so gay*. There is no real sense of homosexuality involved, though in origin this usage stems from the homophobic use of gay as a term of abuse. Has been in use since at least the early 1990s.

gay and hearty Aussie rhyming slang for 'party'. Dates back to the 1960s.

gay boy a young male homosexual.

gaydar the ability to recognise gay men on sight.

gazunder **1.** a chamber-pot. It 'goes under' the bed. **2.** in cricket, a mullygrubber.

G-banger a G-string showing above the top of the pants.

G'day the ubiquitous friendly Australian greeting. Recorded in this abbreviated form since the 1900s. *G'day mate, how're you goin'?* Sometimes written out in full as **good day**, but it is always pronounced as 'G'day'. Occasionally written as **gidday**. When pronounced as two separate words, this was formerly used as a parting comment, generally when the person leaving was annoyed. *Good day to you sir!* This old-fashioned use is occasionally still used nowadays, but only in a joking way.

GDT a **golden drinking token** (see entry).

gear **1.** any illegal drug of addiction, often marijuana or heroin. To be **on the gear** is to be taking heroin. **2.** the apparatus used to prepare and inject drugs, especially heroin. **3.** clothes. *Get your gear off.* **4.** used loosely to refer to whatever is being discussed; stuff; type of thing. *I don't want any whinging or complaining, or that sort of gear.*

gee a thousand dollars. From *g*, standing for 'grand'.

the Gee a nickname for the Melbourne Cricket Ground or MCG.

gee-gee with children, a horse. However, with adults, the **gee-gees** are the horseraces.

geek **1.** a look. *Have a geek at this.* Aussie slang dating from World War I. Taken from Cornish dialect. **2.** generally, a nerd or any person who is uncool. In school contexts, a diligent student, much reviled by cooler kids. In computing contexts, a complete computer fanatic, one whose whole life revolves around their computer. In this last sense, often used by computer geeks in a positive way of themselves, as in *I'm a big computer geek, the geekiest of them all.* Which doesn't really wash with the non-geek world, but makes the geeks feel good about themselves. In origin the word is from British dialect where it is a variant of *geck*, a fool, which comes from Low German or Dutch. In Australia it appeared in the 1980s, borrowed from US slang.

geek boy a male computer geek. Also called a **geek guy**.

geek girl a female computer geek. Also called a **geek chick**.

geekspeak the jargon used by computer geeks.

geekster a computer geek.

geeky of the nature of a geek; befitting a geek; socially awkward; dorky.

gee up to excite or stir up, as in *Her act really geed the audience up.* Aussie slang since the 1950s. Hence, as a noun, an instance of stirring up enthusiasm, raising spirits or the like. *The big crowd gave the players a much needed gee up.*

geez **1.** holy cow! *Geez, word gets around quickly.* This is a euphemistic contraction of *Jesus!* **2.** (pronounced with a hard 'g') a look. *Give us a geez, will ya?*

geezer **1.** an odd or funny old man. **2.** a look. *He came over for a geezer at my new bike.*

GEHA (pronounced 'gee-ha') in WA, relating to subsidised housing provided to government employees, such as teachers or police officers, in regional areas. Standing for Government Employees' Housing Authority.

gen information; all the necessary information about a subject; the good oil. *She gave me the gen about our new boss.* Short for *general information.* Original British RAF slang from World War II.

gene jockey a genetic scientist.

gent among fishos, a maggot used for bait. Way back in the 16th century anglers used to call maggots *gentles*, from an old meaning of the word *gentle* 'soft to the touch'.

gen up to learn or read up on.

geo a geologist or rock doctor.

geri an old person. Short for *geriatric.* Also spelt **gerry** or **jerry**.

Germaine Greer Aussie rhyming slang for 'beer'. Dates from the 1980s.

Geronimo! a cry used when making a parachute jump.

Gestapo Melbourne slang for ticket inspectors.

get a bag! in cricket, a derisive cry directed at a player who has dropped a sitter.

get a black dog up you! meaning 'Get stuffed!' Actually, the dog doesn't necessarily have to be black as you can say 'Get a dog up ya!'

get a guernsey originally, to be selected for a football team. Hence, to be selected for any team, or for anything. Aussie slang since the 1900s.

get a leg over to crack it for a bit of sex.

get a life! Stop being so hopeless! A catchphrase expressing derision at another's behaviour. Became popular in Oz in the 1990s. Borrowed from the US.

get a load of to have a look at. *Get a load of that mug.* Originally US slang of the 1920s. Used in Australia since the 1960s.

get amongst it to get actively involved in something; to take part with enthusiasm. *It's time to hit the pub and get amongst it.* Aussie slang since the 1960s.

get a wriggle on to hurry. Aussie slang since the 1940s. Some people say **get a wiggle on**, which is a US borrowing.

get fucked! Leave me alone! Piss off! Recorded earliest in a glossary of AIF slang written in 1924, thus potentially an Australian original. Slightly less forceful variations are **get rooted!** and **get stuffed!**

get it off to have sex.

get it up **1.** of a male, to achieve erection. **2.** of a male, have sex with someone. **3.** to scold, abuse or stir. *They really got it up me about my new haircut.*

get knotted! a euphemism for 'get fucked!', used in Oz since the 1960s. Of similar age, and also Aussie in origin, is **get nicked!**

get off at Redfern to pull out before ejaculating as a form of contraception; to practise 'coitus interruptus', as they say in the classics. There's only one thing to call people who use this birth control method – parents! Referring to Redfern Station, the stop immediately before Central Railway Station in Sydney. The phrase has been around since at least the 1950s.

get off on **1.** to get your thrills about something. **2.** to become sexually stimulated by something or someone.

get on to place a bet. *Number 4, race 3. Did you get on?*

get on your goat to really annoy you.

get set to place a bet.

get some pork on your fork of a male, to obtain some sexual intercourse.

gettas thongs. From Japanese. Also called **getties**.

get the axe to be dismissed from work; to get the sack. You can also get *the arse, the boot, the chop,* or *the spear.*

get the money of a racehorse, to win the race. *Looks like Tulloch gets the money.*

getting any? a short way of asking 'Are you getting any sexual intercourse?'

get up **1.** to win. *He was trailing at the bend, but managed to get up by a neck at the finish.* Aussie slang since the 1900s. **2.** to annoy greatly. *His continual whingeing really gets up me.* **3.** of a male, to have sex with someone.

get with a adolescent's term for kissing and canoodling. *Did you get with Sandra the other night?* Can also mean to have sex.

get your arse into gear to get ready for action.

get your end in of a male, to obtain sexual intercourse.

get your flaps off me! Leave me alone!

get your rocks off **1.** to orgasm. **2.** to get pleasure from. *He gets his rocks off on heavy metal.*

get yourself outside of to eat something. *Here, get yourself outside of this ice-cream.*

get your wick wet of a man, to lose your virginity.

the GG the Governor-General. Slightly disrespectful, but in a joking way.

the 'Ghan a train on the Adelaide to Alice Springs (now Darwin) route.

Ghan a Afghan camel driver of outback Australia, a common character before the land was opened up to road and train.

GHB the designer-drug gamma hydroxybutyric acid used as a stimulant and hallucinogen and also for bodybuilding purposes; grievous bodily harm.

gibber **1.** a small stone suitable for throwing. See **yonnie** for the full set of regionalisms. From the extinct Aboriginal language Dharug, spoken in the Sydney region. **2.** technically, a geologist's term for a pebble or stone of chalcedony, or other hard silica, covered with desert varnish (a dark coating, composed principally of fine-grained clay minerals, found on rocks or stone in arid regions). Gibbers are found covering the surface of parts of the arid Australian inland. A region covered with gibbers is called a **gibber plain**, a **gibber desert**, or **gibber country**. The local rag in Woomera is called *The Gibber Gabber.*

gidgee in WA, a hand-held spear fired from a thick band of elastic, used in spearfishing. From the name of a type of Aboriginal spear in the Nyungar language of south-western WA.

gift of the gab innate skill in talking.

gig **1.** a fool. As in the common Australian admonishment, *Don't make a gig of yourself!* Borrowed from British slang. **2.** to kid or tease. *Are you gigging me?* Australian slang since the 1890s. From British dialect. **3.** a police informer. Short for **fizgig**. Aussie slang dating from the 1950s. Hence, a stickybeak or busybody. **4.** a look. Aussie slang dating from the 1920s.

giggle hat the standard Army issue hat for jungle wear. Floppy things made from cotton twill. Known officially as 'hats utility, jungle green'. Also called **hats ridiculous** or simply **bush hats**.

giggle house an asylum for the insane. Digger slang from World War I. Also called a **giggle factory**.

giggle suit army greens.

gilgai **1.** a natural soil formation of undulating mounds and depressions occurring extensively in inland Australia. From the NSW Aboriginal languages of Wiradjuri and Kamilaroi. **2.** a natural depression or hole in the ground which forms a reservoir after heavy rain. Also called a **melon hole**.

gilgie (pronounced with an initial soft 'g') in WA, a type of freshwater crayfish, related to the yabby. From the Nyungar language of south-west WA. Also spelt **jilgie**, and colloquialised as **joogie**.

gilgies' piss in WA, a derogatory term for piss-weak beer.

Gilligan's Island a small grassy knoll with palm trees formerly next to Taylor Square in Sydney.

gillion a very large number or sum of money. A person with a gillion dollars is, of course, a **gillionaire**. Similar sums are **jillion**, **squillion**, **squintillion** and **zillion**.

gimp a fool or idiot.

gin this word for an Aboriginal woman originally came from the Dharug language, spoken by the Aboriginals living in the Sydney district at the time of white settlement. As used by whites the word took on all the negative associations that the colonists had for the native inhabitants, and thus the word has remained a racist term ever since.

ginder in Bunbury WA, a haircut, especially a short one. To get a haircut was to be **gindered**. Said to be derived from the name of one Arthur Ginder, a resident of Bunbury in the 1960s, who had a medical condition which caused him to lose all of his hair.

ging (pronounced with an initial hard 'g') a child's catapult or slingshot. Perhaps imitative of the sound made when fired. Aussie slang since the 1930s. Now chiefly used in WA and Qld.

ginger **1.** the backside or bum. *I gave him a swift kick up the ginger.* From **ginger ale**, rhyming slang for 'tail'. Aussie slang dating from the 1960s. If someone is **on your ginger**, then they are chasing you. If you are in a car, then the bastard is tailgating you. **2.** of a prostitute or their accomplice, to thieve from a client's clothing.

ginger beer Aussie rhyming slang for 'engineer', especially an engineer in the armed forces. Dates back to the 1940s.

gin jockey a racist term for a white man who has sexual relations with an Aboriginal woman. A term of great disparagement. Recorded since the 1950s. Also found in the form **gin shepherd**, dating back to the 1920s.

gink **1.** old slang for a silly person. Has been around since the 1920s, but is little heard today. Origin unknown. **2.** a look. *Give us a gink at that.* Aussie slang dating from the 1940s. Perhaps a variant of **geek**.

ginormous incredibly huge; of outstanding size.

gin's handbag a term for a cask of wine. A racist slur referring to Aboriginal problem drinking.

gin's piss really piss-weak beer. Racist Aussie slang since the 1970s.

Gippo a variant spelling of **Gyppo**.

Gippy a local nickname for Gippsland, in Victoria.

girlie a girl or young woman. Used as a disparaging term for effeminate things that should be masculine. As in, *I don't drink none of them girlie designer beers.* Also used to refer to naked photos of women, as in *girlie magazines*.

girl of... a girl or woman by the name of... Thus, 'He married the girl of Jones, who lived next door to the butcher's.' Particularly used in rural NSW.

girl's blouse a timid, ineffectual male; a wuss. A variant of **big girl's blouse**.

girl's germs among children, a supposed contagion of girlness avoided by boys. See **boy's germs**.

girls' night out an evening on which a group of women have a night out together.

girl's week the menstrual period.

girly-girly excessively effeminate, in the manner of a small girl.

gism semen. A variant spelling of **jism** (see entry).

git a fool; a stupid person. From British slang.

give it away to give up on. *I used to smoke, but I've given it away now.* Yep, it's Aussie. Dating back to the 1940s.

give the game away to abandon whatever it is you're doing. Aussie slang dating from the 1940s.

glacio Antarctic slang for a glaciologist.

gladdie a gladiolus. An Australianism dating from the 1940s. Also shortened to **glad**.

glad rags your best clothes, reserved for special occasions.

glamour a stunningly beautiful woman. *She's an absolute glamour.*

glass in WA and Vic if you order a **glass** of beer you will get a serving of seven fluid ounces (200 ml). This usage is also heard in Tas and Qld, but it is more commonly known as a **seven**. In Vic, WA and Qld simply ordering a **beer** will get you the same thing. In other states asking for a beer will get you the question 'What size?' In SA a seven is called a **butcher**.

glass can a stubby.

glassie **1.** a glass marble obtained from a bottle. See **bottle-oh** for more information. **2.** a person employed to clean away used glasses and rubbish and empty ashtrays in a hotel or club.

Gloria Soames in Strine, glorious homes. Australian domestic architecture at its best. If you don't know what Strine is – you can look it up at the entry for **Strine**.

glory hole a hole in a wall, as between toilet cubicles, used for sexual purposes, as the insertion of penis, voyeurism, etc.

glum bum a pessimistic person.

gnarly among adolescents, excellent, terrific, wonderful. *Check out the gnarly surf.* 1970s US slang, originally used by surfers.

go **1.** an attempt. *I'll give anything a go.* Hence the great Aussie barracking cry: *Have a go ya mug!* **2.** a fight. *When the rival fans met in the pub, boy, then you'd see some goes.* Commonly found in that great Aussie challenge to fisticuffs, *Do you want a go, mate?* Hence, as a verb, to attack, as in *I was itching to go him.* **3.** an opportunity fit for taking. *Here's a go!* A fair chance, as in *There's no chance of getting a go here.* **4.** to say, as in *So I go to him, 'Shut your face!'* Used mostly by schoolkids, but also common in the speech of ethnic Australians. Kylie Mole of the hit TV show *The Comedy Company* was a past master at this idiom: *Mum went to me that Dino went to her to go to me that he isn't wif Amanda anymore.* **5.** to eat or drink with pleasure. *I could really go a beer right now.* Aussie slang since the 1940s. **6.** a goanna. *You should have seen that go go!* A great example of the Aussie penchant for abbreviation.

go all the way to have full sexual intercourse.

goal sneak in Aussie Rules, a player who catches the opposition unawares and scores a goal.

goanna Aussie rhyming slang for 'pianner', that is, a piano. Dates back to World War I.

go apeshit to go crazy.

goat **1.** a fool. **2.** a lecherous old man. **3.** a racehorse that is no good. **4.** if something **gets on your goat**, then it annoys the hell out of you. **5.** if a racehorse **runs like a hairy goat**, then it won't be winning any races.

goat boat a surf ski.

goat's head a Qld and NSW term for a three-corner jack or doublegee. See **doublegee** for the complete set of regionalisms.

gob **1.** the mouth. *Shut up, or I'll smack you in the gob.* **2.** to gobble down. *I just gobbed half a packet of lollies.* **3.** to spit or expectorate.

gobble off to suck off. Also shortened to **gob off**.

gobsmacked astonished, flabbergasted. British slang from the 1980s.

go-cart another term for a billy cart. Not to be confused with the motorised Go-Karts.

God nickname of AFL player Gary Ablett – one of the greatest ever to pull on the boots.

go down on to perform fellatio; sometimes used to refer to cunnilingus. US slang from 1910s.

go down the tubes to fail miserably; to go to ruin.

God's gift to a truly wonderful person in a particular sphere of interest. People who think they are this, aren't. *He thinks he's God's gift to women.*

God's own in Australia this refers to Australia. Well, of course it bloody does! We live in a paradise. In Kiwiland they use it about New Zealand, but I guess that stands to reason. But, in America, they use this term to refer to the USA. How weird is that? Don't those Yanks know nothing?

goer **1.** a person who displays great energy and drive. **2.** a keen and energetic sexual partner. **3.** a speedy horse or vehicle. **4.** a racehorse that is being run to win – as opposed to a **dead'un** (see entry). **5.** a project having evident prospects of success.

goey speed (the drug).

goffer military slang for a soft drink. Originally British RAF slang, from the brand name *Goffa*.

go figure an expression of surprise or confusion. Often used sarcastically.

go for the doctor to go all out; to go as fast as you can. Also, to bet all your money on a race. In horseracing, it is the moment when the jockey gets the whip out and goes for broke. Aussie slang since the 1940s.

go fuck yourself Piss off and may evil befall you!

go gangbusters to go along terrifically. Also, **go great guns**.

goggles glasses, especially strong ones.

go-in a fight. *They had a bit of a go-in behind the pub.* Aussie slang since the 1900s.

gold-digger a person who marries for financial gain.

golden arches a McDonald's Family Restaurant.

golden drinking token a fifty dollar note. Also known as a **GDT**.

golden duck in cricket, a dismissal on the first ball. Worse than a **duck**, and slightly less worse than a **diamond duck**.

the Golden Mile a gold-bearing reef lying between Kalgoorlie and Boulder in WA.

golden shower urination onto another for sexual pleasure.

goldfish bowl any room with a large window at street-level.

gold head among used car salesmen, a home-owner with a good credit rating.

Goldie the Gold Coast.

Goldsborough Morts Aussie rhyming slang for 'shorts'. Goldsborough Mort was a large Australian trading company.

go like the clappers to move very rapidly.

golly saliva and mucus collected in the mouth and spat out. Hence, as a verb, to spit. Aussie slang since the 1930s. Perhaps from British dialect *golls* 'mucus dripping from children's noses'.

gonads the testicles.

gone **1.** pregnant. *She's five months gone already.* Aussie slang since the 1940s. **2.** ruined or undone. *If he catches us we're gone.*

gone a million completely and utterly undone; defeated. Aussie slang dating from the 1910s.

gone to Gowings NSW slang, absolutely gone; gone in all respects. Originally an advertising slogan from the 1940s for Sydney department store *Gowing* Bros Ltd. The ad campaign consisted of witty cartoons of someone making a hasty departure with the explanation that they had 'Gone to Gowings'. When notorious criminal Darcy Dugan escaped from jail in the late 1940s he scrawled on the cell wall 'Gone to Gowings'. Specifically the expression can mean destitute, drunk, hungover, losing a race or game dismally, insane, or merely, and in the original sense, departed in great haste.

gong **1.** a medal. **2.** an award.

the Gong **1.** the city of Wollongong, just south of Sydney. **2.** nickname for Australian tennis legend Evonne Goolagong (Evonne Cawley).

gonk a kid's catapult or slingshot. A word from the north coast of NSW. Dating from the 1950s. See **slingshot** for synonyms.

gonnie a small stone suitable for throwing. Used chiefly in Qld. Also found in SA. See **yonnie** for the full set of regionalisms.

gonzo bird an ibis. So called from the resemblance of the ibis beak to the nose of the *Sesame Street* muppet Gonzo.

goober a stupid or annoying person. From US slang, where the word also means a peanut.

gooby a mass of nasal mucus ejected from the mouth. Also called a **golly**, or in Victoria, a **gorby**.

good-bye muscles the flabby triceps of an overweight or matronly woman.

good call a good decision.

good guts useful information; the good oil; the drum. World War II Aussie slang.

good hair day a day in which your hair is manageable. See **bad hair day**.

good-looker an attractive person.

good nut in cricket, a good delivery that is difficult to play.

good-oh all right, okay. *Everything was good-oh.* Commonly used as an exclamation. Aussie slang since the early 1900s.

good oil reliable information; the lowdown; the drum. Aussie slang dating from the 1910s. Also called the **dinkum oil**, or simply, **the oil**.

good on you! Well done! Bravo! Classic Aussie encouragement dating way back to the 1900s. Commonly heard as **good onya**, or shortened simply to **onya!** In the plural, it is, of course, **good onyas!**

good shit excellent quality marijuana.

good sort **1.** a spunky woman. Aussie blokes have been referring to delectable sheilas as good sorts since at least the 1940s. In recent years the term has been adopted by women to refer to spunky men. **2.** a reliable and likeable bloke; a decent chap. This meaning is on the wane nowadays.

good thing a racehorse tipped to win.

good trot a run of good luck. Aussie slang from at least the 1940s.

good wicket an advantageous position. *He's on a good wicket.* Aussie slang since the 1910s.

goof a clumsy fool. Hence, as a verb, to **goof** or **goof up** is to slip up, botch or bungle. To **goof around** is to play the fool to entertain others. To **goof off** is to loaf. All American slang terms which we picked up in Oz in the 1960s.

go off **1.** of a party or similar event, to be thrilling. *The dance floor was really going off*, or *It was a great night, it really went off.* **2.** of the surf, to produce excellent waves. **3.** to vent anger volubly; to hit the roof. **4.** of an illegal establishment, to be raided by police. Aussie underworld slang dating from the 1940s. **5.** to be arrested by the police. **6.** of a racehorse, to make a proper run in a race after being previously held back to give an impression of poor form in order to obtain good odds. Aussie racing slang dating from the 1930s.

go off like a frog in a sock to really go off.

goofy **1.** stupid and clumsy; silly. **2.** pathetically amorous. *He's gone all goofy.* **3.** of a surfer, skater or snowboarder, left-footed. **4.** as a noun, a left-footer, as in, *He was the only goofy out in the surf.* Also called a **goofy-foot** or **goofy-footer**.

goog (pronounced with a short vowel, as in 'good') a kid's word for an egg. Also called a **googy** or a **googy-egg**. This word actually comes to us from Scotland where it was a *goggie*, which originates with the Scots Gaelic word *gogaidh*.

googie hut in the Australian Antarctic Territory, a type of fibreglass hut that resembles an egg in an egg cup.

googly (pronounced with a long vowel, like in 'goon') in cricket, a delivery bowled by a wrist-spinner which looks as if it will break one way but in fact goes the other; a bosie or wrong'un.

googol an enormously large number; zillions and squintillions. Technically a googol is 10 to the power of 100 (written as 1 with 100 zeros after it). Even bigger is a **googolplex**, which is 10 to the power of a googol (written as 1 with a googol of zeros after it). For maths terms, these two have popular appeal so that they turn up in quite unmathematical contexts. *When I go on holidays I take a googol of pictures.* There is also the pun on *google* as in *a googol of sites*.

gook **1.** a racist term for an Asian person. Especially common in the military, and widely used by soldiers. American slang dating back to the 1920s and picked up by Australian soldiers during the Korean and Vietnam wars. The American application of the word is much wider, including Filipinos, Pacific Islanders, southern Europeans, etc. **2.** as an adjective, of South-East Asian origin: *gook food, gook speak.* **3.** the hole aimed for in a game of marbles. This has a different origin to that of the previous two definitions.

goolie **1.** a small stone suitable for throwing. See **yonnie** for the full set of regionalisms. Probably from an Aboriginal language. **2.** a testicle. Originally British slang, dating back to the 1920s. Possibly from Hindi *golee* 'ball'. **3.** a glob of phlegm.

goom methylated spirits drunk by alcoholics. First recorded in the 1960s, and perhaps from an Aboriginal language.

goomie a person addicted to drinking methylated spirits.

goon **1.** originally, a flagon of wine. First appears in the 1980s. Some have suggested that it is from *flagoon*, a jocular pronunciation of *flagon*. They might be right. **2.** cheap cask wine; plonk. This meaning first appears in the 1990s. Also called **goonie**.

goona Aboriginal English for excrement. Also **guna** or **kuna**. From various Aboriginal languages. Also used as a verb meaning to defecate.

goon bag the silver bladder of wine inside a wine cask. Also called a **goonie bag** or **goon sack**.

goon bag soccer a game of drunken soccer played with an inflated silver bladder from a wine cask.

goon box a cask of cheap wine. Also called a **gooner**.

goonie party a backyard party at which the bladders of wine casks are hung from a Hills hoist and accessed by spinning the hoist around. Also called **goon-of-fortune**.

goon juice a drink made from soft drink mixed with cask wine.

goon monkey a lover of the goon; a cheap wine drinker.

goonya in SA, an Aboriginal English derogatory term for a white person. From an Aboriginal word meaning excrement.

goose **1.** a silly or foolish person; a simpleton. **2.** to poke someone between the buttocks, usually in fun and unexpectedly. Thus, an unexpected poke between the buttocks. Originally US slang dating back to the 1900s. Probably coming from the 19th century rhyming slang term *goose and duck* 'fuck'.

goose club in Qld, a fundraising raffle, with a number of small prizes donated by the organising groups.

goose juice booze.

goozy in WA and SA, a gob of phlegm spat out. Hence, covered in a slimy substance, as *There is something goozy in the fridge.* As a verb it means to spit. *The baby has goozied all over her bib.*

go postal to go crazy; to go berserk. Borrowed from the US, this originally referred to postal workers who went berserk and attacked their co-workers, often fatally.

gorby a chiefly Victorian word for a mass of nasal mucus ejected from the mouth. Elsewhere called a **gooby** or **golly**.

gorilla **1.** an ugly, brutal fellow. **2.** the sum of $1000. Because it is twice the size of a **monkey**.

gormless slow and stupid. From British dialect.

Gosford dog Aussie rhyming slang for 'wog', a person of Mediterranean background (see **wog** for more info). From Gosford, north of Sydney, where greyhound races are held.

Gosford skirt a very short skirt. So called because Gosford is close to The Entrance. Similar to the **Gosford boots**, knee-high boots, also close to the entrance.

gospel truth the absolute truth.

goss the latest news; the gossip. *What's the goss?*

goth a person belonging to the goth subculture, affecting a style and look inspired by Gothic novels, that is, pasty white skin, black (and royal purple) clothes, black hair, silver jewellery, and often dramatic black eye make-up and lipstick. All the rage in the 1980s and still to be found in most big cities, but now mostly a fashion statement.

go the knuckle to attack with the fists.

go the whole hog to go all the way.

go through **1.** to decamp; to bugger off; to abscond. Aussie slang dating from the 1940s. **2.** a crass term referring to a man having sex with a woman. *They all got pissed and went through her.*

go to the pack to decline or deteriorate. Dates back to World War I. Aussie variant of the older, originally British, slang phrase **go to the dogs**. Metaphorically referring to an old horse sent to the knackers to become dog meat.

government stroke the easy pace at which work is done, supposed to be typical of those working for the government; originally used specifically of convict road labourers.

govie in the ACT, a government-funded residence, usually offering low-cost accommodation. Also spelt **guvvie**.

go walkabout **1.** of an Aboriginal, to withdraw from white society by taking a journey on foot. Originally Aboriginal pidgin English, dating back to the 1920s. **2.** of a thing, to go missing. *My pen's gone walkabout again.*

go walkies to set out on a journey. Mimicking the usage by British dog trainer Barbara Woodhouse, famed for her amazingly successful television show.

gozunder **1.** a chamber-pot. It 'goes under' the bed. **2.** in cricket, a mullygrubber.

grab in Aussie Rules, a mark. It is interesting that a mark can be called a grab, but never a catch. Anyone using 'catch' immediately gives themselves away as a coming from a non-AFL background.

graft hard work. Aussie slang since the 1890s. Also as a verb, *We'd been grafting all day long.* Hence, **grafter**, a hard worker.

grand the sum of $1000. Originally American underworld slang.

Granny an affectionate name for the *Sydney Morning Herald*. Originally used derisively, back in 1851.

Granny Smith a variety of green apple, first produced in the Sydney suburb of Eastwood, by Maria Ann Smith. Commonly shortened to **granny**. *I had a granny at lunch today.*

grano granolithic concrete, a type of concrete with 7mm aggregate, used to surface floors, fill cavities, and the like.

grape cocky a winegrower.

grape on the business an interloper; an unwelcome person.

grass **1.** marijuana. Originally 1930s US slang. Came to Australia in the 1960s. **2.** to inform on a colleague; to dob in to the authorities. Also, **grass up**. Hence, **grasser**, an informer. **3.** among fishos, to land a fish.

grass castle a large mansion paid for from the proceeds of marijuana cropping.

grasshopper a derogatory term for a tourist.

gravel rash what you get from being a crawler. *He's covered in gravel rash from crawling to the boss.* In use since World War I.

graveyard chompers false teeth.

grease-ball a racist appellation for a person of Mediterranean or Latin-American origin. American slang dating back to the 1920s. Also in the form **greaser**. Never very common here.

greasies fish and chips.

greasy **1.** a shearer. 1930s Aussie slang. **2.** a disdainful or disapproving look. Short for **greasy eyeball**. **3.** a racist term for a Greek, Italian or other Mediterranean person.

greasy eyeball a disdainful or disapproving look. Also called a **hairy eyeball**.

greasy spoon a cheap and nasty hamburger joint, or the like.

great Australian adjective the word *bloody* used as an intensifier; once ubiquitous in Australian colloquial speech. So called since the 1890s.

great nut in cricket, a very good delivery.

the Great South Land Australia, Down Under, this wide brown land of ours. A translation of the 16th century Latin term *terra australis*.

greeblies **1.** spermatozoa. **2.** germs.

Greek anal intercourse. Also called **Greek love**. Hence, to **go Greek** is to have anal sex.

green and gold the Australian international sporting colours. Proclaimed Australia's national colours by the Governor-General on 19 April 1984. Prior to that there were no official colours.

green baggy the Australian Test Cricket cap. More commonly called the **baggy green**.

green can a can of Victoria Bitter beer. As opposed to a **blue**, **red**, **white** or **yellow can** (see entries).

green death Victoria Bitter beer – according to those who hate it.

green giant a plastic $100 note.

greengrocer a type of green cicada.

greenie **1.** a conservationist. Now used worldwide, but originally an Australian coinage back in the 70s. Although the association of green with environmentalism was first made in German politics of the early 1970s, and first appeared in English in the name *Greenpeace*, the addition of *-ie* to form a noun was an Australian contribution. **2.** any of various green parrots, especially the scaly-breasted lorikeet. **3.** a green yabby. **4.** in the navy, an electrician. **5.** among surfers, a large unbroken wave. **6.** a lump of mucus ejected or picked from the nose.

greenlight in police slang, to allow an illegal activity to take place in return for bribery.

green room among surfies, the tube of a breaking wave.

the green sponge a nickname for Macquarie Island – an Australian subantarctic possession lying about 1370 km southeast of Tasmania.

Gregory Peck **1.** rhyming slang for 'cheque'. **2.** rhyming slang for 'neck'.

gremmie a derogatory term for a young inexperienced surfer. From **gremlin**, in the same sense. Both US and Aussie surfie slang dating from the 1960s. Also called a **grommet**.

grenade a small bottle of beer, smaller than a stubby; a throwdown.

grey **1.** a double-headed or double-tailed penny. Used to cheat in the game of two-up. First recorded in an Australian convict slang glossary from 1812. **2.** a grey kangaroo.

grey death in prison, weak, pathetic stew.

grey ghost a parking inspector. Used in NSW, Vic and SA. In Vic they are also called **grey meanies**. See **brown bomber** for the full set of regionalisms.

greylead in Vic, a lead pencil.

grey nomad an older person, often retired, who travels around the country in a caravan or motorhome.

grey nurse an old paper $100 note. From its colour. Now replaced by the **green giant**.

grid a bicycle. Old Aussie slang dating from the 1920s.

grief the leafy parts of a marijuana stash, after all the buds and heads have been smoked. Apt Aussie rhyming slang for 'leaf'.

grievous bodily harm the designer-drug gamma hydroxybutyric acid; GHB.

grill an Australian of Greek or Italian background. An old racial slur referring to the fact that after World War II many immigrants from southern Europe opened hamburger and fish and chip shops. Not heard much any more.

grizzleguts a person given to complaining.

grog **1.** alcohol, particularly cheap alcohol. Aussie slang since the 1830s. Originally 18th century British naval slang referring to watered down rum. 'Old Grog' was the nickname of Admiral Vernon (from *grogram*, the material his cloak was made of) who in 1740 ordered water to be issued with sailors' pure spirits. **2.** a glass of some alcohol drink. *I'm just going to have a few grogs with the old mates.* In this sense since the 1960s.

grogan a piece of excrement; a turd. A tops bit of Aussie kids' slang dating back to the 1980s at least. Origin unknown.

grog artist a heavy drinker.

grog bog a particularly noisome excrement produced the morning after a night of heavy drinking. Affectionately called a **groggy**. See **after grog bog** for more synonyms.

grog on to take part in a piss-up.

grog shop a shop selling alcohol.

grommet a derogatory term for young inexperienced surfer. Also shortened to **grom** or **grommie**. Aussie slang at least since the

1980s. Now also used by snowboarders for novice snowboarders. Also called a **gremmie**.

gronk a fool or idiot.

groover **1.** a person who is cool; a groovy person. **2.** a person grooving to music. Hence, **groovers and shakers**, dancers.

groovy **1.** excellent, cool. Also, stylish, fashionable. Originally jazz slang from the US, then associated with the hippie movement of the 1960s. Became a bit passé after that, but has recently become an acceptably cool word again. **2.** of music, having a good groove; danceable.

grope to fondle sexually; to feel up. Venerable slang dating back to the 14th century. Hence, as a noun, an act of sexual fondling. From the 19th century. The phrase **go the grope** is an Aussie original since the 1950s.

Groper a West Australian. A derogatory term from as far back as the 1890s. A shortening of **Sandgroper**. Hence, **Groperland** is Western Australia. See **Cornstalk** for similar terms of derision for people from other states.

gross disgusting or revolting. A 1980s borrowing from US Valspeak. Commonly used as an exclamation. *Ooh, gross!*

gross out to disgust.

gross-out something disgusting.

grot **1.** a filthy person. **2.** filth. *Wipe that grot off.* **3.** a schoolkid's word meaning to spit on someone.

grotty dirty, filthy, squalid. Originally British slang from the 1960s, and apparently originally Liverpool slang. Perhaps The Beatles had something to do with the spreading the word since the earliest record comes from the Beatles movie *A Hard Day's Night*, which was released in 1964, at the height of Beatlemania, and was watched by millions of Beatles fans the world over.

ground lice sheep.

group grope an orgy.

groupie **1.** a spunky young thing who has sex with members of a pop or rock group. British slang of the 1960s. Originally referring to a young woman who travelled with, and made herself sexually available to, the male members of a rock group, but nowadays also used of males, and with reference to either hetero- or homosexual sexual relations. **2.** a fanatic fan who goes to every gig.

group stoop a gang bang.

grouse **1.** Aussie slang for very good. *We had a grouse time, but it's back to work now.* Been around since the 1920s, and still very much in favour. Origin unknown. Can also be used as a noun, as in *My new car is the grouse.* **2.** in prison, tobacco that isn't jail-issue – in other words, good quality tobacco.

grouter to **come in on the grouter** is to arrive after the work's finished, either through luck or contrivance. Laying the grout is the last job to get done when tiling. Hence, to be lucky, to have things fall your way; to take advantage of an opportune circumstance. Used in a disparaging way by those who haven't had the luck. *Have you noticed how the bludger always manages to come in on the grouter?*

growl a crass term for the vagina. From *growl and grunt*, rhyming slang for 'cunt'. Recorded in Aussie slang dating from the 1940s. Also heard as **growler**. To **growl out** or **go the growl** is to feel a woman up. As a verb, to **growl** is to perform oral sex on a woman.

grub **1.** food or victuals. Old slang from the 17th century. **2.** a non-union worker who enjoys benefits provided by the union.

grumblebum a cantankerous whinger.

grumpy bum a person who is always grumpy.

grundies Aussie rhyming slang for 'undies'. Short for **Reg Grundies**.

grunt **1.** power; strength; of an engine, torque. Hence, a **grunty** engine is one that is very powerful. **2.** military slang for an infantry soldier.

gubba a derogatory word used by Aboriginals for a white person. Commonly shortened to **gub**. Origin uncertain, but perhaps related to *gubment*, an Aboriginal pronunciation of 'government'.

guddiyah a variation of the word **kartiya** (see entry).

guff foolish talk; nonsense.

guido a guidance officer or school counsellor.

guilts feelings of remorse. *I've got the guilts about not writing.*

gullie in the Riverina, a derogatory word for a westie, bevan or bogan.

gully-raker **1.** a cattle thief who combs wild country and steals unbranded stock. **2.** a stockwhip. **3.** in Qld and NSW, a thunderstorm bringing heavy rain.

gully wind a strong evening wind that blows from the Mount Lofty Ranges over Adelaide.

gumby **1.** a fool or nong. Probably after the animated plasticine children's TV character Gumby, whose name no doubt comes from the Yorkshire dialect word *gomby* 'a silly fellow'. **2.** a calf raised on the bottle. **3.** in Vic, a public transport employee. Their uniform was green, as was Gumby. **4.** in the Antarctic, a construction worker.

gum digger a dentist. Also called a **gum puncher**.

gumi in the Riverina, a raft made predominantly of tyre inner tubes. There is a **gumi race** down the Murrumbidgee River held annually. Interestingly, the word *gumi* is pidgin English for rubber.

gummies gumboots.

gumpy military slang for a chocolate bar.

Gumsucker a disparaging appellation for a person from Victoria dating from the 1840s. This originally referred to the habit of chewing on the gum exuded from wattle trees. See **Cornstalk** for similar terms of derision for people from other states.

gumtree the beautiful Australian eucalypt, so named from their gummy sap. A term first used by James Cook in 1770. Used in some slang expressions, namely, **up a gumtree**, in all sorts of strife, and **mad as a gumtree full of galahs**, stark raving bonkers.

gumtree mail a system of letter delivery in remote bush areas, whereby the sender places a letter is a cleft stick from a gumtree, and waits for a passing train. The driver or guard snatches up the letter as the train passes, thereby getting it into the mailbag.

gun **1.** a champion shearer. Aussie slang since the 1890s. Hence a champion at any endeavour. **2.** a large surfboat for riding big waves. **3.** to rev an engine; hence, to drive at great speed.

guna a variation of the word **goona** (see entry).

gundy see **no good to gundy**.

Gundy the southern Qld township of Goondoowindi. Most non-locals mispronounce the first syllable of the town with a long 'oo' rather then the correct 'u'.

gunge **1.** marijuana. A colloquial variant of **ganja**. **2.** filth; disgusting muck. Hence, **gungy**, as in, *What a gungy house, you couldn't set foot in it.*

gunna a person who is always 'gunna' do something, but never gets around to it.

gunyah an Aboriginal shelter made from bark and boughs; a humpy. From Dharug, the extinct language of the Sydney region. Hence, any rough shelter or hut in the bush.

gunzel a railway enthusiast. Originally a derogatory term for someone who was *too* enthusiastic, but now used as a term of self-pride. Apparently started at the Sydney Tramway Museum with reference to Mexican (i.e. Victorian) railway fans who were taking their hobby a little too seriously. It is actually an application of the US slang term *gunsel* 'a fool', ultimately from Yiddish *gendzel* 'gosling'.

gut a brief in police slang, to remove vital documents from a brief in order to foil successful prosecution. Compare **pull a brief**.

gutless wonder an immense coward. Aussie slang since the 1950s, though used in America since the 1930s.

guts **1.** essential information. *We need to get to the guts of the matter.* Digger slang from World War I. Hence, the **good guts** is useful info, the good oil, the drum. **2.** in two-up, the amount of money bet by the spinner which must be covered before any side bets can be made. **3.** to **drop your guts** is to fart.

guvvie flat the same as a **govie** (see entry).

guy a fellow or bloke. Originally American slang dating back to the 19th century. Has been used in Australia since the 1930s, but did not become common until the 1970s. Since the 1980s it has been used by teenagers to refer to people of either sex, especially as in the plural, as in, *Hey you guys, wait up!*

guy-magnet a woman who is attractive to many men.

guy thing something that only males are concerned with or know about. The opposite to a **chick thing**.

guy-watch to ogle males.

gym junkie a person addicted to the gym.

gyno laconic Australian way of saying gynaecologist.

gyp **1.** to swindle, cheat or defraud. Generally only applied to a minor rip-off. **2.** a rip-off. *Don't waste your money on it, it's an absolute gyp.*

Gyppo an age-old racist term for an Egyptian. British slang has used *Gippy* since the 1880s, but this version with the *-o* suffix is recorded first in Anzac slang of World War I. Can also be spelt **Gippo**.

H heroin.

hacker **1.** a computer enthusiast who enjoys programming, exploring computer systems, and working out how to get beyond the supposed limitations of a system. **2.** a person who illegally accesses a computer system, especially with malicious intent. This meaning is now Standard English, but is deprecated by hackers who prefer to use the term **cracker** for a person who breaks computer security systems.

had the chad broken; ruined or wrecked; useless.

had the dick ruined, busted, worn out, wrecked, or, in other words, 'fucked'. Also found in the forms **had the rod** and **had the stick**, and euphemised to **had the Richard**, where Richard means Dick.

ha-ha pigeon a kookaburra. Since the 1930s.

hair dryer a hand-held police radar gun.

hair of the dog (that bit you) an alcoholic drink taken to relieve a hangover.

hair pie cunnilingus.

hairy armpit brigade a derisive term for radical feminists viewed collectively.

hairy chequebook sexual intercourse used by a woman as a payment. *I had to pull out the hairy chequebook.*

hairy eyeball a disdainful or disapproving look. Imagine an eye with a partially lowered eyelid. Also called a **greasy eyeball**.

hairy goat a poor racehorse. If a racehorse **runs like a hairy goat**, then it won't be winning any races. Aussie slang since the 1940s.

hairy leg in NSW, a railway fettler. See also **snake charmer** and **woolly nose**.

hairy Mary **1.** a hairy male homosexual. **2.** a kiwifruit.

half a mo! wait just a moment!

half caser old slang for half a crown. See **caser**.

half-inch rhyming slang for 'pinch', as in, steal. Originally British.

half-pie not fully; halfway. *He was half-pie serious.* An Aussie borrowing, from at least the 1970s, of NZ slang dating back to the 1910s. Possibly from Maori *pai* 'good'.

half spot the sum of $50.

half-tanked half-drunk. Compare **tanked**.

half your luck! Good on you! A compliment given since the 1930s upon someone else's good fortune. Actually short for 'I wish *I* had half your luck'.

hambone especially in the 1970s, a male striptease. *Phil did this king hambone on the kitchen table.* Also called a **hammie**.

hammer **1.** heroin. Short for *hammer and tack*, Aussie rhyming slang for 'smack'. **2.** also rhyming slang for 'back'. Thus if someone is **on your hammer**, then they are following you closely, or, when in a car, tailgating you. **3.** to drive at speed. *We were hammering up the freeway.* **4.** to beat comprehensively.

hammered drunk.

hammie **1.** the hamstring. *He's out with an injured hammie.* **2.** a male striptease; a hambone.

handbag an attractive male used by a woman as a showpiece when going out to social functions. Aussie woman's slang since the 1960s.

handball a common schoolyard game played with a tennis ball which is hit with the hands in a court, consisting usually of either four or six squares, drawn on the asphalt. The positions, in descending order of importance, are King, Queen, Jack, and Dunce for four squares, or Ace, King, Queen, Jack, Dunce and Double Dunce, for six squares. In Sydney also called **king ping**. The version with four squares also gets called **four square**.

handbrake a man's wife or girlfriend viewed as an obstacle to enjoyment. *Davo's not coming to the footy, he's got his handbrake on tonight.*

handbrakie a turn made in a car by slamming on the handbrake when driving at speed, and turning the steering wheel sharply; a handbrake turn.

hand grenade a small bottle of beer, smaller than a stubby; a throwdown.

hand job a manual bringing to orgasm of a male. Also affectionately called a **handie**.

handle **1.** a person's name. **2.** in NT, a beer glass with a handle, about the same size as a middy or pot (10 fluid ounces or 285 ml). Used in Australia since the 1940s, but much older in NZ where it is still prevalent.

handraulic operated by hand.

hands up among used-car sellers, an easy deal which did not involve bargaining.

hang **1.** to change course. *Hang a right at the post office.* **2.** to perform a bodily function: *hang a bog*; *hanging a piss.* **3.** to frequent; spend time in. *I'm going to hang in Indonesia for a while.* **4.** a place you frequent; a hang-out.

hanger a spectacular mark in Aussie Rules in which the player seems to magically hang suspended in the air.

hang five to ride a surfboard standing on the nose of the board with the toes of one foot over the edge.

hanging completely eager; dying for. *I'm hanging to see them when they make it to Sydney.*

hang shit on to denigrate.

hang ten to ride a surfboard while standing on the nose of the board with all your toes over the edge.

hang with spend time with someone.

happening **1.** superlatively good or cool; really going off. As in *This place is really happening*, or *What a happenin' jacket*. A **happening thing** is an event or venue which is currently the coolest thing going. Originally US slang from the 1970s. **2.** a roaring party or piss-up. Aussie slang dating from the 1970s.

happy as a bastard on Father's Day unhappy. There's nothing like Father's Day to remind the bastard of their fatherlessness. Classic Aussie saying since the 1950s.

happy as a pig in shit very happy; well contented.

happy as Larry extremely happy. Aussie slang dating from the 1900s. Just who the gladsome Larry was, and how he could have been happy enough to become a byword for joy, is unknown.

happy camper a person who is very pleased, but usually used with a negative to express just the opposite. *He was not a happy camper after he lost his licence.* From US slang of the 1980s.

happy chappie a male who is very pleased. Frequently used in the negative. *His wife left him and he's not a happy chappie.*

happy juice **1.** alcohol. **2.** any pain-relieving medicine in liquid form.

happy little vegemite a person in a good mood. *Look at the happy little vegemites working away in there.* First appears in the 1980s in this slang sense, originating in the well-loved advertising jingle for the spread Vegemite which first filled Australian air-waves back in 1954.

happy pill an anti-depressant drug.

the Harbour City Sydney.

hard case a highly individual person who will not conform to what others think; an incorrigible eccentric; also, a hard drinker. Good old Aussie slang dating back to the 1870s.

hard cheese! Tough luck! Originally British slang from the 1870s, but used in Oz since the 1910s. Similar to **stiff cheese!** (see entry).

hard doer a person who 'does it hard', but battles on bravely. Aussie slang since the 1910s.

hard graft hard work. Australians have been rolling up their sleeves and getting down to the hard graft since the 1870s.

Hardly Normal a jocular perversion of the department store name Harvey Norman.

hard-on an erect penis.

hard stuff **1.** spirits; hard liquor. An Aussie original dating from the 1830s. **2.** hard drugs.

hard word a fervent request. See entry for **put the hard word on**.

hard yakka good, solid, back-breaking work. See the entry for **yakka** for more information.

hard yards exacting work that is necessary in order to achieve some desired end. Originally a Rugby Union metaphor, thence used in wider sporting contexts, and now everywhere. *This diet will work provided you do the hard yards.*

Harold Holt Aussie rhyming slang for 'bolt', meaning flee. Referring to former Australian PM who disappeared while swimming in the ocean. Also simply shortened to **Harold** or **Harry**. Occasionally used as a rhyme for 'salt'.

harp a harmonica or mouth organ.

Harry High Pants a derisive nickname for anyone wearing their pants too high.

hash a preparation of the resin of marijuana. Originally US slang from the 1940s. Abbreviation of *hashish*, from Arabic.

hash cookies biscuits made with hashish in them.

hat rack **1.** a thin or scrawny animal, as a horse or cow. **2.** a very thin person.

hats off to... congratulations to... Recently popularised by Roy and HG, but this locution has been around in Oz since at least the 1940s.

hats ridiculous in army slang, a giggle hat.

hatter a lonely and eccentric bush dweller. Originally a miner who works alone rather than with a partner. Aussie slang dating from the 1850s. Perhaps from the old saying 'his hat covers his family', that is, he is a loner. But also influenced by 'mad as a hatter'.

have **1.** to have sex with someone. **2.** to fight someone. *I'll have you any day, ya big pussy.*

have a cow to become majorly upset. Generally used to admonish someone for overreacting. Brought to Australia by Bart Simpson.

have a go to make a gutsy effort. An Australian tradition. Often used to exhort someone who isn't having a go. A common cry when barracking, especially in the form *Have a go ya mug!*

have a good head for radio to have an unattractive head. Similarly **I've seen better heads on a glass of beer**.

have a good innings to have a long life or long and successful career.

have a shot at to attack verbally. *He had a shot at me about me swearing.* Aussie slang since the 1820s.

have by the short hairs to have someone at your mercy. Also commonly to **have by the short and curlies**. Both refer to pubic hair.

have had when Aussies 'have had' something, then they are totally fed up with it. *I've had this joint, I'm off to the pub.*

have hollow legs to have a prodigious appetite for food or alcoholic beverages.

have it off to have sex. Unromantic Aussie sexual slang since at least the 1960s.

have the painters in to have your menstrual period.

have tickets on yourself to have an inflated view of yourself. Aussie slang since the 1910s.

have your shit together to be in complete control.

Hawkesbury Rivers Aussie rhyming slang for 'the shivers'.

hawk the fork to work as a prostitute.

hay burner a horse, especially a racehorse. Aussie slang since the 1920s.

Hay, Hell and Booligal hot and uncomfortable places; places to be avoided. From the Banjo Paterson poem by this name. Hay and Booligal are towns on the plains of inland NSW.

he in kids' games, the player who must catch the other players; the person who is 'in'. The commonest term in SA, but also big in Vic and WA. See **it** for the full set of regional variations.

head **1.** a person who uses drugs regularly, especially hard drugs. **2.** the tops of the marijuana plant, having a higher concentration of drug-containing resin. *Got any good head?* **3.** fellatio. *He gives good head.*

head case a nutter.

head down and arse up busily working. Aussie slang since the 1940s.

head 'em **1.** in two-up, to make the coins land with heads upwards. The opposite of **tail 'em**. **2.** to play two-up. *He spends Sunday arvo headin' 'em down at Thommos.*

head honcho the boss; the person in charge. See **honcho**.

headie **1.** in two-up, a person who consistently bets on heads. As opposed to a **tailie**. **2.** a head job.

head job an act of fellatio. Originally US slang of the 1960s.

headless chicken to **run around like a headless chicken** is to act without rhyme or reason. A classic Australianism since the 1950s. Of course, even more Australian is to use the variant **headless chook**.

headless chookery extreme foolishness.

headlights the breasts. A twee blokey word from as far back as the 1940s. Nowadays commonly used to refer to erect nipples.

head like a... Someone with an ugly head is said to have a **head like a half-sucked mango**. Even worse is to have a **head like a half-sucked mango and a body like a burst sausage**. Other sad cases include a **head like a half-sucked**

cheezel, or a **head like a dropped meat-pie**. Still more include a **head like a racing tadpole**, a **head like a revolving mallee root**, a **head like a Turkish trotting duck**, and a **head like a busted sofa**. Man, there are some ugly heads out there! Compare **face like a...**.

head over turkey head over heels; arse over tit. An original Aussie variant dating from the 1910s.

head rush a sudden thrilling sensation in the head, as caused by certain drugs or a flood of adrenaline.

head serang the person in charge; the boss. Aussie slang dating from the 1910s. Sometimes spelt **sherang**. From an old term of the British Raj in India where it referred to the skipper of a native vessel. The word *serang* ultimately comes from Persian.

headshrinker a psychiatrist. Also called a **shrink**.

head swell a conceited person.

head-turner **1.** an attractive person. **2.** a shoplifter's accomplice who distracts staff.

healy another spelling of **heelie**.

heap an old dilapidated car.

heaps **1.** typical Aussie way of saying 'many'. *There will be heaps of people there.* **2.** used as an intensifier. *I will be heaps grateful*, or *She was heaps curious.* **3.** to **give someone heaps** is to bawl them out.

heap shit on to denigrate or criticise harshly.

heart-starter a cup of strong coffee or tea taken early in the day as a remedy for a hangover. Sometimes refers to **hair of the dog**.

heave to vomit. Hence, the act of vomiting. *I had a heave in the laundry.*

heave-ho a rejection; the toss. *Me girlfriend's just given me the old heave-ho.*

heaven on a stick something delicious, especially a sexually attractive person.

he can put his shoes under my bed any day a quaint phrase used by women to indicate that they are sexually attracted to a particular man. Pretty old-fashioned nowadays.

Hector a violent thunderstorm occurring almost daily over the remote Tiwi Islands north of Darwin during November and December.

hector protector in cricket, a hard protective covering for the genitals, worn inside the pants. Also, simply, the **hector**.

heel a despicable person; a cad, bounder or rotter. Originally US underworld slang for a double-crosser or sneak-thief.

heeler a blue heeler.

heelie obsolete Aussie underworld slang, a confidence trick, or the device by which a confidence trick or swindle is worked, such as the ballast in loaded dice, or the brake on a crooked roulette wheel. Also spelt **healy**. Perhaps an aspirated variant of **eelie** (see entry).

heifer a derisive term for a woman. Originally 19th century British slang.

heifer paddock a girl's school. Aussie slang since the 1880s.

height challenged short.

heiny a spelling of **hiney**.

helicopter a dragonfly.

hell **1.** the abode of the devil, evil spirits and damned souls. The potential destination of those who use about half the words in this dictionary! Formerly a powerful swearword, but now greatly reduced in force, though still in common use, especially as an intensifier, as in *Get the hell out of there!* People who cause great trouble are commonly said to be **from hell**, as in *the flatmate from hell*, or *the neighbours from hell.* **2.** in recent use, extremely good or excellent. *He had a hell card collection.*

hella among adolescents, exceedingly or terrifically; used as an intensifier, as in *hella good*, or *hella cool*. American 1980s slang recently adopted here.

hellish great, wonderful, excellent, as in *We went to this hellish resort*. Adolescent perversion of the usual meaning, on the pattern of *sick* and *wicked*.

hell man an aggressive, radical dude, especially a surfer or snowboarder. Also, in the feminine form, **hell woman**.

hello an interrogative expressing disbelief. *We were told that if we laminated our citizenship certificate it would become invalid. Hello?*

helluva a spelling of the phrase *hell of a*, used as an intensifier to denote a very good or extreme example of something. *We had a helluva good time.*

helm to be in charge of a project; specifically, to direct or produce a film.

helo a helicopter.

hen **1.** a fussy old woman. **2.** the bride-to-be when out on her hen's night.

Henry the Third rhyming slang for 'turd'. Originally British. Both **Richard the Third** and **William the Third** have been honoured in rhyming slang in precisely the same way. But, for some reason Edward and George have not.

hen's night **1.** a party, exclusively for women, thrown for the bride-to-be before the wedding day. Traditionally marked by such things as lots of drinking, obscene pranks, and buffy male strippers. The female counterpart of the **buck's night**. **2.** an evening on which a group of women have a night out together; a girls' night out.

hepatitis roll Vietnam War slang, a meat and salad roll bought at a local market. Also called a **heppo roll**.

heppo hepatitis.

herbs engine horsepower. *This car's got plenty of herbs.* Also, fuel supplied to the engine. *I gave it the herbs and took off like a rocket.* Aussie slang since the 1950s. Origin uncertain. Could it be alluding to herbs, meaning hay, fed to horses to give them energy, with a pun on *horse*power?

Hershey Highway the rectum as used in anal sex. An obvious Americanism from the brand of chocolate popular in the States. The Aussie term is of course **Vegemite Valley**.

hetero a dismissive term for a heterosexual person used by gay people. Also shortened to **het**.

he went mad and they shot him an expression to put off an inquirer when you are asked about a bloke and you don't know where he is.

Hexham grey a large and voracious species of mosquito found in the locality of Hexham, NSW.

hey-diddle-diddle **1.** Aussie rhyming slang for 'middle'. As in Aussie Rules. *He's dobbed it straight through the hey-diddle-diddle.* **2.** rhyming slang for 'piddle', as in urination. This meaning originally British.

hickey a haematoma caused by erotic sucking of the skin; a love bite.

hiddy extremely or completely. *I found this hiddy rare record at a sale.* From *hideously*.

hide effrontery or impudence. Unbeknown to most people, this is an Australian original, dating back to the 1900s. To have **more hide than Jessie** is to be supremely impudent. The Jessie in question was a well-loved elephant at Sydney's Taronga Zoo.

hide the sausage of a male, to engage in sexual intercourse. Also known as **hide the salami**.

hidey a common children's game in which some hide and others seek them. This term is more common in Vic, SA and WA. Generally called **hide-and-seek**, though sometimes **hide-and-go-seek**, which is particularly favoured in Tasmania.

high-diddle-diddle a variant of the rhyming slang term **hey-diddle-diddle** (see entry).

high flyer in Aussie Rules, an adept at taking high marks.

high jump **1.** in underworld slang, a higher court than a magistrate's court. As opposed to the **low jump** (see entry). To be **for the high jump** is to be up for trial, or to be up for some punishment or reprimand. **2.** execution by hanging.

the Hill **1.** a sloping area of open ground for spectators at Flemington Racecourse, Melbourne. **2.** a similar place that was formerly situated in front of the scoreboard at the Sydney Cricket Ground. **3.** a local name for Broken Hill.

Hill Ainslie in the ACT, a derisive term for the rather piddling Mount Ainsley.

Hills hoist the classic Australian rotary clothesline. Invented by Australian mechanic Lance Hill in 1945.

Hills people a Melbourne term for people who live in the Dandenong Hills.

hill trolley a Western Australian term for a billy cart.

himbo a superficial, stupid man, who is overly concerned with his looks. The male version of the **bimbo**.

hiney the buttocks or backside. Originally US slang, from *hindquarters* or *hinders*.

hip having inside knowledge, in the know; well-informed about current styles, fashionably smart and sophisticated, in fashion, up on what is cool. Now virtually synonymous with *cool*. US slang from the early 1900s where the word appears alongside its variant **hep**, which fell out of favour in the 1960s. Originally associated with jazz and swing music. Origin unknown. Source of the word **hippie**, who were originally 'hip', but now most hipsters would view hippies as dags.

hippie hop a style of hip-hop with new-agey lyrics and feel. Imagine blending the Mamas and the Papas with the Sugar Hill Gang.

hip-pocket nerve an imaginary nerve which is sensitive to demands for your money.

hipster someone who is hip; a cool person up with the latest.

hissy fit an attack of hysterics; a temper tantrum.

hit and giggle non-competitive tennis.

hit-and-run a game of kids' cricket with the rule that every time the ball is hit the person batting is obliged to run, regardless of whether they can be easily run out or not. No other children's game has spawned so many different names. **Hit-and-run** is the most common name throughout the country, closely followed by **tip-and-run**, and then, trailing by some distance, **tippety run** and numerous variations on that theme. Victorians are the odd ones out here, actually preferring the terms **tippety** and **tippety run**. In SA the two most common terms are **hit-and-run** and **tippy go** or **tippy-go-run**. Qld uses both **hit-and-run** and **tip-and-run**, but also favours the terms **tipsy** and **tipsy-run**. And in WA the most common term is **tip-and-run**, followed by **hit-and-run**. The less common terms, in no special order, are **nick-and-run**, **snick-and-run** and **tip-and-go**.

hitched married. From US slang dating back to the 1840s.

hit for six to confound or stun. A cricket metaphor.

hit on to make a pass at. Originally US slang of the 1950s.

hit the bottle to begin drinking immoderately; to get on the grog.

hit the hay to go to bed.

hit the road to begin a journey; to set out. Also, **hit the bitumen**.

ho a slut or bitch. An Americanism recently making its way to our fair shores via the medium of rap music. It is the American Black English pronunciation of the word *whore*, and is used, generally by teenagers, as an insult to a female with the suggestion of promiscuity. See **skanky ho**.

hock **1.** prison slang, a male who takes the active part in homosexual practices in prison, but does not consider himself homosexual. As opposed to a **cat** or **queen**, who take the passive role, and hence are regarded as unmasculine. Aussie slang since the 1940s. Origin unknown. **2.** pawn. *I put my stereo in hock.* Also, as a verb, to put in pawn. *He had to hock his watch.* This was originally slang, but now is virtually Standard English.

hock a loogie to spit out a ginormous golly.

hockey puck a urinal disinfectant lozenge.

hodad a swimmer who annoys or impedes surfboard riders. Originally 1960s Californian surfing slang. Origin unknown.

hoe into to attack a task with vigour; specifically, to eat with enthusiasm. *I was caught hoeing into a packet of chips.* Aussie slang since the 1930s.

hog **1.** a selfish, gluttonous person who takes more than their fair share. Hence, as a verb, to refuse to share. **2.** a large motorcycle, especially a Harley-Davidson.

hoist **1.** to throw or chuck. **2.** in underworld slang, to steal.

holding having a supply of ready cash. Especially common in the question **How are you holding?** meaning, 'How are you off for money?' Aussie slang since the 1920s.

hole **1.** a filthy, disgusting, boring, or otherwise objectionable place. **2.** any of certain apertures of the body, as the mouth, anus, or vagina. **3.** to **put a big hole in** something is to eat or drink a large proportion of it. *Well, I may not have finished it, but I put a big hole in it.*

Hollyweird Hollywood, USA, noted for its tolerance of weirdos.

hols holidays. Typical laconic Aussie abbreviation. Also called the **hollies**.

holy boon-boon! Good lord! Heavens above! Chiefly used in Queensland, where you can also find the expression **holy snapping duck-shit!** There are many variations on this theme, dating back to the 19th century, including the religious **holy Christ**, **holy Jesus**, **holy Moses**, **holy Mother** and **holy Mother of God**. One of the oldest of these is **holy Moses**, which has since been euphemised to **holy mackerel** and **holy moley** – both of which are originally American, but can be heard here. Another 19th century version was **holy smoke**, which is not uncommon in Australia. Of Australian origin seems to be **holy dooley**, which is also found in the form **hooley dooley**. Finally, there are the cruder expressions that employ very unholy expletives, such as **holy fuck** and **holy shit**.

Home an obsolete way of referring to England or the British Isles. Naturally with the first colonists this was an accurate use of the term, and their children would have learnt the term from their parents. But after a few generations it started being a bit silly. By the 20th century there were all these Aussies still calling England 'home' without ever having been there.

home and hosed of a racehorse, having won by a great length. Hence, finished successfully, done with. Aussie slang dating from the 1950s.

home boy a male member of a youth gang. Commonly in the shortened form **homey**. In Australia mostly an affectation in conscious imitation of American gangs as portrayed in rap music. Aussie home boys are generally at odds with westies and surfies.

home on the pig's back certain to succeed.

homer World War II slang for an injury bad enough for a soldier to be sent home, or at least away from the battlefront. Similar to the World War I **blighty**.

homers in the Australian Antarctic Territory, home-brewed beer.

homo homosexual; a male homosexual. Used disparagingly.

hon a term of endearment. Short for *honey*.

honcho the boss. Originally World War II slang, from Japanese.

honey 1. an extremely good-looking person. **2.** a term of endearment; darling. Also in the forms **honey bun**, **honey buns**, **honey bunch** and **honey pie**.

honey pot the vagina. One of the few pleasantly positive terms for it. A survival of a metaphor found in 18th century poetry.

honker a nose, especially a large one.

Honkie a person from Hong Kong.

honky a chiefly US Black English racist term for a white person. Not really used in Australia but well known here from American TV and movies. First appearing in the 1940s, honky is a variant of the US slang term *hunky*, originally meaning a person from eastern Europe, probably derived from *Hungarian*.

honky nut in WA, a type of large gum nut, especially from the marri gum. In use from at least the 1950s. Origin unknown.

the 'hood a neighbourhood; local area. From US slang, dating back to the 1960s there.

hoodie a jacket with a hood.

hooer a prostitute. In origin a representation of a dialect pronunciation of the word *whore*. By the 1950s in Australia it had become a general term of abuse applied to either sex. Little heard any more.

hoof the human foot. *Get your bloody big hoofs off it*. Venerable slang, dating back to old Bill Shakespeare.

hoofa in WA, a slang name for Aussie Rules.

hoof it to travel by foot.

hoo-ha a fuss; turmoil. Borrowed from US slang, originally from Yiddish.

hook 1. in horseracing slang, to illegally pull a horse to prevent it from winning when it could. **2.** to capture in marriage. *She's managed to hook a rich man.*

hooker a prostitute. An American term for prostitute not uncommonly used in Australia and not really slang any more. So called because they *hook*, that is, entice, their clients.

hooley dooley! an Australian exclamation of amazement or surprise. Also heard as **holy dooley**.

hoon 1. a hooligan or lout. The original sense, dating back to the 1930s. Origin unknown. **2.** a man who lives off the earnings of prostitution; a pimp or bludger. This usage dates back to the 1940s. **3.** a fast, reckless driver of a car, boat, or the like. Now the most common meaning. Thus, a speedy drive, as in *I'm going out for a hoon tonight*. As a verb, to drive fast and recklessly.

hoop 1. a jockey. So called from the circular bands of their silks. **2.** a circular pattern made on the ground by driving a car in a tight circle at high speed and causing the rear wheels to skid; a doughnut. *I've been cuttin' hoops in my ute.*

hoop snake a fictitious type of aggressive and venomous snake which is supposedly able to chase people by holding its tail in its mouth and rolling along swiftly like a hoop.

hooray typically Aussie way of saying farewell. Recorded in the *Bulletin* way back in 1898. Also used in NZ. In origin this is merely an alteration of the word 'hurrah', which has also been used as a farewell. Unique to Australia is **hooroo**, and its unaspirated version, **ooroo**. This can be reliably dated back to 1916.

hoot money. From NZ slang, from Maori *utu* 'payment'.

hooter the nose.

hooters a crass term for the breasts.

hophead a drunkard. A bit of 1950s slang that has pretty much disappeared now.

hop in for your chop to step up and take your fair share.

hop into to tackle with gusto. *Don't just stand there, hop into it!* Aussie slang dating from the 1930s.

Hopoate to goose the anus of another. After the famous goosing activities of Rugby League player John Hopoate.

hopper a kangaroo, wallaby or the like.

hoppo bumpo a kids' game of hopping on one leg and trying to knock over other players similarly disadvantaged. Played by Aussie kids since at least the 1950s.

hops beer. Aussie slang since the 1930s. Hence, **on the hops**, on a drinking binge.

horizontal folk dancing sexual intercourse. Also known as the **horizontal hula**.

horizontally challenged fat or obese.

horn **1.** the telephone. Originally US slang from the 1940s. **2.** an erect penis. Something that is extremely arousing to the male is said to be able to **put a horn on a jellyfish**.

hornbag someone who is sexually attractive and active. Aussie slang dating from the early 1980s.

horny sexually excited; randy. US slang recorded as early as 1826. Even earlier was the now obsolete term *horn-mad*, dating back to the 18th century.

horrie in surfing, a large and dangerous wave. Also known as a **hozzo**.

horse users' slang for heroin. Originally US, from the 1950s.

horse bite a stinging slap to the skin, usually someone else's bare legs, with a cupped hand. In use by schoolkids. In WA called a **camel bite**.

horse's doover a jocular mispronunciation of 'hors d'oeuvre'. Aussie slang since the 1970s.

horse's hoof rhyming slang for 'poof', that is, a gay man. An Aussie original. Commonly shortened to **horse's**. Unlike 'poof', this is generally used in a fun way.

horsey a jump into water with one leg tucked under your arms and hugged into the chest and the other extended straight out. Also called a **banana**, **can opener** or **peg leg**.

hospital pass a pass to a player who is under imminent threat of being crash-tackled. In Aussie Rules, when the ball is kicked high and straight up in the air it is called a **hospital kick**.

hostie an air hostess. An Aussie abbreviation from the 1960s.

hot **1.** sexually attractive or stimulating; spunky or horny. **2.** fashionable and exciting; cool. **3.** performing well; peaking. *The bassist is really hot tonight*. **4.** recently stolen or otherwise illegally obtained. **5.** of a person, wanted by the police. **6.** the latest and freshest. *The hot news is he's getting the sack.*

hot pot in horseracing, a hot favourite. Racing slang since the 1900s.

hots to have the **hots** for someone is to have a strong sexual attraction to them.

hot shit **1.** a proficient person; an expert. *So you think you're hot shit, do you?* **2.** an expression of enthusiasm or excitement.

hot-shot **1.** exceptionally proficient. *He's engaged a hot-shot lawyer*. Hence, an exceptionally proficient person. **2.** to inject someone with heroin laced with some dangerous chemical in order to cause injury.

hot stuff **1.** a sexually exciting person. **2.** something or someone of great excellence or interest.

hottie **1.** a hot-water bottle. **2.** a total hornbag.

hot to trot raring to go.

hot-wire to start a car using a wire to bypass the starting key.

the House a local nickname for Parliament House, Canberra. Also called **the House on the Hill**.

the house that Jack built a VD clinic.

how embarrassment! How embarrassing! A jocular use of a common grammatical error made by small children or second-language speakers. *I introduced her as Lena instead of Nina – how embarrassment!*

how're you going? typical Aussie form of greeting. Does not require a precise answer. It's been in use since the 1930s at least. Another common form is **how's it going?** Or, more recently, **how're you travelling?** Elsewhere in the world they say 'How are you?'

how's it hanging? How are you? A greeting generally used among men. Literally with reference to the male genitalia. Also in the form **how are they hanging?** or **how's your left testicle?**

how would you be? used as a greeting this is equivalent to 'How are you?'

howzat in cricket, an appeal by the fielding side to the umpire to declare the person batting out.

hoy **1.** to throw. **2.** a call. *I'll give the kids a hoy.* **3.** a game of chance, similar to bingo, in which playing cards are used.

hozzo among surfies, a wave that is large and dangerous. Ockerised version of the word *horror*. Also known as a **horrie**.

hubba hubba an exclamation of admiration for a sexually attractive person, generally used leeringly by males, but often more comically than seriously. A borrowing from the US.

hubby husband. Venerable slang dating back to the 17th century.

Huey a jocular name for the powers above used when encouraging a heavy rainfall, or good snow or surf. *Send her down, Huey!* or *Whip 'em up, Huey!* Also spelt **Hughie**. Aussie slang since the 1910s.

hum to really stink. *God, those footy socks really hum.*

humbug **1.** nonsense. Venerable slang from the 18th century. **2.** to pester or annoy. **3.** to cadge or beg.

humdinger a person or thing remarkable of its kind. Originally US slang from the 1900s, but in Australia since at least the 1920s.

hump **1.** to have sexual intercourse. Originally 18th century British slang. Hence, as a noun, an act of sexual intercourse; a sexual partner; a person rated on the sexual performance. **2.** to carry. This one is Aussie, dating back to the 1850s. *He wandered up the hill humping a sack of potatoes.*

hump the bluey to live the life of a swagman, carrying a swag and seeking work.

humpy any rough or temporary dwelling; a bush hut. Originally an Aboriginal dwelling. The word comes from the language Yagara of the Brisbane region.

humungous of huge size or extent. A borrowing from the States that became popular in the 1980s.

Hun in both World Wars, a disparaging term for a German soldier, or Germans in general.

hung of a male, possessed of a large penis; well-hung.

hungry bum a backside in pants that have crept up into the butt cleft.

hunk a solid, well-built, sexually attractive male. Recorded in America as far back as the 1940s. Hence, **hunky**, virilely handsome.

hunky-dory perfectly satisfactory; splendid. Commonly abbreviated to **hunky**. Originally US slang from the 1860s. Apparently introduced by a popular variety performer of the day named Japanese Tommy, who derived it from the name of a street or bazaar in Tokyo.

hurdy-gurdy a merry-go-round.

hurl to vomit. Hence, an act of vomiting. Aussie slang dating from the 1960s.

hurry-up an urging to action. *Go and give them a hurry-up.* Also called a **hurry-on**.

husband beater a very long, narrow, loaf of bread. Conversely also called a **wife beater**.

hush money a bribe to keep silent about something.

hydro **1.** in Tas, short for the Hydro-Electric Commission. Hence, the power supplied them. The **hydro bill** is the electricity bill. **2.** hydroponically grown marijuana.

hydro pole in Tas, a power pole.

hyge hydroponically grown marijuana. A shortened form of *hydroponic.*

hyper over-stimulated or over-excited. An abbreviation of *hyperactive.* Also found in the form **hypo**.

the Hypodermic in Canberra, the Telstra Tower.

I

ice **1.** a crystallised form of methamphetamine hydrochloride smoked like crack; shabu. **2.** diamonds. Originally US underworld slang.

iceberg a regular winter swimmer. An Australian institution since the 1930s.

ice-cold a cold beer. *Let's have a few ice-colds before the game.*

ice-cream licker among used-car sellers, a person who has no intention of buying; a tyre-kicker.

ice-cream sandwich an ice-cream wafer. The common term in WA, but also found in all other states.

ice queen a woman who is extremely cold towards anyone making romantic advances.

ickle a childish way of saying 'little'. *Poor ickle diddums.*

identity an odd, interesting or well-known person; a 'character'. An Australianism since the 1870s. The **oldest identity** is the oldest person in a community.

idiot box a television set.

idiot lights warning lights on a dashboard.

-ie **1.** a suffix used originally to create affectionate diminutives, as *doggie*, a dog; *littlie*, a child. This is common throughout all Englishes but in Australia we have really taken to it and use it to create slangy forms of ordinary words where the sense of smallness is not present, such as *Aussie*, an Australian; *brickie*, a bricklayer; *budgie*, a budgerigar; *conchie*, a conscientious objector; *footie*, football; *goalie*, a goalkeeper; *mozzie*, a mosquito; and *truckie*, a truck driver. Often spelt **-y**, but in this dictionary the *-ie* form has been preferred for simplicity's sake. **2.** used to form colloquial versions of place names, as *Charnie*, Charnwood, *Crowie*, Crows Nest, *Lonnie*, Launceston, *Winnie Hills*, Winston Hills. See the entry at **-o** for more information

iffy dubious or suspect. *The deal is a bit iffy.* Hence, unsure or undecided. *I was a bit iffy about it.*

if it moves, shoot it – if it doesn't, chop it down a jocular summing up of the Australian attitude to clearing and settling the land.

if it was raining palaces I'd be hit on the head by the dunny door the great Aussie cry bewailing your misfortune and chronic bad luck. First appears in the 1950s. There are many variations on this theme – such as **if it was raining soup I'd have a fork**, and the wonderful **if it was raining virgins I'd be locked in the dunny with a poofter.**

Ikey a racist term for a Jewish person. Originally British slang from the 1860s. Also in the form **Ikey-Mo**. From the common names Isaac and Moses.

I kid you not I am speaking the truth, no bullshit.

illywhacker a con artist or swindler. Dates back to underworld slang of the 1940s. Literally, a person who **whacks the illy** (see entry).

imaginitis the problem of having an overactive imagination. Many panic attacks can be put down to imaginitis.

I'm all right Jack an expression of selfish complacency on the part of the speaker. Used to stereotype a society where everyone is out for what they can get with no regard to others.

imbo a fool or imbecile.

impro improvisation.

imshi a word used by Aussie soldiers in both World Wars to mean 'go away'. They originally picked the word up from Arabic when stationed in Egypt during World War I.

in **1.** in kids' games, the player who must catch the other players. See **it** for the full set of regional variations. **2.** among adults, assured of sexual success. *I'm definitely in with the redhead.*

in a quander undecided, confused. *I'm in a quander and need some advice.* Jocular back-formation from the regular English 'quandary'.

in a shit in a bad mood.

inbreeder a derogatory term for a person from a remote area.

incoming a cry used to warn that something thrown is approaching. A bit of military jargon picked up from war movies.

indeedy certainly. *Yes, indeedy, here we are.* Also in the form **indeedy-do**.

Indo a dismissive term for Indonesia, or a person from Indonesia. Aussie slang since the 1950s.

Indro laconic local way of saying Indooroopilly, a suburb of Brisbane.

ink booze. *He's been on the ink.*

inked drunk, intoxicated. Aussie slang since the 1890s.

in like Flynn assured of consummating a sexual encounter. Occasionally used in a non-sexual way to mean easily successful in a particular enterprise. Referring to Australian Hollywood actor Errol Flynn, notorious for his real-life sexual adventures. Interestingly this term has been used in the US since the 1940s, but only in the non-sexual sense.

in more shit than a Werribee duck a peculiarly Victorian phrase meaning in deep shit. For the information of non-Melburnians, the Melbourne sewerage treatment works are located in the suburb of Werribee.

in more trouble than Speed Gordon in dire straits. For more information see the entry for **Speed Gordon**.

innie a recessed belly-button; a navel that goes in, as opposed to an **outie**. Hence, a person with such a navel.

innos in schoolyard games, a call claiming that an interference occurred and upset play, thus requiring a restart of play. In some playgrounds it is **intos** – both a shortening of the word *interference*.

insane among adolescents, fantastic, wonderful, terrific. See **mad**.

inside in prison.

intestinal fortitude strength of will; guts.

in the altogether in the nude; naked as a newborn babe.

in the buff naked.

in the chair being the person buying the drinks.

in the doghouse in disgrace; in trouble; unpopular. American slang from the 1920s.

in the nick in the nude; naked. Also, **in the nuddy**.

in the pudding club pregnant.

in the shit in trouble. Also, **in deep shit**, in deep trouble.

in the wars going through a period of trouble, illness, or the like.

intro an introduction.

invo an invitation. *I cracked it for an invo to Parliament House.* Also called an **invite**. *I can't come 'cause I didn't get an invite.*

in your dreams! not on your life!

in-your-face confronting.

Ippo the city of Ipswich, just west of Brisbane. Also known as **Ippie**.

Irish **1.** illogical, like the Irish in Irish jokes. *Sorry that was pretty Irish of me.* People who use this term for some reason don't think they are being derogatory. **2.** if you **get your Irish up**, then you become enraged.

Irish as Paddy's pigs very Irish in character.

Irish curtains cobwebs.

iron out to flatten a person.

iron pony a motorcycle.

irrits a feeling of annoyance or irritation. *That bastard really gives me the irrits.*

the Isa the north-west Qld town of Mount Isa.

is the Pope a Catholic? a rhetorical question to emphasise an affirmative. *Do you like beer? Is the Pope a Catholic?*

it **1.** in kids' games, the player who must catch the other players. Other terms are **in**, **he** and **up** and there is some regional variation in this set. The most common term in all states, except SA, is **it**, by a big margin. In NSW, ACT and Tas, the second most common term is **in**, whereas in Vic and WA it is **he**. Only in SA is **he** the most common form. The use of **up** is a Qld specialty, though it has been recorded in Tas as well. **2.** sexual intercourse. **3.** sex appeal. **4.** the one chosen for a specific task, job, etc. *Okay, you're it.*

Italian lawn great slabs of concrete that commonly fill the front or back yards of the homes of people of Mediterranean background. Also called **Lebanese lawn**.

item If two people are an item, then they are involved in a romantic relationship.

Itie a disparaging term for an Italian. Also spelt **Eyetie** (see entry).

it isn't over till the fat lady sings the outcome is unknown until the end. An Americanism adopted here in 1990s, reputedly coined by San Antonio sports editor Dan Cook in 1978.

it's all good a recent, faddish way of saying that everything is bonzer. Borrowed from the US of course.

jack **1.** venereal disease. Aussie slang since the 1940s. In origin from *jack in the box*, rhyming slang for 'pox'. **2.** a police officer; a police detective. World War I Aussie slang. Little heard these days. **3.** nothing. *I don't know jack about it*. A shortening of **jack shit**. **4.** underworld slang for a double-headed penny. **5.** to increase. *The swell jacked again mid-afternoon*. **6.** among druggies, to flush blood in and out of a hypodermic needle in order to get the last remnants of the drug in the syringe. **7.** in military slang, deserving contempt for lack of effort or fairness; slack; shithouse.

Jack and Jill rhyming slang for 'bill' (what you're up for at a restaurant). Also, for 'pill' (the contraceptive), 'dill' (a fool), and 'till' (the cash register variety).

jackass the kookaburra. An old term dating back to 1805. Referring to the bird's loud braying call. Also called the **laughing jackass**.

jacked-up infected with venereal disease.

jackeroo an apprentice station hand on a sheep or cattle station, especially one who wishes to learn how to manage a property. As a verb, to work as jackeroo. *He's jackerooing in Queensland this year*. In use since the 1840s. The suggestion of an Aboriginal origin for this word is unfounded. Perhaps it is a blend of kangaroo with the male name Jack.

jack it up of a male, to enter a woman.

jack jumper the Tasmanian name for a type of aggressive bull ant whose bite is sometimes fatal. Elsewhere called **hopper ants** or **jumper ants**.

Jack Lang Australian rhyming slang for 'Australian slang'. Jack Lang was a Labor premier of NSW twice in the 1920s and 1930s.

Jacko **1.** the kookaburra. Also known as **Jacky**. **2.** in World War I, a Turkish soldier.

jack of fed up with; sick and tired of. Aussie slang since the 1890s.

jack off of a male, to masturbate.

jack shit nothing. *We owe you jack shit*. Originally US slang of the 1960s.

Jack the dancer Aussie rhyming slang for 'cancer'.

Jack the painter a strong green tea which discolours utensils, formerly used in the bush.

Jack the Turk obsolete Gallipoli slang for a Turkish soldier.

jack up **1.** to refuse or resist; to be uncooperative. Aussie slang since the 1890s. **2.** to raise or increase something. *They had been jacking up their prices*.

Jacky a nickname given to Aboriginal men by white people. In full it was **Jacky Jacky**. Hence the phrase **to sit up like Jacky**, to sit up in a cheeky posture.

Jacky Howe a navy or black sleeveless woollen singlet traditionally worn by labourers and bushmen. Named after John Robert Howe, world champion shearer of 1892.

jaffa **1.** in cricket, a very good delivery. After the proprietary name for the well-loved orange-flavoured chocolate lollies. **2.** mining slang for *Just Another Fucking Field Assistant*. Actually this acronym can be used for many thing, like *Just Another Fat Fucking Arsehole*, or *Just Another Fucking Accountant* (you don't have to worry about using both f's). In NZ it is commonly used to stand for *Just Another Fucking Aucklander*. In the Australian Antarctic Territory, it is used derisively for *Just Another Fucking Academic*, as opposed to a labourer or tradesman. An alternative term is **jafo**, *Just Another Fucking Observer*.

jaffle a type of circular toasted sandwich cooked in a **jaffle iron**, that is, a double-sided hinged pie-shaped iron mould with a long handle for holding over a hotplate or fire. Good tucker this. This is a generic use of a brand name.

jaffy any annoying first year student at a tertiary institution. Standing for *Just Another Fucking First Year*.

jag a drinking binge. Hence, any binge or sustained activity, as an *eating jag*, or a *fishing jag*.

jail bait a girl or boy below the legal age of consent.

jake **1.** all right. *She'll be jake, mate.* Originally US slang. Origin unknown. In World War I Aussie soldiers came up with their own version of this word, namely **jakeloo**. This has sadly died out now. **2.** a toilet. Age-old slang. In the 16th century it was *jackes*, probably from the male name *Jakes* or *Jacques*, similar to the modern use of *John* for a dunny.

jam tart a spunky young woman. Originally rhyming slang for 'sweetheart'. 19th century British slang that survived in Australia up until the 1960s.

Jane Doe a name used to refer to any unknown or unspecified woman who is dead or unconscious. The female counterpart of the **John Doe**.

Jap a shortening of Japanese, used as a noun or adjective. Used in a racist or contemptuous manner, especially during World War II. Upon being served terrible food Aussies might be heard to say **I wouldn't feed it to a Jap on Anzac Day**.

Japanese safety boots a pair of thongs. Also called **Chinese safety boots**.

Jap crap Japanese-made cars.

Japper a derogatory term for a Japanese motorcycle.

jar **1.** a glass of beer. *Had a few too many jars last night*. **2.** especially among schoolkids, to embarrass or upset someone with an insult, witty comeback, or cutting remark. Also, to fool someone or suck them in. *Ha, ha, jarred you severely!*.

jarrah jerker in WA, a timber-getter or other bush worker.

J Arthur an act of masturbation. Short for *J. Arthur Rank*, rhyming slang for 'wank'. Originally British.

Jatz crackers the testicles. From rhyming slang for the 'knackers'. Aussie slang since at least the 1990s.

jaw breaker **1.** a hard word to pronounce. **2.** a large, hard or sticky sweet.

jay a marijuana cigarette. From the first letter of *joint*.

Jeff in Victoria, to treat someone or something in the manner of Jeff Kennett, Liberal state premier from 1992 to 1999. Thus, to downsize, to reduce funding to, or to scrap an institution, government department, or the like; to retrench or fire staff; or generally, to ruin or destroy in a heartless and unfair way; to fuck over. *Our hopes of getting a fair wage deal have been Jeffed.* Occasionally people have used to **Kennett**.

Jeff's Shed in Vic, a derisive name for the Melbourne Exhibition Centre on the south bank of the Yarra.

jelly blubber a jellyfish.

jelly cake lamington-style cake rolled in half-set pink jelly and coconut, sometimes with a cream filling. Also called a **pink lamington**.

jerk an annoying, stupid person; a prize wally or nong. First recorded in US slang of the early 20th century. Perhaps originally meaning a male masturbator.

jerk off to masturbate. Originally British sexual slang of the Victorian era.

jerk-off **1.** an act of male masturbation. **2.** a male masturbator; hence a fool, idiot or wanker.

jerk the gherkin of a male, to masturbate.

jerry **1.** a chamber-pot. Thought to come from *jeroboam* a very large wine bottle, though this is just idle speculation. If you are **full as a family jerry**, then you are completely full, especially of alcohol. **2.** an old person. A shortening of *geriatric*, and hence also spelt **geri**. **3.** If you **jerry to** something, or **take a jerry to** it, then you understand it or come to a realisation about it. Been around since the late 1890s; origin unknown. **4.** During both World Wars a German was known as a **Jerry**. Probably from *Ger*man.

Jerusalem screw a brutal prison warder. In World War I the British in Palestine trained Aussies in the art of breaking really tough prisoners.

Jesus bird the comb-crested jacana or lily-trotter. So called because it 'walks on water'. Also called the **Christ bird**.

Jesus freak an overtly enthusiastic and obtrusive Christian.

Jesus handle a fixed handle inside a vehicle cabin, grabbed by passengers when in fear of their lives.

jet to leave or get going. *Let's jet!*

jew typical Aussie shortening of the *jewfish*. Also known as the **jewie**

jeweller's shop mining slang for a rich deposit of gold or opal.

jewels the testicles. Venerable slang, dating back to the 1400s. Also called the **crown jewels** or the **family jewels**.

jezza in Aussie Rules, an extremely high and spectacular mark. Named in honour of Alex (Jezza) Jesaulenko.

JFL the blissful facial expression and accompanying mood of someone who has recently had sex. Standing for the *Just Fucked Look*.

jiffy a very short time. *Hang on, I'll do it in a jiffy.* Commonly shortened to **jiff**. *I'll be with you in a jiff.*

jig to play truant. *They were caught jigging school.*

jigger **1.** what you call a mechanical device when you can't think of its proper name. **2.** in prison, an illegally made crystal radio set. **3.** in horseracing, an illegal apparatus which gives a shock to a horse during a race in order to increase its speed. **4.** a type of electric cattle prod.

jig-jig sexual intercourse. Also called **jiggy** or **jiggy-jig**.

jilgie a variant spelling of **gilgie** (see entry).

jilleroo a female station hand on a sheep or cattle station. Modelled on **jackeroo**.

jillion an inordinate amount. A person with a jillion dollars is, of course, a **jillionaire**. Similar sums are **gillion**, **squillion**, **squintillion** and **zillion**.

Jimmy Brits Aussie rhyming slang for 'the shits', meaning either diarrhoea, or a bad mood. Jimmy Britt was a boxing champion who toured Australia during World War I.

Jimmy dancer Aussie rhyming slang for 'cancer'. Dates back to the 1980s at least.

Jimmy Riddle rhyming slang for 'piddle'. Originally British, from the 1930s.

Jimmy Woodser a person who drinks alone in a bar; also, a drink consumed alone. After 'Jimmy Wood' the loner in the 1892 poem of the same name by the bush balladist Barcroft Boake. Claims that it refers to an actual person have not been substantiated.

jinx among kids, a call made when you coincidentally say a word at exactly the same time as someone else. That person is then forced to keep silent until relieved of the jinx by the utterance of their name.

jism semen. Spelt with great variation, such as **gism**, **jissom** and **jizzom**, and shortened to **jizz**. A recent adoption from US slang, only common here since the 1990s, but in America going back to the 19th century. Perhaps from the British dialect word *chissom* 'a shoot or sprout', 'to germinate'.

jizz **1.** a spelling of **jism**. **2.** among birdos, the general shape of a bird from which it is possible to identify its family. *It had the jizz of a thrush, but I couldn't see any details.* The story goes that it is an adaptation of airforce slang for the general shape of a plane, reported to be an acronym from *General Impression Shape and Size* (GISS).

Joan of Arc rhyming slang for 'shark'. Originally British.

job **1.** to hit or punch. *I'll up and job the bastard.* Aussie slang dating from the 1900s. A variant of the Standard English word *jab*. Hence, a punch or hit delivered. *He copped a hefty job of the nose.* **2.** the product of an act of defecation. **3.** in underworld slang, a theft or robbery, or any criminal deed. English criminal slang from the 18th century.

jobbies kidspeak for defecation.

jobs for the boys preferential treatment for your mates.

jock **1.** a jockey. **2.** a jockstrap. Hence, in the plural, men's underwear. **3.** a male athlete. Chiefly US slang, but used here in a disparaging way for overly keen sporty types.

Joe in colonial times, a military police officer or trooper. The story goes that it is after Charles *Joseph* La Trobe, lieutenant-governor of Victoria in the 1850s, whose mining regulations were enforced by the police. On the goldfields the cry of 'Joe!' was used to warn of the approach of police.

Joe Blake Aussie rhyming slang for 'snake'. Dates back to 1905. Also simply shortened to a **Joe**.

Joe Blakes Aussie rhyming slang for 'the shakes', that is, delirium tremens. Dates back to the 1940s. Also shortened to the **Joes**.

Joe Bloggs the man in the street; the average citizen. Also known as **Jow Blow**.

joes a fit of depression or irritation. *That bastard gives me the joes.* Aussie slang from the early 20th century.

joey **1.** a baby kangaroo. Actually, originally used as far back as the 1820s for a young possum. Now commonly used for the young of any marsupial, as a wallaby, koala, bilby, quoll, quokka, potoroo, bettong, pademelon, even a wombat. Also used in a slang sense for the young of the human species. To have a

joey in the pouch is to be pregnant. No-one seems to know just where this word comes from. It may merely be an application of Joey, the common boy's name. **2.** a disparaging term for an Anglo-Australian used by people of other ethnic background. Similar in origin, but not as common as, **skip** (see entry). **3.** in the Newcastle region of NSW, a local name for the dreaded **bindi-eye** (see entry).

john **1.** a toilet. **2.** a police officer. An abbreviation of *John Darm* 'gendarme'. **3.** a prostitute's client.

John Doe a name used to refer to any unknown or unspecified man who is dead or unconscious. The male counterpart of the **Jane Doe**.

John Dory Aussie rhyming slang for 'story'. *What's the John Dory?* Dates back to the 1980s.

John Hancock a signature. An Americanism referring to the American statesman who was the first signatory of the Declaration of Independence.

John Hop Aussie rhyming slang for 'cop', as in the police. Since the 1900s. Sometimes spelt **jonnop**.

Johnny Bliss Aussie rhyming slang for 'piss'. Dating from the 1960s.

Johnny Cash Aussie rhyming slang for 'hash' (the drug).

Johnny Coward a disparaging nickname for Prime Minister John Howard used by opponents of the Iraq war.

Johnny Raper Aussie rhyming slang for 'newspaper'. After the Australian Rugby League legend.

John Thomas the penis. Originally British slang from the Victorian era.

joint **1.** a place of business, especially a stall, tent, or small shop. **2.** your house, unit, office, or the like. *Come round to my joint.* Can even be used to mean the entire country. *They bloody come out here and act like they own the joint!* **3.** a marijuana cigarette.

jo-jo in WA, the dreaded lawn weed **bindi-eye** (see entry).

joke a person who is laughable. *He's not a cricketer, he's a bloody joke.*

joker a fellow or bloke. *He's a funny sort of joker.* An Australian original this one, recorded in the *Sydney Gazette* in 1810. Now used in the US.

jollies cheap thrills. Generally used in a disparaging way. *He gets his jollies watching mud wrestling.*

jonnic genuine or true. A traditional Australianism dating back to the 1870s, but dying out in the 1960s. It had a good innings I suppose. Originated in British dialect.

joogie a **gilgie** (see entry).

josh to joke in a teasing way. *Don't worry, he was just joshing.*

jostle an annoying person; a dickhead.

journo a journalist. Aussie slang dating from the 1960s.

joystick the penis.

the Js the national radio station Triple J.

jug an old slang word for a glass of beer. Not heard much any more as it has been replaced by the convention of selling actual jugs of beer from which you can pour glasses.

jugs the female breasts.

juice **1.** electric power. **2.** fuel used to run an engine. **3.** any alcoholic beverage. **4.** any sexual secretion.

juicy fruit Aussie rhyming slang for 'root', as in an act of sexual intercourse. Dating from the 1950s. Named after a brand of chewing gum.

jumbuck a sheep. Formerly quite common, now virtually obsolete except for its prominent placement in the national song *Waltzing Matilda*. Originally Aboriginal Pidgin English, where it seems as though it might be related to the phrase *jump up*. Apparently it was an Aboriginal belief that after dying they would 'Jump up, white fellow', that is, rise again reincarnated as a white person. Could it be that jumbuck is an alteration of *jump up*? Another theory has jumbuck as an Aboriginal word for 'a white mist preceding a shower', to which sheep supposedly bore a resemblance. A fanciful idea.

jump **1.** the bar in a pub. **2.** to board a train, bus, or ferry without paying the fare. **3.** to have sexual intercourse with someone. Hence, the act itself. **4.** of a horse, to start a race. *The bookie got caught with a large bet just before they jumped.* Hence, the start of a race.

jump the shark of a TV series, to reach a point where it starts to go downhill. Referring to an episode of *Happy Days* in which The

Fonz performed a waterski jump over a live shark, seen as indicative of the show's decline.

jump the twig to die.

jump-up a point where a road or track rises abruptly from one level to another; a sharp rise in otherwise flat country; an isolated mesa. The area around Tibooburra in northwestern NSW is known as **jump-up country**.

jumpy as a wallaby extremely nervous.

jungle juice **1.** in World War II, a rough alcoholic drink originally made by soldiers in New Guinea. Recorded first among Australian troops, but also commonly used by American soldiers. **2.** any strong and rough booze.

junk heroin. *She's back on the junk.*

junkie **1.** a drug addict, especially one addicted to hard drugs. **2.** an addict to anything. *I'm a bit of a chocolate junkie.*

JW a Jehovah's Witness.

kack a variant spelling of **cack**.

kai food or tucker; sometimes used for drink. Used in many Pidgin Englishes. Ultimately from Polynesian, though we probably borrowed it from the Kiwis, who got it from Maori.

Kal the WA mining town of Kalgoorlie.

kalamazoo in WA, a hand-pumped railway trolley used by fettlers. The term has been around since at least the 1940s.

kambrook among car sellers, a group of four or more customers of Asian background. From the brand name of a maker of power boards – because there are four or more **power points** (see entry).

kamikaze 1. in surfing, a deliberate wipe-out. **2.** dangerous, suicidal. *He was a kamikaze drinker.*

Kanaka a derogatory term for a Pacific islander. Originally applied to those brought forcibly to Queensland as indentured labourers in the sugar and cotton industries. The word is Hawaiian for 'man'.

kanga 1. a kangaroo. **2.** money, dosh. *How much kanga have got on you?* **3.** prison rhyming slang for 'screw', as in warder.

kangaroo 1. well-known indigenous marsupial that looms large in Australian culture, history and slang. There is a widely-told story that when Captain Cook first arrived on the east coast he (or Joseph Banks) asked the local Aboriginals what the name of this strange new animal was and they replied 'Kangaroo', which meant 'I don't know what you're saying' or 'I don't understand' in their language, and thus the name was born of this misunderstanding. Even worse was the theory that kangaroo was a crude term, a joke on the white strangers. Of course, this is utter nonsense. Kangaroo is actually a word from the Aboriginal language Guugu Yimidhirr, from the Cooktown region of Qld, which both Cook and Banks recorded in their journals after visiting that region in 1770. To have **kangaroos loose in the top paddock** is to be slightly insane, a bit bonkers. Little known to most Aussies is that fact that across the Pacific Ocean in America they use the word kangaroo as well – as a derisive slang word for an Australian! **2.** to make a car jump along by unskilful clutch management. Also, **kangaroo-hop**. **3.** to squat over a toilet seat in order to do your business while avoiding contact with it. **4.** rhyming slang for 'screw', as in a prison warder.

kangaroo dog a breed of dog closely related to the greyhound but stronger, used for hunting roos.

kangarooer a kangaroo hunter.

kangaroo tail the grass tree or xanthorrhoea.

Kangaroo Valley the suburb of Earls Court in London. It has long been the major haunt of yobbo tourists from Down Under.

kangawallafox a mythical monstrous beast, a cross between a kangaroo, a wallaby and a fox, tales of which are used to frighten tourists.

kaput smashed, broken, ruined. From German.

kark a variant spelling of **cark**.

kartiya in northern WA, an Aboriginal English word for a white person. Also spelt **gaddiyah** or **guddiyah**.

Kate's Folly Bruce Stadium, the premier football ground in Canberra. From Kate Carnell, Chief Minister of the ACT from 1995–2000, nicknamed 'can do Kate' for her grand schemes.

keen as mustard extremely enthusiastic.

keeper the ringkeeper of a two-up game.

keepings off chiefly in Vic and Tas, the children's game piggy-in-the-middle.

keep nit to act as a lookout, especially when an illegal activity is taking place. Also known as **keeping yow**.

keg-on-legs 1. a person who drinks an inordinate amount of beer. **2.** an obese person.

keg party a traditional Aussie party at which a keg of beer is provided.

kelly an axe. This is a generic use of a brand name dating back to the 1900s. Rare nowadays.

Kelly country a nickname for parts of north-eastern Vic and just across the border into NSW where the Kelly Gang operated.

kelpie a breed of sheepdog developed in Australia from imported Scottish collies, having pricked ears and a smooth coat of variable colour. The breed's name comes from a dog by the name of Kelpie (from the Lowland Scottish word for a type of water sprite) which won the first ever sheepdog trials at Forbes, NSW, in 1872. She then became the progenitor of the breed.

Kembla Grange Aussie rhyming slang for 'change', that is, in the monetary sense. *Don't forget your Kembla Grange.* After the name of the racecourse at Wollongong, NSW. Usually shortened to **kembla**. Been around since the 1950s.

Kenmore tractor in Brisbane slang, a derogatory term for a city-only 4WD. See **Toorak tractor** for a host of synonyms.

Kennett same thing as to **Jeff** (see entry).

'kenoaf (spoken with a strong Australian accent) a euphemistic variant of the exclamation *fuckin' oath!*

kerb-crawling driving a car slowly along a street seeking sexual partners, or at least targets for sexual banter.

kerfuffle an argument, commotion or rumpus. Also spelt **kafuffle**.

kero typical laconic Aussie way of saying 'kerosene'.

kerosene language a cryptolanguage used by schoolchildren. For an explanation see **arpie-darpie**.

kewl a spelling of the word *cool*, representing an expressive pronunciation.

Khyber Pass rhyming slang for 'arse'. After the famous pass in the Hindu Kush mountains between Pakistan and Afghanistan. Generally shortened to **Khyber**. *He got a swift kick up the Khyber.* Originally British slang from the 1940s.

KI local nickname for Kangaroo Island.

kibosh a variant spelling of **kybosh**.

kick 1. a trouser pocket. *Here, put this in your kick.* Hence, your financial resources. *Sorry, mate, I've got nothing in the kick.* To **hit the kick** is to delve into the pocket for money, in other words, to front up the money. **2.** in Aussie Rules, a player viewed in terms of his kicking skill. *He's the best/worst kick the club's ever had.* **3.** of a racehorse, to put on a sudden burst of speed. *The big mare didn't kick till half way down the straight.* Hence, of a jockey, to urge a horse to greater speed.

kick arse 1. to be totally amazing; to really go off. *This band really kicks arse.* An Americanism borrowed here in the 1980s, along with its cousin **kick butt**. Hence, as an adjective, **kick-arse** means terrific, excellent, superlative. **2.** to defeat overwhelmingly. *We really kicked arse last Saturday.* This Americanism dates back to the 1960s there, but once again only came to Oz in the 1980s.

Kickastickalong an imaginary remote country town.

kick back to relax.

kick-flip a skateboarding manoeuvre in which the board is flipped over whilst in motion, twisting lengthwise so that it lands back on the wheels enabling the skater to land and continue riding.

kick for the other team to be homosexual.

kick in to contribute money.

kick off to start. *The band kicks off at seven o'clock.* Hence, the **kick-off** is the beginning. A football metaphor.

kick on to carry on or continue. *The party kicked on until the wee small hours.*

kick the arse off an emu if you feel you could do this, then you are feeling in tip-top condition, ready for anything.

kick the bucket to die. Dating back to the 18th century, this perhaps comes from the practice of hanging a pig to be slaughtered from a beam called a 'bucket'. Another theory is that it relates to people hanging themselves by standing on a bucket and kicking it away after fastening the noose.

kick the tin to make a donation.

kiddie 1. a young child; a kid. **2.** in colonial times, a flashily dressed young criminal or larrikin. The earliest meaning of the word, recorded in the US and Britain back in the late 18th century. Now long obsolete.

kiddo a familiar form of address to a young person.

kidney wiper a crass bragging term for a large penis.

kids' beer 1. low alcohol beer. **2.** KB brand beer, jokingly supposed by children to be the meaning of the initials. This joke died out in the 1970s when KB was knocked off the top of the popularity ladder by VB.

kidstakes childish behaviour; kidding around; kid's stuff. Aussie slang dating from the 1910s. From *stakes* 'something wagered', thus, literally, what a kid might bet, hence, child's play.

kiff marijuana. The common name in north Africa, from the Moroccan Arabic word for pleasure.

kill a brown dog of food, to be disgustingly repulsive.

killer **1.** absolutely fantastic. *We had a killer mud cake.* **2.** an animal ready to be slaughtered.

Killiecrankie diamond a type of colourless topaz found near Killiecrankie on Flinders Island, used as a gemstone.

kill the pig to work your heart out.

kindy common abbreviation for kindergarten. Also called **kinder**, especially in NSW and Tas. Both can also be used to refer to kindergarten-aged kids. *We took the kindies to the zoo.*

king **1.** excellent, top-notch, wonderful, the best. A popular word among young men, especially in the 1960s. *There were some king birds at the party.* **2.** formerly, a title given to an Aboriginal leader. **3.** an expert at something specified. *He was a two-up king.* Aussie slang since World War I. **4.** as a verb, to **king** someone is to king-hit them.

the King If you are a Rugby League follower you will know that this title refers to the one and only Wally Lewis. However, if you follow Aussie Rules, it is none other than Wayne Carey.

king brown in WA, a 750 ml bottle of beer. Generally called a **longneck** elsewhere, except Qld, where the term **tallie** is favoured.

king hit originally, a knock-out blow. Now, a cowardly punch from behind. Aussie slang since the 1910s. Hence, as a verb, to deliver such a blow. *He king-hit the boss and fled.*

king hit merchant a cowardly thug.

kingie **1.** a king prawn. **2.** a kingfish.

king of the ring a prominent bookmaker.

king pair in cricket, a batsman's demise on the first ball in both innings. See **pair**.

kingpin the top person in an organisation; a leader. Aussie slang dating from the 1900s.

king ping a Sydney schoolyard term for **handball** (see entry). Sometimes abbreviated to **KP**.

King River prawn Melbourne slang for a floating piece of human excrement in the ocean. See **blind mullet** for a swag of synonyms.

Kings Annoyed a jocular nickname for the Sydney suburb of Kings Cross.

king's ransom an exorbitant amount of money.

kip **1.** in two-up, a flat, thin piece of wood used for spinning the coins. Recorded as far back as 1887. Perhaps from Yorkshire and Lincolnshire dialect *kep* 'to toss up into the air'. **2.** a sleep or nap. As a verb, to sleep. Hence, to stay somewhere on a temporary basis. *He's kipping at Tom's for a couple of days.*

kipper a sailor in the Royal Navy, hence, any English person. Aussie slang from World War II. One unkind commentator remarked that the name derives from the similarity of the English and their favourite breakfast fare – 'both are spineless, two-faced, and smell.'

Kirup Syrup a red wine obtained by the flagon produced in Kirup, a small town south-east of Donneybrook in south-western WA. Rumoured to contain all sorts of fabulous ingredients.

kiss arse to fawn; to behave sycophantically.

kisser the mouth.

KISS method a very simplistic method of explaining or teaching. Standing for *Keep It Simple, Stupid!*

kiss my arse! an expression of derision. *The working class can kiss my arse / I've got a foreman's job at last.* In Aussie English also found as **kiss my bum!**, **kiss my quoit!** or **kiss my ring!**

kite **1.** among sailors, a spinnaker. **2.** an aeroplane. **3.** a hang-glider. **4.** prison slang, a newspaper. **5.** underworld slang, a blank cheque, or a forged or stolen one. Hence, to **fly a kite**, to pass off a forged cheque.

kittle the collection of empties which accumulate on a table while having beers with mates.

Kiwi **1.** a New Zealander. After the well-known flightless native bird, emblem of NZ. **2.** in financial slang, the New Zealand dollar.

Kiwiland New Zealand.

klutz a clumsy, awkward person. 1950s US slang, from Yiddish.

knackered exhausted; worn out.

knackers **1.** the testicles. First found in 19th century British dialect, picked up by Aussies during World War II. From the verb to *knack*, 'to make a sharp cracking noise'. **2.** a friendly term of address from one man to another. *How ya going knackers?*

knee trembler the act of sexual intercourse when both parties are standing. Aussie slang dating from the 1950s.

knight of the road a swagman.

knob **1.** the penis, or rather, specifically, the head of the penis. **2.** hence, an annoying or stupid person; a dickhead.

knobbies speedos. For a full set of synonyms see **sluggos**.

knob end the head of the penis; hence, a prick or dickhead.

knob jockey a homosexual man. Hence, used as an insult.

knock **1.** to criticise; find fault with. *People are always knocking the Government*. This meaning dates back to the 1890s in Australia. **2.** to kill. In World War I slang it meant to kill or wound severely. Hence, as a noun, a wound received in battle. **3.** to exhaust or debilitate. *I tell you, malaria can really knock you.* **4.** to have sexual intercourse with someone. Venerable slang, dating back to the 1500s. Hence, an act of sexual intercourse. **5.** in old Australian slang of the 1930s and 40s, to **do a knock with** someone, was to go courting with them. **6.** in cricket, an innings. *He got out LBW after a good knock.* **7.** in horseracing, to **take the knock** is to admit that you are unable to settle your debts.

knock about **1.** to roam about; to lead an irregular existence. *I spent my early years knocking about down south.* **2.** to be found at. *There should be some pain-killers knocking about in the kitchen cupboard.*

knockabout leading a rough life travelling about the country and living by your wits. *He's a genuine knockabout bloke, who's led a hard knockabout life.*

knock around with to spend time with someone; to companion someone.

knock back **1.** a refusal or rejection. Aussie slang since the 1910s. As a verb, to refuse. **2.** to consume quickly. *They knocked back a couple of beers.* This one is borrowed from US slang.

knock down to spend the entirety of your wages from a seasonal job, generally through going on an unrestrained drinking binge. *He knocked down his cheque at the local pub.* A former habit among shearers, frequently because they were victims of **lambing down** (see entry).

knockdown a formal introduction. Aussie slang dating from the 1910s. No longer in use.

knocked up exhausted; tuckered out.

knock 'em down rains violent thunderstorms in the Top End, with strong winds, lashing rain and plenty of lightning and thunder. Also called a **knock 'em down**. *Looks like we're in for another knock 'em down tonight.*

knocker **1.** a person who's always putting others down; one that doesn't have anything good to say about anything. The kind of ratbag that Aussies have been hating under this title since at least the 1920s. **2.** to be **on the knocker** is to be precisely accurate. *He was there on the knocker.* It can also mean right away or immediately. *They want cash on the knocker.*

knockers **1.** a bloke's word for large breasts. That is, they are so large they knock together. **2.** a brothel. *After six months out bush he headed straight for the knockers.*

knock for six to stun or astound; to blow away. A cricket metaphor. Also in the form **knock for a sixer**.

knocking shop a brothel.

knock it off **1.** Stop it! Give it a break! **2.** to have sexual intercourse. *A mate of mine said his missus was knocking it off with the bloke that reads the meters.*

knock off **1.** to finish up; to quit working. *We knock off at six sharp.* Hence, the end of a shift. *Only half-an-hour till knock-off.* **2.** to stop anything. *I've tried to knock off swearing.* **3.** to steal. **4.** to kill. **5.** to complete or finish with ease and speed. *I knocked off a letter to the PM.* Also used of eating and drinking. *Let's knock off these last few sambos.* **6.** to have sex with; to fuck. **7.** to copy or plagiarise something. Hence, a **knock-off**, a poor copy of something; a rip-off.

knock-off time the end of the working day; the end of a shift.

knock out **1.** to earn. *She knocked out a decent living as a journalist.* **2.** to make or produce. *Pete knocked out a few toy horses for the kiddies.*

knock over **1.** to drink with alacrity. *We knocked over a few nice cold ones.* **2.** to rob. *The bank had never been knocked over.* **3.** to raid a premises.

knockover an easy success; a pushover.

knock rotten to daze or stun with a heavy punch.

knock shop a brothel.

knock together to assemble something hastily or roughly.

knock up **1.** to arouse or waken by knocking. **2.** in prison, to attract the attention of the warder on duty by hammering on the cell door. **3.** to put together something hastily or roughly; to improvise. **4.** in sport, to amass a good score. **5.** to exhaust or wear out. **6.** to make pregnant.

know-all a person who likes displaying their knowledge to others; an intellectual show-off. Frequently they don't know what they are talking about. Also known as a **know-it-all**.

know your shit to really know your subject well.

knuckle to assault with the fists. To **go the knuckle** is to fight. To be **fond of the knuckle** is to be keen on solving differences with the fists.

knucklehead a fool or bonehead. US slang from the 1940s.

knuckles a game in which two contestants hold closed fists knuckle-to-knuckle and take turns at hitting the other player's knuckles. A change of turn takes place when one player misses a strike.

knuckle sandwich a punch in the mouth. *Are you looking for a knuckle sandwich, mate?*

Kodak poisoning in the Australian Antarctic Territory, the supposed deleterious effects suffered by wildlife from being madly photographed by group of tourists.

k one w one a New Zealander. A fanciful spelling-out of *Kiwi* with 'one' substituted for 'i'.

konk a variant spelling of **conk**.

kook **1.** a strange or eccentric person. A bit of 1920s US slang, never very common here. Hence, **kooky**, bonkers, weird. Ultimately from *cuckoo*. **2.** in surfing, a novice surfer, the bane of real surfies.

kooka a kookaburra. Also called a **kookie**.

kool a deliberate misspelling of the word *cool*.

Kossy (pronounced 'kozzie') affectionate name for Australia's highest peak, Mt Kosciuszko.

KP the same as **king ping** (see entry).

Kraut an old racist term for a German, formerly very popular while we were at war with them and still heard occasionally today even though all that was long ago and is way behind us. Actually it is the German word for cabbage.

kuna a variation of the word **goona** (see entry).

kybo a temporary toilet constructed for use when camping. Reportedly an acronym of *Keep Your Bowels Open*.

kybosh to **put the kybosh on something** is to put an end to it; to foil or quash something; to upset someone's plans. Occasionally spelt **kibosh**. Originally British slang from the 1830s, now also used here and in the US. Origin unknown.

kylie **1.** a boomerang having one flat and one convex side. From the Aboriginal language Nyungar of south-western WA. This is the origin of the popular Australian female name. **2.** in south-western WA, a flat piece of metal shaped and thrown like a boomerang, used to catch fish in shallow waters.

lace-out in Aussie Rules, describing the supremely perfect kick that delivers the ball to the intended marker with the lace facing outwards. *He received a beautiful lace-out pass at full forward.*

lack among currency traders, one hundred thousand dollars. From Hindi *lakh* = 100,000.

lacky band an elastic band. This word is used all over Australia, but is most common in WA, where it also gets shortened to **lacky**. Elsewhere it is called a **lacker band** (also spelt **lacka band** and **lacquer band**), especially in Victoria.

lad originally a word for a boy, but now also commonly used for an adult man who behaves like an obnoxious boy and in a particularly chauvinistic way – like mooning a busload of old ladies, drinking till he pukes, having pissing competitions, and worse. This is known as **laddish** behaviour. **The lads** is a term for a group of male friends when out together, not necessarily behaving in a laddish way, but it often depends on how much they drink.

lady among currency traders, five million dollars. Short for **Lady Godiva**, rhyming slang for 'fiver'.

Lady Blamey in World War II, a drinking glass made from an empty bottle with the top cut off. A string soaked in kerosene was wrapped around the bottle and then set alight. After the string had burnt through, the glass would separate where it was fire-weakened. This trick was taught to the troops by Lady Blamey, the wife of the commander of the south-western Pacific Allied Forces, Sir Thomas Blamey.

lady in the boat a cask of Coolibah moselle. It has a picture of a woman in a boat on the side.

lady killer an attractive man popular with women.

lady's waist a small, waisted glass used for serving alcoholic drinks, formerly common in Australian pubs.

lag 1. originally, to transport a convict from Britain to Australia. Hence, a transported convict. After being freed, a convict was commonly known as an **old lag**. As the transportation of convicts was phased out, this word remained in circulation and was used to refer to imprisoning (as opposed to transporting) a convicted criminal, and hence, a prisoner, especially a hardened prisoner. **2.** to report someone to the authorities; to inform on. Also, **lag on**. *He got done over for lagging on his mates.* **3.** among children, to illegally move your hand over the line when shooting in a game of marbles. See **fananny-whacking** for a full set of synonyms.

lagerphone a traditional Aussie folk music percussion instrument made from a stake to which beer bottle caps have been nailed. You bang it in time with the music.

lagger a police informer. See **lag** (def. 2).

lair a flashily dressed young man of brash and vulgar behaviour. Also known as a **mug lair**. Classic Aussie slang. This word is first recorded back in the 1920s and is a back-formation from **lairy**.

lair about to behave in a brash and vulgar manner; to show off. Also, to **lair up** or **lair it up**.

lairise to behave like a lair; to show off; to indulge in exhibitionism. Original Aussie slang coined in the 1940s.

lairy flashy in a vulgar way; ostentatious. Used in Australia since the 1890s. A particular Aussie use of a Cockney slang term. In Cockney it was rather more positive, meaning wise, knowing or awake up.

la-la the toilet. A euphemism in Australia since the 1960s.

lambing down the practice of extracting the entire pay packet of a seasonal worker by getting them drunk and keeping them intoxicated until their money runs out. This reprehensible activity was a commonplace in the outback in days of yore. The original meaning of **lamb down** is to tend ewes during lambing time.

lamington an Australian culinary treat essentially consisting of sponge cake pieces dipped in runny chocolate and then rolled in desiccated coconut. Apparently named after Baron Lamington, governor of Qld, 1895–1901. Colloquially shortened to either **lammie** or **lammo**, making it one of the few words that can take either the *-ie* or *-o* suffix.

lance jack Australian Army slang for a lance corporal. Originated in World War I.

land in horseracing, to win. *She has only landed moderate stakes up till now.*

Landie a Landrover. Also known as a **Lannie**.

land lice sheep.

Land of the Long Weekend Australia.

Land of the Wrong White Crowd **1.** New Zealand. **2.** the beachy suburb of Bondi, Sydney, heavily populated by Poms and Kiwis.

langers drunk. A bit of Irish slang that has been picked up in Oz. Not common.

La Perouse Aussie rhyming slang for 'booze'. After the Sydney suburb south of Botany Bay. Named in honour of Comte de La Pérouse, the French navigator who narrowly missed claiming Australia for the French by showing up in Botany Bay about five days after Governor Phillip planted the Union Jack in Sydney Harbour.

lappies circuits of a street block in a car for the purpose of entertainment. This term is chiefly used in Qld. Compare **blockies** and **bog laps**.

Larpa the Sydney suburb of La Perouse. Hence, rhyming slang for 'booze', as well.

larrikin a good-natured, independent and wild-spirited person, usually having little regard for authority. This word comes from the British dialects of Warwickshire and Worcestershire, and has been used in Australia since the 1860s. However, contrary to current usage, in 19th-century Australia the most prominent meaning was a negative one, referring to a petty criminal or thug, especially one who was a member of a street gang. Larrikins were the teenage delinquents of the 19th century and hung around in gangs called pushes (see **push**). The media of the day went to town on this subject, widely decrying what they termed **larrikinism**. This negative meaning can still be seen in the modern adjectival use of the word, such as 'larrikin behaviour' or 'the larrikin element', where it implies socially irresponsible activities.

Larry Dooley If you **give someone Larry Dooley**, it means you give them a hiding or beating. Aussie slang dating from the 1940s.

lash **1.** an attempt. *I'll have a lash at it.* Aussie slang since the 1840s. **2.** an act of sexual intercourse.

later a common shortening of the farewell 'I'll see you later'. *Later, dudes!* A 1980s borrowing from American slang which dates back to the 1950s.

laughing in a favourable or fortunate position. *One more result like that and you'll be laughing.* Aussie slang since at least the 1960s.

laughing gear the mouth; to **wrap your laughing gear around** something is to eat it. *Here, wrap your laughing gear around this sanger.* Aussie slang since the 1960s.

laughing jackass the kookaburra. An old name dating back to 1789. Referring, of course, to the bird's loud territorial call.

laughing sides elastic-sided boots. Aussie slang since the 1930s. Also called **laughing-side boots**.

laugh like a drain to laugh in a loud and undignified manner.

Laura Norda Strine for 'law and order'. If you don't know what Strine is – you can look it up at the entry for **Strine**.

lay **1.** to have sex with someone; to root or screw. Hence, an act of sexual intercourse. Hence, a person rated by their sexual performance. *He was a great lay.* **2.** to bet or wager. *I'll lay you six to one you can't do it.* To **lay off** is to make a secondary bet on another competitor to offset money already wagered. **3.** to **crack a lay** is to divulge information. Old slang from the 1940s, not heard much any more.

lay a cable to defecate. A charming metaphor recorded in Oz since the 1970s.

lay down misère something that is a certainty.

lazy wind a bitterly cold wind. It is too 'lazy' to go around you – it goes right through you instead.

lead swinger a lazy person who **swings the lead** (see entry).

leaf the leaves of the marijuana plant dried and prepared for smoking.

Leagues a Rugby Leagues Club. *I met him down Wenty Leagues.*

leaguey a player or follower of Rugby League.

leak an act of passing water. *Hang on, I've got to hang a leak.* Hence, as a verb, to urinate. The noun sense is originally US slang of the early 20th century, but the verb is first recorded in Shakespeare's play *Henry IV, Part I* in 1596!

leather dyke a homosexual woman who dresses in leather.

leather man a homosexual man who dresses in leather.

Leb a Lebanese person. Commonly used by Anglos in a disparaging way but, like 'wog', used within the Lebanese community without any negative connotation. Also in the extended form **Lebbo**.

Lebanese lawn great slabs of concrete that commonly fill the front or back yards of the homes of people of Lebanese background. Also called **Italian lawn**.

lech a variant spelling of **letch** (see entry).

ledge an absolutely cool person. Short for **legend**.

leery doubtful or suspicious. If a man is scared of getting married, he is said to be **leery of the brush**.

left-footer a Roman Catholic – from the Protestant point of view.

leftie 1. a left-handed or left-footed person. **2.** a punch with the left arm. **3.** a turn to the left in a vehicle. **4.** a person holding socialist ideas; a leftist.

left right out a spurious position on a sports field, or rather, off a sports field.

legend an absolutely cool person. Adolescent slang from the 1980s.

legend in your own mind a person who is fabulously conceited but has no right to be.

leggie in cricket, a leg spin delivery or a leg spin bowler.

leg it to decamp; to flee with great celerity. *The cops showed up, so we had to leg it.* Can also be simply used to mean to walk. *The engine's kaput, we'll have to leg it.*

legit genuine; truthful. Short for *legitimate.*

legless very drunk, to the point where the basic human action of walking cannot be executed even though you've been practising it most of your life.

leg man a male who is sexually aroused by legs.

leg of lamb an absolutely cool person. A jocular elaboration of **legend**.

Lego Land any new suburb with cul-de-sac upon cul-de-sac of nearly identical houses.

leg opener an alcoholic drink calculated to facilitate the seduction of a woman. Aussie slang since the 1940s.

leg-over an act of sexual intercourse. To **get your leg over** is to crack it for a bit of sex – half your luck!

legs 1. in sport, the ability to keep running or playing; staying power. Hence, metaphorically, to **have legs** is to be able to endure or continue, to go the distance. **2.** When used leeringly by males, this refers to long, shapely female legs. The simple statement **She's got legs** means she has beautiful legs. Along the same line is the phrase **She's got legs right up to her bum**. Of course, these locutions can be used of males' legs, if that's your leaning.

Leichhardt grass Sydney slang for the great slabs of concrete that commonly fill the front or back yards of people of Mediterranean background. After the expansively concreted Sydney suburb of Leichhardt.

lemon 1. a lesbian. Aussie slang from the 1980s, but perhaps earlier. So called because lemons are fruits (i.e. punning on *fruit* = homosexual). No doubt also influenced by the similarity of the first syllable of *le*mon and *le*sbian. **2.** a car which looks all right but actually is mechanically unsound. **3.** anything that is no good; a dud or turkey. **4.** a swindler's victim.

lemon head a surfie with bleached hair.

lemony annoyed. *I got lemony at the kid.* Aussie slang dating from the 1940s – formerly common, but very scarce today.

length a rather unpoetic way of referring to the penis. To **slip someone a length** is to have sex with them.

lesbie a lesbian. There are many ways to shorten the word *lesbian.* **Lesbie** is used in Britain, Australia and the US, as is **lezzie**. The form **lesbo** is originally American but is also found in Oz. Unique to Australia is **lezzo**, which has been around since the 1940s, and the less common **lezzer**.

lesbie friends a lesbian couple, punning on the phrase 'let's be friends'. Generally used by schoolkids when maligning other girls who are close friends.

letch 1. a disparaging term for a lecherous man or womaniser. Hence, a sexual predilection or a kink. Old British slang from as far back as the 18th century. **2.** as a verb, to behave lecherously; to ogle or perve. Also spelt **lech**.

let go to fart without restraint. Also, to **let off** or **let one go**.

let her rip! Begin! Commence! Don't hold back!

let rip **1.** to give free rein to anger or passion. **2.** to fart unabashedly.

let's blow this popsicle stand let's leave. A recent adoption from the US. It is strange that this blatant Americanism could find any favour in Australia, especially since it uses the term 'popsicle stand' which has no meaning in Oz. Nevertheless, it seems to be here to stay, as is the variant **let's blow this candy store**.

leviathan a wealthy man who bets big on the horses. Aussie racing slang from the 1870s.

levna See **elevener**.

lezzie/lezzer/lezzo a lesbian. See **lesbie**.

lick out to perform cunnilingus on woman.

lick you to death said of overly friendly dogs.

lid an old term for a hat. Now only heard in the phrase **dip your lid** (see entry).

lifer a person sentenced to life imprisonment.

life sucks and then you die a catchphrase expressing a rather dismal outlook on life, generally used after suffering some misfortune. It first appeared on the scene in the 1980s. Also found in the form **life's a bitch and then you die**.

the lights are on but nobody's home a phrase used to refer to a brainless dimwit.

like **1.** so to speak; as it were. *It was a bit tough, like.* Placed after a statement in order to weaken it. This is a common feature of Australian English, especially in rural areas and among the working class, and has been so since the 19th century. The next three definitions are all newcomers from the States, and as such are anathema to many true blue Aussies. Of course, at the same time they are prefectly normal and natural-sounding to the younger true blue Aussies who use them on a daily basis. **2.** used before a number, around about or almost. *It's like six in the evening.* **3.** used to introduce and emphasise a statement. *There was like this big guy, like really big.* This is an American usage that originated in the 1950s among jazz musicians, but was taken up by beatniks and hippies, and by adolescents, where it made its way into the Valspeak of the 1980s and hence was transported to Australia. In the speech of some people it appears so frequently it has little meaning and acts as a mere filler, like the word 'um'. *He like said to me like that he wanted to like go to the beach.* **4.** used with the verb 'to be' or 'go' to introduce reported speech. As in *So I was like 'No Way!'*, or *He would go like 'Shut up!' really loud.* This is also from the US, but originated there only in the 1980s, once again associated with Valspeak. It appeared in Oz not long after and is now almost universal among teenagers and young adults.

like a blue-arsed fly in a bottle racing about furiously in a highly agitated state.

like a hole in the head not at all. *Would you like some black sausage? Yeah, like a hole in the head.* A literal translation of a Yiddish metaphor.

like a rat up a drainpipe with great speed. *I'd be up her like a rat up a drainpipe.* Aussie slang dating from the 1960s. Also heard as **like a rat up a rope**.

lily on a dustbin a person or thing rejected or neglected. Hence, someone who looks incongruous, as being overdressed at an informal gathering.

limp dick a weak-willed, ineffectual person; a soft cock.

limp-wristed of a man, homosexual.

line **1.** a measure of cocaine laid out for inhalation. **2.** a pick-up line. *That's the oldest line in the book.* This was originally American slang but has virtually become Standard English now. In old Australian slang there was the phrase to **do a line with someone**, which meant to court or date them. *Now, there's a man I could do a line with any day.* This was around from the 1930s to the 1950s. **3.** an attractive woman. *He has dated some slashing lines.* Aussie slang dating from the 1940s and 50s. Not heard any longer.

linie a person who works on telephone line installation and maintenance.

lippy lipstick. Aussie women's slang since the 1950s.

lipstick lesbian a lesbian who wears conventional women's clothing and make-up. Also called a **lipstick dyke**.

liquid laugh an act of vomiting, as you might experience after a lengthy liquid lunch.

liquid lunch alcoholic drink, usually beer, consumed instead of food at the normal lunchtime.

little aths laconic Aussie way of referring to Little Athletics.

little Aussie battler a typical member of the working class in Australia.

little blister Aussie rhyming slang for 'little sister'.

little boy a cocktail frankfurt. In Qld and northern NSW also called a **cheerio**.

the Little Digger nickname of Billy Hughes, the Australian Prime Minister during World War I.

little green cart the supposed waggon that comes to take you to the lunatic asylum. Dating back to the 1940s.

little house an outside toilet. Aussie euphemism from the 1880s. Also known as the **little boy's room** or **little girl's room**, depending on who is going there.

Little House on the Prairie a local nickname for Parliament House, Canberra.

little jobs a word for urination, used when speaking to ankle biters.

Little Johnny a disparaging nickname for Prime Minister John Howard. In reference to his small stature. He is also known as **Little Johnny Jackboots**.

little tacker a little kid. The word *tacker* is from the Devon and Cornwall dialects of southern England.

little white mouse a euphemistic way of referring to a tampon.

littlie a child.

live on the smell of an oily rag to survive on the barest amount of food and money. This phrase has been around since the 1900s.

Liverpool kiss a headbutt. Also called a **Balmain kiss**.

livestock maggots infesting a dead body. A word used by police and ambos.

living shit used as a substitute for *hell*. *He beat the living shit out of it.*

lizard 1. the penis – as used in the phrases **drain the lizard** meaning to urinate, and **flog** or **gallop the lizard** meaning to masturbate. **2.** If you are working at full capacity or going at top speed, then you are **flat out like a lizard drinking**. **3.** A formerly common exclamation of surprise was **starve the lizards!** Also found in the form **stiffen the lizards!** Now rare.

LKS water. A long way around this one! From the *LKS Mackinnon Stakes*, a 10 furlong horserace, which in imperial measure is a mile and a quarter. *Mile and a quarter* is rhyming slang for 'water'. Not very common.

load 1. a venereal infection. **2.** an ejaculation of semen. **3.** to **get a load of** something is to look at it. *Get a load of that drongo!*

loaded 1. unjustly incriminated; framed. Also **loaded up**. **2.** very wealthy. **3.** drunk. **4.** stoned on drugs.

load up to falsely charge someone with crimes they did not commit; to frame.

lob 1. to arrive, especially unexpectedly. *He lobbed here this afternoon.* Aussie slang since the 1910s. Also, **lob in** or **lob up**. **2.** to land. *My bag fell and lobbed on the rockery below.* **3.** to win a race. *He was hoping the horse would lob.*

lobby a name for the yabby in Qld. See **yabby** for an explanation of the regional variants.

lobster a twenty dollar note. So called from its colour.

the local your local pub. *See you later at the local.*

local yokels the local inhabitants of a town, suburb, or the like.

logodile a half-submerged log mistaken for a crocodile.

lollipop 1. rhyming slang for 'cop', as in the police. Originally British. **2.** in cricket, a piss-weak delivery that is easy to play.

lolly 1. a sweet or piece of confectionery. A peculiarly Aussie (and NZ) term since the 1850s. **2.** money or dosh. *I'm running out of lolly.* **3.** the head. To **do your lolly** is to lose your temper. Aussie slang dating from the 1950s.

lolly bags speedos. For a full set of synonyms see **sluggos**.

lolly legs long, skinny legs, or a tall, lanky person with long legs.

lolly water carbonated soft drink. Sometimes used to refer to cordial. Aussie slang dating from the 1900s.

London to a brick extremely likely. *It's London to a brick that he'll chicken out.* Coined by famous race caller Ken Howard who used it to unofficially announce winners in a tight finish while awaiting the official decision. In racing parlance it is a statement of betting odds in which a punter is so certain of the outcome that they are willing to bet London to win a measly brick (that is, ten quid – see **brick**). Technically the phrase should be 'London to a brick *on*'. Many people unaware of betting lingo leave out the vital word *on*, thus making the phrase the opposite of what is intended, i.e. the odds of laying a brick to win all of London. Not much of a risk.

long as a wet weekend depressingly long.

long drop **1.** a type of pit toilet with a deep shaft. **2.** underworld slang, death by hanging. No longer used as we no longer have the death sentence.

long flat dog a crocodile.

long grass the edges of the township of Darwin, where large numbers of displaced Aboriginals live. Such inhabitants are known as **long grassers** or **long grass people**.

long hair **1.** an intellectual. **2.** a hippie.

long hop in cricket, a delivery pitched very short so that it loops up and curves downwards when approaching the wicket.

long in the tooth elderly.

long neck a 750 ml bottle of beer. Also called a **longie**. In Qld they prefer the term **tallie**, and in WA, a **king brown**.

long paddock grassed roadsides used for grazing cattle or sheep.

long streak of misery a tall, thin, miserable person.

long streak of pelican shit an uncomplimentary way of referring to a tall, thin person.

long time no see a greeting used when you haven't seen someone recently. Of all the pieces of pidgin English to cross over into general slang, this is the most common.

Lonnie the Tasmanian town of Launceston. Locals pronounce the town's name 'Lon-cess-ton', and pronouncing it 'Lawn-cess-ton' immediately marks you out as an ignorant Mainlander.

loo a toilet. From British slang of the 1940s. Origin unknown. Supposed by some to be from the long-obsolete cry *Gardyloo!* shouted in old Edinburgh before throwing dirty water out the window into the street. Another theory is that it a clipping of *Waterloo*, a British toilet manufacturer of the early 20th century. Neither suggestion is particularly convincing.

the 'Loo the Sydney suburb of Woolloomooloo.

look a million dollars to look terrific.

looker a good-looking person. *A bit long in the tooth, but a real looker.*

look like death warmed up to look dreadful, especially from being ill.

look-see a visual examination. Originally pidgin English of the 19th century.

loony bin a lunatic asylum.

loop a crazy person; weirdo.

loop-the-loop Aussie rhyming slang for 'soup'. Dating back to the 1960s.

loopy mad or eccentric.

loose stuff bits of leaves, stems, and whatnot, of marijuana, of poorer quality than tightly packed, moist heads.

loppy a handyman on a station; a rouseabout.

loser a person who is hopeless at everything; an out-and-out no-hoper; a complete dag. Originally US slang from the 1950s. Picked up in Australia in the 1980s.

lose the plot to no longer fully understand what is going on.

lose your rag to lose your temper.

the lot Aussie prison slang for a life sentence. Dates back to the 1940s.

love glove a condom.

love handles the sides of the roll of fat running around the abdomen which can be grasped during copulation.

love juice sexual secretions.

lovely a sexually attractive woman; a honey or spunk-rat.

love machine a passionate lover.

love muscle the penis.

lover's balls pain in the testicles caused by unrelieved sexual arousal. Also called **blue balls**.

love shack a retreat for lovers, especially illicit. Popularised by the B52s hit song of 1990.

lower than a snake's belly mean, despicable, contemptible. Another way of saying this is **lower than shark shit.**

low heel a derogatory term for a female prostitute or a promiscuous woman. Originally referring to a streetwalker who has worked so much that she has worn her highheels down. Aussie slang dating from the 1930s.

lowie **1.** a female prostitute. A shortening of **low heel**. **2.** a contemptible person; a scumbag or low-life.

low jump underworld slang, a magistrate's court. As opposed to the **high jump** (see entry).

low-life **1.** the seamy elements of society, as those involved in vice. **2.** a despicable person;

a scumbag. Also used adjectivally, as in *You low-life scum!*

lubra a word for an Aboriginal woman which probably came from an Aboriginal language of south-east Tasmania. First recorded in the 1830s, it quickly spread throughout the country and just as quickly took on all the negative associations that the colonists had for the native inhabitants. Nowadays, it is avoided by anyone with a skerrick of racial sensitivity.

lubra lips large lips. See above.

lubricate the larynx to drink booze.

luck out to run out of luck; to have bad luck. Borrowed from American English. Curiously, in the US it is also used to mean the opposite – that is, to have exceptionally good luck. Australians have picked it up only in the negative sense.

Lucky Country Australia seen as a fortunate country enjoying the benefits of prosperity, opportunity, stability, and the like. This appellation comes from the title of an influential book written in 1964 by Australian academic Donald Horne. It was originally intended by Horne as an ironic rebuke, describing Australians as having survived by 'luck' rather than good management – that we lazed around enjoying the good life, instead of concerning ourselves with productivity, international competitiveness, striving for the future, and stuff like that. Horne's negativeness was of course ignored by the average Aussie and the phrase has ended up being self-complimentary.

lucky shop in Victoria, a TAB premises.

lug 1. the ear. To **chew someone's lug** is to talk at them incessantly. Among musicians, to **lug** a piece of music is to work it out by ear. **2.** a big, clumsy person. *Out of my way, you great lug.*

lumber 1. to leave someone with something unwelcome or unpleasant. *We got lumbered with the bill.* **2.** to place under arrest. Aussie slang since the 19th century. Derived from the older sense, 'to put into pawn'. A variant of *Lombard* 'a pawnbroker', ultimately from Old French. **3.** to pick someone up and take them back to your place for sex. Also, of a prostitute, to pick up a client.

lunatic soup alcoholic drink; booze or grog. Aussie slang since the 1930s.

lunch 1. the penis or male genitalia. Also called a **packed lunch**. **2.** to **cut someone's lunch** is to make a move on or steal their girlfriend or wife. **3.** to **drop your lunch** or **open your lunch box** is to fart.

lunch cutter someone who steals another's girlfriend.

lungs a crass, laddish term for large breasts.

lurgy a cold or flu. *I've come down with a bit of a lurgy.* Commonly in the phrase **the dreaded lurgy**. *I've caught the dreaded lurgy.* Coined by Spike Milligan and popularised by the Radio Goons where it referred to some fictitious infectious disease.

lurk a dodge; a slightly underhanded scheme. Aussie slang since the 1890s. Commonly used in a positive way to refer to some easy way of making money. *He's on a good lurk.* Also frequently coupled with the word 'perk'. *She knows all the lurks and perks.*

lurk merchant a person who is adept at organising lurks for personal benefit. Also known as a **lurk man**.

lush 1. a drunkard. Originally 19th century British slang. **2.** sexually attractive. *She is one of the lushest babes on the planet.* **3.** terrific, great, wonderful. Commonly used by teenagers.

maaate a long, drawn-out way of saying **mate**. Used in various contexts, such as a friendly greeting when two mates are pleased to see one another, as a way of cajoling a mate into agreeing with you, or as a way of placating a mate who is getting a bit hot under the collar.

Mac attack a strong desire to eat food from a McDonald's Family Restaurant.

macca **1.** a recruit in the armed forces. Common in World War II. Origin unknown. **2.** a macadamia nut.

Macca a nickname for Macquarie Island. Hence, a **Macca-ite** is a resident on this remote subantarctic Australian outpost.

Maccas **1.** a McDonald's Family Restaurant. **2.** food from a McDonald's Family Restaurant. Also spelt **Mackers**.

mad among teenagers, extremely good; excellent; cool. *She's got a mad outfit.*

mad as a cut snake extremely mad, either in the angry sense, or the crazy sense. Formerly it used to be just **mad as a snake**.

mad as a gumtree full of galahs absolutely crazy; all over the place.

mad as a meataxe stark staring bonkers.

mad mick Aussie rhyming slang for a 'pick'. Dates back to World War I.

Madonna's bra a local nickname for Sydney's Anzac Bridge – which, from a distance, vaguely resembles the pointy bra formerly worn by the pop star Madonna.

mag **1.** to chat or natter. An Australianism dating back to the late 19th century. **2.** a sociable chat. *Just having a bit of a mag.*

maggered extremely drunk.

maggie an affectionate name for the magpie, a bird which during the breeding season will less than affectionately attack you.

maggot **1.** an utterly loathsome person. **2.** especially among surfies, a term of contempt for a woman. **3.** drunk. *I got totally maggot last night.*

maggot bag a meat pie. Also, **maggot sack**.

maggoted extremely drunk. *Chris got totally maggoted at my place.*

maggots in white Aussie Rules umpires.

maggot taxi a sheep.

maggoty in a bad mood.

magic mushie any of various mushrooms, as the liberty cap or fly agaric, which contain psilocybin, a hallucinogenic substance.

magic sponge a sponge applied by trainers to supposedly injured players (read: players who are faking it) who then recover miraculously.

-magnet **1.** a person who attracts much sexual interest from others due to their beauty and personality. *chick-magnet*, *stud-magnet*. **2.** any person or thing with the power to attract that which is specified by the first element. *an ugly-magnet.*

magpie lark the official name for the common black and white bird commonly known as the peewee. See **peewee** for the full list of regionalisms.

magsman **1.** a superb teller of stories; a raconteur. **2.** a confidence man.

Mainland in Tasmania this refers to continental Australia. However, if you are on King or Flinders Island then it refers to Tasmania. If you are from the Mainland, then you are, of course, a **Mainlander**.

main man your best mate; a man for whom you have great admiration. A usage borrowed from American Black English.

major **1.** in Aussie Rules, a goal, as opposed to a behind. **2.** among the youth of today it means complete, total, utter. *She has the major hots for him.*

majorly to a great extent; in a major way. *He was majorly upset.*

make to seduce someone; to have sex with someone.

make babies to have sex, but not exactly for the purpose of having children.

make it to have sex.

make old bones to grow old; to reach a ripe old age.

make out **1.** to have sexual intercourse. *We made out last night.* **2.** to kiss, pet and fondle sexually. *Just some kids making out at the movies.*

make whoopee **1.** to engage in uproarious merry-making. **2.** to have sexual intercourse.

make your marble good to improve your situation or prospects.

makings the tobacco and paper used to hand-roll a cigarette.

mal among surfies, a malibu surfboard.

Malabar Hilton the Long Bay Correctional Centre, Malabar, NSW.

malaka a wanker. From Greek. A fairly common insult among Aussies of Greek descent. Even worse is to be called a **malaka pousti** (the word **pousti** means homosexual).

malish! it doesn't matter! A word borrowed from Arabic. Common among soldiers during both World Wars.

mallee technically, a species of eucalyptus, but in slang **the mallee** refers to the remote outback, as in *Been stuck in the mallee for a week.* If you are as **fit as a mallee bull**, then you are superbly fit.

mallie (pronounced 'mawley') a listless youth who habitually hangs around a shopping centre.

malt sandwich a beer.

man a term of address to a man – or woman – as in *Hey, man. Long time no see.* It is quite common among teenage girls to call one another 'man'. An old borrowing from US English. More recently teenagers have adopted the American Black usages **my man**, **my main man**, and **to be the man**, as positive affirmations of friendship and admiration.

man boobs the flabby, boob-like contouring of the overweight male's chest. Also called **man boobies**, **man tits**, or, more crudely, **bitch tits**.

man fern a Tassie term for a tree fern.

mangare (pronounced 'mun-jar-ay') eating; food. From Italian *mangiare* to eat. *A good place for serious mangare.*

mango madness a feeling of oppression that descends upon residents of the Top End during the build-up to the wet season.

mangulate to mangle; to bend or twist out of shape; to wreck.

man in the boat the clitoris. Sometimes called the **boy in the boat**.

man in white the Australian Rules referee or umpire.

mankad in cricket, when a bowler runs out the non-facing batter who is backing up, especially after pretending to bowl. Named after Indian cricketer Vinoo *Mankad* who was dismissed in this manner in the Test series of 1947–8.

manky rotting, mouldy, scabby, or otherwise repulsive.

man on the land the farmer, the stockman, the cocky, or other rural worker, who scrapes a hard-won living from this wide brown land.

man outside Hoyts the commissionaire outside Hoyts Theatre, Melbourne, in the early part of last century, used as a scapegoat for any crime, misdemeanour, rumour, or the like. *Who left this here? The man outside Hoyts!*

a man's not a camel! give me a drink before I die of thirst!

Maoriland New Zealand. Hence, **Maorilander**.

map of Tasmania the female pubic area. Aussie slang since the 1970s. Also called the **map of Tassie**.

Maralinga breadbox a microwave oven.

margarine legs the legs of a promiscuous woman. Because, like margarine, they 'spread well'. *Not a bad-looker, and she's got margarine legs.* Boyishly blokey word.

mark a person who is the target of a swindle. An **easy mark** is a complete gull who falls prey to a con or swindle with the greatest of ease.

marley a sideways skid on a bike. This term is most common in Qld.

Marrickville Mercedes in Sydney, a derisive term for a Chrysler Valiant. Marrickville has a large ethnic population among whom this make of car is popular.

marvie marvellous.

Mary **1.** a homosexual male. **2.** formerly a common appellation among men for an Aboriginal, Papuan or Islander woman.

Mary Jane marijuana.

Mary Pickford in three acts a quick, perfunctory wash of the face, hands and crotch.

masher a man who makes aggressive sexual advances to women. A somewhat old-fashioned term rarely heard these days.

Ma State New South Wales.

mate **1.** a friend or cobber – the great Australian expression of true and undying friendship among men. Equivalent to the British *chum* and American *buddy* or *pal*. As in *They've been good mates from way back*, or *Never let a mate down*. This masculine bond is known as **mateship**, and almost made its way into our national Constitution, except hardly anyone voted for Prime Minister Howard's Preamble. Anyhow, **mate** is a very serviceable word and is also commonly used as a form of address, as in *G'day mate* – and this can be said to someone who is a true mate, or just an acquaintance, or even someone you don't know but are meeting for the first time. Mate can also be used to refer to some bludger who ain't your mate in the slightest, like *You got a problem with that, mate?* **2.** as applied to women, **mate** has for a long time, since at least the 1930s, been used to refer to a close female friend that a bloke does not have a romantic relationship with. Also, it is not too uncommon for men to refer to their wives as mates either. *Me missus is a great mate.* **3.** among women, at least in recent years, the traditional male usage has been adopted, so that a woman can refer to her female friends as *mates*.

mates rates especially cheap rates or prices for friends.

matey a slangy variant of **mate**, especially as a term of address. *Come on matey – we'll be late.*

maths in space the simplest level of mathematics offered at high school.

Matilda a swag, hence the phrase **waltzing Matilda** means carrying your swag, in other words, being on the wallaby track, travelling from place to place looking for work. A lot of people blithely sing the song *Waltzing Matilda* without exactly knowing what the lyrics mean – which is a little bit funny since it is our national song after all.

matinee the sex act when performed in the afternoon. Also called **afternoon delight**.

mattress muncher a homosexual man. See **dung puncher** for a swag of synonyms.

max the maximum. Hence, **to the max**, to the utmost degree.

maxed out of surf conditions, too big to ride. *The Shorey was maxed out and unrideable.*

max out to reach the maximum. *I've maxed out my credit card again.*

mazuma money or dosh. Originally American slang of the 1900s, from Yiddish.

me the fair dinkum Aussie way of pronouncing 'my'. *Me and me mates, Where's me car keys?*

meat **1.** male or female genitalia. **2.** people considered as sexual objects. *There was plenty of meat at the party.*

meat hangers a chiefly Qld term for speedos. For a full set of synonyms see **sluggos**.

meat head a fool or idiot.

meat injection the intromission of the penis in sexual intercourse. In use since the 1940s.

meat market a venue at which casual sexual partners are to be easily acquired.

meat pie **1.** a small, hot pie with a filling of gravy. Oh yeah, and a little bit of meat too. The ubiquity of the meat pie has made it a national dish, and has given rise to the phrase **as Aussie as meat pies**. **2.** Aussie rhyming slang for 'eye'.

meat-pie bookie a small-time bookmaker.

meat tag an identity disc worn by members of the armed forces. Also called a **meat ticket**.

meat wagon an ambulance.

Meccano Set an enormously large set of traffic lights at the intersection of the Hume Highway and Henry Lawson Drive, near Liverpool in Sydney. *Turn left at the Meccano Set.*

Mediterranean back a supposed back injury faked in order to get out of work. A racial slur on immigrants of Mediterranean background who are sometimes accused of putting in too many workers' compensation claims.

meet an appointment. *Are we on for a meet this arvo?*

megababe an extremely attractive person, male or female; a major spunk.

megabucks a large amount of money.

megahunk a very attractive male.

-meister used to create nicknames, as *Bruciemeister* (Bruce). From German *Meister* 'master, chief'.

mellow to relax; to chill out.

melon **1.** the head. **2.** a stupid person; a fool.

melonhead a fool; an idiot.

melon hole a natural depression or hole in the ground which forms a reservoir; a gilgai.

melons large, full breasts.

member the penis.

men in white coats fictitious employees of a mental asylum who come and take people away to be institutionalised. A phrase used when someone is acting crazy.

mental **1.** driven to distraction; acting crazy: *He'll go mental when he finds out.* Hence, an outburst of rage, as in to **chuck a mental**, to completely lose your temper. **2.** extremely drunk. **3.** (especially among children) a stupid person. *Shut up, you mental!*

mental attack a sudden fit of rage.

the Mental Coast the Central Coast, NSW.

me'n'u a restaurant menu. Punning on the phrase *me and you.*

Merc a Mercedes-Benz motor car.

merchant a person noted for a certain aspect of their character or behaviour. *panic merchant, standover merchant.*

merkin **1.** an artificial hairpiece to cover the vagina. This word goes back to the 1600s, when it was common for prostitutes to shave their vaginas in order to pass themselves off to customers as pre-pubic virgins. **2.** an artificial vagina used for autoerotic purposes. **3.** a derisive term for an American.

mermaid a weighbridge inspector – so called because they are **scaly** (see entry).

merry monk a now obsolete term for the sum of £500.

meself the fair dinkum Aussie way of pronouncing 'myself'. *That's the way I see it meself, I'll take you on meself.*

messages small errands to the shops. *Mum sent me down the street to do the messages.*

metalhead a fan of heavy metal music.

Met cop a ticket inspector on Melbourne's public transport system.

meth methedrine.

metho **1.** methylated spirits. Also, **meths**. **2.** a metho drinker.

Metho a Methodist.

Methodist gate a gate that is extremely difficult to open – that is, only a Methodist can open it without swearing.

mettie the sausage meat mettwurst.

Mexican someone from 'south of the border'. So, in Qld, it can mean a person from New South Wales or Victoria, but in NSW, it means a person from Victoria.

Mick **1.** a Roman Catholic (especially of Irish extraction). **2.** an Irish man or woman.

mickey a mouse – after the Disney character.

mickey drip a Roman Catholic.

Mickey Finn **1.** a drink spiked with an incapacitating drug. **2.** obsolete rhyming slang for 'spin', the sum of £5.

Mickey Mouse **1.** rhyming slang for 'grouse' – excellent, terrific, wonderful. Aussie slang since the 1970s. **2.** of a mechanical item, cheap and poorly made. Note how these two definitions are pretty much opposites – so you have to rely on context to get the meaning.

micky **1.** the female genitalia. Also, rarely, **mick**. **2.** a young, wild bull. Also, **mickey**. **3.** to **chuck a micky** is to throw a tantrum. **4.** to **take the micky out of someone** is to tease them.

micky juice vaginal secretions produced during sexual arousal.

micky muncher one who practises cunnilingus.

microdot a type of LSD trip.

Microsloth a computer geek's jocular derogatory term for the Microsoft operating system, with reference to its supposed lack of speed. Compare **Windoze**.

middy a beer glass of 10 fluid ounces (285 ml). Used in NSW and the ACT, WA, NT and parts of Qld. Presumably so called because it occupies the *mid*dle spot between a schooner and a glass. In Tas, Vic and Qld this is equivalent to a **pot**. Not surprisingly, this used to be called a **ten**, which name is still used in Tas and Qld. In SA, and some country areas, a 10 ounce glass is sometimes confusingly known as a **schooner**, a fact that has caused great shock, disappointment, anger, etc., to travelling New South Welshmen. In NT and Tas if you simply order a **beer** you will get a 10 ounce glass.

mile-high club a supposed club, the members of which have all had sex in an aeroplane in flight.

milkie **1.** a white marble, usually with swirls of another colour. **2.** same as a milko.

milko a person who sells or delivers milk.

Millennium Bug among Aussie rail enthusiasts, the CityRail (Sydney) Millennium Train, supposed to begin service in 1999, but endlessly delayed by technical problems.

millihelen a spurious measurement of beauty: one millihelen is the amount of beauty required to launch a single ship. A thousand millihelens is, of course, a 'Helen', powerful enough to launch a thousand ships!

minda in South Australia, a stupid or clumsy person. Generally used as an insult by schoolkids. From *Minda*, the name of a home for people with intellectual disabilities. Not exactly PC is it? For similar non-PC terms see **moonya** and **crowl**.

mind-fuck something that blows you away; literally, something that fucks with your mind.

minge a crass, blokey word for the vagina. Originally British slang, and first recorded in the Suffolk dialect of England, back in 1903.

Ming the Merciless a nickname of erstwhile Prime Minister, Sir Robert Menzies. So called after the evil ruler of Speed Gordon comic strips (for more information see **Speed Gordon**).

min-min light a type of bright light of mysterious origins seen at night in the outback.

minnow a small-time gambler. As opposed to a **whale**.

mint in WA, excellent, tops, terrific, cool. This was common from the 70s onwards. The idea is that mint is cool to the taste, and thus means 'cool', though it probably also owes something to the word 'mint' meaning in perfect condition. Anyhow, **mint** was later extended to become **mintox**, as in *That movie was mintox* or *I read a mintox book the other day*. This comes from the brand name of an oral antacid.

minute man a derogatory term for a man afflicted with premature ejaculation.

miserable as a bandicoot on a burnt ridge totally and utterly miserable.

miseryguts a person who is always whingeing or complaining.

the Missos the Miscellaneous Workers Union.

missus **1.** the wife; the little woman; the cheese and kisses. **2.** the woman of the house on a rural property or station, traditionally having jurisdiction over the affairs pertaining to the homestead. Counterpart to the **boss**.

mitt the hand.

mix mulled-up marijuana.

mix it to fight.

mix-up a fight.

mixup in Tasmania, cordial concentrate to be mixed with water. See **cordial**.

mizzle off to depart; to leave.

mo **1.** a moment. Hence, **half a mo!** hang on a sec! **2.** a moustache. Hence, **curl the mo!** struth! crikey!

mob **1.** a crowd of people. **2.** in Aboriginal English, a tribal or language group, or a community. **3.** a group of people, as friends, not necessarily large. *We'll invite the mob over for Saturday night.* **4.** a collective noun for certain animals, as cattle, sheep and kangaroos. **5.** If there are **mobs of** something or some things, then there is a lot of it, or a large number of them. If there are still more, then it is a **big mob**, and an even larger number is denoted by **biggest mob**. *There were big mobs of people at the race meeting. I'll have big mobs of mashed potato, please. Biggest mob of cattle over that hill!*

mobile ready to leave immediately.

mocca a Melbourne term for a westie, bogan or bevan. From their habit of wearing moccas.

moccas moccasins. No, not the Native American ones – the daggy suede leather shoes.

mocker to **put the mocker on** is to jinx or bring bad luck to someone. You can also **put the mockers on** or **put the mocks on** someone.

Mockery a mocking name for the Tasmanian newspaper *The Mercury*. Also a local name for the *Illawarra Mercury* of coastal NSW.

mods modifications made to a standard car engine.

moff a rural word for an hermaphroditic kangaroo. Perhaps borrowed from South African English.

mofo an abbreviated and somewhat euphemistic way of saying **motherfucker**. It is an Americanism of the 1960s, and made its way to Oz in the 1980s.

moggy a cat. Originally Cockney slang from the 1910s.

moi the French word for 'me', used in mock affectation. *Pretentious? Moi?*

moisty a nubile young female.

mojo personal magical power; your essential coolness and sexuality. Popularised by Mike Myers' *Austin Powers* movies. Originally American Black English, and ultimately from an African language. *I've gotta get my mojo back, man.*

moke a horse.

mole **1.** a spy. Originally US slang of the 1970s. **2.** a variant spelling of **moll** (see entry).

moll **1.** a promiscuous woman; a prostitute. A very harsh word equivalent to *slut*. Something egregiously out of place is said to be **like a moll at a christening**. **2.** the girlfriend or mistress of a gangster, crook, bikie, etc.

moll patrol a scathing term for a group of schoolgirls as viewed by a rival group.

mollydooker a left-handed person. Aussie slang since the 1930s. Probably from British dialect *molly* 'an effeminate man' and *dook* 'the hand'.

Molly the Monk Aussie rhyming slang for 'drunk'. Dating back to the 1960s.

molo drunk. Formerly quite common, but now outmoded. Origin unknown.

money for jam easily made money.

mong **1.** a mongrel dog. **2.** a stupid person; a dork. A shortening of *mongoloid*. Non-PC Aussie kids' slang since the 1990s. Hence, as an adjective, stupid, hopeless, worthless, or the like. *What a mong car.* Also heard in the forms **monger** or **mongo**. Hence, the adjective **mongy**: *Jim's a bit mongy dropping the ball like that.*

mong out to hang around wasting time doing nothing; to veg out.

mongrel **1.** a detestable person. One of the great Aussie insults, formerly used in Britain but now obsolete there. **2.** something difficult. *It's a mongrel of a job.* **3.** despicable; detestable; rotten; ratshit. *You filthy rotten mongrel bastard.*

mongulated very stupid. *You are so mongulated.*

moniker **1.** a person's name or nickname. **2.** a person's signature.

monkey an obsolete term for £500, and then, after decimal currency, $500. A monkey is about half the size of a **gorilla** (see entry). Has sometimes been recorded as meaning £50 or $50.

monkey on your back any obsession, compulsion, or addiction, seen as a burden, such as a compulsion to work or an addiction to drugs.

monkey suit a dinner suit.

monobrow a person with one long eyebrow stretching across both eyes and the nose.

monster to harass or hassle.

month of Sundays a very long time.

monty a certainty.

moo a stupid person, especially a woman; a dork. *Give it here, ya stupid moo.*

mooch **1.** to hang or loiter about. **2.** to slouch or saunter along.

moo juice milk.

moolah money. Originally US slang dating back to the 1930s. Origin unknown. Also commonly spelt **moola**.

moon to display the buttocks publicly, as from a car window.

moonbeam a plate, cup or piece of cutlery which was not used at an evening meal, and does not need washing up. The night-time equivalent of the **sunbeam**.

moonface a person with a large round head. **Old Moonface** is the affectionate nickname of TV star Bert Newton.

moonie a public display of the buttocks. *We were horrified when she flashed a moonie.*

moon tan the extremely pale skin of a person whose flesh barely ever sees sunlight.

moonya a stupid or clumsy person. Used by schoolkids in Gippsland in the 70s. Comes from the Moonya South West Gippsland Centre for Intellectually Handicapped. See **minda** and **crowl**.

moop in the Australian Antarctic Territory, a person whose circadian rhythms have become disoriented due to the odd length of day and night in polar regions. Standing for *Man Out Of Phase*.

moo poo cow manure.

moosh **1.** (rhymes with 'shush') the mouth; the face. Originally British slang of the mid-19th century, of unknown origin. **2.** prison food, especially porridge. A different word this, coming from the US, and perhaps an alteration of *mash*.

moot (rhymes with 'foot') the female genitals. An indelicate word that women generally eschew. It is used in Aboriginal English and is perhaps from some Aboriginal language. Occasionally spelt **moote**.

moped a blokey word for a woman who you are sleeping with but ashamed of in public. In other words 'nice to ride, but you wouldn't want your mates to see you on one'.

moral a certainty. *They're a moral to win.*

more front than Myers overly impudent. From the Melbourne department store which has a large frontage. A similar phrase is **more hide than Jessie**, referring to a well-known elephant formerly at Sydney's Taronga zoo.

Moreton Bay fig underworld rhyming slang for 'gig' or 'fizgig', in other words, an informer. Aussie slang since the 1940s.

morning glory **1.** sexual intercourse had upon awakening in the morning. **2.** an erection of the penis upon awakening. **3.** a horse which performs well in morning track work, but not in races.

morning sticks a Tasmanian term for kindling gathered at the start of the day. In WA and SA called **morning's wood**.

morph morphine.

Moscow a pawnshop. Thus if something is **in Moscow**, it is pawned. Hence, as a verb, **to Moscow** something is to pawn it.

mosey to amble, stroll, saunter, as in *Just moseying along minding my own business.* A word popularised by US Westerns.

mosh **1.** to dance in a mosh pit. Perhaps a variant of *mash* 'to squash'. **2.** the crush of moshers in a mosh pit.

mosher one who takes part in moshing. Also called a **moshie**.

moshing vigorous dancing in a tightly packed crowd at the front of a stage.

mosh pit the area in front of a stage at a concert where moshing takes place.

Mosman tractor Sydney slang, a derogatory term for a city-only 4WD that never sees off-road driving. Also known as a **Mosman shopping trolley** or a **Mosman truck**. See **Toorak tractor** for a host of synonyms.

mossie a mosquito. Aussie slang from the 1930s. Also spelt **mozzie**.

Moss Vegas the township of Moss Vale, in south-east NSW. Modelled on the earlier term **Bris-Vegas**.

mother **1.** an abbreviated way of saying **motherfucker**. Not very complimentary to your mother, or anybody else for that matter. **2.** the most extreme example of its kind. *the mother of all wars.*

motherfucker an utterly contemptible person. Similar to a *prick* or *bastard* or *mongrel*, but a lot worse. An Americanism dating back to the 19th century. Common in Black English and sometimes spelt **muthafucka** in order to represent the pronunciation. The abbreviated form **mofo** is only occasionally heard here in Oz.

motherfucking an intensifier, used in negative contexts, like *You motherfucking arsehole!*, but also in positive ones, as *We had this motherfucking enormous chocolate cake.*

motherless broke completely destitute.

mother's milk any beer the speaker wishes to lionise as the greatest. To many, mother's milk equates to VB. Northern Tasmanians will use it of Boag, and the southerners will use it for Cascade. Queenslanders mean XXXX by it – either that, or Bundy rum.

motorhead a car enthusiast.

motormouth a person who just won't shut up.

motza a large amount of money, especially a gambling win. An Australianism that first appears in the 1930s. Perhaps from Yiddish *matse* 'bread', as in *bread* = money. Also spelt **motser**.

mountain maggot a sheep. From a distance they look like little white blobby things infesting a hillside.

mountain oyster a testicle of a castrated bull or ram, eaten as food. The same thing as a **prairie oyster**.

Mount Isa by the Sea a nickname for Townsville, Qld, alluding to its lack of greenery. Also called **Brownsville**.

mouse potato a person addicted to surfing the internet.

mouth like the bottom of a cocky's cage the sort of mouth you get after a big night out on the piss.

move a choice or decision about a course of action. *So you've decided to forgive him? Bad move!*

move it, or lose it a warning indicating that one should move whatever it is one has in the way.

mow someone's lawn to have sex with another's partner; to cuckold someone. Also, to **cut someone's grass**.

mozz to **mozz** someone, or to **put the mozz on** them, is to jinx them or bring them bad luck.

mozzie a mosquito.

Mrs Kerfoops a fictitious woman used as a put-off to a question you can't answer or don't wish to. As in, 'Who were you talking to?' 'Oh, Mrs Kerfoops down the street'. She is also used as a scapegoat, as in, 'Who used the last of the milk?' 'Mrs Kerfoops did'. Also, used as a term of endearment to a young girl. Sometimes it is **Madame Kerfoops** or **Lady Kerfoops**. The spelling of her name is quite variable, such as *Kuffoops* or *Kafoops.*

Mrs Palmer and her five lovely daughters a metaphor for the hand used in male masturbation. Dating back to the 1950s.

muchly very much. *Ta muchly.*

muck-up day the last day of attendance at high school, traditionally a day of student pranks.

Mudbank the Sydney suburb of Meadowbank, on the Parramatta River, having large mud flats at low tide.

muddie a mudcrab.

mud gecko a crocodile.

Mudguard a nickname for a bald bloke who's a bit stupid – because he's shiny on top and shit underneath.

mud lark **1.** a racehorse that performs well on wet tracks. Also called a **mud runner**. **2.** a name for the magpie lark, most commonly found in Vic and WA. See **peewee** for the full list of regionalisms.

mud map a map drawn in the earth with a stick. Common out in the bush.

mud stump a termite mound.

muff **1.** the female genitalia. **2.** a failure. **3.** to make an error when doing something; to bungle. *He muffed it.*

muff diver a person who indulges in cunnilingus. Also called a **muff muncher**.

muff-diving cunnilingus. Also, **muff-munching**.

mug **1.** a fool. Hence, stupid, as in the *mug punters* or a *mug copper*. **2.** a criminal's victim or 'mark'; also, anyone who is not a member of the underworld. **3.** a prostitute's client. **4.** among showies and carnies, a customer. **5.** the face. **6.** in olden days, to **mug** someone was to smooch them.

mug lair a flashily dressed young man of brash and vulgar behaviour.

mugs away the losers go first (in the next round of a game, etc.).

mug's game a foolish enterprise; an occupation a mug is likely to get involved in. *Gambling is a mug's game, Married life is a mug's game.*

mulga technically, any of several species of acacia, but in slang **the mulga** means the outback. *She's been out in the mulga for a few years.*

mulga wire the rural gossip mill; the bush telegraph.

mulie in WA, a pilchard used as bait.

mull **1.** a preparation of dried leaves, as mint, comfrey, or tobacco, used to mix with marijuana or hash. *What are we gonna use for mull?* **2.** marijuana or hash mulled up or prepared for smoking.

mull bowl a small bowl used to mull up marijuana.

mullet **1.** a type of haircut, commonly worn by males, with the hair short on the top and sides but long at the back. This haircut was very popular among 1970s rock stars, and nowadays is common in North America, Britain and Europe – not to mention Australia. In North America it is especially popular with male country-and-western artists, athletes, and professional wrestlers, while in Australia it is in fashion among westies, bogans, and bevans, and is despised and ridiculed by inner city trendies, goths, surfies, bank managers, the judiciary – well, it is pretty much despised by anyone who doesn't have one.

According to a list I found on the internet this haircut has numerous other names around the English-speaking world such as: *ape drape, beaver paddle, bi-level, Billy Ray, business in the front – party in the back, butt-rocker, dirtmonkey, dirtstick, Grand National, hockey hair, hockey player, Kentucky waterfall, Mississippi grapevine, Missouri compromise, mudflap, neck blanket, schlong, seven, sho-lo, skirted eggshell, soccer-rocker, 10/90,* and *wrestlemania*. But none of these terms are as common as *mullet*, which appears to have had its origin in the Beastie Boys song *Mullet Head* of 1994.

2. a stupid person.

mull head a heavy marijuana user.

mull mix dried herbs for mulling with marijuana, used to soften to the harsh effect of marijuana smoke on the throat.

mullock the refuse from mining, thus, rubbish, nonsense. From British dialect. To **poke mullock at** is to ridicule.

mull up to prepare marijuana or hash for smoking, often by mixing it with some other substance such as tobacco.

mullygrubber in cricket, a low bowl which trundles along the ground (technically, which bounces more than once).

mumble pants very tight-fitting gym shorts worn by a woman. So called because you can see the lips move, but you can't hear the c#@% talk. (Sorry about that.) Also called **mumblers**.

mummy's boy a male who is mollycoddled by his mother; hence, a wimp or wuss.

munch among car sellers, a tyre-kicker who takes a car on a test-drive and still has no intention of buying.

munchie a shark.

munchies **1.** anything to eat, especially snacks between meals. **2.** a craving for food, especially as resulting from smoking marijuana. You have to inhale to get the munchies.

munchkin a person small in stature; someone with duck's disease. From the dwarfish race in the film *The Wizard of Oz*.

mundowie the foot. Especially common in northern Qld. Can also be used to refer to a footprint. From an Aboriginal language.

mung **1.** food. **2.** a stupid person; a fool. **3.** under the influence of marijuana; totally stoned. *He's wasted man, he's mung.*

munga food. Chiefly used by soldiers in both World Wars. It is originally British slang and probably comes from the Italian *mangiare* to eat. Sometimes it was **mangaree** or **mungey**.

mung bean **1.** a New Age, greenie, leftie, vego, feral type. **2.** a stupid or annoying person; a loser.

mungo a derogatory term for a Rugby League player. Been around since the 1960s. It is also used to mean a player who has committed the sin of switching from Union to League. Sometimes it's pronounced **mongo**. The origin of the term remains a mystery though many have sought it. The mostly likely is that it is derived from *mongrel*.

mung out to eat.

munted **1.** incapacitated from too much alcohol or drugs. **2.** totally ruined or wrecked.

Mur'bah Murwillumbah, in northern NSW, as pronounced by the locals.

Murphy's law a mock-scientific law which states 'If something can go wrong, it will go wrong'. Apparently it originally referred to a Captain E. *Murphy* of the Wright Field-Aircraft Laboratory in 1949.

Murray magpie in SA, a name for the magpie lark. See **peewee** for the full list of regionalisms.

Murrumbidgee whaler a swagman who frequented the Australian inland rivers and sustained himself by both begging and fishing. A *whaler* was a person who fished for Murray cod.

muscle car a souped-up and tricked-up car.

muscle mary a strong, masculine homosexual man.

muscles on your piles said of an extremely strong man.

mush (rhymes with 'shush') prison food, especially porridge. Also spelt **moosh**.

mushie a mushroom.

mushroom a person who is deliberately kept ignorant and misinformed, in other words, 'they are kept in the dark and fed on shit'.

muso a musician.

muss up to make a mess of. *Her hair was all mussed up.*

mustard hut Tasmanian slang for a musset hut, a transportable classroom used in schools.

mute very drunk.

muthafucka a spelling of **motherfucker**, meant to represent an American Black English pronunciation.

mutt **1.** a dog, especially a mongrel. **2.** a simpleton; a stupid person.

muttai on the north coast of NSW, a corncob. Origin unknown. Perhaps from an Aboriginal language.

mutton the penis.

mutton dressed up as lamb something made out to be better than it really is. Specifically, a tarted-up woman.

myall an Aboriginal living traditionally.

my arse! I think not! No way! Rubbish! Bullshit!

my bloody oath You bet! Certainly! Too bloody right! Also, you can drop the 'bloody' and just say **my oath**. Formerly it was common to replace 'bloody' with the euphemistic 'colonial' and say **my colonial oath**.

my dog's are barking my feet are sore.

myst all critey! a deliberate Spoonerism of *Christ Almighty!*

mystery bag **1.** a sausage. **2.** a meat pie. Also called a **mystery box**.

mystery bundle a pastie.

my word You bet! Certainly! An original Australianism dating as far back as the 1850s.

myxo the viral disease myxomatosis introduced to control the feral rabbit population. Also called **myxie**.

N

nada nothing. *Best of all it's free, zip, zero, nada.* From US slang, from Spanish.

nads the testicles. Shortened from *gonads.*

nag a bulb of nitrous oxide or laughing gas, inhaled for recreational purposes. *After a few drinks we got out the whipped cream bottle and did nags.* Also called a **nang**.

nags the horseraces. *He spends Sundays at the nags.*

nail **1.** to catch, apprehend or arrest. **2.** to kill. **3.** of a male, to have sex with someone; to fuck. **4.** to do something perfectly and confidently.

nana a banana. To **chuck a nana** is to throw a tantrum. This is also known as **doing your nana**. If you are **off your nana** you are crazy.

nancy boy an effeminate man; an effeminate homosexual man. Also simply called a **nancy**.

nanny goat rhyming slang for the 'tote'. Originally British.

nanosecond a very brief period of time. *Be with you in a nanosecond.*

Nappy Valley a derisive name for Tuggeranong in the ACT, alluding to the high birth rate there.

narc a police officer from the narcotics squad.

nard a piece of excrement; a turd.

nark **1.** a police informer. The original meaning in Australia. From British underworld slang of the 1860s, originally meaning to watch, from Romani (the language spoken by Gypsies) *nāk* 'nose'. Now obsolete. **2.** a whingeing, whining person; one who is always interfering and spoiling the pleasure of others; a spoilsport or wowser. **3.** a fit of annoyance. *Stay out of her way, she's got the nark properly.* Old slang, not heard any longer. **4.** to irritate or annoy. *Jack'll be narked about this.*

narkie in Tasmanian, a local name for the native hen, a small, flightless, water bird endemic to the island. Also called a **bush chook** or a **racing chook**.

narky irritable; bad-tempered.

Nasho the National Service. Hence, a National Serviceman. National Service was a system of compulsory military training for all young fit men of 18 years of age, which ran from the years 1951 to 1974.

Natasha Spot Destroyer a jocular nickname for Democrats politician Natasha Stott Despoja.

natch an abbreviation of the word 'naturally'.

national game Actually, Australia has two national games – **Aussie Rules** and **two-up**.

natural foot a surfer who rides with the left foot in front of the right.

naughty an act of sexual intercourse. First recorded in 1959.

Naussie a recent immigrant. This cute little blend of *New* and *Aussie* had a brief life in the 1950s when the term *New Australian* was in common use for an immigrant of non-English-speaking background.

Nazi anyone with dogmatic prejudices and a dictatorial attitude about a certain topic or thing. *You're such a remote-control Nazi.*

NBG no bloody good.

near and far rhyming slang for 'bar' (of a hotel). Originally British.

neck **1.** to kiss, cuddle and pet. Originally US slang, adopted here in the 1940s. **2.** underworld slang, to rob a person by seizing them about the neck. **3.** to commit suicide by hanging. *He necked himself.*

Necknock a joking way of referring to the town of Cessnock, NSW. Also, **Nicknock**.

neck oil booze or grog. Because it lubricates the larynx.

neddy a horse. Aussie slang since the 1880s. In early British slang this was used for a donkey – Australians seem to have borrowed the word but changed the meaning. Hence, the **neddies** are the horseraces.

Ned Kelly **1.** Australia's most famous bushranger and unofficial national hero. Used in a negative way to refer to anyone who is a bit of a crook, or in a positive way to mean a person who courageously stands up against overbearing authority. To be **game as Ned Kelly** is to be outstandingly gutsy. If you are **in more shit than Ned Kelly**, then you are in big strife.

2. rhyming slang for 'belly'. *Get that into your Ned Kelly.*

need your head read you are acting insane. A quaint Aussie way of disparaging another's point of view. It's been around since the 1950s.

neenish tart especially in NSW, ACT and Vic, a small tart, sometimes made with almond flavoured pastry, with a mock cream filling, and a topping half one colour and half another, usually a combination of white and chocolate or white and pink. Recipes for this Aussie pastry date back to the 1930s when it was spelt 'Neinich Tart'.

neg driving the offence of negligent driving.

Nellie Bly Aussie rhyming slang for 'meat pie'. Has been around since the 1960s. Originally this was British rhyming slang for 'fly', the insect, that is, and comes from the name of a character in the popular ballad *Frankie and Johnnie*. In Australia it also gets used to mean the fly of a pair of pants, or a lie, or a tie. Sometimes spelt **Nelly Bligh**.

Nelson's blood rum. Originally British naval slang. The story goes that when Lord Nelson died at sea his body was preserved in a cask of rum so that it could be transported back home for burial. Supposedly sailors on the ship, having finished the supply of rum and getting desperate, tapped the cask containing their erstwhile captain and drank the rum. Yum!

Nelson's number in cricket, a score of 111 – thought by the English to be unlucky. So called, because after his injuries, Lord Nelson retained 1 arm, 1 leg, and 1 eye.

nembie a nembutal tablet, used as a downer.

nerd a geek, drip, drongo or dag. US slang from the 1950s. Origin uncertain, but perhaps from the name of a character in Dr Seuss's *If I Ran the Zoo* (1950). Sometimes spelt **nurd**.

nervous Nelly an overly timid or nervous person.

nest the vagina. To be **on the nest** is to be engaged in sexual intercourse.

net head an internet addict.

netiquette the etiquette of good and bad behaviour on the internet.

netizen a user of the internet.

never-never **1.** sparsely inhabited outback regions of Australia. Aussie slang since the 1830s. **2.** the hire-purchase system. *We bought our lounge on the never-never.* This one is originally British slang.

Neville an unpopular person; a nerd, dag or geek. Same as a **Nigel**.

newbie a novice or newcomer.

new chum **1.** originally, a newly transported convict; later, any newly arrived immigrant from Britain. The butt of much humour and scorn because of their naivety regarding Australian life and ways. This term was first used at the beginning of the 19th century, but began to die out in this sense in the first decades of the 20th. The opposite was, naturally, the **old chum**. **2.** a novice or inexperienced person. *I was the new chum on the job.* This meaning first appears in the 1850s and is still in use.

newie something completely new; a novelty. Often used sarcastically. *My, that's a newie!* Aussie slang since the 1920s – so not exactly a newie itself.

Newie **1.** the city of Newcastle, north of Sydney. **2.** the beachy suburb of Newport. Either the one in Sydney or the one in Melbourne.

Newkie the city of Newcastle, NSW.

Newkie Brown Newcastle Brown brand beer.

NFI no fucking idea.

Niagara Falls rhyming slang for 'balls'. Originally British from the 1950s. Commonly shortened to **Niagaras**.

nibble pie a party pie.

nibs an ironic title for an important person, or a self-important person, especially an employer. *His nibs has asked us to work a little harder.* Generally used of men, though **her nibs** is sometimes used. Originally British slang.

nice try, but no cigar a phrase indicating that someone has made a good, but nevertheless incorrect, guess. Sometimes rendered as **nice try, but no banana**, which, although a cheaper prize, is at least healthier. If someone guesses correctly then you can say **give the man** (or **lady**) **a cigar**.

nick **1.** prison. Aussie slang since the 1880s. In British slang it is used for the police station. **2.** to capture or arrest. **3.** to steal. **4.** to go or move with speed. *I'll nick across the road.* Aussie slang since the 1890s.

nick-and-run a variant name for the kids' game **hit-and-run** (see entry).

nicker one dollar. Originally British slang for one pound sterling. Origin unknown.

Nicknock a joking way of referring to the town of Cessnock, NSW. Also, **Necknock**.

nick off **1.** to leave hurriedly; to decamp. *Let's nick off before the boss gets back.* **2.** a polite way of saying *piss off!*

nick out to go out for a short period. *I'll just nick out and get a few things from the shops.*

nicky swim in WA, a skinny dip.

nig a shortening of the word **nigger** (see entry). Recorded in Australia from as early as 1880.

Nigel an unpopular person; a nerd, dag or geek. Same as a **Neville**. Also known as **Nigel No-Friends**.

nigger a dark-skinned person of African descent, especially an African American. Long used as a term of great contempt by white people, and now so taboo that it is generally referred to as 'the N word' in the US and increasingly elsewhere. In colonial Australia it was naturally used by white settlers to refer to the indigenous peoples, recorded as early as 1845. The attitude of the colonists to Aboriginals is evident in these lines penned by the famous Australian poet Henry Kendall in 1880 – *I never loved a nigger belle / My tastes are too aesthetic! / The perfume from a gin is – well, / A rather strong emetic.* As racial prejudice is basically only skin-deep, the term nigger is often applied to any non-white or swarthy peoples, such as Pacific islanders, Kanakas, Indians, Arabs, and even southern Mediterraneans. Not common in Australia nowadays except among unabashed racists.

nigger-lover a term of contempt used by racists for non-racists.

the night's a pup the night is young. Aussie slang dating from the 1910s.

nightwatchman in cricket, a low order batsman, who is sent in to bat late in the afternoon when the batting-side captain wishes to preserve the better batsmen for the next day's play.

nimby **1.** a person who is against having necessary developments such as new prisons, hospitals, airports, and the like, built in the vicinity of their home, although they would support such development elsewhere. An acronym from *Not In My Back Yard.* **2.** any development nobody wants built nearby.

niner a nine-gallon keg of beer. Also called a **nine**. Aussie slang dating from the 1940s. Died out with the introduction of metrication.

nineteenth hole the bar in a golf clubhouse.

ning-nong a simpleton. An Australian variant of the British dialect form *ning nang.* Been around since the 1950s.

Nip a racist name for a Japanese person, especially a Japanese soldier. Short for *Nipponese.* First used in World War II.

nipper **1.** a small child; a kid. **2.** a young lad on a construction site or in a mine who does small odd jobs, such as making tea and buying lunch. Aussie slang dating from the 1910s. **3.** a junior lifesaver.

nit **1.** a word used to warn people engaged in some illegal activity that the police are coming. Thus, to **keep nit** is to keep watch or act as a lookout. Recorded in Australia from as early as 1882. Probably a variant of British slang *nix*, used in the same way, which is from the German word *nichts* 'nothing'. However, German dialect also has *nit* meaning 'no'. **2.** a foolish or stupid person.

nit keeper a person who keeps watch for authorities while illegal activities are taking place; a lookout or cockatoo. Aussie slang since the 1930s.

nitwit a slow-witted or foolish person.

nix **1.** nothing. *She bought it for next to nix.* **2.** No! Not at all! From cant and flash language, ultimately from German *nichts.*

Noah's ark **1.** rhyming slang for 'shark'. Aussie slang since the 1940s. Commonly shortened to **Noah**. **2.** rhyming slang for 'nark', as in a spoilsport. Much older this one, dating back to the 1890s, but now obsolete.

no Arthur Murrays Aussie rhyming slang for 'no worries'. From the famous Arthur Murray Dance Studios.

nob **1.** the head of the penis. Hence, an annoying person; a social reject; a dickhead. *He sat there by himself, looking like a real nob.* Also known as a **nob end**. **2.** obsolete two-up slang for a counterfeit coin having two heads.

nob-sucker a contemptible person; a scumbag.

nod **1.** permission; the go-ahead. *We got the nod for our new extension.* **2.** credit. *The bookie usually allowed me to bet on the nod.*

no David Murrays South Australian rhyming slang for 'no worries'. From David Murray's, a well-known furniture store in Adelaide.

nod bet a bet taken on credit.

nod your head underworld slang, to plead guilty or accept blame or responsibility for something. Aussie slang since the 1950s. Also in the form **nod your nut**.

no flies on you a complimentary phrase meaning you are clever. Aussie slang since the 1840s. This is one Australianism that has made its way to the US.

nog a strongly racist term for an Asian person, especially common in the military. In the Korean War this word and the variant **noggy** were used by Australian soldiers to refer to Koreans and Chinese. Subsequently, in the Vietnam War, the terms were applied to the Vietnamese. The prevailing theory is that these come from British slang *nig-nog* 'an African' – but this isn't terribly convincing as there is little similarity between African and Asian peoples.

noggin the head. Originally US slang from the 1850s.

no good to gundy no good at all. Aussie slang since the 1900s. Who (or what) 'Gundy' was has been lost in time.

no-hoper **1.** an unpromising racehorse or greyhound; an outsider. Aussie slang dating from the 1940s. **2.** a hopeless case. *He is a real no-hoper at tennis.* Borrowed into the US in the 1950s

nointer in Tasmania, a mischievous child or brat. From British dialect, a shortening of *anointer* 'a mischievous fellow'. This relates to an obsolete verb *anoint* 'to chastise or thrash', in other words to 'consecrate' by beating.

nollie in skateboarding, a manoeuvre similar to an ollie but off the nose of the board rather than the tail. See **ollie**.

no more Mr Nice Guy no more acting nicely; no more being kind or generous.

no-neck a muscular, stupid man.

nong a fool or idiot; a drongo. Aussie slang since the 1940s. A shortening of **ning-nong**.

non-starter something which has no chance of success.

no-nuts an effeminate or gutless male; a wimp or wuss.

noogie a harsh and painful rubbing of the knuckles across someone's head, especially used by children as a form of bullying. Originally US slang of the 1970s. Origin unknown.

nooky sexual intercourse. Recorded in the US from the 1920s and common in Australia since the 1970s. It has been suggested that it is from Dutch slang *neuken*. The Dutch word is etymologically related to the English word 'knock', which has been used since the 1500s to mean 'fuck'. However, the Dutch pronunciation is *no-ken*, and definitely not *nook-en*.

no plum pud Aussie rhyming slang for 'no good'.

no problems! Everything is okay! No worries! Dates back to the 1960s. Also common in the shortened form **no probs** and the faux Spanish **no problemo**. The latter was picked up in Australia from *The Simpsons* and the movie *Terminator II*.

noras breasts.

no risk! an exclamation of reassurance or approval. Aussie slang dating from the late 1950s – slightly earlier than **no worries**.

norks breasts. First recorded in the 1960s. Also rarely found in the form **norgs**. The suggestion that it is from *Norco* butter, the wrapping of which at one time featured a cow's udder, is barely worth consideration.

noromo (when *The X-Files* was popular) a fan who did not want to see Mulder and Scully get together romantically. As opposed to a **finishipper** or a **shipper** (see entries).

north and south rhyming slang for 'mouth'. Originally British slang from the 1850s.

the North Island in Tasmania, an ironic nickname for the Mainland.

North Shore Holden Sydney slang for a Volvo car.

North Shore tank Sydney slang, a derogatory term for a city-only 4WD. Also called a **North Shore Kingswood**. See **Toorak tractor** for a host of synonyms.

North Snore the North Shore of Sydney, noted for its prevalence of boring farts.

nosebag to **put on the nosebag** is to begin a meal. Aussie slang dating from the 1910s.

nosh food. This word made its way to Oz from the US in the 1980s. Ultimately from Yiddish *nashn* 'to nibble'.

noshery an eating house, restaurant or cafe.

no shit? Really? Is that true? Also, commonly used sarcastically when someone has stated the obvious.

no-show an instance of not turning up for an appointment. Hence, a person who fails to turn up. *He was a no-show at last night's game.*

no show without Punch a phrase used to mean that the most important guest was not present. It is also used to have a go at some show-off who always needs to be the centre of attention.

nosh-up a meal.

no spring chicken not a young person any more.

nosy parker a person who continually pries; a meddler or stickybeak.

not used after a sentence to negate the previous statement. *That's a nice shirt. Not!* This humorous locution originated in the 1890s in the US. It recurred in the 1980s in the TV comedy show *Saturday Night Live*, and then the 1992 movie *Wayne's World*, whence it made its way to Australian shores.

not a sausage absolutely nothing. It has been suggested that this derives from rhyming slang *sausage and mash* 'cash'. But that hardly makes sense as 'not a cash' is meaningless.

not bat an eyelid to be unconcerned.

not give a rat's arse to not care at all.

not give a shit to not care at all.

not have a bar of to have nothing to do with; to totally repudiate. Aussie slang since the 1930s.

not in the hunt not in contention.

not know from a bar of soap to be completely unfamiliar with. *He doesn't know me from a bar of soap.* Aussie slang since the 1910s.

not know shit to be a complete ignoramus.

not much chop no good. Aussie slang since the 1840s. From *first chop* 'highest quality', a term originating in the Anglo-Indian English of the Raj, and ultimately coming from Hindi *chāp* 'a stamp or brand'.

not on your nelly! Absolutely not! No way!

not playing for sheep stations a phrase used to describe a game that is not all that important. If someone is taking their sport a little too seriously they often need to be reminded that they are not playing for sheep stations.

not the full quid not having a full complement of intelligence. Aussie slang from at least the 1940s.

not the sharpest tool in the shed not very bright.

not worth a bumper to be worth little or nothing; to be worthless. There are many variations on this theme. In culinary terms, things can be **not be worth a cracker/a crumpet/a mintie** or **a pinch of salt**. In financial terms we have **not worth a brass razoo/two bob** or **a zack**. A worthless document is said to be **not worth the paper it's written on**.

not worth a pinch of shit entirely worthless.

noughties the first decade of the new millennium.

nous brains, intelligence. Venerable slang from the 18th century. Originally academic slang, from the ancient Greek word for the mind or intellect.

no way José not under any circumstances!

no worries **1.** don't you worry about that! *No worries, trust me, I'm good!* Aussie slang since the 1960s. **2.** don't mention it! you're welcome! *'Thanks for bringing those beers over.' 'No worries, mate.'*

no wucking furries a deliberate spoonerism of 'no fucking worries'. Also shortened to **no wuckers** or **no wucks**.

nubile an attractive young woman.

nude nut a bald person.

nuff **1.** cool, excellent, terrific. *What a nuff car.* **2.** in Vic, stupid or silly; also, daggy or nerdy.

nuff nuff in Vic, an annoying or idiotic person; a nong. Also called a **nuffy**.

nugget **1.** a lump of naturally occurring gold. First used in the 1850s, from British dialect. No longer slang. **2.** a short muscular man or animal. **3.** an unbranded calf. **4.** a hard knob of faeces.

nuggets the testicles.

nuggety solidly and sturdily built; stocky and tough. Aussie slang dating from the 1860s.

nuke **1.** a nuclear weapon. Hence, to strike with a nuclear weapon, or, metaphorically, to utterly destroy. **2.** to cook in a microwave oven.

the Nulla the Sydney seaside suburb of Cronulla.

nullabat a cryptolanguage used by schoolchildren in which normal words are modified by adding into each syllable the sounds 'ullab'; thus *hug* becomes *hullabug*; *You are a pig* becomes *Yullaboo ullabar ullaba pillabig*. Also called **alibi**. Similar secret languages are **arpie-darpie**, **aygo-paygo**, **obo language**, **pig Latin** and **rechtub kelat**.

Nullarbor Nymph a beautiful, blonde, semi-naked woman who supposedly lived wild on the Nullarbor Plain near Eucla back in the 1970s. The entire story was a hoax, but was swallowed by a gullible public, both Australia- and world-wide.

number ones urination.

number twos defecation.

numb nuts **1.** a weak, gutless man; a man without any balls. **2.** a fool or goof; a klutz.

numbskull a dull-witted person; a blockhead. Age-old British slang from the 1700s.

numero uno **1.** the leader or most important person in any situation. From Italian for 'number one'. **2.** oneself. *You've gotta look after numero uno.*

nurd a variant spelling of **nerd**.

nurries the testicles. A term especially common in WA.

nut **1.** an insane, foolish or eccentric person. US slang from the 1900s. **2.** an enthusiast. *He was an absolute car nut.* **3.** a testicle. **4.** the head. To be **off your nut** is to be deranged. To **do your nut** is to lose your head.

nutbar a fool; a crazy person. Also called a **nut bag**.

nut case a foolish or eccentric person. Aussie slang since the 1940s.

nut house a mental hospital. Also called the **nut factory**.

nutmeg in soccer, to pass the ball between an opponent's legs.

nut out to work out or solve. World War I Aussie slang.

nuts **1.** the testicles. To **do your nuts over** someone is to be infatuated with them. **2.** crazy. *He's nuts about cricket.* **3.** an expression of disbelief, disgust, anger, defiance, or the like. *Nuts to you!* An Americanism from the 1910s, not very common in Australia. Most famously used by Brigadier General McAuliffe in the World War II Battle of the Bulge. His official reply to the German army's demand for the surrender of the town of Bastonge, Belgium, was 'Aw, nuts'.

nutso crazy.

nutter a crazy or foolish person. British slang of the 1950s.

nutty silly or stupid; crazy.

nutty as a fruitcake exceedingly mad; completely insane.

nylon disgusters speedos. For a full set of synonyms see **sluggos**.

nympho a nymphomaniac. Generally used by men to disparage women.

-o **1.** a suffix used to create slangy forms of ordinary words and names. First used in occupational names of itinerant street vendors such as the *rabbit-o* and *bottle-o*. Such vendors announced their arrival by crying out their wares followed by 'oh' – *Rabbit Oh!*, *Bottle Oh!*, *Milk Oh!*, etc. Later it was added to the first syllable of multisyllabic words, such as *arvo*, afternoon; *compo*, compensation; *demo*, demonstration; *kero*, kerosene; *muso*, musician; *panno*, panel wagon; *reffo*, refugee; *Salvo*, Salvation Army officer; and *smoko*, smoking break.

The **-o** suffix alternates with the **-ie** suffix, which is used in pretty much the same manner, though often with a diminutive sense as well. Very few words can take both suffixes – *alko/alkie, arvo/arvie, flanno/flannie, lammo/lammie* and *sammo/sammie* are a few of the exceptions. Of course, there is a very big difference between a *sicko* and a *sickie*! Knowing just when to use the **-o** and when the **-ie** suffix is a skill that defines whether or not someone is a natural speaker of Australian English.
2. used in positive responses or assurances, as *goodo* and *righto*. **3.** used to form colloquial versions of personal names, especially male names, as *Gibbo*, Gibson, *Tommo*, Thompson, *Davo*, Dave, *Peto*, Peter. **4.** used to form colloquial versions of place names, as *Baulko*, Baulkham Hills, *Belco*, Belconnen, *Ermo*, Ermington, *Penno*, Pennant Hills.

OAF SA slang for an Old Adelaide Family.

oater a Western movie.

obo language a cryptolanguage used by schoolchildren in which normal words are modified by adding into each syllable the sound 'ob'; thus *hug* becomes *hobug*; *You are a pig* becomes *Yobu obar oba pobig*. For similar secret languages see **alibi**, **arpie-darpie**, **aygo-paygo**, **pig Latin** and **rechtub kelat**.

ocker **1.** the archetypal uncultivated Australian working man. Also spelt with a capital, **Ocker**. Generally used in a negative way to depict a chauvinistic, misogynistic, sports-loving, beer-gutted, esky-carrying, rubber-thong-wearing yob. Totally lacking in sensitivity, compassion, gentleness and insight. Exactly the same 'bloke' can be seen also in a positive way, as an honest, laid-back, fair dinkum, fun-loving larrikin. An Australian cult figure – popularly satirised in the 1970s by the likes of Paul Hogan and the Barry Humphries creation Bazza McKenzie.

In origin, the term derives from the typically Aussie way of colloquialising the name Oscar. From as early as 1916 blokes named Oscar were called Ocker. In the late 1960s a TV comedy called *The Mavis Bramston Show* had a character named Ocker, played by Barry Creyton, who was your typical uncultivated Australian male, and it is probably from this show that the word was first disseminated throughout the country. As an adjective, **ocker** has come to mean quintessentially Australian. *He had an ocker sense of humour.* And although principally designating men, it can also be used of women. *She was ocker through and through.*
2. Australian English. *I lapsed into ocker and yelled 'Dice it!'*

ockerdom the society of boorish, uncouth, chauvinistic Australians.

ockerina the female counterpart of the ocker.

ockie an octopus.

ockie strap an octopus strap.

odd bod an eccentric person, especially one with a particular fixation.

odds-on certain. *It's odds-on he'll be at the pub.* Racing jargon that made its way into Aussie slang in the 1890s.

off absolutely disgusting; revolting. Especially used by teenagers. *That skirt is totally off!*

offa off your head on either drugs or alcohol.

offal box a meat pie.

office a hint. *You'd better give him the office before he makes a fool of himself.* Originally British sporting slang and underworld slang, brought to Australia as part of the flash language.

office bike a derogatory term for a woman who has sex with many different men in her place of employment.

offie **1.** in cricket, a ball bowled so as to change direction from leg to off when it pitches; an off break. **2.** a bowler who specialises in off-break deliveries.

off like a bride's nightie off or away with the utmost speed.

off like a bucket of prawns in the midday sun extremely rotten; stinking.

offsider an assistant or partner; a workmate. An Australian original from the late 19th century. Originally a bullocky's term for a bullock yoked to the offside (the right-hand side), and hence a bullocky's assistant who attended to the bullocks on the offside of a team.

off the rails mentally unsound or eccentric; not in touch with reality; daydreaming. This is old British slang from the 19th century, and is in origin a railroad metaphor. The 1980s saw some more up-to-date versions appear, namely, **off the air** and **off the planet**.

off with the fairies daydreaming; mentally unsound or eccentric; not in touch with reality. You can also be **off with the pixies**, which is the same thing.

off your face really drunk, stoned or tripping out. Also, **off your tits**.

oi See **oy**.

oic in the Australian Antarctic Territory, an 'Officer In Charge' of a station. Hence, the **oicery** is the sleeping quarters of an oic.

oil news or information. Aussie slang dating from the 1910s. As 'oil' lubricates a machine, so 'information' greases the wheels of progress. Generally qualified in some way, as **dinkum oil**, **good oil**, **inside oil** and **straight oil**.

oiled drunk. Venerable slang of the early 18th century.

oil the tonsils to drink booze. Also heard in the form **oil the larynx**.

oinker **1.** a pig. **2.** an ugly person; a person with piggish habits.

okay all right, correct, fine. *That's okay with me.* A versatile word which can be used in many parts of speech. As an adverb, it means 'well' or 'correctly', as in *I can manage it okay.* As a noun, it signifies approval, as in *She gave it her okay.* As a verb, it means to allow or endorse, as in *He okayed their application.* Finally, it can also be used as a positive answer to a request, where it means 'yeah' 'sure', 'fine' or 'go ahead', or as a question where it means 'is that all right?' 'are you sure?' or 'do you agree?' Also spelt **O.K.** and **ok**, and reduplicated to make the jokey sounding **okey-doke** and **okey-dokey**.

Originally US slang from the 1830s, **okay** made its way to Australia as early as the 1910s, but only became popular here from World War II onwards. Over the years much speculation as to the origin of this strange word has taken place, including derivations from French, Greek, Finnish, various African and Native American languages, British dialect, Old Norse, and even the Scottish *Och aye!* None of these are supported by available evidence. In reality O.K. is the first two letters of *orl korrect*, a jocular misspelling of 'all correct'.

old bastard **1.** a form of genial address among males. *G'day you old bastard. How are the kids?* **2.** a member of the Australasian Order of Old Bastards, a charity organisation which raises funds for health institutions. According to the rules, the greeting between members of the order is, 'G'day you Old Bastard', and if the member so addressed is not carrying his card at the time, he is up for shouting drinks for ALL present.

old bat an unpleasant old woman.

old bloke **1.** your father. **2.** the penis.

old boy **1.** your father. **2.** your husband. **3.** your boss. **4.** the penis. **5.** the captain of a vessel.

old boy network a system of male nepotism among old school buddies.

old cheese your wife. Aussie slang dating from the 1970s. From *cheese and kisses*, rhyming slang for 'missus'.

old chum in colonial times, an experienced colonist, a person who had spent some years in the colony, especially in the outback, and was thus accustomed to Australian life and conditions. The opposite of **new chum** (see entry).

the Old Country generally England or Britain, though, among non-Anglo-Saxon migrants, it refers to whichever country they came from.

the Old Dart England. Has been used in Australia since the 1890s. Dart is the same word as 'dirt', as pronounced in the Essex dialect of southern England. Thus Old Dart = Old Dirt, a person's native land.

old fart any old person. *Even old farts can have fun.*

old fellow **1.** your father. **2.** the penis.

old folks your parents. Aussie slang since the 1950s.

old girl **1.** your mother. **2.** your wife.

old identity a long-term and well-known inhabitant of a community.

oldie **1.** an elderly person. **The oldies** are your parents. **2.** any old thing.

old lady **1.** your mother. **2.** your wife.

old lag **1.** an ex-convict or ex-prisoner. **2.** a hardened prisoner who has been in jail many times or is serving a long sentence.

old man **1.** your father. **2.** your husband. **3.** your boss. **4.** the penis. **5.** the captain of a vessel. **6.** a male Aboriginal elder. **7.** a large, fully grown, male kangaroo.

old man kangaroo an adult male kangaroo. Recorded as early as 1827.

old mate **1.** a term of address to a man, usually by another man. *G'day old mate, how're ya going?* Commonly used after a man's name as an encouragement. *Davo, old mate, don't worry about that.* **2.** the protagonist of a yarn. *Then the old mate took off up the hill.*

olds your parents. Aussie slang from the 1970s.

olds and bolds military slang, older officers, usually given cushy jobs.

oldster an old person.

old timer's disease a jocular alteration of 'Alzheimer's disease'.

old woman **1.** your mother. **2.** your wife. **3.** a fussy, silly person of either sex.

Olivia Neutron Bomb a nickname given to Olivia Newton-John.

ollie a skateboarding manoeuvre in which the rider and board jump together while rolling on a flat surface. This is the essential move behind most skateboarding tricks. Invented by Florida skater Alan 'Ollie' Gelfand in 1979. See **nollie**.

on **1.** to have a bet placed. *Make sure you get on before the price drops too much.* **2.** under way; begun in earnest. *It was on for young and old.* **3.** willing to take part. *I'm on for a deal with him.*

on a good wicket in a great position; successful or poised for success. Aussie slang since the 1910s.

on a promise of a man, having been promised sexual intercourse from a woman. *Nah, I'll give the pub a miss, I'm on a promise from the wife.* The implication is that men are always wanting it and women are reluctant to comply. A rather sad reflection on Australian sexual life. Dates back to the 1960s, but no longer very common, which would indicate some progress in terms of sexual maturity.

oncer **1.** something done or made once only. **2.** an obsolete term for a one pound note.

the One Day of the Year Anzac Day, the 25th April.

one-dog night a reasonably cold night, not as cold as a **two-dog night**. From the bushmen's practice of sleeping with their dogs – the colder the night, the more dogs needed. See **dog**, def. 7.

one 'em in two-up, to throw a head and a tail, requiring the coins to be tossed again.

one-eyed trouser snake the penis.

one for Ron a cigarette borrowed for later on. (Get it? – Later Ron). *Can I have a ciggie, and one for Ron?*

one-handed reading pornographic literature. I'll leave it to your imaginations as to what the hand not holding the book is up to.

one out by yourself; on your own. *He always fishes one out.*

one-pub town a small country town with only one pub. A term first used by Henry Lawson.

ones in two-up, a throw of a head and a tail, requiring the coins to be tossed again. Also called **two ones**.

onesies a childish term for urination. Compare **twosies**.

1SM Sydney slang for a cup of coffee, or tea, made with one sugar and milk. See **2SM** for an explanation of the origin of this term.

on for young and old wild, unrestrained and involving everyone – used of a fight, argument, or the like. Aussie slang since the 1940s.

onkaparinga Aussie rhyming slang for 'finger'. From the name of a blanket manufacturer. Also shortened to **onka** or **onker**. Since the 1960s.

onkus no good, hopeless, crap; broken, out of order. Old Aussie slang, dating from the 1910s. Dying out or already dead. Origin unknown. It is also used in New Zealand, but in the completely opposite sense, meaning good.

on the battle working as a prostitute. Aussie slang since the 1940s.

on the blink not working properly. Originally US slang of the 19th century.

on the boil **1.** in football, running or going at full speed. Also known as **on the burst**. **2.** in a state of continuous activity; doing something without pause. *He's been on the boil day and night.*

on the bugle stinking to high heaven. Aussie slang dating from the 1940s. The bugle here is, of course, the nose.

on the burst **1.** in football, running or going at full speed. Also known as **on the boil**. **2.** in old slang, on a drinking spree. Aussie slang from the 1850s up to about the 1940s. No longer heard.

on the coat in prison, ostracised; out of favour. Derived from the practice of signalling the approach of a warder by pulling on the lapel of your coat, thus effectively ending conversation.

on the game working as a prostitute.

on the improve improving. Aussie slang since the 1950s.

on the job actively engaged in sexual intercourse.

on the land working as a farmer. An Australian phrase dating back to the 1900s.

on the make **1.** intent on personal gain. **2.** looking for a sexual partner.

on the money absolutely correct. US slang of the 1940s.

on the Murray cod Aussie rhyming slang for 'on the nod', that is, on credit – used of wagers. In use since the 1960s.

on the never-never on hire purchase.

on the nod of a bet, taken on credit. Originally British slang of the 1880s.

on the nose **1.** smelly, stinking. *Man, this bait's a bit on the nose!* Aussie slang since the 1940s. **2.** unpleasant, distasteful.

on the outer ostracised. Aussie slang since the 1900s. See **outer** for an explanation of the origin.

on the Q.T. on the quiet; secretly. From British slang of the 1880s.

on the scoot on a drinking binge. Aussie slang dating from the 1910s.

on the square **1.** living an honest, law-abiding life. **2.** in a faithful monogamous relationship with someone; going steady. Old Aussie slang dating back to the 1940s, now outmoded.

on the take in receipt of bribes, as a corrupt police officer, politician, or the like.

on the tit of a baby, breast-feeding.

on the toe **1.** fleeing; in flight. **2.** nervous; wishing to be gone.

on the track travelling as a swagman. Short for **on the wallaby track**.

on the trot **1.** one after another; in quick succession. *He won three races on the trot.* **2.** in a state of continuous activity.

on with romantically involved with. Aussie slang since the 1900s.

onya an abbreviated form of *good on you!* Also, in the plural, **onyas**. Been around since the 1940s.

on your hammer following closely, or, when in a vehicle, tailgating. From *hammer and tack*, rhyming slang for 'back'.

on your knees a command for someone to assume a kneeling position in order to pay deference to you by performing oral sex. Used in a joking way.

on your lonesome all alone.

on your Pat Malone Aussie rhyming slang for 'on your own'. Commonly shortened to **on your Pat**. Dates back to the 1900s.

oodles a large quantity. *She's got oodles of money.* Originally US slang of the 1860s. Origin unknown.

Oodnawoopwoop an imaginary remote town. *His parents had a station out Oonawoopwoop.* A blend of *Woop Woop* and *Oodnadatta*, which is a fairly remote town in north central SA, far from Adelaide. Another similar remote and backward town is **Oodnagalahbi**.

oo-er an exclamation of pretended shock.

oont a camel. Used by Australian Camel Corps in World War I, and also throughout the outback where camels were used for transport. The word comes from Hindustani and Urdu.

oo-roo Goodbye! See ya! An unaspirated version of the more common **hooroo**.

op **1.** a surgical operation. *He hasn't been the same since his op.* **2.** a military operation. **3.** an operator.

open go a free chance; an unhindered opportunity. Aussie slang since World War I.

open slather a situation in which there are no restraints, often becoming chaotic or rowdy;

a free-for-all. Aussie slang dating from the 1910s.

oppo in the navy, a chum or companion; a person's opposite number.

op shop an opportunity shop. Aussie slang dating from the 1970s. Op shops are known elsewhere in the world as 'charity stores'.

optic an eye. *A patch covered his left optic.* Aussie slang since the 1860s.

optic nerve Aussie rhyming slang for 'perve'. Commonly shortened to **optic**. *Give us an optic at that.*

-o-rama a suffix used as an intensifier. As *tack-o-rama* (incredibly tacky), or *spunk-o-rama* (an incredible spunk).

orchestras the testicles. Short for *orchestra stalls*, rhyming slang for 'balls'. Originally British.

order of the boot the sack; dismissal; forcible ejection.

ordinary no good; nothing special; nothing out of the box. *'How was your day?' 'Oh, pretty ordinary.'*

Orstralia a representation of the high-falutin' British pronunciation of Australia. Hence, **Orstralian**.

ort the anus. *Stick that in your ort, sport.* Aussie slang since the 1950s. Origin unknown.

oscar ready money. Short for *Oscar Asche*, rhyming slang for 'cash'. Aussie slang dating from the 1900s. Oscar Asche was a famous actor and stage producer who died in 1936.

Ossie a pretty poor way of spelling **Aussie**, but you see it from time to time.

osteo laconic Aussie way of saying 'osteopath'.

othersider in WA, a person living on the other side of the Nullarbor Plain.

our Harbour Sydney Harbour. An affectionate appellation since the 1880s.

out **1.** to publicly expose someone as gay or lesbian. **2.** to reveal or unmask an impostor, charlatan, or the like. **3.** to suspend from playing a sport. *He was outed for the rest of the season.* This one is an Australian original, dating back to the 1960s at least. **4.** to dismiss or sack. **5.** used with a specifying number, in a group of that many, thus *one out* – alone, *two out* – in company with another, *three out* – in a group of three, and so on. **6.** a **run of outs** is a succession of bad luck or unfortunate events.

outback the remote, sparsely inhabited parts of Australia. The symbolic heart of the nation. The term first appears in the 1890s. An inhabitant of this region is occasionally called an **outbacker**. And bush life and ways are sometimes termed **outbackery**.

out dipper in cricket, a ball bowled so that it swings from leg to off.

outer an open betting place at a racecourse designated for non-members. In two-up, the area around the ring where the gamblers gather. Hence, to be **on the outer** is to be excluded.

out-gun to beat convincingly in a contest.

outie a protruding belly-button; a navel that goes out, as opposed to an **innie**. Hence, a person with such a navel.

outlaw a horse that is difficult to handle or impossible to tame. Rural slang since the 1900s.

outlaws a joking term for your in-laws.

outside prison slang for the world outside prison.

outta here leaving. *I'm outta here, see ya tomorrow.*

over the falls in surfing, where one goes when wiping out from the top of a wave. Very dangerous.

over-the-shoulder boulder-holder a joking term for a bra.

Oxford scholar rhyming slang for a 'dollar'. Originally British. Can be shortened to **Oxford**.

oxygen thief an idiot; a useless human being. That is, they waste oxygen by breathing.

oy an exclamation calling for attention, equivalent to 'hey'. Not exclusively Australian, but an icon of the Aussie working class. Also, especially since the 2000 Olympics, fixed in Australian cultural history by being part of the Aussie sporting cheer: Aussie, Aussie, Aussie, Oy, oy, oy! Also spelt **oi**.

Oz Australia or Australian. Has been around since the 1940s, but only became common from the 1970s onwards.

Ozzie another way to spell **Aussie**.

packed lunch the penis or male genitalia as seen through clothing.

pack of poo tickets **1.** something that is in an unholy mess. For an explanation of this term see **pakapoo ticket**. **2.** a roll of toilet paper. This meaning seems to have arisen through a complete ignorance of the original term.

pack shit to be almost shitting yourself in fear. This uniquely Australian phrase first appears in the 1940s. Also found in the variant form **pack the shits**. The earliest examples are of the euphemistic forms **pack 'em** and **pack it**, because the word 'shit' was not allowed in print or polite conversation back in the 40s or 50s. Another euphemistic form that appears in the 1970s is **pack death**. By the 1980s the object can be dropped altogether. *We were packing that our mum would notice the stain on the carpet.*

Paddo the suburb of Paddington, either the one in Sydney or the one in Brisbane.

paddock **1.** a sporting field. Aussie slang since the 1830s. **2.** a spectator's enclosure at a racetrack. An Australianism from the 1890s.

paddock-basher **1.** an old car, generally unregistered, used for driving around paddocks. **2.** any old bomb for bashing around the bush. Both can also be called a **paddy-basher** for short.

paddock chicken a wild rabbit.

Paddy's lantern the moon.

Paddy's poke a cut made to a deck of cards by pushing out the middle section with a finger and placing those cards on top.

paddy wagon a police van for transporting people under arrest.

paddywhack Aussie rhyming slang for 'back'.

pain in the arse an annoying person or thing. More politely called a **pain in the neck**.

pair in cricket, getting out for zero in both innings. Compare **king pair**.

pakapoo ticket Something that is in an unholy mess, especially written work, is said to look like a **pakapoo ticket**. Aussie slang since the 1950s. This originally referred to the tickets used in a type of Chinese gambling game, which were marked with Chinese characters. To western eyes, they just looked like messy scribble. The game was recorded in Australia from as early as 1886. Through mis-hearing the term, some people have come to say **pack of poo tickets** (see entry).

Paki a Pakistani person. This is generally used as a racist label, and in the UK this usage has a particularly high taboo. In Australia it is not very common except in the plural form, **the Pakis**, meaning the Pakistani Test Cricket team. This is not used or meant with any disrespect.

pal a good friend; a mate or chum. Although considered a blatant Americanism by many Aussies, it is in fact venerable British slang dating way back to the 17th century. It has been in constant use in Australia since colonial times. In origin it is a borrowing of the word for 'brother' in Romani, the language of Gypsies. Hence, to **pal up** is to become someone's buddy or mate.

Palmie the northern Sydney suburb of Palm Beach.

palooka a hopeless boxer or wrestler. Hence, any hulking, stupid male. After a comic strip character named Joe Palooka who appeared in the US *Variety* magazine in the 1930s and 40s.

palsy-walsy noisomely friendly.

panic merchant an inveterate panicker; a worry wart. Aussie slang since the 1960s, at least.

pan licker a dog.

pannikin boss a person with a modest amount of authority, such as a foreman. Often used in a negative way to mean a boss's man.

panno **1.** a panel van. Aussie slang since the 1970s. **2.** a **pannikin boss** (see entry). Dating back to the 1950s.

pansy a derisive label for a gay man. Originally British slang from the 1920s. Also used as a gibe at any man considered lacking in masculinity.

pants to pull someone's pants down as a prank. *I got pantsed standing on the sideline.* A more Aussie way of saying it is **dack**.

pants man a womaniser. Aussie slang since the 1960s.

panty-waist an effeminate male; a wimp or wuss. A very recent borrowing of a US slang term that dates back to the 1930s.

paperbag job an ugly person – they are so ugly that you need to cover their head with a paperbag when having sex with them.

papers cigarette papers. Nowadays most commonly called **tally-hos**, after a popular brand. In Tasmania called **tissues**.

para **1.** completely drunk. A 1980s shortening of **paralytic**. **2.** among surfers, a derogatory term for a boogie boarder. Short for 'paraplegic'.

paralytic completely drunk. Aussie slang since the 1890s.

park a tiger to vomit.

parkie **1.** an itinerant semi-resident of a city park. **2.** a parking inspector. **3.** a park ranger. **4.** someone suffering from Parkinson's disease.

parking kissing, petting, and other amorous activities carried out in a parked car.

Parko's Parkinson's disease.

park the carcass to take a seat.

parra a derogatory term used by locals for a tourist or visitor to a beach area. Been around since the 1970s. Originally Sydney slang, referring to the westie suburb of *Parramatta*. Common also on the Central Coast.

Parra the city of Parramatta, in Sydney's west.

party animal a person who parties hard.

party pooper a spoilsport, especially at a party.

pash **1.** a long, passionate, deep kiss. Aussie slang from the 1960s onwards. **2.** a session of passionate kissing, especially French kissing. **3.** to kiss passionately; to French kiss; to suck face. Hence, **pash on**, to have a prolonged kissing session, and **pash off**, to kiss someone until fully satisfied.

pass in your marbles to die.

passion wagon a panel van used as a place of sexual encounter.

Pat Malone see entry at **on your Pat Malone**.

pav laconic Australian way of saying 'pavlova'.

Pavarotti among currency traders, ten million dollars. Because Pavarotti is a 'tenor', punning on **tenner**.

pavement pizza a dried splash of vomit left on the street. Hence, to **dial a pavement pizza** is to vomit.

pavlova a large meringue dessert with a soft centre and topped with fruit and cream. An iconic item of Australian cuisine. Named after Russian ballerina Anna Pavlova. Originally called a *pavlova cake*, this dish appears to have originated in New Zealand back in the 1920s when the ballerina visited there.

pay out to berate or scold someone; to give someone heaps.

pay your dues surfing slang, to earn your place in the line-up.

pea horseracing slang, a favourite or certainty in a race; a horse being run to win after being kept dark in previous races. A metaphorical use of the 'pea' in the swindler's game of pea and thimble.

peabrain an idiot or fool.

peach **1.** an attractive young woman. **2.** an exceptional person or thing.

peachy excellent, wonderful, great.

pea floater a meat pie served floating in pea soup.

peak **1.** to climax sexually. **2.** to reach the height of drug-induced euphoria. **3.** to reach a climax of enjoyment. **4.** of a wave, to reach its greatest height. Aussie surfing slang.

peanut **1.** a fool. Aussie slang since the 1930s. **2.** a small penis.

peanut paste the name in Qld, WA and SA for what the rest of the country calls peanut butter. Apparently these three states had at some stage legislation that prevented the word 'butter' being used for any non-dairy product.

peanuts a piddling amount of money.

pearler something exceptional or superlative. *Her new dress was a real pearler.* In cricket, a very good delivery. Sometimes spelt **purler**. Aussie use of British English term for a knock-down blow, from *purl* 'to overturn'. Been around since the 1930s.

pearl necklace blobs or beads of sperm ejaculated on the chest of a sexual partner. Also called a **string of pearls**.

pear-shaped badly awry. *Everything has gone pear-shaped.*

pea soup a thick fog. Also called a **pea souper**.

ped a paedophile.

pedal to the metal to be driving a vehicle at top speed. *We were pedal to the metal when we passed a cop.*

pee to urinate. Also, an act of urination. *I've gotta go for a pee.* Originally 19th century British slang. Euphemistically from the first letter of the word 'piss'.

peel to take your clothes off or strip.

peen the penis.

peepz people; hence, friends. A new cool word found mainly on the internet.

peewee 1. the common black and white bird with a loud piping voice known officially as the magpie lark. Peewee is the common name, and is the most common term in Qld, NSW, ACT, and Tasmania. In Vic and WA it is more commonly known as the **mud lark**. And in SA it is mostly called the **Murray magpie**. Not to be confused with the SA **piping shrike**. **2.** a black and white playing marble.

peg 1. to throw or toss something. Most common in Qld and NSW. An Aussie original. Recorded since the 1940s. **2.** to observe, look or watch. Hence, to comprehend the true nature of someone. *I've got you pegged.* **3.** a look or peek. *Have a peg at this.* **4.** an obsolete term for a shilling.

peg leg a jump into water with one leg tucked under your arms and hugged into the chest and the other extended straight out. Also called a **banana**, **can opener** or **horsey**.

peg out to die. Originally 19th century British slang.

pelican an idiot or fool. Among car sellers, it refers to a customer who buys a vehicle without attempting to haggle over the price.

pen and ink Aussie rhyming slang for 'drink' – an alcoholic drink, that is. Dates back to the 1960s.

pencil to work as a bookmaker's clerk writing out betting tickets. Hence, a bookie's clerk is called a **penciller**. Aussie slang since the late 19th century.

pencil-neck a geeky person with a thin neck.

penguin a nun.

penguin suit a dinner suit.

Percy the penis. Generally heard in the phrase **point Percy at the porcelain**, referring to male urination.

perfection surfing slang for perfectly formed waves – the dream of all surfies.

perform to throw a temper tantrum; to make a fuss; to bung on an act. Aussie slang since the 1890s.

performer 1. a person who habitually throws tantrums or makes a fuss. **2.** a keen and energetic lover. Generally a blokey word used when gloating about women they've been with. *She's a great little performer.*

perk 1. any fringe benefit of a job. A shortened form of *perquisite*. Originally British slang of the 1860s. Now commonly found in close association with the word 'lurk'. **2.** to vomit or puke. Aussie slang since the 1940s. Also, as a noun, vomit. *There was a big stain of perk on the carpet.* **3.** of percolator coffee, to bubble up and make that spitting noise. *The coffee's almost ready – I can hear it perking.*

persuader a whip or crop used by a jockey, bullocky, or the like.

perv 1. a sexual pervert; a person with an abnormal kink. Obviously a shortening of the word *pervert*. Also spelt **perve**. Aussie slang dating from the 1940s. Hence, a leering, voyeuristic man; anyone whose sexual advances are unwanted. *Rack off, you old perv.* **2.** an act of voyeurism; a look taken for the sake of sexual observation. *Just having a bit of a perv.* **3.** an attractive person; one who is worth perving at. **4.** to watch a person lustfully; to look at someone in a sexual way. **5.** to look or gawk at (but not in a sexual way). *They all just stood around perving at the couple fighting.*

pervy 1. sexually perverted or kinky. **2.** overtly sexual.

peter 1. a prison cell, hence jail. Aussie slang since the 1890s. *I never thought I'd end up in the peter.* **2.** a till of a cash register. Originally British slang from the 1850s. Hence, to **tickle the peter** is to steal from the till while using it. **3.** the penis.

peter thief in jail, an inmate who steals from other cells.

petrol bowsers Aussie rhyming slang for 'trousers'. Has been around since the 1970s.

petrol head a car nut. Aussie slang since the 1980s.

pew a jocular way of referring to a chair or any place where one can sit down. *Please, take a pew.*

PGB a **post grog bog** (see entry).

phat excellent, cool, groovy. *Everything is phat*. A 1990s adoption from US slang.

phernudge another spelling of **fnudge**, that is, to cheat at marbles. See **fanannywhacking** for a full set of synonyms.

phizgig another spelling of **fizgig**, a police informer.

phlegm cake a vanilla slice. Also called a **phlegm sandwich**.

phone in prison, a toilet bowl in a cell emptied of water and spoken into – the sound waves travel along the water pipes to other toilet bowls in other cells.

phoof/phoofy the same as **foof/foofy** (see entries).

phwoar an exclamation expressing keen appreciation of a sexually attractive person. Also spelt **fwooar**.

physie abbreviation of 'physical culture', a type of athletics program for after school. It's an eastern states thing.

physio laconic Australian way of saying 'physiotherapy' or 'physiotherapist'.

piano arms the arms of an overweight or matronly woman with flabby triceps.

piccaninny an Aboriginal child. Recorded from the early 19th century and commonly used by non-indigenous Australians up until the 1940s and 50s, after which it started to die out as it was seen to be colonial and patronising. The word itself was first used in the West Indies and probably comes from the Portuguese word for 'very small'.

piccaninny daylight the first light of day. Has been used since the 1860s. Also called **piccaninny dawn**.

piccy a picture, either a photograph or illustration.

pick to start a fight with someone. *Do you know who you're picking?* Aussie bloke's slang dating back to the 1950s.

pick a winner to pick a large piece of snot from the nose with your finger. Referring to infantile games of snot comparison.

pickled drunk. Venerable slang of the 17th century.

picnic **1.** something easy; a doddle. This is old British slang of the early 19th century, and used in Australia at least since the 1890s. **2.** something difficult or unpleasant. A sarcastic expression found only in Australia. First recorded in the 1890s. Has died out now.

piddle to urinate. Venerable slang from 18th century England. Also used as a noun to mean an act of urination. *He's just stepped out for a piddle.*

piddle about to fiddle about or trifle. Also, **piddle around**. This term has been around since the 1500s.

piece **1.** a woman seen solely as a sex object. *She's a nice little piece.* In use since the late 18th century. **2.** a sandwich. A word generally used when talking to children. A regionalism from WA, SA, Vic and far west NSW. In Vic it can also mean a slice of bread with a topping, which is also called a **piecey**. **3.** to **take a piece out of** someone is to chastise or rebuke them. Aussie slang dating from the 1950s.

piece of piss to a trained digger an easily achieved enterprise or undertaking.

piece of skirt a belittling term for a woman viewed as a sex object. Also called a **piece of fluff**.

pie-eater a person of little or no importance. Metaphorically referring to a person whose narrow view of the world is given away by the fact that they eat nothing but meat pies. Has been around since the 1940s.

pie-eyed drunk. Originally US slang.

piff a slang term in Victoria meaning to chuck or throw. Dates back to the 1950s.

pig **1.** a person with piggish attributes like eating too much, being messy, not sharing, or the like. **2.** a derogatory word for a police officer. First recorded in England in 1811, this term has persisted as the commonest term of abuse for the constabulary up to the present day. Absolutely despised by police officers. **3** in Rugby Union, a forward.

pig dog **1.** a bull terrier. **2.** a dog used for hunting wild pigs.

pigging the hunting of wild pigs with a dog and a knife.

pig ignorant extremely ignorant.

Pig Iron Bob a nickname of erstwhile Prime Minister, Sir Robert Menzies. Stemmed from his selling of pig iron to Japan while Minister for Industry in the period before World War II.

pig Latin a cryptolanguage in which the first letter or syllable of a word is transferred to the end and the syllable 'ay' is added. Thus *scram* becomes *amscray*.

pig out **1.** to eat like a pig; to gourmandise or gluttonise. **2.** a session of overeating; a meal at which there is excessive eating.

pigs arse! Nonsense! Rubbish! Bullshit! Also heard as **pigs tit!** If you want to be less rude you can euphemise it to **pigs bum!** or **pigs ear!** or shorten it simply to **pigs!**

pig's ear rhyming slang for 'beer'. Originally British, from the late 19th century.

pike **1.** to **pike on** someone is to let them down or abandon them. *Don't pike on me now.* **2.** to **pike out** is to go back on an arrangement or to opt out of something in a cowardly manner. *He piked out on the deal.*

piker **1.** a person who in a cowardly fashion opts out of an arrangement or challenge; a person who lets you down at the last moment. In Australia, pikers are pretty low down on the scale of things. **2.** a timid gambler who hasn't the guts to risk big money.

pile driver a powerful punch, kick, or the like.

pile it on to exaggerate; to bullshit in a big way.

pill in Aussie Rules and Rugby, the football.

Pilliga yowie a yowie said to live in the Pilliga Scrub of northern central NSW.

pillow **1.** a person who is a wimp, especially when playing sport; a gutless player. **2.** a kids' name for a Spicy Fruit Roll, a type of biscuit made by the Arnott's company, resembling a pillow in shape.

pillow biter the passive partner in anal intercourse.

pillow hair messy hair caused from sleeping with the head on a pillow.

pimp **1.** a person who lives off the earnings of a prostitute. Hence, to act as a pimp or pander. British slang from the 17th century. **2.** an informer. This one is Aussie slang, dating from the 1890s. In the underworld this referred especially to a police informer, but among children it was formerly a common term for a dobber or tattle-tale. Hence, to **pimp** on someone was to dob them in. Little heard these days.

pimples a derogatory term for small breasts.

the Pin the local nickname for Jumpinpin – the southern tip of North Stradbroke Island, Queensland – a famed fishing spot.

pinch **1.** to steal. Old slang from the 17th century. **2.** to arrest. Originally British criminal slang of the early 19th century. Hence, an arrest. *He was set up for a pinch.* **3.** a steep hill or sudden steep rise in a road. Recorded earliest in the US, but common in Australia since the 1840s.

pineapple a fifty dollar note. From its colour.

piner in Tassie, a timber-getter employed in the Huon pine trade.

ping **1.** to penalise for an infringement of the rules. *I got pinged for holding my player.* **2.** of a racehorse, to put on a sudden burst of speed. *About 200 metres out she pinged for the line.*

ping off a euphemism for *piss off* used by children. Has been around since the 1970s.

pin head a stupid or contemptible person; a jerk.

pink bits the female genitalia.

pink fit a burst of anger; a tantrum. *He had a pink fit.* If you would not do something **in a pink fit**, then you would never do it. *I wouldn't shake his hand in a pink fit.*

pinkie in Vic, a parking ticket.

pink lamington a lamington-style cake rolled in half-set pink jelly and coconut, sometimes with a cream filling. Also called a **jelly cake**.

pinko a Communist or Leftist sympathiser. Now most commonly found in jocular combinations maligning non-right-wing types. *Poofo, commo, pinko, basket-weavers.*

pinky in SA, the lesser bilby, now thought to be extinct. From the Aboriginal language Kaurna of the Adelaide region.

pinned high on an injected drug, especially heroin; high on any drug.

pinnies pinball machines. Aussie slang since at least the 1970s.

pins the legs. Venerable slang from the 16th century.

pipe loaf a loaf of bread, usually white, baked in a cylindrical tin with corrugated sides resembling a water tank. This is the common term in Tas, Vic and SA. The other states call it a **tank loaf**.

pipe opener **1.** an alcoholic drink taken early in the day, often as a remedy for a hangover. **2.** any drink, as strong coffee, taken at the beginning of the day.

pipes the respiratory passages.

pipi an edible bivalve mollusc, commonly used as bait. From Maori. In Qld called a **eugari**.

piping shrike the emblematic representation of the white-backed subspecies of the Australian magpie, found on the state badge of South Australia. Note that this is not a peewee.

pipsqueak a small or insignificant person or thing.

piss **1.** to urinate. Also, as a noun, urine or urination. Actually, although very old, this is technically not one of the original Anglo-Saxon four-letter words, as it originally came into medieval English from Old French. If you have a low regard for someone you **wouldn't piss on them**. If you have even less regard you **wouldn't piss on them if they were on fire**. Utter contempt can further be expressed by saying you **wouldn't piss in their ear if their brain was on fire. 2.** as a noun, urine or an act of urination. *I'm hanging for a piss.* An insignificant amount of something is styled **a piss in the ocean**, and something easily achieved is **a piece of piss** or **a piece of piss to a trained digger**. **3.** alcoholic drink, especially beer. Hence, **on the piss**, on a binge. **4.** to **take the piss out of** someone is to stir or make fun of them. **5.** used as an intensifier, the word **piss** can be prefixed to the beginning of adjective. *That was piss-awful* = extremely awful. Also, can be substituted for 'the hell', as in *He scared the piss out of me.*

piss about to mess about. *Stop pissing about and get some work done!* Also, **piss around**.

piss along to move quickly; to travel at a good bat.

pissant **1.** a type of greenish black ant with a strong formic acid smell. This word dates back to the 17th century in England, where it is preceded still further by the word *pismire* (from *piss* + *mire*, an obsolete word for 'ant'), which was used by Geoffrey Chaucer back in the 1300s! The formic acid produced by various ant species smells a lot like urine. **2.** in a negative sense, an annoying little bastard. Aussie slang since the 1850s. **3.** in a positive sense, a small but aggressive person. Hence the phrase **game as a pissant** = very brave. **4.** to be **drunk as a pissant** is to be very drunk. **5.** as an adjective, small and insignificant, but annoying as well. *I'm sick of pissant politicians.*

pissant around to mess about; to waste time in frivolous activity. Aussie slang since the 1940s.

piss artist an inveterate drinker; a drunkard.

piss away If you **piss something away**, you waste or squander it. *He pissed away his inheritance.* An alternate expression is **piss it up against the wall**.

piss bolt to run at your top speed; to go for your life.

piss cake a urinal disinfectant lozenge.

piss down to rain heavily.

piss-easy extremely easy.

pissed **1.** drunk. There are numerous similes, the most common in Australia probably being **pissed as a parrot** (not that parrots are known for their drinking habits) – this has been around since the 1970s and seems to be an Aussie original. But you can be **pissed as a bastard/fart/newt/owl**, or **pissed as forty arseholes**. You can also be **pissed to the eyeballs**. **2.** extremely annoyed; in a bad mood. *He was pretty pissed about getting the sack.* This is a recent adoption from US slang. The usual Australian form was **pissed off**, but since the 1990s the US form **pissed** has been gaining ground, especially among teenagers and young adults. At the moment both forms exist side by side.

pissed off disgruntled; fed up; thoroughly discontent.

piss-elegant with pretensions to elegance.

pisser **1.** something bad; a bad outcome; a bummer. **2.** something extremely funny – it makes you piss yourself laughing. **3.** a pub. **4.** a urinal. **5.** a criminal who pisses their pants when caught by the authorities.

piss-fart to waste time.

piss fat an morning erection caused by a full bladder. Also called a **piss horn**.

piss flaps a none-too-charming word for a woman's labia.

piss head a big drinker; a booze merchant or drunkard.

piss house a toilet.

piss in someone's pocket to flatter someone; to ingratiate yourself to someone. Aussie slang since the 1940s.

piss into the wind to waste time striving for the unachievable.

piss it in to win easily.

piss off **1.** to leave or depart with haste. *Let's piss off before he gets back.* Has been around since World War I. Euphemised to **P.O. 2.** as a command: go away! fuck off! A harsh expression of rejection. **3.** to get rid of someone. *I decided my last boyfriend was a drongo, so I pissed him off.* **4.** to annoy someone. *His constant whingeing really pisses me off.*

piss on **1.** to beat comprehensively. Also, to **piss all over**. **2.** to continue on with drinking; to booze on.

piss-poor shabby; third-rate.

pisspot **1.** a drunkard or alcoholic. Aussie slang since the 1960s. **2.** a chamber pot. An age-old term, dating back to the 1400s.

piss-proud of the penis, erect as a result of an overfull bladder.

piss-take a satirical version; a send-up. Formed from the phrase *take the piss out of.*

piss-up a drinking session.

piss-weak **1.** mean, despicable, shabby, substandard. *It was a piss-weak thing to do.* **2.** cowardly.

piss whacker any cicada which urinates when held in the hand.

pissy **1.** wet with urine. **2.** mildly drunk; also, given to drinking. *I'm sick of your pissy mates coming around.* **3.** irritable. **4.** insignificant or puny. *It's just a pissy little thing.*

piss yourself **1.** to quail in fear. **2.** to laugh uproariously.

pit **1.** the hollow tube of a breaking wave. **2.** a cement bowl for skateboarding. **3.** a mosh pit.

pits **1.** the most unpleasant or obnoxious place, circumstance, or condition. *This job is the pits.* **2.** the armpits.

Pitt Street in Sydney, used allusively to refer to any extremely busy place. *It's like Pitt Street in here.*

Pitt Street farmer in NSW, a person who owns a country property, often for purposes of tax avoidance, but who lives and works in Sydney. See **Collins Street cocky**, **Queen Street bushie**.

pizza face a person with a bad case of acne.

pizzling an overwhelming defeat; a thrashing. *We really copped a pizzling last Saturday.*

planet Zorg an imaginary distant planet used to explain odd or weird behaviour. *I asked him to put the red wine in the fridge and he looked at me like I was from planet Zorg.*

plank an old-fashioned type of long surfboard.

plastered drunk.

plastic a credit or ATM card, or such cards collectively. *Have you brought your plastic?*

plate face a racist designation for an Asian person.

plates of meat rhyming slang for 'feet'. Originally British from the 1850s. One of the earliest recorded pieces of rhyming slang.

play it cool to be cautious and shrewd; to maintain composure.

play silly buggers to muck around.

play stink finger to engage in erotic play of the female genitals with the fingers.

pleased as Punch delighted; highly pleased.

pleb a commonplace or ordinary person. A shortened form of *plebeian.*

plink old slang for really cheap wine, even worse than **plonk**. First appears in the 1940s – but has not stood the test of time.

plod card an employee's time sheet.

plonk **1.** cheap wine. Can be used jokingly to refer to really excellent wine. *That's not a bad bottle of plonk you've got there.* Originally Aussie slang, first recorded in the 1930s. Probably a corrupt pronunciation of French *blanc*, as in *vin blanc* 'white wine'. Possibly originating with Australian troops in France in World War I. Now commonly used in Britain. **2.** racing slang, a large amount of money bet on a horse or greyhound; a plunge.

plonk artist an immoderate drinker of wine. Also called a **plonk fiend** or a **plonk merchant**.

plonko an alcoholic who drinks wine. Also called a **plonkie**.

plonk shop a bottle shop.

pluggers thongs with only one plug under the foot – as opposed to **double pluggers**.

plug-ugly extremely ugly.

plum an exceptional person or thing.

plumber's smile the portion of a buttock cleft showing above the top of someone's pants; the coin slot. Also called the **plumber's crack** or the **plumber's bike rack**.

plunge **1.** a large sum of money bet on a horse or greyhound. Hence, to bet a large sum of money. **2.** a large sum of money bet on a horse or greyhound in such a way as not to alert the bookies. If bookmakers notice a lot of money bet on one competitor, they then shorten the odds. Plunges are normally organised by the connections of a horse or greyhound whose abilities have been kept secret. **3.** in Qld, a bath.

plunger one who bets large amounts on horse or dog races.

plurry the word *bloody*, used as an intensifier, as pronounced in pidgin English. In Australia, used occasionally by native speakers as either a joke or as a euphemism (more common in the past). In NZ, commonly used to represent Maori pronunciation.

pluto pup a battered sav on a stick. Also called a **dagwood dog**, or in SA, a **dippy dog**.

po a word for a chamber pot which we borrowed from the French. In French it is actually *pot de chambre* – but they don't pronounce the 't' so it became *po* in English. Chamber pots aren't much seen these days but the word persists in the phrase **full as a family po**, meaning completely full, and in the delightful insult **po-faced**.

P.O. a euphemism for *piss off*.

poached egg a traffic dome or silent cop. Also called a **fried egg**.

pocket in Tassie, a sack of potatoes.

pocket billiards a game played by some boys in the first flushes of puberty. The rules are pretty simple: 1. walk around with your hands in your pockets and fondle your testicles. 2. try to look like you are merely walking around completely innocently and your hands just happen to be in your pockets even though it isn't cold in the slightest. Sometimes called **pocket pool**.

poddy **1.** a young calf, especially if unbranded. **2.** a calf, lamb or foal that has been handfed. Hence, to handfeed a young stock animal.

poddy-dodge to steal unbranded cattle. Hence a proponent of this is known as a **poddy-dodger**.

poet's day Friday, the end of the working week, on which people often leave a little early. An acronym from Piss Off Early Tomorrow's Saturday.

pogo army slang, a member of the non-combatant staff; anyone stationed further back from the enemy than yourself. From *pogo stick*, rhyming slang for 'prick' – but also because they are viewed as useless bludgers who bounce around all day on their pogo sticks and are of no use to the fighting soldiers.

point Percy at the porcelain of a male, to urinate into a toilet bowl.

point the bone to indicate a guilty person; to point the finger. Alluding to the Aboriginal ritual practice of pointing the bone in order to will someone's death.

poisoner a cook, especially a shearers' cook.

poke **1.** of a male, to have sex with someone. Originally British slang recorded as early as the 1860s. Hence, an act of sexual intercourse; a person rated on their sexual performance. **2.** the penis. **3.** a street name for the drug Viagra, when used as a sexual stimulant rather than to remedy impotence.

poke borak at to ridicule or make fun of someone. Identical in meaning to **poke mullock at**, although these phrases originate from quite separate sources. See **borak** and **mullock**.

pokey jail. Originally British slang of the late 19th century.

pokies poker machines. Aussie slang since the 1960s.

pole on to bludge on others. *He's always poling on his mates, never buys anything himself.* Been around since the early 1900s. An adept at this is known as a **poler** – not a compliment. The origin of this phrase goes back to bullock-driving days where 'polers' were the bullocks harnessed to the pole of the dray and apt to do less pulling than the others.

poley cup a cup which has lost its handle. This is a classic Australianism dating back to the 19th century when people were so hard-up that even if your cup broke its handle you couldn't afford to throw it away. Now that's really battling. The word *poley* is a rural term for hornless cattle.

police pimp a police informer. Aussie slang since the 1940s. See **pimp** (def. 2).

pollie a politician. Aussie slang since the 1960s.

Pollyanna a girl with her hair up in front and hanging loose at the back.

pollywaffle a floating piece of human excrement in the water you are swimming in. See **blind mullet** for a swag of synonyms.

Pom usual abbreviation of **Pommy**.

Pommy a term, sometimes derogatory, for an English person. It first appears in documentary evidence in 1912 and was originally used to refer to immigrants from Britain (not only England), as opposed to long-term or native-born Australian residents. For a long time Pommy was quite derogatory, but nowadays it carries less negative connotation than it used to and can even be used affectionately.

As for the origin – well, the much repeated suggestion that it derives from an acronym of Prisoner Of Mother England (POME), or Prisoner Of Her Majesty (POHM), or any other of numerous variants is clearly wrong – it is nothing but urban legend. Firstly, there is no documentary evidence of such phrases and acronyms ever being in use. Secondly, acronyms were extremely rare before the 1950s. Thirdly, the period of transportation had been over for about 75 years before the word Pommy ever appeared. Fourthly, the word Pommy was applied to immigrants and never to convicts or prisoners. The actual source of the word is *pomegranate*, rhyming slang for 'immigrant'. This piece of home-grown rhyming slang first appears in 1912, the same time that both *Pommy* and *Pom* arrive on the scene, hence the conclusion that the latter two are abbreviations of the first is unavoidable.

Pommy bastard an English person who embodies the very antithesis of all things Australian. This collocation has been around since the 1950s. Nowadays it is generally used jokingly.

Pommyland England. Also called **Pomland**.

ponce **1.** a derogatory term for a gay man. Also used as a gibe at any man considered lacking in masculinity. **2.** a pimp; a man who lives off the earnings of a prostitute. Originally British slang from the 1850s. Recorded in Australia as early as the 1880s. **3.** an obsolete term for the vagina or vulva. This is perhaps the original sense, as the word comes from the Yiddish *punse* (from German dialect *punze*) 'the female genitals'.

ponce about to flounce; to behave in a foolishly effeminate fashion.

poncy effeminate; like a ponce. An elaboration of this is **poncy as a gay parrot**.

Pond Tuggeranong in the ACT, a derisive term for Lake Tuggeranong.

pong a bad smell. Hence, to stink. First recorded in a glossary of Australian digger slang from World War I. Sometimes in the form **ponk**.

pont in the Antarctic, to pose for a photograph whilst uncomfortably exposed to the harsh climatic conditions. So called after Herbert George Ponting, photographer on Robert Scott's polar expedition of 1910–13.

pony **1.** in WA, a beer glass of 5 fluid ounces (140 ml). Sometimes used for a 4 ounce glass. In the days before refrigeration, beer was often difficult to chill and thus was served in small glasses as the beer in larger glasses would get warm before they were finished. Obsolescent. **2.** an old slang term for the sum of twenty-five pounds. Recorded in England since the 18th century. After decimal currency, it was used for twenty-five dollars. Sometimes has been used for fifty dollars (which was the monetary equivalent of twenty-five quid).

poo excrement or faeces. Also, as a verb, to excrete. Commonly used by and with children. Often euphemistically substituted into other slang phrases in place of the word 'shit'. Thus, *in the poo*, *to poo yourself*, *to have the poos*, and so on. Occasionally spelt **pooh**, or reduplicated as **poo-poo**.

the Poo a nickname of Australian tennis star Mark Philippoussis. Popularised, and perhaps originally coined, by Roy and HG. Also known as 'the Scud'.

poo-brown of a yucky brown colour reminiscent of faeces.

poo bum an annoying person. An insult used by children, and jokingly by adults.

pooch a dog. Originally US slang of the 1920s. Origin unknown.

poof a derogatory term for a male homosexual. Also used as a gibe at any man considered lacking in masculinity. Around since the 1830s and may ultimately derive from the French *poufiasser* 'a homosexual prostitute of either sex'. Occasionally spelt **pouf**. In Australia, it dates back to at least the 1890s and was elaborated into the form **poofter** (see entry).

poofo homosexual; used in jocular combinations maligning non-right-wing types. *Poofo, commo, pinko, nancy-boys.*

poofteen any number of; umpteen.

poofteenth a very small quantity or measure. *Move it just a poofteenth.*

poofter a derogatory term for a homosexual man. Also used as a gibe at any man considered lacking in masculinity. This word is an Australian original, dating back to the 1890s. Presumably it is from *poof* + *-er*, with the *-t-* thrown in to make it sound nicer. Sometimes spelt **poufter** or **pooftah**. Since the 1970s it has become common in Britain as well.

poofter-bashing the practice of assaulting homosexual men, as is carried out by certain homophobic men, often in cowardly groups. A man who does this is called a **poofter-basher**.

poofter-rorter **1.** prison slang for an inmate who persuades or induces other men to have sex with him. **2.** a person who assaults and robs homosexual men.

poofter shot a shot played with a pool rest – seen as gutless.

poofter stick a pool rest; a cheat stick.

poofy effeminate; camp; wimpish.

poo head a childish insult. Also, **poo-poo head**.

poo jabber **1.** a male homosexual. See **dung puncher** for a swag of synonyms, including **poo denter, poo puncher, poo pusher** and **poo shooter**. **2.** among kids, a mild term of abuse. They seem to be unaware of the literal meaning of the word.

poon **1.** a fool or idiot; a dill. **2.** an obsolete term for a homosexual male. Presumably a clipping of the word *poonce*. Perhaps the original meaning.

poonce a derogatory term for a gay man. Also used as a gibe at any man considered lacking in masculinity. An Australian pronunciation of **ponce** (see entry).

pooncey effeminate.

pooned up dressed up to go out; togged out in your finest.

poontang a crass term for the vagina. Hence, sexual intercourse. Originally US slang from the 1920s and adopted in Oz in the 1980s. Perhaps from French *poutain* 'prostitute'.

poop (pronounced with a short vowel, like in 'put') excrement. Hence, to excrete. *He pooped his pants*. Hence, to be **in the poop** is to be in trouble. From British dialect. This same word exists in both American and British English, except that there the pronunciation is with a long vowel, like in 'loop'.

poop cart a horse-drawn cart used to collect sanitary cans. Same as a **dunny cart**.

poota a jokey shortening of the word *computer*.

poove the word **poof**, said in an affected hoity-toity manner.

Pope's phone number a nickname or jocular codeword for 'Vat 69' whisky.

pop off to fart.

poppycock nonsense; rubbish. Originally US slang from the 1860s, from Dutch *pappekak* soft dung.

pops a powdery substance spread on wooden dance floors in the 1950s and 60s to make them slippery.

Pop's sop stale white bread and dripping soaked in hot water, eaten with tomato sauce and salt. An old one – not around any more.

P.O.Q. the politest way of saying *Piss Off Quick!* First recorded in Australian digger slang of World War I.

porcupine an alternate name for the echidna. Formerly common, but now mostly restricted to Tasmania.

pork of a male, to have sex with someone. US slang of the 1970s, picked up in Oz in the 1980s.

pork and bean Aussie rhyming slang for 'queen', that is, a homosexual man. Originally prison slang of the 1940s.

pork chop **1.** to be **silly as a pork chop** is to be really, really silly. Similarly, to **carry on like a pork chop** is to behave in a silly fashion. Why pork chops are especially silly, as opposed to other cuts of meat, is one of those unanswerable mysteries of slang. **2.** something unwanted is said to be **like a pork chop at a Jewish wedding.**

porker **1.** a pig. **2.** a fat person.

porkie short for **pork pie**, rhyming slang for 'lie'. *There was trouble when he started telling pork pies.* A bit of British slang adopted here in the 1980s.

pork sword a crass and rather infantile term for an erect penis.

porn and prawn night a social function for men where pornography is watched, booze is drunk and prawns are devoured.

port a suitcase or a school bag. A word peculiar to Qld and north coast and inland NSW. Short for *portmanteau*. Hence, **port rack**, a shelf outside of a classroom for holding school bags.

portergaff a drink of stout with a dash of lemonade. Aussie drinking parlance from the 1890s.

posh elegant and luxurious; first-class; snobbishly opulent. Hardly slang any more. There is a long-standing story that this was originally an acronym from the phrase *Port Out; Starboard Home*, referring to the better (i.e. cooler) accommodation on vessels sailing between Britain and India, Australia, etc. Unfortunately hard evidence to back up this assertion is painfully lacking. There was an older slang word *posh*, meaning a dandy, and this seems to be the more likely origin.

posse **1.** a gang of youths. **2.** specifically, a gang of graffiti artists.

possie a place or position. *Save me a possie next to you.* Also spelt **pozzie**. Originally World War I digger slang which referred to a position or shelter, or a hiding place taken up by a sniper.

Possie a half-Pom, half-Aussie, or a Pom that has become naturalised.

possum **1.** well-known Australian marsupial. Now generally regarded with affection, but in many rural areas seen as nothing but a pest. Absolutely despised in New Zealand where they were introduced from Australia in the 19th century and have since bred like crazy and caused the destruction of much native fauna and flora. In Australia the word was first used by Captain Cook way back in 1770. The word itself is a shortening of *opossum*, which is an American word from a Native American language. **2.** to **stir the possum** is to create a disturbance. **3.** a term of affectionate address. *How are you, possum?* Popularised by Dame Edna Everage. **4.** a victim of a swindle or confidence trick. Aussie underworld slang from the 1940s.

possum stomp to jump up and down on with large boots.

poster in Aussie Rules, a kick which hits one of the goal posts, scoring a point.

post grog bog particularly noisome excrement produced the morning after a night of heavy drinking. Abbreviated to PGB. See **after grog bog** for more synonyms.

postie a postman or postwoman. Aussie slang since the 1950s.

pot **1.** marijuana. Originally US slang of the 1930s – common in Australia since the 1960s. Probably from Mexican Spanish *potiguaya* 'marijuana leaves'. **2.** a beer glass of 10 fluid ounces (285 ml). Used principally in Tas, Vic and Qld. For other synonyms see the entry for **middy**. **3.** a heavily backed horse; the favourite.

pot and pan Aussie rhyming slang for 'man', in the sense of your partner or boyfriend. Been around since 1905.

potato **1.** a woman or girl. From *potato peeler*, rhyming slang for 'sheila'. Aussie slang since the 1950s. **2.** a small hole in a sock through which skin is showing.

pothead a marijuana user or addict.

pot luck **1.** a meal made from whatever happens to be at hand. **2.** a shared meal concocted from all the ingredients everyone brings.

poultice a large bet. *There was a poultice laid on by the connections.* Also, any large sum on money. Aussie slang since the 1900s. Still used in racing circles.

pound the punishment cells in a prison.

pousti a homosexual. From Greek. A fairly common insult among Aussies of Greek descent. Even worse is to be called a **pousti malaka** (the word **malaka** means wanker).

pov **1.** poor. A shortening of the word 'poverty'. Hence, a poor person. *They're such povs they can't afford new thongs.* Recent Aussie slang from the 1990s. **2.** bad, pathetic, uncool. Used chiefly by adolescents who associate poverty with lack of sophistication, style, and the like – kids can be so cruel. Also, **povvo** or **povvy**.

pov cone a 30c McDonald's ice-cream cone – cheap enough to be affordable to povs.

pow powdery snow, good for skiing on.

powder puff a weak or effeminate male.

powder your nose an age-old euphemism for a woman to visit the ladies' room or toilet. It can also be a joking way to refer to snorting cocaine.

power point a racist term for an Asian person.

pox a venereal disease. Interestingly this word derives from *pocks*, small pustules on the skin which are a feature of advanced syphilis (hence our modern word *pock-marked*). Now not in common use except in imitation of Elizabethan insults like **a pox on that!** This is at least one tangible enrichment of modern life attributable to the forced study of old Bill Shakespeare at high school. Thanks Bill.

pox doctor a doctor treating venereal disease. If you are **all dressed up like a pox doctor's clerk**, then you are dressed in a flashy manner that reveals a rather poor taste in clothing.

poxhead a contemptible person.

pox off another way of saying *Piss off!*

poxy no good, rubbishy, crap.

pozzie an alternate spelling of **possie** (see entry).

prairie oyster a testicle of a castrated bull or ram, eaten as food. Otherwise called a **mountain oyster**.

prang to crash a car, bike or other vehicle. Hence, such a crash. Originally RAF slang of the 1930s referring to aeroplane crashes. In World War II it was also used to refer to bombing raids.

prat **1.** the arse. Venerable slang originating in thieves' cant of the 16th century. **2.** a fool or jerk. British slang from the 1960s.

pratfall **1.** a heavy fall onto the buttocks. **2.** a specially practised fall onto the buttocks, as by a clown.

prat yourself in to butt in or intrude. Aussie slang since the early 1900s.

prawn **1.** a fool or jerk; an insignificant or objectionable person. *He's a bit of a prawn.* Australian slang since the 1890s. Also called a **prawn head**. See also the phrase **don't come the raw prawn with me**. **2.** a person with an attractive body but an ugly head. **3.** to be **off like a bucket of prawns** is to be really rotten; to stink.

prawn and porn night the same as a **porn and prawn night** (see entry).

preggers pregnant. Originally British slang but quite common here. The Aussie variant **preggo** has been around since the 1950s, and the form **preggie** since at least the 1970s.

pregnant rollerskate the original Volkswagen car.

Presbo a Presbyterian.

pressie a variant spelling of **prezzie**.

prezzie a present or gift. Aussie slang since at least the 1960s. Also called a **prezzo**.

prick **1.** the penis. A taboo swearword – worse than *dick* or *cock*. Recorded as far back as 1592! **2.** a contemptible person; a dick or cock. This dates back at least to the 1820s. Synonymous compounds are **prick features** and **prick nose**.

prickle farmer a suburban or urban resident who takes up working a small block of land in a rural area.

prickteaser a woman who leads a man on but doesn't come across. Can also be used of a gay man who behaves in the same way. Also called a **cockteaser**.

Prisoner of War a local nickname for the Prince of Wales Hospital, Sydney. Both have the initials POW.

pro **1.** a professional. **2.** a prostitute. **3.** problem. *No pro, bro.*

prob a problem. *What's the prob?* Gives rise to the familiar reassurance *No probs!*

Proddie a Protestant. Also called a **Proddy dog**. As used by school children, especially Catholic school children.

prole a member of the proletariat or working class.

prong an erect penis.

pronto promptly; quickly. From Spanish.

prossie a prostitute. Australian slang since at least the 1940s. Occasionally spelt **prozzie**. Also called a **prosso**.

Protto a Protestant.

provo a military police officer. Short for *provost marshal*. World War II slang.

psycho **1.** crazy, insane. Hence, wild, furious, angry. *They went absolutely psycho.* **2.** an insane person.

pub a hotel. Short for *public house*. Recorded since the 1850s in Britain, and at least the 1880s in Australia.

Pubbo a kid from a public school.

pub crawl an outing in which you drink at a series of pubs in succession.

pube **1.** a pubic hair. **2.** a derisive term for a public servant – clearly punning on the previous sense.

pub golf a type of pub crawl in which nine pubs are visited, each of which have a certain 'par' of how many beers are to be drunk.

pub suck the attraction a pub seen from the air can have on a hang-glider pilot, often causing an otherwise unplanned landing. Compare **cloud suck**.

puggle a baby echidna. This is actually a trademark name for a fictitious Australian bush animal that has appeared in numerous children's books and as soft toys. The fictitious Puggles also happen to look quite like infant echidnas. The word itself was invented by Tony Barber (former drummer for Billy Thorpe and the Aztecs – not the quiz show host) in 1979 but was not applied to echidnas until the early 1990s when an echidna specialist saw some Puggle soft toys in a shop and noticed the uncanny resemblance. She started using the term and thus it spread to the general population. It even got to the point of being applied to baby platypuses for a while as well. However, generally echidna and platypus specialists use the term 'nestling' for young in the nest, and 'pouch young' for young in the pouch. The owners of the copyright have made efforts to undo this unwarranted application of their invention, which has met with some intitial success, but only time will tell if the name will stick.

pug hole a hole in a dried-up watercourse.

puke to vomit. Old slang, first recorded in Shakespeare's play *As You Like It*, written in 1600! Hence, as a noun, that which is vomited. *There was puke all over the floor.*

pull **1.** of a jockey, to prevent a horse from running on its merits. **2.** to successfully bed someone. *He's an expert at pulling the chicks.*

3. of a male, to wank. Hence, an act of wanking. *He always has a pull before dropping off to sleep.* **4.** to suck down a cone of marijuana.

pull a brief to remove or steal a brief in order to foil successful prosecution.

pull a chick to successfully woo a woman into bed.

pull a fastie to deceive; to take an unfair advantage.

pullie a pullover.

pull off **1.** to achieve or do. *She's pulled it off.* **2.** of a male, to masturbate until orgasm.

pull on the wobbly boots to prepare yourself for going out and getting drunk.

pull up of a jockey, to prevent a horse from running on its merits.

pull your finger out to get on with the job; to stop fiddle-farting about.

pull your head in! Mind your own business! Aussie slang since the 1940s.

pull your pud of a male, to masturbate.

pump to have sexual intercourse. Old sexual slang from the 18th century.

pumpie a pump-action shotgun.

punch buggy a children's game in which punches are dealt out to others upon seeing a Volkswagen Beetle. There are many variations on the rules.

punchy punch drunk.

punt **1.** to bet or wager. Hence, a bet or wager. To **take a punt** is to have a gamble on something, to take a chance. **2.** gambling in general. *He could just make a living on the punt.*

punter **1.** a gambler on horse or dog races; the prey of the bookie. **2.** a customer; the person who is paying out money for something.

pure merino a member of an old and established Australian family not of convict descent.

purler another way to spell **pearler** (see entry).

purse-carrier a derogatory term for a homosexual man.

pus ball a pimple.

pus face a person badly affected with acne.

push **1.** formerly, a gang of vicious city hooligans. Known by the area they frequented, as 'the Rocks push' or the 'Cardigan Street push'. Especially common in the 19th century and early 20th century. **2.** a group of friends or associates.

pushie a pushbike.

push shit uphill with a pointy stick to attempt the impossible; to waste time on the unachievable.

pus pie **1.** a vanilla slice. **2.** a custard tart.

pussy **1.** the vagina or vulva; the female genitals. British sexual slang of the Victorian era. **2.** crudely used to refer to women considered as sexual objects. *There'll be plenty of pussy at the party.* **3.** sexual intercourse. *Getting much pussy lately?* **4.** an ineffectual or weak man; a wimp or wuss.

pussy-whipped of a man, dominated by a wife or female partner; under the thumb. US slang from the 1950s. Recently adopted in Australia.

put a cork in it Shut up!

put in the fangs to cadge from or borrow off someone. You can also **put in the hooks**.

put lead in your pencil to excite a man sexually.

put on dog to behave pretentiously.

put out of a woman, to let a man have sex with her; to come across.

putrid excellent, cool, unreal. Used by teenagers. Along the same lines as **sick** and **filthy**.

put some wood in the hole please shut the door!

put the acid on to pressure someone into doing something they are reluctant to do, especially to come across with sexual favours.

put the boot in **1.** to attack savagely by kicking. **2.** to attack unfairly and without restraint.

put the hard word on **1.** to be persistent in asking for a favour. Aussie slang since World War I. **2.** to be persistent in pursuing sexual favours from someone. *The boss put the hard word on the new secretary.* This nuance has been around since at least the 1930s.

put the mocker on to jinx or bring bad luck to someone. Same as **put the mozz on**.

put the scarers on to frighten.

put up or shut up to be prepared to support what one says or else remain silent.

pyjama game one-day cricket, especially when it first began in the 1980s. So called because of the colourful uniforms worn – as opposed to the (then) usual cricket whites.

pyramidiot a person who believes in the mystic properties of pyramids, such as their having been built by aliens, pyramid power, and the like.

pyro laconic way of saying 'pyromaniac'.

QG a Queensland Government vehicle. They sport number plates beginning with these letters.

quack originally a swindler who claimed to be a medical practitioner and sold cure-alls or other fabulous medicines, but in Australia any doctor at all – with the joking implication that they are all phoneys. First used during World War I.

quacker a derisive term for a Kawasaki bike.

quad **1.** a quadrangle or courtyard. **2.** a four-wheeled rail motor.

Quaint Arse a jocular nickname for QANTAS.

quandong a person who cadges or imposes upon another.

queen an effeminate male homosexual. Originally British slang of the 1880s. Sometimes spelt **quean**, especially formerly. See **beat queen**, **drag queen**, **drama queen**, **size queen**.

Queenslander a high-set weatherboard house such as is common in Qld.

Queen Street bushie in Qld, one who owns a country property, often for purposes of tax avoidance, but who lives and works in Brisbane. Can be used to mean any wannabe farmer. Also called a **Queen Street ringer**. See **Pitt Street farmer**, **Collins Street cocky**.

queeny effeminate; camp.

queer of a male, homosexual. Hence, a homosexual man. This is the original meaning, dating back to the 1920s and probably of US origin. Long used in both the gay and straight community, and frequently used disparagingly by homophobes. It has recently been reclaimed as a positive term by the gay/lesbian/transgender community and is now applied widely to refer to any sexual practices or proclivities that are not straight-up-and-down heterosexual.

queer for infatuated or in love with.

Queer Street a state of financial embarrassment.

quiche-eater a derogatory term for a man who is kind, sensitive, politically correct and a bit new-agey; the antithesis of the rugger-bugger or ocker. After the title of the popular book *Real Men Don't Eat Quiche* (1982) by Bruce Feirstein.

quickie **1.** sex on the fly, and often through the fly. **2.** a quick drink. **3.** anything done rapidly or in a short space of time. **4.** in cricket, a fast bowler.

quick quid a modest amount of money earned with little effort.

quid **1.** a pound note or the sum of one pound. Originally British slang dating back to the 17th century. Used in Australia up until the introduction of decimal currency in 1966. Despite its demise as a term for currency, quid still lingers in a number of slang expressions. For example, someone who is lacking in intelligence is said to be **not the full quid**. **2.** money, especially a large amount. *It must have cost a quid.* A **quick quid** is a modest amount of money earned with little effort. If you won't do something **for quids**, then you won't do it under any circumstances. *I wouldn't miss it for quids.* And, finally, the great Aussie expression of lust for life: **I wouldn't be dead for quids**.

quietie a quiet drink.

quim the female genitalia. Venerable slang from the 18th century. Origin unknown. Common in pornography.

quince **1.** a homosexual man. Aussie slang since the 1940s. **2.** to **get on someone's quince** is to annoy or irritate them.

quiver a surfie's word for a set of surfboards catering for different conditions.

quod prison or jail. Venerable slang from 17th century cant.

quoit **1.** the anus. Aussie slang dating from the 1910s. To spell it out – from the resemblance of the brown rope ring to the sphincter. Sometimes spelt **coit**. **2.** the backside or arse. *You lot – get off your quoits.* **3.** an annoying or obnoxious person.

quokka soccer the so-called 'sport' of kicking quokkas on Rottnest Island. The small endangered marsupial known as the quokka still exists in large numbers only on fox-free Rottnest Island about 12 km off the coast from Perth. Each year post-exam schoolkids descend on the island and get roaring drunk – and thus quokka soccer was invented. The local population of quokkas were used to people as some 400,000 tourists a year visit the island – and so they were fair game for drunken youths. They usually die from internal injuries after being kicked. The sadistic practice is now banned and warrants a $10,000 fine.

rabbit **1.** a fool. **2.** in cricket, a player who is not very good at batting. Also called a **bunny**. Neither of which are as bad as being the **ferret** (see entry). **3.** to **root like rabbits** is to indulge in sex – to go at it hammer and tongs.

rabbit cooker a woman whose obsession with a partner verges on the psychotic. So called after the character played by Glenn Close in the 1987 hit movie *Fatal Attraction*. More often known as a **bunny boiler**.

rabbit ears **1.** an indoor television antenna with two adjustable arms. **2.** in Canberra, a derisive name for the American war memorial at Blamey Square, Russell Hill.

rabbit on to talk on and on, generally about nonsense. Perhaps originally from rhyming slang *rabbit and pork* 'talk'. Originally British slang.

racehorse **1.** a thinly rolled cigarette or joint. So called because it is smoked quickly. Aussie slang since the 1940s. Originally prison slang. **2.** in WA, a sand goanna.

race off To **race someone off** is to take them to a secluded spot for sex. *He races his wife off to the bedroom as much as possible.* Aussie slang since the 1960s.

racers speedos, as opposed to boardies. For a full set of synonyms see **sluggos**.

racing chook in Tasmania, the endemic flightless native hen which runs swiftly to cover when disturbed. Also called a **narkie**.

rack **1.** a pair of large, prominent, breasts. *She had a magnificent rack.* **2.** among adolescents, a French kiss or pash. Also, as a verb, to French kiss or pash on. **3.** to rob; to steal or shoplift.

racket **1.** a dishonest scheme or trick; a swindle or fraud. **2.** legitimate business or occupation. *He's in the advertising racket.*

rack off to leave or depart with haste. *Let's rack off before he gets back.* Aussie slang since the 1970s. Often used as a command meaning Piss off! Fuck off! Perhaps originally a euphemism for these. In 1975 Bob Hudson had a hit record in Australia entitled *Rack Off Normie*. A common comic rejoinder is **rack off, hairy legs!**

radical great, wonderful, fantastic. Almost equivalent to cool, but better. Originally US slang, adopted in Oz in the 1980s. Commonly shortened to **rad**.

Rafferty's rules no rules at all. Probably a use of the Irish surname as a slur on their supposed unruliness. Aussie slang since the 1910s.

rag **1.** a newspaper or magazine, especially a local one. **2.** a harshly derogatory term for a woman, usually implying that she is promiscuous. **3.** a woman **on her rags** is menstruating.

rager a person who parties hard and long.

rails the railings surrounding the track at a racecourse. Hence, that part of the ground for spectators next to the rails where the leading bookmakers are situated – as opposed to the **flat**. Hence, a **rails bookie** is a leading bookmaker at a race meeting.

railway tracks dental braces.

rainbow in both World Wars, a serviceman that joined a fighting unit after conflict had ceased. So called because a rainbow follows a storm.

rainbow dozen a mixed dozen of the range of Cascade beers (Blue, Red, Green).

raincoat a condom.

rainmaker in Aussie Rules, a very high kick.

rake-off a share or portion of a sum or profit. Originally used of money illegally gained.

ralph to vomit. Imitative of the noise of spewing. Also spelt **ralf**.

ram **1.** a highly-sexed man. **2.** a swindler's accomplice who sets up the victims. Hence, to act as swindler's confederate.

Rambo an aggressive, macho male. After the character in the movie *First Blood* (1982).

rammies pants. An alteration of *round mes*, short for *round me houses*, rhyming slang for 'trousers'. Recorded since 1906.

ramp to search a prisoner or prison cell. Hence, as a noun, such a search. Ramps are conducted in order to search for contraband items, but also commonly done in order to harass prisoners by junking their cells. Australian slang since the 1910s.

rancid cool, excellent, unreal. Used by adolescents. Along the same lines as **filthy** and **sick**.

random a non-local or outsider; a blow-in.

ranger danger the potentiality of running into a park ranger. *Is there any ranger danger in this park?*

ranking in Adelaide, reverse parking or parallel parking.

rap 1. a favourable appraisal; a compliment. *She gave it a real rap.* Also known as a **rap-up**. Also spelt **wrap**. **2.** a review. *The movie got a bad rap.* **3.** punishment or blame, especially for a crime one did not commit. *She had to take the rap.* **4.** a criminal charge. *He's trying to beat a housebreaking rap.*

rare as hen's teeth exceedingly scarce. Also, something scarce can be as **rare as rocking horse shit**.

rashie a lycra garment worn under a wetsuit for prevention of wettie rash; a rash vest.

raspberry tart rhyming slang for 'fart'. Originally British, from the late 19th century. This is the origin of the term 'raspberry', that is, a derisive sound made by blowing sloppily with the tongue stuck out through the lips. The noise so made is meant to sound like a fart. Hence, it is also the origin of the verb **razz**, and possibly of **razoo** (see entries).

rat 1. a contemptible person. **2.** a person who betrays others. Specifically, a police officer who blows the whistle on corrupt coppers. **3.** a derogatory term for a chihuahua. **4.** in Tas, an undersized crayfish. **5.** to desert someone in times of trouble. *Three of the delegates ratted this morning.* **6.** to continue at work during a strike; to work as a scab. **7.** to renege or pike out. **8.** to rob or steal from. *The soldiers were ratting dead bodies for souvenirs.* (See **souvenir**). Aussie slang dating from the 1890s. **9.** to steal opal by working another's mine.

ratbag 1. a worthless, despicable, unreliable person. Aussie slang. Recorded as early as 1890, but not common until the 1940s. **2.** an eccentric or queer person; a weirdo. Hence, **ratbaggery**.

rat cunning shrewdness; slyness.

rat house a psychiatric hospital. Aussie slang since 1900.

rat on to betray; to dob in or inform on someone.

rat on stilts a racing greyhound.

rat's arse If you **don't give a rat's arse**, then you don't care at all. Aussie slang since the 1970s.

rat's coffin a meat pie.

ratshit no good; useless; broken. Aussie slang since the 1970s. Politely abbreviated to **RS**.

rat's tail a single, long thin lock or plait of hair.

rats with wings a derogatory term for the much hated feral pigeons that infest Australian cities and towns.

rat tamer a psychologist or psychiatrist.

rat through to rifle through hurriedly and carelessly.

rattler any of various types of trains noted for their loud rattling. To **jump a rattler** was to board a moving train and thus obtain a ride without buying a ticket – a practice common among swagmen during the Depression.

rattle your dags Hurry up! Get a move on! For an explanation of this idiom, see **dag**.

ratty 1. mad or crazy; eccentric. Aussie slang since the 1890s. **2.** worn-out; shabby.

Ravo the Launceston term for a westie, bogan or bevan. From the suburb of Ravenswood.

raw prawn a naive fool. See the phrase **don't come the raw prawn**.

razoo a fictional coin of little value. To have no money is to **not have a razoo**, and to be worth nothing is to be **not worth a razoo**. Commonly called a **brass razoo**. Such a coin never existed. The origin of this term has led to much speculation over the years, most of which is not worth a brass razoo. However, one intriguing possibility is that it is a euphemistic alteration of *arse razoo* = a fart. The word *razoo* was used in American slang since the late 19th century to mean a fart, being a variant of *raspberry*, from rhyming slang, *raspberry tart* 'fart'.

razz to deride or make fun of; to chiack. Originally US slang, derived from *raspberry*, the derisive fart-like sound made with the tongue and lips.

Razzle an RSL club. Also **the Razza**.

readies ready cash. *I'm a bit short on the readies.*

reality check a moment of self-reflection; a bringing of oneself back down to earth.

ream 1. to sodomise someone. 2. to suck or lick another's anus for sexual gratification.

rear-end loader a prisoner who hides things up their rectum.

rec grounds in Tas and formerly Vic, the town recreational grounds, in other words, the local footy oval.

rechtub kelat a cryptolanguage used by butchers in which normal words are pronounced backwards (roughly). For instance if you wanted to say '*butcher talk*' in **rechtub kelat**, you'd say *rechtub kelat*, which is where the name comes from! Curiously in 19th century Britain this linguistic game was popular among costermongers (that is, apple sellers), where it was known by the rather unimaginative name **backslang**.

record in Vic and Tas, a booklet containing information about the week's round of AFL games. Called the **budget** in WA and SA.

recovery party a party held after a big event at which people who have been out all night can continue partying by lazing around and coming down.

red 1. a red kangaroo. 2. a Communist or Leftist sympathiser.

red back a twenty dollar note.

red can a can of Melbourne Bitter beer. As opposed to a **blue**, **green**, **white** or **yellow can** (see entries).

the Red Centre the desert interior of Australia. So called since the 1930s. Also called **the Red Heart**.

red handbag a cask of cheap red wine.

red-headed rabbit rooter a common appellation directed at any red-headed bloke. Somewhat derogatory, but a bit too schoolboyish to cause serious offence.

red hen 1. in SA, any of various diesel railcars used on urban services from 1955 onwards which were painted red. Compare this with **blue bird**. 2. an obsolete slang term for a ten pound note. So called from its colour.

red-hot 1. enthusiastic, keen, avid. *She's a red-hot Wallabies supporter*. 2. unfair. *These prices are a bit red-hot*. Aussie slang since the 1890s. Scarcely heard since the 1950s. 3. highly sexually aroused or arousing. 4. by a long margin. *Hyperno was the red-hot favourite*.

red hots harness racing. Aussie rhyming slang for 'the trots'. Dates back to the 1960s.

red myrtle in Tas, corned beef.

red ned cheap red wine. Aussie slang since the 1940s.

red plate a Victorian government car. Because Victorian government car registration plates are red.

red ragger a derisive term for a Communist or Leftist sympathiser. Aussie slang dating from the 1910s. A red flag is a symbol of socialism.

red rattler any of various passenger trains with dark red carriages which rattled noisily when travelling at speed.

red rover a common schoolyard chasings game, which is usually banned by teachers. Also called **red rover cross over**. This term is used in all states, but is most common in Qld, NSW and SA. For the full set of regionalisms, see **British bulldog**.

red sails in the sunset menstruating.

red suitcase a cask of red wine.

reefer a marijuana cigarette. Originally US slang from the 1930s. From *reef* 'part of a sail which is rolled up'. But perhaps influenced by Mexican Spanish *grifo* 'marijuana'.

reffo a derogatory term for a refugee. Aussie slang. First used for European refugees during World War II.

Reg Grundies Aussie rhyming slang for 'undies'. After *Reg Grundy*, Oz television producer. Also called **Reggies**, **Reginalds** or **Grundies**.

rego registration. *The vehicle was out of rego*. Laconic Aussie shortening since the 1960s.

rehab rehabilitation; the rehabilitation ward of a hospital. Aussie slang since the 1940s.

reject a socially unacceptable person; a nerd, turkey, loser or the like.

rellie a relative. Also common in the form **rello**. One of the few words which has both an *-ie* and an *-o* form. Your relatives are also known as the **rels**.

rent boy a young male homosexual prostitute.

rents the parents of one living at home. Emphasising the pecuniary nature of the relationship, as seen from the adolescent point of view.

reo 1. a surfing manoeuvre where the surfboard partially leaves the wave and then re-enters it. Short for *re-entry*. 2. military slang for member of a reinforcement troop. 3. reinforcing steel, as used to strengthen concrete.

repo man a repossession agent. Originally US slang of the 1960s.

repro a reproduction, as of an antique.

reptile an unscrupulous news reporter.

resto an antique, vintage car, or any other old thing that has been restored.

retard an awkward or clumsy person. Hence, a socially unacceptable person; a nerd.

retent an excessively meticulous person. Short for **anal retent** coming from **anally retentive**.

retic in WA, an automatic garden sprinkler system. Short for *reticulation*. Pronounced 'REE-tik', with stress on the first syllable.

retread a person who has come out of retirement to take up work again.

retro **1.** a fashion and music taste harking back to the previous decades. **2.** deliberately old-fashioned. In terms of music, referring to any pop music dating from the 1950s to the 1980s. As time goes on, the meaning of 'retro' will inevitably change.

reverse biceps flabby, down-hanging triceps.

rev head a car enthusiast. Aussie slang since the 1980s.

rhodie a rhododendron.

rhyming slang a technique of forming slang terms by using terms that rhyme with another, as in *elephant's trunk* for 'drunk'. Rhyming slang first appeared in London in the 1840s where it was popular among 'chaunters' (men who sang ballads and carols, recited dying speeches and the like) and 'patterers' (street pedlars selling miraculous products). Rhyming slang quickly made its way to Australia and the earliest home-grown list dates back to 1898. Oz took rhyming slang to its heart and has created numerous local terms to add to the many British ones adopted here. Rhyming slang was also transported to America where it was used especially by the underworld, but it was never as popular there as here. Usually the rhyming slang term is two or more words – this allows the actual rhyme word to be dropped and thus make the connection even more obscure, as in *Noah*, rhyming slang for 'shark', a shortening of *Noah's ark*.

ribuck obsolete Aussie slang meaning very good. *He was a ribuck shearer*. Also formerly used as an answer in the positive, meaning 'all right'. In use from the 1890s up until the about the 1950s. An Aussie use of British slang *rybeck* 'profit', which comes from either Yiddish or German. Sometimes spelt **rybuck** or **ryebuck**.

rice grinder a derogatory term for a Japanese motorcycle.

Richard the third a piece of excrement. Also the act of defecation. Rhyming slang for 'turd'. Originally British. Right royally related to **Henry the third** and **William the third**.

ride to have sexual intercourse with someone; to fuck. Venerable slang dating back to the 17th century. Hence, an act of sexual intercourse.

ride shotgun to sit in the front passenger seat when on a journey. From the practice of acting as a shotgun-toting security guard on a stagecoach in the Wild West. Actually, it is interesting to note that this phrase first appears in the 1960s, and so was probably just made up for movie Westerns.

ride the tan track to be the active partner in anal intercourse.

ridgy-didge **1.** true, genuine, dinkum. First recorded in the 1950s. This great Ockerism comes from the earlier *ridge* = genuine, which dates back to the 1930s, and probably comes from underworld slang *ridge* = gold or gold coins. **2.** Aussie rhyming slang for 'fridge'. *Just whack it in the ridgy-didge.*

R-ie an RSL club. *They have an under-18s disco every Friday night at the R-ie.*

rig a great big insulting term, especially when directed towards Rugby League legend Gordon Tallis's mother. This term came to prominence in the State of Origin series in 2002 when a spectator incurred the wrath of Gordo by holding up a sign saying 'Your mother's a rig'. Gordo was not backward in coming forward with what he thought about this, and the television cameras diligently broadcast his reaction – the nature of which even the poorest of lip-readers could not mistake. Actually, the precise meaning of the term in question is a bit of a mystery. The press were able to track down the hapless signwriter the next day, who turned out to be a rueful 17-year-old boy who would only be identified as 'Scott'. He claimed there had been a misunderstanding and that *rig* only meant 'a dominant person'. Suffice to say, despite its brief spot in the limelight, the term has not caught on.

righto All right! Sure! Okay! Aussie slang since the 1890s. Also common in Britain. Also in the form **righty-oh**, which is old in Britain, but has only become common in Oz since the 1980s.

right stuff alcohol, grog, booze. Aussie slang since the 1910s. Last heard in the 1960s. No longer in use.

rim to suck or lick another's anus for sexual gratification.

ring **1.** in two-up, the circle of punters within which the coins are tossed. Aussie slang dating from the 1890s. **2.** the area of a racecourse where the leading bookmakers congregate. Hence, the leading bookmakers themselves. *All sorts of rumours are spread about in an effort to deceive the ring.* Aussie horseracing slang since the 1870s. **3.** the anus or backside. *They've been sitting on their rings doing nothing all day.* Used in Australia since at least the 1950s. **4.** in shearing, to **ring the shed** is to beat all other shearers with your tally. Recorded since the 1890s.

ringdinger a derogatory term for a two-stroke motorcycle. So called from the noise of the engine.

ringer **1.** the fastest shearer in a shearing shed. Recorded since the 1870s. This word comes from an earlier, now obsolete, sense, where a ringer was any person or thing that was superlatively good. For more information see the entry for **snagger**. **2.** a stockman or drover. So called because they circle the stock and keep them together. Dates back to the 1900s. **3.** a substitute racehorse or greyhound; a ring-in or ringtail. Aussie racing slang since the 1930s.

ringie the person running a two-up game.

ring in **1.** to substitute a racehorse or greyhound for another in a race. Aussie slang since 1918. **2.** in two-up, to substitute a double-sided coin for a genuine one. *If you got caught trying to ring a two-header in, you'd probably be kicked to death.*

ring-in **1.** a racehorse or greyhound substituted for another in a race. **2.** a person or thing substituted for another at the last moment. *Joe couldn't come, so I'm the ring-in.* **3.** a person pretending to be someone else; a phoney. **4.** someone from another place; an outsider.

ring keeper the person running a two-up game. Also occasionally called the **ring master**.

Ringwood Reeboks Melbourne slang for daggy suede moccasins.

rinsed drunk. *We really got rinsed last night.*

rip **1.** to move along at great speed. **2.** to surf, skate, ski or snowboard, outstandingly. **3.** to be excellent. *His latest movie really rips.*

rip off to swindle; to overcharge.

rip-off **1.** something not worth its price; an overpriced item or thing. **2.** a system or situation in which people are unfairly done out of money. **3.** a poor copy of some successful piece of literature, entertainment, etc.; a knock-off

ripped heavily under the influence of drugs or alcohol; stoned.

ripper **1.** something or someone exciting extreme admiration. *You little ripper!*. Also used as an adjective to mean absolutely excellent. *It's a ripper movie.* Originally 19th century British slang, but has since died out there. It has been used in Australia since the 1850s. **2.** an excellent surfboard rider, skater, skier or snowboarder.

ripsnorter an outstanding or remarkable person or thing. From US slang of the 1840s. Probably introduced to Australians from American troops during World War II. Hence, the adjective, **ripsnorting**.

rissole **1.** an RSL club. Chiefly NSW slang. Hence, for entertainers to **do the rissoles** is to make a tour of RSL clubs. **2.** If someone farewells you with 'See ya round', the stock reply is 'Yeah, like a rissole.'

roach **1.** a cockroach. **2.** the butt of a marijuana cigarette. As a joint is smoked, the end of it becomes black and shiny and vaguely resembles a cockroach.

roadie **1.** a road manger for a rock group or the like. Slang back in the 1960s, but virtually Standard English now. **2.** a bottle or can of beer consumed while driving. Also called a **traveller**. **3.** a measure of driving distance equivalent to the distance travelled while consuming one bottle or can of beer. *It's a three-roadie trip.* **4.** one for the road. *Have you got time for a roadie?*

robber the fluffy airborne seed of various plants, such as the moth vine or Scotch thistle. See **Santa Claus** for synonyms.

robber's dog a dog such as would be owned by a petty thief – used in slang as a metaphor for either speed as in *She was off like a robber's dog*, or ugliness as in *He's got a head on him like a robber's dog.*

rock **1.** to be excellent. *Club Retro really rocks.* **2.** to go or travel some place. *We're all going to* *rock along to the party later. We all rocked over to his place.* **3.** to gobsmack someone with a cutting remark or witty come-back.

rock ape **1.** a lout or hooligan. **2.** a racist term for an Aboriginal person.

rock box a ghettoblaster.

rock chick a female rock 'n' roll musician.

rock chopper a Roman Catholic. Originally this term was applied to navvies, that is, labourers employed to make roads, railways, canals and the like – because they spent their days breaking up rocks. It was used in a derogatory way to refer to Irish Australians, with the imputation that they were all descendants of convict rock choppers. The matching up of the initial letters 'r' and 'c' no doubt helped in firming the connection.

rock doctor a geologist.

rocker **1.** a rock 'n' roll performer or fan. **2.** In the early '60s, there was a whole sub-culture of rockers, characterised by delinquent behaviour and American-influenced dress, such as leather jackets and greased-back hair. The motorcycle was their steed.

rocket **1.** a severe reprimand. **2.** to **put a rocket under** someone is to stir them to action.

rocket scientist a very intelligent person; a brainiac. If something is **not rocket science**, then it is easy to understand.

rock hopper a person who fishes from coastal rocks.

Rockie a member of the Royal Australian Naval Reserve.

rock lobster a twenty dollar note. So called from its colour.

rock 'n' roll **1.** Aussie rhyming slang for the 'dole'. **2.** to set about doing something. *Okay everyone, let's rock 'n' roll.*

rock spider prison slang for a child molester. A term of great opprobrium. Has now become part of general slang.

rock up to arrive. *Look who's just rocked up.*

Rock-Vegas the north Qld town of Rockhampton. Modelled on the earlier term **Bris-Vegas**.

Rocky Rockhampton, the principal city of central Queensland.

rod **1.** an erect penis. To have **had the rod** is to be ruined, busted, worn out, wrecked – in other words, 'fucked'. **2.** a pistol.

rod walloper a male who masturbates; a wanker. Used as a term of abuse.

roger **1.** of a man, to have sex with someone; to fuck. Venerable slang from the 18th century. In 17th and 18th century literature the word name Roger was used to mean the penis (as with the names Dick, John Thomas, and Percy). Thus to Roger someone was to give them the penis. **2.** to treat harshly; to ruin; to shaft.

rogue a racehorse that is difficult to handle.

roid rage an attack of aggressive or violent behaviour characteristic of steroid abuse.

roids steroids, especially when used as a drug of abuse.

roll **1.** to assault and rob a person. **2.** to convince a person to turn witness and incriminate others. **3.** a bankroll. This dates back to the mid-19th century. In Australia a very big bankroll can be described as **a roll so big Jack Rice couldn't jump over it.** Jack Rice was the name of a successful steeplechase and hurdles racehorse of the 1910s.

Roller a Rolls Royce car.

rollie a hand-rolled cigarette; a roll-your-own.

roll in the hay an act of sexual intercourse.

roll over to turn witness and incriminate others after initially claiming innocence. A person who does this is known as a **roll-over** in police slang.

Rolls-Canardly a dilapidated car; a 'bomb'. So called because it rolls down one hill and can hardly get up the next.

ronnie a small stone suitable for throwing. Used chiefly in SA. See **yonnie** for the full set of regionalisms.

Ronny an act of sexual intercourse. From rhyming slang *Ronny Coote* 'root'. After Ron Coote, Rugby League giant of the modern era.

roo **1.** a kangaroo. This shortening dates back to the 1890s. Commonly spelt with an apostrophe, **'roo**. **2.** a jackaroo. This shortening also dates back to the 1890s.

roo fucker a derogatory term for an Australian. A similar racist slur is **dingo fucker**.

a rooster one day and a feather duster the next a phrase expressive of the ups and downs of life.

root **1.** to have sexual intercourse; to screw or fuck. Aussie slang this one. Dates back to the 1940s. Also used in NZ. Never as rude as the F-word, and in fact, can be used as a slightly euphemistic substitution. Thus you could say *Don't root it up* instead of *Don't fuck it up.*

No one seems to be very sure just where this word stems from. It most probably a metaphorical use of *root* = to turn up soil with the snout, as swine do. Which is a pretty unpleasant image, but the word root has never had any pretensions to elegance. The connotation has always been of raw and unrefined sex – like most slang words for sex: bang, bash, hump, plug, pork, pump, shag, and so on. Rooting is quite different to 'making love'. Another suggestion is that root is related to the word *root* = penis. This meaning has existed in pornography since the 17th century, but has never been common in Australia, and so seems less likely than the first theory.
2. metaphorically, to ruin, spoil or wreck. *You've rooted me best chisel.* Also, used to mean astound or amaze. *Wait a moment - this'll root you.* **3.** to kick. *I rooted him fair up the behind with a boot.* **4.** as a noun, an act of sexual intercourse. *I haven't had a root in months.* Or, a person rated on their sexual performance, as in *a great root* or *a dud root*. Also, a sexual partner, as in *He was my first root.*

rootable sexually desirable; fuckable.

rooted **1.** exhausted. **2.** frustrated; thwarted. **3.** broken; ruined.

rooter a person noted for their rooting. Often used as a jocular nickname. *Rita the Rooter.*

root like rabbits Aussie version of *fuck like bunnies.*

root rat a person who is famed for their sexual endeavours.

root ute a panel van fitted out in the back with mattress and curtains as a retreat for sexual liaisons. See **fuck truck** for synonyms.

root your boot! a comic way of saying 'Get fucked!'

ropeable seething with anger; literally, 'fit to be tied'. Aussie slang from the 1870s, and still going strong.

rort **1.** a trick, lurk, or underhand scheme; a confidence trick. Hence, as a verb, to swindle, dupe or gyp. Aussie slang since the 1910s. In origin a backformation from **rorty**. Now commonly used of election rigging, embezzlement, and other dodgy practices indulged in by the nation's politicians – in this sense the word is hardly slang any more. **Rort** can also be used to describe a job that's a bit of a bludge. *Nice rort you're on here.* **2.** a wild party. Quite common in the 1950s and 60s, but now scarcely heard, if at all.

rorter a person who perpetrates a rort; a con artist or swindler.

rort horse a horse whose form has been kept secret; a smokie.

rorty **1.** wild and rowdy, as of a party. Originally British slang of the 19th century. **2.** of an engine, emitting a deep, throaty growl, suggestive of a grunt.

Rose Bay shopping trolley Sydney slang, a derogatory term for a city-only 4WD that never sees off-road driving. See **Toorak tractor** for a host of synonyms.

rotgut alcoholic liquor of inferior quality.

rotten extremely drunk. Aussie slang since the 1860s.

rottie a Rottweiler.

Rotto Rottnest Island, opposite the mouth of the Swan River in WA.

rough as bags extremely rough, uncouth, dirty, and ugly to boot. Aussie slang since the 1910s. Variations include **rough as guts**, which has been around since at least the 1960s, and **rough as hessian undies** – Ouch!

rough diamond an honest, fair dinkum, essentially good person who lacks refinement.

rough end of the pineapple a raw deal; the worst part of a bargain.

roughie **1.** a rough or crude person. **2.** a swindle or shrewd trick. Aussie slang since the 1910s. **3.** a starter with little chance of winning the race; a long shot. Aussie slang since the 1920s.

rough it to live without even the ordinary comforts or conveniences. *We roughed it all month long.*

rough trade homosexual slang for casual sexual partners or pick-ups. Originally used specifically to mean a man who takes the active part in casual homosexual encounters, but never the passive role, and who doesn't identify as gay.

rough trot a spell of bad luck or misfortune. Aussie slang since the 1940s.

round chiefly WA, a sandwich. To ask for a round of cheese and tomato is the same as asking for a cheese and tomato sandwich.

rouseabout a person employed to do odd jobs on a station or rural property. Recorded from the 1880s. Also called a **roustabout**. Hence, as a verb, to work as a rouseabout. Common in NZ also.

rouse on to scold or upbraid. You can also **rouse at** someone. Aussie slang since the 1890s. In origin, a variant of Scottish *roust* 'shout or roar'.

royal flush a schoolkid prank in which a student's head is shoved into a toilet bowl which is then flushed. Often done as an 'initiation' to a new student.

Royce a fart. From rhyming slang *Royce Hart*, famous Aussie Rules player.

roziner a healthy serving of booze. Sometimes spelt **rosiner**. Aussie slang since the 1930s – possibly borrowed from Irish slang where it is also used.

rozzer underworld slang, a police officer. Perhaps from French slang *rousse*, *roussin* 'a detective'.

RS a euphemism for **ratshit** (see entry).

RTFM problem in computing, any problem which arises from the user assuming things rather than actually learning how to use the software or hardware first. Standing for Read The Fucking Manual!!!!

rub-a-dub-dub Aussie rhyming slang for 'pub'. In use since the 1940s. A variant of **rubbity-dub**.

rubber 1. a condom. **2.** car tyres. *I've got to put new rubber on.* To **burn rubber** or **lay down rubber** is to drive like a demon.

rubberneck a gawker; a stickybeak; hence, a derogatory term for a tourist. Also, as a verb, to gawp or stare; to wander about idly gazing at things. *They were just hanging around rubbernecking.*

rubber nut a stupid or annoying person.

rubber van a van which, in popular fancy, takes people to a lunatic asylum. Also called the **rubber cart** or the **rubber truck**.

rubbish to denigrate or put down. Aussie slang since the 1950s.

rubbity-dub Aussie rhyming slang for 'pub'. Been around since the 1890s. Commonly shortened to **rubbity**.

rub uglies to have sex.

ruddy a euphemism for *bloody*. Aussie slang since World War I.

rude bits a twee way of referring to the genitalia.

rugger bugger a derogatory term for a Rugby Union player seen as the bastion of coarse tastes and loud behaviour.

rug rat a small child, especially one at the crawling stage. Compare **ankle biter**.

rule to be the best or greatest. *Wogs rule okay.* Commonly used in graffiti. Became popular in Australia in the 1980s. Can also be used in sporting contexts to describe the best competitor on the day. *Rob ruled with the cleanest ollie kick-flip of the day.*

Rules Australian Rules Football. Shortened thus since at least the 1940s.

rum odd, strange, or queer. Originally British slang of the 18th century.

rum do a lively party. Formerly more common than now, except in Tasmania where it still survives.

rum go an obsolete term for harsh or unfair treatment. *He was given a rum go by the coppers.*

rumpy-pumpy sexual intercourse.

rum 'un in Tasmania, an eccentric person, a character or wag, a cheeky person or scallywag. Formerly common all over the country but now restricted principally to Tasmania. Also spelt **rumun** and **rumin**. From *rum* 'odd' and *'un* 'one'. Aussie slang from the 1890s, but ultimately from British dialect.

run a banker of a river, to be completely full, right up to the top of the banks.

run like a dog to run very slowly. Generally said of an engine or a computer.

runners women's sports briefs worn over underwear and under a skirt. See **scungies** for the full set of regionalisms.

run of outs a succession of bad luck or unfortunate events. Aussie gambling slang since the 1960s.

run-through an act of sexual intercourse, from the crass male's perspective.

runway the catwalk of a fashion parade.

rush a strong feeling of exhilaration and pleasure induced by a narcotic or stimulant drug.

Ruski a derogatory term for a Russian. This is actually the Russian word for 'Russian'.

rust bucket a badly rusted motor vehicle. An Australian original from the 1960s.

ryebuck a variant spelling of **ribuck**.

sack **1.** dismissal; discharge from employment. Hence, as a verb, to dismiss or fire. **2.** bed. *He was great in the sack.* To **hit the sack** is to turn in for the night.

sack of shit a lazy, good-for-nothing.

sacred site a place of great significance. *I got to finally stand on that sacred site of Australian sport – the SCG.* A jocular extension of the concept of the Aboriginal sacred site.

saddling paddock a place where sexual activities take place. Originally the nickname of the bar and vestibules of Melbourne's Theatre Royal, famed for its prostitution in the 19th century.

said the actress to the bishop a catchphrase used to make a sexual innuendo out of an innocent statement.

Saigon tea in the Vietnam War, a drink of whisky and cola, popular with bar girls.

salad dodger an obese person.

Sallie a member of the Salvation Army. Sometimes shortened to **Sal**. Aussie slang since the 1930s. Hence, **the Sallies**, the Salvation Army. Compare the much earlier **Salvo**.

salmon **1.** a twenty dollar note. From its orange colour. **2.** formerly used of both the ten and fifty pound notes.

saltie a saltwater crocodile.

salt mine an unrelenting workplace.

salute the judge to win a horse race.

Salvo a member of the Salvation Army. Aussie slang since the 1890s. Hence, **the Salvos**, the Salvation Army. Compare the much later term **Sallie**.

sambo a sandwich. Also **sammo** or, with the *-ie* ending, either **sambie** or **sammie**.

same diff there is no difference.

same ol', same ol' the usual or customary thing.

Sandgroper a derisive term for a Western Australian. This has been around since the 1890s. See **Cornstalk** for similar terms of derision for people from other states.

sandshoe crusher in cricket, a ball aimed at the feet of the person batting.

Sandy the Melbourne suburb of Sandringham.

Sandy McNab rhyming slang for 'cab'. Originally British.

sanger **1.** a sandwich. From the pronunciation 'sangwich'. **2.** a sausage. Also spelt **sanga**.

sanno the sanitary man – that is, a man employed to empty sanitary cans in the good old days before flush toilets.

Santa Claus the fluffy airborne seed of various plants, such as the moth vine or Scotch thistle. Also called a **Father Christmas**, a **fairy**, a **robber** or a **wish**.

sarky sarcastic. *No need to be sarky.*

sarvo this afternoon. Just another way of writing *this arvo*. Now also written *the sarvo*.

satched soaked through. A short form of *saturated*.

satchel swinger a bookmaker.

sausage **1.** the penis. Usually to be found in the phrase **hide** or **sink the sausage**, to have sex – well, from the male perspective anyhow. **2.** the phrase **not a sausage** means 'absolutely nothing'.

sausage roll in Aussie Rules, rhyming slang for 'goal', as opposed to a behind. Shortened to merely **sausage**, or even just **saus**.

saver a secondary bet on another competitor to offset money already wagered. Aussie racing slang since the 1890s.

sawbones a surgeon. A grisly term dating back to the 1830s in Britain.

sawn-off of a person, suffering from duck's disease – in other words, short.

SBD a fart that, while inaudible, has an extremely unpleasant bouquet. Standing for 'Silent But Deadly'.

scab **1.** a person who is mean or stingy. **2.** a person who cadges from others. **3.** to cadge; to borrow without intending to repay.

scabby **1.** poor quality; bad; pathetic. **2.** mean or contemptible. *That was a scabby trick.*

Scabs the Perth suburb of Scarborough.

scag heroin. Originally US slang of the 1960s. Origin unknown. Hence, **scagged-out**, under the influence of heroin, or debilitated from heroin addiction.

scale to board a train, bus, or ferry without paying the fare. *They scaled a rattler up to Newcastle.* This was a common mode of transport among swagmen during the Depression.

scaly a weighbridge operator.

scarce as hen's teeth exceedingly rare. Also, **scarce as rocking horse shit**.

scarper to flee or decamp. Originally British slang of the 1840s. Probably from Italian *scappare* 'to escape'. But influenced by Cockney rhyming slang *Scapa Flow* for 'go'.

scheisse a euphemism for the exclamation *shit!* From the German word for it.

Schindler's drunk. Short for *Schindler's List*, rhyming slang for 'pissed'.

schizo **1.** a schizophrenic, hence a crazy person. **2.** suffering from schizophrenia; hence, mad or crazy. Also called **schizoid**.

schlep **1.** to carry, cart or lug. Originally British slang of the 1920s, from Yiddish. **2.** to drag yourself.

schlock low-grade entertainment. Originally US slang from the 1910s, from Yiddish. Also spelt **shlock**.

schlong the penis. Originally US slang, from Yiddish – literally the word for 'snake'.

schluck in SA, a quick nip of an alcoholic drink. From Barossa Deutsch.

schm- added to the start of, or combined with the initial consonant of a specific word to form a reduplicative pair, and used to reject or deny the importance of that word. *'I can't come – I'm too old.' 'Old, schmold! You can't get out of it that easily.'* Originally in US slang of the 1920s.

schmear the **whole schmear** is the totality of a scheme or activity. From US slang, from Yiddish.

schmick **1.** cool, excellent, terrific; classy and stylish. *He's got a really schmick car.* Also spelt **smick**, or extended with the Aussie *-o* ending to **schmicko**. **2.** neat, tidy, in good nick. In the armed forces, commonly used to refer to immaculate attire or drill. Perhaps from German *schmuck* 'neat', 'spruce', 'smart'. **3.** as a verb, to do up beautifully; to get spruced up. *We got all schmicked up for the photos.*

schmiddy originally, a derisive term for a glass of beer that is supposed to be a schooner but is actually smaller. Now also used for an actual beer glass that is somewhere between the middy (10 fluid ounces) and the schooner (15 fluid ounces).

schmo a foolish person; a goose. Originally 1940s US slang – probably a variant of **schmuck**.

schmooze **1.** to chat idly. Originally US slang of the 1890s, from Yiddish. **2.** to suck up to some important person.

schmuck an idiot or fool. Originally US slang of the 1890s, from Yiddish *shmok* 'penis'. In Australia elaborated to **schmucko**.

schnitter in the Barossa Valley, a sandwich. From Barossa Deutsch.

schnozzle the nose. Originally US slang of the 1930s, from Yiddish. Also shortened to **schnoz** or **snoz**.

schooie a schooner of beer. Also spelt **schooey**.

school a gathering of gamblers, especially if playing two-up; hence, a regular two-up game. Aussie slang since the 1810s.

schoolie **1.** a school student. **2.** a holidaying school student who has just completed their final year exams; a teenager on a holiday during schoolie's week. **3.** a school prawn.

schoolies week a week or so of holiday, especially in Surfers Paradise, Qld, taken by Year 12 students after their final exams.

school port a term for a school bag in Qld and north coast and inland NSW.

schooner a beer glass of 15 fluid ounces (425 ml). The most common size of beer glass in NSW, ACT and NT. Has some use in WA and Tas, and is spreading from northern NSW into southern Qld. However, in SA, a schooner is only a 10 ounce glass – what is normally called a **middy** or **pot** in other states. This great Australian word has been in use since the 1890s.

schtick a stage routine or gimmick. Originally US slang of the 1960s, from Yiddish. Also spelt **shtick**.

schtup to have sex; to fuck. Originally US slang of the 1960s, from Yiddish. Also spelt **shtup**.

schwing a newish, cool way of saying 'swing', when referring to music and dancing. *The joint was schwingin'.*

scoff to eat something in a hurry; to devour or gobble down.

scone the head. Aussie slang since the 1940s. Hence, as a verb, to strike on the head. *Sconed him a beauty with a wet tennis ball.*

scoob a marijuana joint. Also called a **scooby**.

scope to watch, look for or look about. Originally US slang of the 1970s, borrowed into Australia in the 1990s.

score **1.** latest news; what's what. *What's the score on Malcolm?* **2.** a prostitute's customer. **3.** the sum of twenty dollars. Before decimal currency was introduced in 1966, this was, of course, used to refer to twenty pounds. **4.** to get or obtain. *I scored the job!* **5.** to obtain a partner for casual sex. Recorded since the 1900s in both Australia and Britain. **6.** to obtain illegal drugs for personal use. **7.** to win a race.

Scott Neville an unpopular bloke; a real loser; a complete dag. *Check out the Scott Neville sitting under the tree by himself.* So called because 'He's got no mates, and never will'.

scotty annoyed or cranky; tired and irritable.

scozzer a Victorian term for a bogan, bevan or westie. Also spelt **scozza**, or even better, **skozza**. Origin unknown.

scrag **1.** a highly derogatory word for a woman. **2.** a dirty, unkempt person. **3.** a crass, blokey word for sex. *Had a great scrag last night.*

scranno a coffee break or smoke-oh.

scrap **1.** a fight or struggle. **2.** a bicycle. From 'scrap iron'. Old slang from the 1950s.

scrape **1.** an act of sexual intercourse. Also, as a verb, to have sex, to fuck. Not very charming Australian slang, amazingly dating back as far as 1865! It was originally used in Aboriginal English and is still common there, but also used by whites. **2.** a dilation and curettage of the uterus. **3.** an abortion.

scraps batter scraps from a fish and chip shop, formerly sold cheaply to those who wished for a death-defyingly fatty meal.

scratch money; dosh.

scratchie **1.** an instant lottery ticket. **2.** in Victoria, a type of public transport ticket.

the 'Scray the Melbourne suburb of Footscray. Their footy team was also known as **the 'Scrays** up until they were renamed the Western Bulldogs in 1997.

screamer **1.** someone who is very vocal during sexual intercourse. **2.** a person who cannot hold their liquor. Always qualified by an piddling amount of alcohol, as a *two-pot screamer* or a *one-schooner screamer*. **3.** a remarkable or superlative thing. In surfing, a large wave. In Aussie Rules, a spectacular mark. *He pulled down a terrific screamer, right on the buzzer.*

screw **1.** to have sexual intercourse; to root or fuck. Venerable slang from the 18th century. **2.** metaphorically, to ruin or wreck. *You've screwed it this time.* Also, to cheat or swindle. *I got screwed for fifty bucks.* **3.** used as a swearword or word of abuse, it is a much stronger equivalent of *damn*. *I don't give a screw* = I don't give a damn. *Screw you!* = Damn you! **4.** as a noun, an act of sexual intercourse. *I haven't had a screw in months.* Or, a person rated on their sexual performance. *She was a terrific screw.* **5.** a prison warder; a turnkey. Originally British slang of the early 19th century. Referring to the turning of the key in the lock. **6.** a look. Aussie slang since the 1900s. Presumably referring to screwing the face up when squinting to look closer. **7.** a wage. *He made a decent screw.* Originally British slang of the 1850s.

screw about **1.** to engage in casual sex; to cheat on someone sexually. **2.** to waste time; to fiddle about. **3.** to treat unfairly. Also, **screw around**.

screwed ruined or wrecked. Also, **screwed-up**.

screw the legs off to have sex with someone energetically; to fuck to the point of sexual exhaustion. There are many variants on this theme, such as **screw senseless**, **screw silly**, and **screw the arse off**.

screw up **1.** to blunder. **2.** to ruin or wreck.

screw with to meddle with.

scrote the scrotum.

scrub basher any old bomb used for hooning around in the bush.

scrub bashing **1.** clearing virgin bush; making a path through virgin bush. **2.** driving a vehicle through virgin bush. Also called **bush bashing**.

scrubber **1.** a derogatory term for a rough, unattractive and especially promiscuous woman. Originally British slang of the 1950s. Used in Australia from at least the 1970s. **2.** a cow or bull gone feral and living in the scrub. Aussie slang dating from the 1840s.

3. a horse bred in the wild, and thus seen as inferior. Aussie slang since the 1870s. **4.** a grey kangaroo or a wallaroo.

scrub up to appear as specified, after grooming. *She scrubs up pretty well.* Aussie slang dating from the 1980s.

scrum down a gathering together of police officers in order to ensure that their bogus statements are consistent.

scrummy scrumptious, delicious. Hence, attractive or spunky. Also shortened to **scrum**.

scull a variant spelling of **skol**.

scum **1.** in cricket, a score of 36 runs. **2.** contemptible people. **3.** to cadge something. *He was trying to scum a cigarette.*

scumbag a contemptible person. A popular 1980s adoption of US slang. Famously used by Prime Minister Paul Keating in parliamentary debate in the 1980s where it quickly became a faddish word among politicians. In America it originally meant a condom, from *scum* = semen, but it has never had that meaning in Oz. Variations on the theme are **scumball** and **scumbucket**.

scum of the earth the worst kind of people.

scum on to scold or rebuke someone.

scum sucker a contemptible or despicable person.

scunge **1.** filth. *I'll clear the scunge off this desk.* **2.** to cadge. Hence, a cadger. **3.** a stingy miser.

scunge-face a contemptible or despicable person.

scungies **1.** a type of woman's full brief underpants worn whilst playing sport. Chiefly used in NSW and the ACT. Qld has **bum shorts** and **bummers**, while the term **bloomers** is known all over, though especially common in Qld, NSW and WA. They are also called **runners**, though this doesn't seem to be regionally restricted. **2.** in NSW, men's speedos. For a full set of synonyms see **sluggos**.

scungy mean, dirty, miserable, unpleasant. Australian and NZ slang since the 1960s. Also sometimes spelt **skungy**.

scunted caught in the act; busted.

scuzz a contemptible person. Also elaborated as a **scuzzbag**, **scuzzball** and **scuzzbucket**.

sea-changer a person who has recently moved to a coastal area after having lived in the city. A relatively new phenomenon, the mass of sea-changers flooding to the coast has radically changed the make-up of many electorates, a fact which has made many politicians very edgy.

seagull **1.** a person working in a fly-in/fly-out job. **2.** a non-union, or casual, wharfie. **3.** a person who makes a lot of fuss, upsets people, and then departs. *That last boss was a bloody seagull, mate. Flies in, makes a lot of noise, flies out leaving shit everywhere!* **4.** a visiting tourist.

seat to sodomise someone. Aussie prison slang since the 1950s.

secko a sex pervert or a person charged with a sexual offence. Also spelt **secco**. Aussie slang since the 1940s.

SEC pole in WA and Vic, a power pole. From State Electricity Commission.

see a man about a dog an euphemism used when leaving a gathering in order to go to the toilet.

sell someone a pup to swindle someone by selling them something that's no good.

send her down Huey! an encouragement to the rain gods to let the rain fall. See **Huey**.

septic tank Aussie rhyming slang for 'Yank', an American. Also shortened to **septic** or, with the *-o* ending, to **seppo**.

serial tyre kicker a person who is always checking out cars with the idea of buying one, but never makes a choice.

servo a service station.

sesh a colloquial shortening of the word 'session', especially in its various slang applications. In WA it is commonly used to refer to the **Sunday session** (see entry).

session **1.** a booze-up. **2.** the hours on Sunday during which a particular pub is open – the **Sunday session**. Especially common in WA. Can also refer to Saturday if the pub has restricted hours on that day. **3.** a dope smoking session. **4.** an extended bout of love making. **5.** a period of surfing, normally a couple of hours.

set **1.** a pair of large breasts. *She had an enormous set.* Leering Aussie slang since the 1960s. **2.** a series of larger than normal waves. Aussie surfing slang since the 1960s. **3.** racing slang, having a bet placed. *Make sure I'm set for a tenner.* This term is an Australian original, dating way back to the 1910s. Also used as a verb: *The bookie set me for five hundred.* And as a noun: *The favourite has taken a big set against it.* **4.** in two-up, to **set**

the centre is to make sure the money wagered by the spinner is covered by other gamblers.

settle, petal! Relax, dear! Calm down! An ironic injunction.

seven in NSW, ACT, Tas and Qld, a seven fluid ounce glass of beer. See the entry at **glass** for other names for this size serving.

seven course meal the highly nutritional six pack and meat pie. Good Aussie tucker that.

Sevo **1.** a Seventh Day Adventist. **2.** the Sydney suburb of Seven Hills.

sex bomb an extremely attractive woman, or man.

sex, drugs and rock 'n' roll a life of partying, drinking, drugs and promiscuous sex, such as is led by the archetypal rock 'n' roller.

sex god a sexually attractive man.

sex goddess a sexually attractive woman.

sex on legs an extremely sexually attractive person. Also known as **sex on a stick**.

shabu a crystallised form of methamphetamine hydrochloride which is smoked like crack; ice.

shackle dragger a derogatory term for an Australian – used by Yanks, Kiwis, Poms and the like. Referring to our convict origins.

shack up **1.** to live together in a sexual relationship. Originally US slang. **2.** to live at a place; reside. *You can come and shack up with us till your house is ready.*

shades sunglasses.

shaft **1.** the erect penis. **2.** of a male, to have sex with someone; to fuck. Also, to sodomise someone. **3.** to betray someone for your own gain. *He got shafted by his workmate.*

shag to have sex with someone; to fuck. Venerable British slang from the 18th century. Also, as a noun, the act of sexual intercourse, or a person rated on their sexual abilities. *He wasn't a bad shag after all.* The origin of the term is unknown.

shagged exhausted from a long bout of sexual activity; hence, exhausted from any activity. Originally British slang of the 1930s, and used in Australia at least since the 1960s. Also in the form **shagged out**.

shagger a person noted for their sexual prowess.

shagger's back back pain as a result of sexual excesses.

shaggin' wagon a panel van fitted out in the back with mattress and curtains as a retreat for sexual liaisons. Aussie slang since the 1970s. Also called a **shag wagon**. See **fuck truck** for synonyms.

shag on a rock a lonely person. *All alone like a shag on a rock.* Referring to the shag or cormorant, a black marine bird commonly seen perched alone on seaside rocks. An Australian metaphor dating back to the 1840s.

shake to steal. *The chain-saw's been shook from the back of the ute.*

shake hands with the unemployed of a male, to urinate. The 'unemployed' in question is the urinator's old feller. A similar phrase is **shake hands with the wife's best friend**.

shake the cow to shake an opened milk carton to see how much milk is left in it.

the Shaky Isles New Zealand – so called from the prevalence of seismic activity there.

shanghai **1.** a child's catapult. Recorded in Australia since the 1860s. Perhaps this word comes from the Scottish word *shangie* 'a cleft stick put onto a dog's tail' – however, that word was pronounced 'shan-gee', which is quite a way from 'shang-eye'. See **slingshot** for synonyms. **2.** old nautical slang, to abduct a man against his will and force him to become part of a ship's crew. Hence, to compel someone to do something they do not wish to. In Australian prisons this term is used specifically to refer to transferring prisoners to another jail without any prior warning. This is generally done as an unofficial form of punishment. Hence, as a noun, an unexpected transfer to another jail.

Shanks's pony your legs, used as a mode of transport. *How'd you get here? Shanks's pony.*

shark bait one who swims where there is danger of a shark attack. Aussie slang since the 1920s.

shark biscuit **1.** a cheap surfboard made from foam rather than fibreglass. **2.** a bodyboard. **3.** a person who is new to surfing. **4.** a bodyboard rider.

shark feeding frenzy a mob of people clambering over the top of one another to get at something.

sharpie a teenage or young adult hoodlum of the late 1960s and 1970s. Developed from the **bodgies** of the 1950s and early 1960s. Generally used of males, but also of females.

shat off upset; annoyed.

sheep fucker an extremely derogatory term for a New Zealander. So called from the prevalence of sheep in their country. Jokes about Kiwi/sheep bestiality are rife in Australia. Not unsurprisingly, in New Zealand, this term does service as a derogatory term for Aussies.

sheep station a supposed prize for a sporting match. Used in the phrase **not playing for sheep stations** (see entry).

sheet anchor in cricket, a player whose batting is very reliable.

sheetie a sheet metal worker.

sheik an old term for a dashing, debonair, handsome man used by women back in the 1920s when Rudolph Valentino was 'it'. One of Valentino's biggest film hits was *The Sheik*, the story of a young woman kidnapped by a desert sheik who turns out to be a titled Englishman. The term survived up until the 1960s, but is no longer heard.

sheila a woman. *A couple of sheilas told me to get lost.* In use since the 1830s in Australia. Also common in NZ and even used in Britain in the late 19th century. It is a generic use of the common Irish girl's name. Sheila is basically a bloke's word – women on the whole do not use it. Some men seem to think it is a neutral word, rather than a derogatory one, but in general women don't like being called sheilas.

shekels money. From the currency of the ancient Hebrews, commonly referred to in the Bible.

shelf an informer. Australian underworld slang since the 1920s. Hence, as a verb, to inform on someone.

shellback in Tasmania, a garden snail. A delightful regionalism.

she'll be right everything will be okay.

shemozzle a confused state of affairs; a muddle. Originally 19th century Cockney slang, from Yiddish *shlimazel* 'an unlucky person'.

shenanigans silly behaviour; frivolous escapades. Can also be used of deceitful practices. Originally 19th century US slang, perhaps from Irish Gaelic *sionnachuighim* 'to play tricks'.

sherbet beer. Aussie slang dating back to the 1900s. From the 1960s used to mean a drink of beer. *Just having a few sherbets down the pub.*

shicer old mining slang for an unproductive mine.

shickered drunk. Also in the form **shicker**. Both Aussie slang dating from the 1890s – ultimately from Yiddish.

shindig a party. Originally 19th century British slang.

shiner a black eye.

a shingle short lacking a full complement of intelligence; mentally deranged. The 'shingle' in question is a wooden roofing tile, thus, in full it is 'a shingle short of a roof'. Aussie slang dating from the 1840s, making it one of the very earliest expressions of this sort. For similar comparisons see the entry for **short of**.

shiny arse a person who works behind a desk; a paper pusher or desk jockey. Also called a **shiny bum**.

shipper (when The *X-Files* was popular) a fan who wished to see Mulder and Scully get together romantically. Also called a **shippie**. As opposed to a **finishipper** or a **noromo**. The internet breeds strange obsessions.

shiralee a now obsolete term for a swag. First recorded in 1892, it was never very common, but was made famous by the 1955 novel of the same name by D'Arcy Niland, and the subsequent 1957 movie starring Peter Finch. The origin of the term is a mystery.

the Shire the common appellation for the Sutherland Shire of Sydney used by residents of that area.

Shirley Temple a child's glass playing marble with an internal net pattern; a birdcage.

shirt-front in Aussie Rules, a head-on charge that knocks an opponent to the ground. Hence, as a verb, to knock down a player in this manner.

shirt lifter a homosexual man. Aussie slang since the 1960s. See **dung puncher** for a swag of synonyms along similar lines.

shish kebab a euphemism for the exclamation *shit!*

shit **1.** to defecate. Hence, as a noun, excrement; also, an act of defecation. *I've got to go for a shit.* One of the genuine Anglo-Saxon four-lettered words. It first appears in documentary evidence from the 1300s, but was obviously around long before then. In Old English there is found the term *scitte*, meaning diarrhoea. Cognate forms appears in other Germanic languages, such as Middle Low German *schiten*, Dutch *schijten*, German *scheissen*, and Old Norse *skita*. It has been a taboo word since at least the 17th century, though nowadays is not considered so bad – depending on which meaning is intended. For instance, 'having the shits' is not nearly so rude as 'I don't give a shit'. The form **shite** is a common British pronunciation that is now used as a euphemistic or jocular variant. **2.** to anger or disgust. *Politicians shit me.* **3.** to mislead or deceive. *You're shitting me aren't you?* This is a shortening of the word **bullshit**. **4.** a contemptible or despicable person. This meaning dates back to the 1500s. **5.** junk. *Don't leave your shit on my desk*, or *He collected stamps, coins, that sort of shit.* **6.** nonsense, rubbish, lies. *Don't give me that shit.* **7.** used as a swearword or word of abuse, it is a much stronger equivalent of *damn* or *hell.* Thus *I don't give a shit* = I don't give a damn. *He beat the shit out of it* = He beat the hell out of it. **8.** drugs, especially heroin. *He's back on the shit again.* Good quality marijuana is often praised by saying that it is *good shit.* **9.** prison slang for tobacco. **10.** very bad, or very badly. *This is shit beer, man*, or *I played shit last weekend.*

shit a brick! Damn! Hell! Drat! – but way, way stronger than these. This peculiarly Australian exclamation of extreme exasperation has been around since the 1950s.

shit-awful dreadful beyond belief.

shitbag to denigrate. *He's always shitbagging his teammates.*

shit box **1.** a disgusting hovel. **2.** a crap car. **3.** a contemptible person.

shit bricks what you do when you are really scared.

shit bucket the receptacle of a sanitary toilet; a bucket or tin can used for a toilet, especially in prison. Also called a **shit can** or **shit tin**.

shitcan to denigrate unmercifully. Aussie slang since the 1950s.

shit catchers knickerbockers. Aussie slang since the 1960s.

shite a jocular or euphemistic way of saying **shit**.

shit-easy terribly easy.

shit-eating grin a great big, stupid-looking grin. The kind of grin one might expect to find on a madman eating shit.

shit eh! How about that! Aussie slang since the 1960s.

shit end of the stick the worst part of a deal or the like; the rough end of the pineapple.

shitface a contemptible person. Originally British slang of the 1930s.

shit-faced extremely drunk. Originally US slang of the 1960s.

shit fight a furious row or disagreement.

shit-for-brains a stupid, annoying person.

shit happens a catchphrase of resignation used after suffering some misfortune. It first appeared on the scene in the 1980s. Sometimes elaborated to **shit happens, and then you die**.

shit head **1.** a mean contemptible person or thing. **2.** a marijuana addict.

shit heap a crap car.

shit heel a contemptible person. Originally US slang of the 1930s.

shit hole a filthy, disgusting, boring, or otherwise objectionable place.

shit-hot extremely good, excellent, terrific.

shithouse **1.** a toilet or dunny. Venerable slang, dating back to the 1700s in England. Long used in Australia, very common from the 1960s onwards. In polite speech sometimes euphemised to **shouse** or **touse**. **2.** foul, wretchedly bad, terrible. Aussie slang since the 1960s.

shit in your own nest to have a romantic relationship with a work colleague.

shit it in to win easily. Also, to **shit in**. Aussie slang since the 1970s.

shit itself If a mechanical contrivance shits itself, then it breaks down; in other words, it is buggered. *The radiator shit itself while I was driving to work today.*

shit kicker an assistant, especially one doing menial or repetitive jobs; hence, a person of no consequence. Aussie slang since the 1950s – originally prison slang for a prisoner serving a short sentence, often employed on sanitary work.

shitless completely or utterly. Generally people are either 'scared shitless' or 'bored shitless'.

shit list a mental list of people you hate.

shit load a great deal. *There were a shit load of people there.*

shit of a thing anything that is annoying or exasperating.

shit off to annoy.

shit on **1.** to denigrate. **2.** to vanquish; to be better than. *Melbourne shits on Sydney for style.* Aussie slang since the 1970s.

shit on the liver the putative cause of bad temper. Aussie slang since the 1940s.

shit packer a gay man, as seen in the eyes of the homophobe. For a swag of similar synonyms see **dung puncher**.

the shits **1.** a bad mood. *Having to work on weekends gives me the shits.* **2.** diarrhoea.

shit scared very frightened; terrified.

shit shoveller someone who does harsh manual labour or other unpleasant work.

shit-stir to make trouble; to provoke or tease – especially just for amusement or simply for the sake of it.

shit-stirrer a trouble-maker, especially one who is only stirring in jest.

shitter **1.** a toilet. **2.** equivalent to 'hell' – used as an intensifier. *They beat the shitter out of them.*

shit tickets toilet paper.

shitty **1.** defiled with shit. **2.** annoyed; bad-tempered. Aussie slang since the 1960s. **3.** a bad temper or foul mood. *He's been in a shitty all afternoon.* Aussie slang since the 1970s. **4.** of low quality; crappy. **5.** in SA, the trumpeter, regarded as a poor eating fish; any other small bony fish.

shit upon to vanquish; to be better than. *They were profoundly shat upon by the opposition.* Aussie slang since the 1970s.

shit work the boring, terrible jobs that no one wants to do.

shit yourself to be terrified. Also known as **shitting your pants**.

shivoo a party or celebration. Aussie slang since the 1830s. In origin an alteration of French *chez vous* 'at your place'.

shocker something dreadfully bad. Commonly used in sport for a bad game. *Had a shocker last Saturday.* Known in rhyming slang as a **Barry Crocker** (from the name of the Australian popular entertainer).

shock jock a radio host who specialises in sensationalism.

shonk a dishonest person; a swindler or con artist.

shonky **1.** of dubious integrity or honesty. *He was a shonky developer.* Aussie slang since the 1960s. A local application of British slang *shonky* = mean, money-grubbing, from *shonk*, a derogatory term for a Jewish person. **2.** counterfeit or phoney. *His report was full of shonky figures.* **3.** as a noun, a dishonest person. *There are a lot of shonkies in this business.*

shoofty **1.** a look; an inspection. *Give us a shoofty.* From Egyptian Arabic *shufti* 'have you seen?' – picked up by Australian soldiers stationed in the Middle East in World War II. It is also found in British slang. **2.** dishonest or sneaky. *She engaged a shoofty lawyer.* Aussie slang dating from the 1960s. Probably a variation of *shifty*.

shoo-in a certainty to win. Originally US slang.

shook on infatuated with someone. *He was really shook on his boss.* Aussie slang since the 1860s.

shoot a euphemism for the exclamation *shit!*

shoot a bunny to fart. Also, to **shoot a fairy**.

shoot blanks of a male, to experience orgasm but not ejaculate any semen, or to ejaculate infertile sperm.

shoot hoops to play basketball or practise shooting baskets.

shooting gallery a place where people go to shoot up heroin.

shooting iron a firearm, especially a pistol or revolver.

shoot through to leave, abscond or decamp. *Instead of going to the exam, he shot through.* Aussie slang since the 1940s.

shoot through like a Bondi tram to depart in haste. Originally Sydney slang dating back to the 1940s, and referring to the trams along the Bondi line which were notoriously fast. Now known and used the country over.

shoot your bolt to ejaculate.

shoot your wad of a male, to ejaculate.

shop till you drop to go on a shopping spree.

short and curlies the pubic hair; to **have someone by the short and curlies** is to have them at your mercy. Similarly, to **have by the short hairs**.

short arm the penis. In the army a **short arm parade** was a medical inspection of the genitalia for signs of veneral disease.

short of Since the 19th century people who are 'not all there' have been described by phrases comparing them metaphorically to some aggregate which is lacking its full complement. One of the earliest examples of this is the Australian phrase **a shingle short** (of a roof, that is). This dates back to the 1840s. And an early British example of similar age is **a button short** (of a coat). A similar notion is found in **not the full quid**. Generally things are a 'few' or 'couple' short, as a **few bricks short of a load** or a **couple of alps short of a range** or a **few sheep short of a paddock**. For some reason, food metaphors are the most common, such as a **few bites short of a bickie**, or **bangers short of a barbie**, a **couple of lamingtons short of a CWA meeting**, or **sandwiches short of a picnic**, or a **few Tim Tams short of a packet**.

shotgun 1. a small hole at the back of a bong which is uncovered in order to get the smoke that has accumulated in the bowl. Also called the **shotty**. **2.** to smoke the entire contents of a bong in one go. **3.** to drink a can of beer by first shaking it up a little, puncturing a small hole near the base with some pointed object, and then placing the mouth over the hole and releasing the tab or ring-pull. **4.** a word shouted to 'bags' the front passenger seat, with reference to **ride shotgun** (see entry). Hence, as a verb, to bags anything. *I shotgun the last Mint Slice.*

shot of 1. rid of. *I can hardly wait to be shot of him.* Aussie slang since the 1960s. **2.** fed up with. *I reckon they must be shot of me.*

shotty a shotgun.

shouse a euphemistic way of referring to the **shithouse** or toilet. Polite Aussie slang since the 1940s.

shout 1. to buy a round of drinks. Aussie slang dating back to the 1850s. Obviously Australian pubs have long been noisy places. Hence, a round of drinks bought for the present company. Someone who **wouldn't shout if a shark bit him** is a stingy bastard who won't buy drinks for others. **2.** hence, to pay for something for another person. *I'll shout you lunch.*

show 1. a chance or opportunity. *Here's a show, better take it.* Aussie slang since the 1870s. **2.** a matter or business. *I'm sick of the whole show.* **3.** a war or military engagement. *I hope to set up my own business when this show's over.*

show bag 1. a sample bag of goods found at agricultural shows. Originally consisting of free samples, but now exorbitant in the eyes of parents. Still, the kids love them. **2.** hence, someone who is full of crap.

showie 1. an amusement stall or fun ride operator at an agricultural show; a carnie. **2.** a person who has a role in an event at an agricultural show.

show pony a lairy show-off. Aussie slang since the 1960s. Alluding to ponies that are specially groomed and trained for agricultural shows, as opposed to working horses.

show time time to begin. *Come on everyone, it's show time.*

show us your tits! the mating cry of the sexist pig. Doesn't work on anything but scrubbers.

shrapnel small change.

shred to surf or snowboard outstandingly. Hence, an excellent snowboarder or surfer is called a **shredder**.

shrewdie a cunning person. Aussie slang since the 1900s. Also called a **shrewd head**.

shrimp 1. a diminutive or insignificant person. **2.** NOT the Aussie word for 'prawn'. See the entry for **throw another shrimp on the barbie** for more info.

shrink a psychiatrist. Also called a **headshrinker**.

shtick another way of spelling **schtick**.

shtoom quiet; to **keep shtoom** is to keep quiet about something. From Yiddish.

shut-eye sleep. Originally British slang of the late 19th century.

shyster a dishonest person or con artist. First used in the US and originally meaning a shonky lawyer. Said by some to derive from an unscrupulous 19th century New York lawyer named *Scheuster*; or alternatively to be derived from the German word *Scheisse* 'shit'. But, basically, no one knows where this word comes from.

sick totally excellent; absolutely cool. *He had a totally sick haircut.* Formed along the same lines as 'wicked' and 'filthy'. A borrowing from US slang which first appears in Oz in the 1990s. Also spelt **sik**.

sickie a phoney sick day taken off work. Aussie slang since the 1950s. Can be used to refer to genuine sick days as well, but that certainly isn't the most common usage.

sicko a disturbingly depraved person.

sick puppy a depraved person. *When he told me what he'd done, I said 'Hey man, you are one sick puppy.'*

side an affectedly superior manner; airs and graces. People either 'put on side' or 'bung on side'. Aussie slang since the 1940s.

sik totally cool. A variant spelling of **sick**.

silent but deadly a phrase used to describe a fart that, while inaudible, is extremely unpleasant to the nose. Also called **silent but violent**.

silent cop a circular steel traffic cone placed at intersections. Aussie slang since the 1930s. Also called a **silent bobby**.

silly as... very silly. Australians have been quite inventive in coining silly phrases, such as **silly as a pork chop** (I've yet to get an intelligent conversation out of a pork chop), **silly as a two-bob watch** (that is, a wristwatch which only cost two bob to buy and not likely to keep good time), and **silly as three wet hens in a row**.

the Silver Bodgie a derisive nickname for erstwhile Prime Minister Bob Hawke.

silver bullet **1.** a can of Resch's Pilsener beer. Especially common in NSW. **2.** in NT, a transportable classroom used in schools.

Silver City a nickname for Broken Hill.

silver pillow the bladder of a wine cask.

silvertail a derogatory term for a person from the upper crust of society. Aussie slang since the 1890s.

sin bin **1.** an area adjoining the playing field set aside for penalised players. Hence, to consign a player to the sin bin. Originally Aussie sporting slang of the 1980s, but now mainstream. **2.** a panel van fitted out in the back with mattress and curtains as a retreat for sexual liaisons. See **fuck truck** for synonyms.

since Archer won the Cup in a long, long time. Referring, of course, to the great racehorse Archer who won the inaugural Melbourne Cup back in 1861. If you want to go even further back in time you can say **since Adam was a pup**.

Sin City a derisive nickname for Sydney, seen as a hotbed of vice and corruption. Give me a break!

sing underworld slang, to turn informer.

the Singing Budgie a nickname for Kylie Minogue.

single-barrelled snot gun a violent expulsion of snot from the nose when performing a bushman's hanky. Same thing as a **snot rocket**.

singlets in pool, smalls. As opposed to **T-shirts**.

sink to drink down (a glass of booze). *Time to sink a few middies.* Great Aussie drinking slang since the 1910s. Also common in NZ.

sink the sausage of a male, to get your end in.

sink the slipper to kick someone when they're down; to put the boot in.

sixer **1.** in Aussie Rules, a goal (as opposed to a behind). **2.** in cricket, a hit scoring six runs by clearing the boundary without touching the ground. To **knock someone for a sixer** is to deal them a nasty blow. To **come a sixer** is to suffer a nasty fall or setback. **3.** prison slang for a six-month jail sentence.

six-finger country a remote area in which the inhabitants are imagined to be inbred.

six o'clock swill a hectic session of beer consumption in a public bar as 6 p.m. approaches. From 1916 to 1955 this was the regular closing time of most hotels.

sixpack a male's well-defined abdominal muscles.

six-pointer three slices of bread with filling, cut diagonally. Not to be confused with the **four-pointer** (see entry).

sixty-nine simultaneous oral sex by two people. Dating back to the late 19th century in Britain, this term is a literal translation of the French term *soixante-neuf*. Also called a **sixty-niner**.

size queen a male homosexual obsessed with penis size.

skank **1.** an ugly, slovenly, or filthy person, either male or female. **2.** an overtly promiscuous woman. **3.** to dance to ska or reggae music.

skanky filthy, dirty, disgusting, contemptible.

skanky ho an insulting appellation directed at a female, roughly equivalent to 'filthy whore'. A recent adoption from US slang, but in Australia generally only used in a bantering way.

skatie **1.** a skateboard rider. **2.** a skateboard.

skeeter **1.** a mosquito. **2.** a nickname for a man of small build.

skeg a derogatory term for a surfie. Aussie slang dating from the 1980s. It derives from *skeg* 'the fin of a surfboard'. Also called a **skeg head**.

skerrick the smallest amount; a smidgin. Aussie slang since the 1850s. Originally used in British dialect.

skid lid a helmet worn by a cyclist.

skid mark a mark or smudge of faeces on underwear, or on the inside of a toilet bowl. Also called **skiddies**.

skimpy in Kalgoorlie, a scantily clad barmaid. In some pubs you can flip a two-dollar coin in order to get a skimpy to flash her breasts. A bit of a Kal institution but, since its fame spread, it has become a tourist attraction and authorities have tried to crack down on it. Skimpies can now be found elsewhere.

skin and blister rhyming slang for 'sister'. Originally British.

skin dog an uncircumcised male.

skin flick a pornographic movie.

skinful a large amount of consumed grog – literally, as much as you can drink. Venerable slang dating back to the 18th century.

skinner **1.** a rank outsider which wins a race. Aussie horseracing slang from the 1890s. So called because the bookies 'skin' the punters of their money. **2.** a large win on a long-odds horse; a betting coup.

skinny made with skim milk. *I'll have a skinny cap to go, thanks.*

skint completely without money; broke. A variant pronunciation of *skinned*.

skip a derogatory term for an Anglo-Celtic Australian, as opposed to a person of Mediterranean or Arabic descent. A shortening of **skippy**.

skip hop Australian hip-hop or rap music.

skippy **1.** the fuller form of **skip**. Obviously it is derived from Skippy the Bush Kangaroo. Coined in the 1980s as a direct counterpart to the word **wog** (see entry). Used derisively. Not uncommonly found in the collocation **skippy poofter**. *As if I care what some skippy poofter thinks.* **2.** in WA, a *skipjack*, a species of trevally found in the waters of southern Australia. So called since it leaps from the water.

skirt **1.** a woman, viewed as a sex object. Old slang dating back to the 19th century. **2.** women collectively, viewed as sex objects.

skite **1.** to boast or brag. *Quit skiting, will ya?* Aussie slang dating from the 1850s. **2.** a boaster or braggart. Also, boastful talk. *That's enough of your skite.*

skol to consume a drink at one draught. Aussie slang dating from the 1970s. A verb use of the Scandinavian toast word. Also spelt **scull**.

skun broke to the wide; skint (see entry).

skungy a variant spelling of **scungy**.

skyhook an imaginary hook hanging from the sky, upon which is hung things of unknown whereabouts.

sky rocket rhyming slang for 'pocket'. Originally 19th century British.

slab **1.** a carboard carton of two dozen cans or stubbies of beer. Aussie slang from the 1980s. **2.** a thousand dollars. **3.** an examination or preparation table at a mortuary or morgue.

slack **1.** unkind, cruel, unfair or mean. If a big kid bullies a smaller one, then he is being slack. Common schoolkid slang since the 1970s. **2.** outstandingly lazy. *Why don't you ever come and visit, you slack bastard.* **3.** no good, hopeless, pathetic, dodgy. *What a slack haircut.* **4.** of a woman, promiscuous, of easy virtue. Commonly in the phrase **slack moll** – one of the vilest insults that can be directed at a woman.

slack arse an incurably lazy person. Aussie slang since the 1970s. Hence the adjective **slack-arsed**.

slacker a person who avoids work. Originally 19th century British slang, and picked up by Aussie soldiers in World War I where it was commonly used to refer to a soldier who shirked his duty.

slag **1.** to spit. Hence, a gob of phlegm spat out. Aussie slang since the 1960s. **2.** a highly derogatory word for a promiscuous or otherwise contemptible woman.

slag off to denigrate. Originally British 1970s slang – picked up here in the 1980s.

slam a heavy fall when skating or blading.

slammer jail. Originally British slang.

slanter a swindle or other piece of dishonest trickery. Aussie slang since the 1840s. Still common in the racing game. Originally spelt **schlinter** or **schlenter**. In South African English this word is used to mean counterfeit and comes from the Dutch or Afrikaans *slenter*.

slant-eye a racist term for an Asian person. Also in the forms **slant-eyes** and **slanty-eyes**.

slap a racist term for an Asian person. Also, in full, **slap head**. Aussie slang since the 1980s.

slapper an ugly or unrefined girl or woman. Originally British slang of the 1970s. Common in Oz since the 1990s.

slapping skins having sexual intercourse.

slaps a kids' game in which two contestants hold out their hands in prayer-position fingertip to fingertip, and take turns at slapping the other player's hands. A change of turn takes place when one player misses a strike.

slash **1.** the act of urinating. **2.** the vagina or vulva.

slaughtered extremely drunk.

sleaze an obnoxiously leering man; a slimy bloke who thinks he's god's gift to women. This word is occasionally applied to women who are overtly sexual in an unpleasant way. To **sleaze onto** someone is to attempt to crack onto them in a slimy manner.

sleazebag a contemptible person; a sleazy person. Pretty much the same thing as a **scumbag**, which word appeared on the scene at the same time. Also known as a **sleazeball** or a **sleazebucket**.

sleazepit a nightclub, bar, or the like, full of sleazy people.

sleazoid **1.** of the nature of a sleaze. *He was a sleazoid PR man.* Also in the form **sleazoidal**. **2.** a sleazy person. *Jake is such a sleazoid.*

sledging the practice of heaping abuse and ridicule on members of the opposing team in an effort to upset their game. Originally Aussie cricket slang from the 1970s, from where it has spread to other sports. The practice is, of course, as old as the game of cricket and there are laws against it dating as far back as 1744.

sleep prison slang for a short jail sentence, usually three months or less.

sleeper gambling slang for an unclaimed bet left through mistake or confusion.

sleepout **1.** a partially enclosed porch or veranda, used as sleeping quarters. Aussie slang since the 1920s. **2.** especially in Vic, a separate outbuilding used as sleeping quarters.

slew **1.** a large number. *There were a slew of leadership hopefuls.* This is originally US slang, where it was borrowed from Irish Gaelic. **2.** to turn your head or look sideways; hence, to spy or act as a voyeur. Aussie underworld slang since the 1950s. Hence, to **slew and blue** is to look at the wrong time and be caught doing so. **3.** to defeat or do for. *That slews you!* Old Aussie slang, now obsolete.

slide a well-known piece of playground equipment for sliding down. This is the most common term in Vic, Tas and WA, but is also used in all other states. Most commonly called a **slippery dip** in SA and NSW. The other alternative, **slippery slide**, is most common in Qld, though both other terms are common there.

slime **1.** a contemptible person. *Some slime stole my bike.* **2.** a leering, sleazy person. *What a slime!* As a verb, to **slime onto** someone is to try and crack onto them in a sleazy manner. *That bloke at the bar tried to slime onto me.* **3.** to crawl or fawn over someone. Aussie slang since the 1950s.

slimebag a contemptible person. Equivalent to the **sleazebag**. First appears in the 1980s, borrowed from US slang. Also known as a **slimeball** or a **slimebucket**.

sling **1.** to give money as a bribe. Aussie slang since the 1900s. Hence, a monetary bribe. **2.** to give a gratuity or tip to someone. Aussie slang since the 1870s. Hence, money paid as a gratuity; a tip. Specifically, a tip given to a jockey by the winning horse's owner or connections.

slinging in Aussie Rules, the act of catching a player by the neck and throwing them on the ground.

sling off to disparage. *He was slinging off at his teachers.* Aussie slang since the 1900s.

slingshot a child's catapult, typically made from a forked stick and rubber bands. Originally British slang. Also called a **dinger**, a **ging** (formerly widespread, but now most common in WA and Qld), a **gonk** (restricted to north coast NSW) or a **shanghai**.

sling your hook old slang for depart or make off.

slip the price of a fare home given to a punter who has done all their dough. So called because it was slipped to the punter on the sly. A fine example of the Aussie sense of fairness and generosity. Aussie slang dating from at least the 1960s.

slippery dip playground equipment for sliding down. See entry for **slide** for regional variations.

slip someone a length of a man, to have sexual intercourse with someone.

slit a crassly anatomic term for the female genitalia. Venerable coarseness, dating back to the 1600s.

slogger in cricket, a disparaging term for someone who just slogs the ball, as opposed to playing shots.

slop choppy sea, no good for surfing.

slope a racist term for an Asian person. Also in the form **slopehead**. Originally US slang dating back to the 1940s. Commonly used by soldiers in the Korean and Vietnam wars.

sloppy seconds to **go sloppy seconds** is to have sex with a woman immediately after another man has. It can also refer to dating a woman who has previously had a partner. *Troy's gone the sloppy seconds.*

slops **1.** beer. Aussie drinking slang since the 1940s. **2.** to **go slops**, on the other hand, is to be the second or subsequent male sexual partner of a woman entertaining a number of men in a row.

slops merchant a great lover of beer.

sloshed drunk. Originally British slang of the 1940s and common in Australia since the 1960s.

slot **1.** a prison cell. Aussie slang since the 1940s. Hence, to lock someone up. **2.** in the Australian Antarctic Territory, a crevasse. Hence, as a verb, to fall or cause to fall into a crevasse.

slouch hat the iconic hat of the Australian soldier. A wide-brimmed, rabbit-felt hat, usually worn with one side of the brim pinned up. Known officially as 'hat, fur felt, troops for the use of'.

slug **1.** a lazy, indolent person. **2.** the penis.

sluggos speedos. Also called **sluggies**, **sluggers**, or **slug-huggers**. Referring to the revealing of the shape of the underlying penis. There are a host of slang terms for tight-fitting, and thus revealing, men's swimwear. These include **ball huggers**, **boasters**, **budgie smugglers** or **budgie huggers**, **cluster busters**, **cock chokers**, **cock jocks** (or **CJs**), **cod jocks**, **dick bathers**, **dick daks**, **dick pointers** or **dick pokers** (both shortened to **DPs**) and, especially in NSW, **dick stickers**. In Qld they are more commonly called **dick togs** (or, in front of grandma, **DTs**). You might think that is enough, but no – there are also **dipsticks**, **fish frighteners**, **knobbies**, **lolly bags**, **meat hangers** and **toolies**. An old-fashioned term, little heard nowadays, was **nylon disgusters**. Surfies, who wear boardies, call them **clubbies**, referring to the preferences of surf lifesavers. And they also get called **racers**, as they are used for competitive swimming, and, in NSW, **scungies**, from their similarity to underwear.

slug it out to fight; to settle an argument by a fight. Hence, to contend vigorously.

slug-slewer prison slang, an inmate who voyeuristically views penises at the urinal or communal shower.

slurry a derogatory term for a promiscuous woman. A variation on the word 'slut'.

Slurry Hills the Sydney suburb of Surry Hills – with the implication of sexual promiscuity.

slush box a derogatory name for a car with automatic transmission.

slushy **1.** a cook's assistant or kitchen hand. Aussie slang since the 1880s. **2.** in the Australian Antarctic Territory, a person rostered on to kitchen and cleaning duties.

slut a highly derogatory term for a promiscuous woman. Often used as an insult to attribute promiscuity or faithlessness to a woman, or merely as a strong term of abuse. This term has been used disparagingly towards women since the 1400s. Now also commonly used of homosexual men, and of promiscuous heterosexual men, often derogatorily, but also braggingly in self-reference.

sly grog illicitly made or supplied alcoholic liquor. Aussie slang since the 1820s. Hence, a person who supplied alcohol illegally was known as a **sly grogger**, and the place where it was obtained was called a **sly groggery** or **sly grog joint**.

smack heroin. Originally US slang of the 1940s. So called because it hits you hard. But, perhaps partly influenced by earlier *smeck*, from Yiddish *schmeck* 'sniff'.

smacked-out heavily under the influence of heroin.

smacker a dollar. Before 1966, used for one pound. Originally 1920s US slang for a dollar. Also called a **smackeroo** or **smackeroonie**.

smackie a person who takes or is addicted to taking heroin. Also called a **smackhead**.

smalls in pool, solid-coloured balls.

smart alec a person who is ostentatious in the display of knowledge or skill, often despite basic ignorance or lack of ability. In more direct speech **smart arse** is used, which has been recorded in Oz since the 1930s.

smarty pants a smug know-all; a show-off. Also in the form of a mock title **Mister Smarty Pants** or **Miss Smarty Pants**.

smashed drunk; pissed. Also, really stoned on drugs.

smeg short for *smegma* 'a secretion of sebum from the penis'. Used as an insult. Hence, the childish term of abuse **smeghead**.

smick a variant spelling of **schmick** (see entry)

smoke marijuana dried and prepared for smoking. *Anybody got any smoke?* Also known as **smokey** or **smoko**.

smoke-oh a rest from work; a tea-break or the like. Australian slang since the 1860s. Originally short for a 'smoking break'. Also spelt **smoke-o** or **smoko**.

smokie a horse whose form has been kept secret; a rort horse.

smoodge **1.** to kiss and cuddle. Aussie slang since the 1910s. **2.** to fawn or crawl to someone. Also Aussie slang, this one dating from the 1890s.

smooey the female genitalia. Hence, a **bit of smooey** is sexual intercourse with a woman. Aussie slang since the 1950s. Origin unknown. Also, shortened to **smoo**.

smoush (pronounced with a long 'oo') a kiss. Aussie slang since the 1960s. Hence, the activity of **smoushing**.

smut to kiss passionately.

snafu a muddled or chaotic situation. Hence, as a verb, to throw into disorder. Standing for *Situation Normal: All Fucked Up*. Originally US military slang of World War II.

snag a sausage. Great Aussie slang dating back to the 1940s. Possibly from British dialect *snag*, a variant of *snack* 'a bite to eat'.

SNAG a New-Agey type bloke who is sensitive and articulate and the complete opposite of the yobbo, ocker or macho man. An acronym from *Sensitive New-Age Guy*.

snagger a poor shearer. Recorded since the 1880s, it appears to have been first used to refer to shearers who were learning the trade and sheared less than 50 sheep a day. Eventually came to mean a poor or slow shearer who wasn't a beginner, or a man who was once a good shearer, but is now old and content to jog along with 100 or so sheep a day. In the song *Click Go the Shears* the snagger beats the ringer (the fastest shearer in the shed) by one stroke: 'The ringer looks around and is beaten by a blow / And he curses the old snagger with the bare-bellied yoe'.

snail mail the normal postal service (as opposed to e-mail).

snail trail dried mucus or semen on clothing.

snake in surfing, to cut in front of another surfer; to drop in. A heinous practice in the etiquette of the sport.

snake bite a drink of Guinness stout and apple cider.

snake charmer in WA, a railway fettler. So called because of the many snakes found along railway tracks. See also **hairy leg** and **woolly nose**.

Snake Gully a mythical remote place in the outback.

snake oil merchant a quack selling phoney medical treatments.

snake's hiss Aussie rhyming slang for 'piss'. Generally only used in the urination sense. Recorded since the 1960s.

snapping log a crocodile.

snark a guy who sniffs girl's bicycle seats.

snatch the female genitalia. Venerable slang dating back to the 1700s.

snatch it to quit from a job. Aussie slang since the 1910s.

sneaker net an office data transferral system in which computer files are copied onto a floppy disc and then taken to other computers on foot.

snick-and-run a variant name for the kids' game **hit-and-run** (see entry).

snig to pull or drag logs in timber-getting. Hence a **snigger**, someone who does it. Especially in Qld, NSW and Tas.

Snives the affluent Sydney suburb of St Ives. Reflecting a toney accent.

snodger fantastic, excellent, awesome. Aussie slang from World War I. Origin unknown. Barely heard any longer.

snog to kiss and cuddle. Hence, an act of kissing and cuddling. *They were having a quiet snog in the corner*. Aussie slang since the 1980s. Origin unknown.

snoozer **1.** any bloke or fellow. *He's not a bad sort of snoozer*. **2.** a senior citizen.

snork **1.** a sausage. Also called a **snorker**. **2.** a baby or young child. Aussie slang since the 1940s.

snorkle the penis.

snot block **1.** a chiefly Victorian term for a vanilla slice. Also called a **snot box** or a **snot brick**. **2.** a small plastic box filled with gel used to protect joints of electrical wiring. Also called a **snotty**.

snot rag a handkerchief.

snot rocket a violent expulsion of snot from the nose when performing a **bushman's hanky** (see entry).

snotsicle in the Australian Antarctic Territory, frozen mucus hanging from the nose.

snottygobble **1.** the fruit of the native *Persoonia* tree. Also used to mean the tree itself. A borrowing from the British dialect of Bedfordshire where it referred to the fruit of the yew tree. **2.** the name of a climbing plant found in mallee scrub.

snow cocaine. Originally US slang of the 1910s.

snow bird a person travelling with a caravan.

snowdrop to steal laundry from clothes lines. From *snow* 'linen hung out to dry' and thieves' slang *drop* 'to steal'.

snow man an old paper $100 note. Because it sported a picture of Antarctic explorer Douglas Mawson. Now replaced by the **green giant** (see entry).

snoz the nose. A shortening of **schnozzle** (see entry).

snuff if to die. Originally 19th century British slang.

soak a heavy drinker of alcohol.

soap box a term for a billy cart, found in both WA and SA.

soapy not predisposed to washing; smelly and dirty. An ironic usage.

sobriety challenged drunk.

sod a contemptible person. Originally a shortening of *sodomite*, used as an insult, but now no longer connected with that word. Can be used affectionately. *You poor old sod.* Note the similar development and usage of **bugger** (see entry).

soda something easy to do; a cinch; a push-over.

sod all nothing. Originally British slang of the 1950s.

sod it! Damn! Hell! Originally used in British dialect.

sod off Go away! Piss off!

soft cock a weak-willed, ineffectual person; a limp dick.

soft cock rock unaggressive, wimpy rock 'n' roll.

softie a non-erect penis.

soft touch a generous soul who readily lends money or does other favours; an easy touch.

soggy Sao a game in which a group of men simultaneously begin masturbating onto an Arnott's Sao biscuit – the last to ejaculate having to eat the biscuit.

s.o.l. a polite way of saying **shit on the liver** (see entry).

soldier a strip or finger of bread or toast for dipping into a soft-boiled egg.

solid **1.** underworld slang, reliable and loyal; loyal to the underworld, especially when under pressure from the police. **2.** thoroughly; completely; without reservation. *She was crying her eyes out, solid.* Common in Aboriginal English, but has filtered into the speech of other Australians.

sollo a solicitor.

son of a bitch a contemptible man; a right bastard; a real prick. Hence, loosely, any person, object or thing which has incurred your wrath. A venerable insult. Essentially the same as calling someone a 'dog' or a 'cur'. In Shakespeare's King Lear we find 'son and heir of a mongrel bitch', and the term 'bitch-son' can be dated as far back as the 1300s!

sook a wimpish, overly sensitive person; a cry-baby. Aussie slang dating from the 1940s.

sooky timid or cowardly; piss-weak. Used in Australia since the 1900s, borrowed from British dialect.

sool to incite a dog to attack. *He sooled his dog onto me.* Hence, to incite or urge someone to some action. Aussie slang dating from the 1840s.

sop **1.** a weak or cowardly person. Old slang, a shortening of the still older insult *milksop*. **2.** stale white bread and dripping soaked in hot water, eaten with tomato sauce and salt. Also called **Pop's sop** – being the kind of food dad might serve up when mum's away. Formerly common, but thankfully no longer.

sort a good-looking woman. *There were some real sorts at the party.* Aussie slang since the 1930s. When unqualified it always means attractive, but it is very commonly used with a qualifying adjective, either positive, as in *great sort* or *top sort*, or with a negative one, as in *rough sort* or *drack sort*.

sorted fixed up; effectively dealt with. A recent borrowing from British English, now existing alongside the normal Australian **sorted out**. *There was a problem with the bill, but we've got it sorted now.*

sosso a sausage.

soul case your whole energies or affections; your whole being. *She's been working her soul case out on it.* Aussie slang since the 1900s.

southerly buster a strong, cool southerly wind which blows after a hot day on the south-eastern coast of Australia, bringing blessed relief from the heat, and often a reviving rainstorm. Aussie slang since the 1850s.

South Seas Pom a derogatory term for a New Zealander. Also called **South Pacific Poms**.

souvenir to steal some minor item as a souvenir. Originally Aussie soldier slang from World War I.

sozzled drunk. Originally 19th century British slang.

spac among schoolkids, daggy and uncool, stupid, clumsy; a general insult. Hence, an uncool person, a dag or geek. A perversion of the word **spastic** that first appeared in the 1980s. Also in the forms **spacca** and **spacko**.

space cadet a vague, stupid person. From the stock science fiction character of a naive cadet at a space academy.

spaced-out in a euphoric or dreamy state brought on by mind-altering drugs, or by tiredness, illness and the like.

spacey **1.** of a drug, hallucinatory. **2.** of a person, vague or empty-headed.

spacies computer arcade games in general. Named from *Space Invaders*, one of the first models to become popular after its appearance in the late 1970s.

spade **1.** a racist term for an African or Aboriginal person. Most common in US white speech, but known and used here. From *spade* 'black playing card suit'. **2.** to attempt to impress a potential sexual partner. *He was over by the bar spading for his life.* A backformation from **spade work**.

spade face a racist term for an Asian person. Also known as a **spade head**.

spade work social interaction preliminary to sexual advance.

spadger a sparrow. From British dialect.

spag **1.** spaghetti. *We're having spag for dinner.* **2.** a contemptuous term for an Italian, or the Italian language. Racist Aussie slang since the 1960s. **3.** a sparrow. From British dialect. **4.** saliva or mucus that is spat out. Hence, as a verb, to spit out a gob of saliva or mucus.

spag bol spaghetti bolognaise. Also called **spag bog**.

spam can aeronautical slang for a mass-produced light aircraft with a thin metal skin.

Spanish dancer Aussie rhyming slang for 'cancer'.

spanner head a car nut.

spanner water extremely cold water. So called because it 'tightens the nuts'.

spare tyre a roll of fat around a person's midriff.

sparrow fart dawn; very early morning. *She was up at sparrow fart.*

sparrowgrass a jocular perversion of 'asparagus'.

spastic **1.** a silly, foolish or clumsy person. Used as a term of mild abuse. Especially common among schoolkids. Not at all PC. **2.** to **go spastic** or **chuck a spastic** is to have a temper tantrum. **3.** extremely drunk. *I got totally spastic last night.*

spaz a colloquial shortening of **spastic**. Hence, to **chuck a spaz** is to lose your temper or throw a tantrum. Also elaborated to **spazzo**.

spaz attack an instance of losing your temper, freaking out, or the like.

spear **1.** If you **get the spear** then you are out of work. **2.** among surfies, a surfboard.

spear the bearded clam of a male, to have sexual intercourse with a woman.

speccy **1.** remarkably good; impressive. A colloquial rendering of the word *spectacular*. **2.** in Aussie Rules, a fantastic mark – one that makes the whole crowd gasp.

Special K the drug ketamine, an anaesthetic and hallucinogen used recreationally by club goers. Too much can cause unconsciousness – known among users as a **K-hole**.

speck **1.** to search the surface of the ground in a mining area for stray bits of gold or opal. **2.** in racing slang, to bet in a highly speculative manner; to place a lot of money on a long shot.

speed a stimulant drug, as an amphetamine; goey. Originally US slang of the 1960s.

speedball **1.** a mixture containing cocaine and heroin. Originally US slang of the 1900s. **2.** a rissole. Perhaps so called because of their speed in travelling through the alimentary canal.

speed demon a person who likes to drive fast. Also called a **speed merchant**.

Speed Gordon the name under which American comic superhero Flash Gordon was for a long time known in Australia. Hence the slang phrase **in more trouble than Speed Gordon** – in other words, in a lot of strife. Back in the 1930s and 40s, when Flash Gordon was first published in Australia, the word *flash* most commonly meant 'ostentatious or showy', and so a figure called 'Flash' Gordon would be expected to be a bit of a lair. Hence the renaming.

speed hump a derisive term used by boaties for a skindiver.

Speewah a mythical outback station used as the setting of many Australian folktales, legends and bush yarns.

spew **1.** to vomit. Hence, an act or instance of vomiting, or that which is vomited. This words feels a bit slangy these days but it is actually the original Anglo-Saxon word for the very natural act of ejecting unwanted stomach contents. We picked up the word 'vomit' from Latin in the Middle Ages. **2.** to become extremely angry and vent that anger verbally. *When he found out we had eaten his dinner he was spewing!*

spewsome nauseating.

spewy **1.** unpleasant, yucky, off. *I just had a really spewy meat pie.* **2.** angry; in a bad mood. *He's been pretty spewy this morning.*

spic a racist term for person of Spanish or Latin American descent. Originally US slang from the 1910s. In origin it is a representation of the Spanish pronunciation of the word *speak*, as in the phrase 'No spic a de Eenglish'.

spiel a persuasive speech designed to explain and hopefully sell a product; a sales talk or patter. Originally US slang, but long used in Australia as well. From Yiddish. Hence, any speech on a particular subject. *I was given this huge spiel about honesty and stuff.*

spieler a swindler or con artist, especially one who deceives others with glib speech. Aussie slang since the 1870s. Originally meaning a card sharp or gambler, from Yiddish. Probably the ultimate source of the word **illywhacker** (see entry).

spike the keg to urinate for the first time when participating in a drinking session.

spill the beans to divulge information. Originally US slang. Another version is **spill your guts** – also American, but both have been in common use here since World War II.

spin old slang term for five quid. Transferred to five dollars after the introduction of decimal currency in 1966. An abbreviation of **spinnaker**.

spin a yarn to tell a tall story. In Aussie naval slang they use **spin a dit** (see the entry for **dit**).

spinebash to lie down and rest or sleep; to loaf on the job. Aussie slang since the 1940s. Hence, a rest or slumber. Formed from the earlier phrase **bash the spine** (see entry).

spinifex grasshopper a kangaroo.

spinnaker an obsolete term for a five pound note or the sum of £5. No longer in use. Served some time as a term for five dollars, but only the shortened version **spin** is still used.

spinner the person tossing the coins in two-up. So titled since the 1910s. See the entry for the phrase **come in, spinner!**

spin out **1.** to cause amazement, shock, or the like; to stun, flabbergast or gobsmack. Hence, as a noun, anything that amazes or shocks. **2.** in two-up, to lose the right to continue spinning the coins by throwing a pair of tails.

spit chips to vent spleen. Great Aussie slang since the 1940s. This originally meant to be in dire need of a drink, that is, your mouth was so dry that if you spat, wood chips came out. Nowadays the metaphor seems to be one of being so angry that you could chew up a log of wood and spit out chips.

spit it out! Say what you have to say!

spitter a person who spits out the proceeds of fellatio – as opposed to a **swallower**.

spit the dummy to throw a tantrum. A relatively new phrase, first appearing in the 1980s. It refers to a baby throwing a tantrum and spitting out its dummy – as they do!

spiv a man who lives by his wits, without working or by dubious business activity, and usually affecting ostentatious dress and tastes. Originally US slang of the 1930s.

splash the boots to urinate.

spliff a marijuana cigarette; a joint. This term has been around since the 1930s, and originated in Jamaica.

split to leave hurriedly; to decamp or bugger off.

split the whiskers of a woman, to urinate.

splosh money. Originally 19th century British slang.

spoggy especially in SA, a sparrow.

spondonicles metal tongs for lifting a hot billy off the fire. Commonly shortened to **spongs**. Also called **billy grips** (see entry).

spondulicks money. Originally British slang from the 1850s. Origin unknown, but the closeness of the Ancient Greek word *spondulikos*, adjective of *spondulos*, 'a vertebra, a round stone or weight, a voting pebble', cannot be overlooked – perhaps it was originally a jocular term created by some learned university wit. Also spelt **spondulix**, or altered to **spondulee** or **spondula**, or shortened to **spons** or **spon**.

spono a sponsor; sponsorship. *Who are your sponos?* Also, as a verb, to sponsor. *I'd love to get spono'd.*

spoof (rhymes with 'hoof') to ejaculate semen. Aussie sexual slang since World War I. Hence, as a noun, semen. *There was spoof all over the sheets.*

spoon a fool.

sport a fellow or bloke – frequently used as a term of address. *How you doing, sport?* Aussie slang since the 1920s.

spot an obsolete term for £100, dating back to the 1940s. Used for $100 after the introduction of decimal currency in 1966.

spottie **1.** a spotlight, especially one mounted on a car, 4WD, or other vehicle. **2.** among fishos, a spotted mackerel.

spotto a game played to relieve boredom on long trips. Various items are listed and the first person to see one calls out 'Spotto!'

the Spout in Canberra, a derisive name for the Captain Cook Fountain in Lake Burley Griffin.

spouting a chiefly Victorian and Tasmanian regionalism for what the rest of the country calls the guttering of a house.

sprag especially in Qld, a sparrow.

spray-on trousers really, really, really tight-fitting trousers.

spring **1.** to catch someone out doing something they shouldn't. *We were sprung jigging school last Tuesday.* **2.** to help someone to escape from prison.

springy a wetsuit covering the body to the knees, elbows and neck. Originally designed for use in spring weather.

sprog **1.** a child or youngster. **2.** a new recruit, as in an air force. **3.** semen. Hence, as a verb, to ejaculate or come.

spruik to make a speech, especially to explain and hopefully sell a product, or gather an audience for a show. Aussie slang since the 1900s. Probably from Yiddish *shpruch* 'a saying or charm'.

spruiker a person who spruiks in order to attract customers to a show.

spud **1.** a potato. An old word dating back to the mid-19th century. Recorded earliest in NZ, but known to be used in Australia from at least the 1890s. Hence, a potato farmer is a **spud cocky** and a potato-growing region is known as **spud country**. The word itself used to refer to a 'type of digging implement', and was thence transferred to the thing dug up. **2.** a hole in a sock through which the skin shows. **3.** a fist. Hence, **spuds** is another name for the game rock, paper, scissors. To **spud** someone is to challenge them to a game of spuds. *I'll spud you to see who goes first.*

spunk **1.** a good-looking person, male or female. Aussie slang since the 1970s. **2.** semen. Originally and chiefly British slang, dating back to the 1860s.

spunkalicious extremely sexually desirable.

spunk bubble a sexually attractive person.

spunkette a female spunk.

spunk rat a sexually attractive person – even spunkier than the usual spunk. Aussie slang since the 1980s.

spunky **1.** good-looking; attractive; drop-dead gorgeous. Aussie slang since the 1970s. **2.** a good-looking person, male or female. This is the earliest sense, dating back to the 1960s. Not so common anymore.

square **1.** ignorant of up-to-date popular culture; daggy. Hence, an uncool person; a dag. Originally a jazz term from the 1940s. **2.** among homosexuals, heterosexual. Hence, a heterosexual person. Aussie gay slang since the 1940s, but now used elsewhere. **3.** a law-abiding person; a goody-two-shoes.

square bear a 700 ml bottle of Bundaberg rum.

square head **1.** a racist term for a German, Dutch or Scandinavian person. Originally 19th century British slang. Commonly used during both World Wars. **2.** underworld slang for a non-criminal. Aussie slang since the 1890s.

squarie Aussie naval slang for a young woman, or a sailor's girlfriend. First recorded in 1917.

squashed fly biscuit a biscuit with dried fruit between two thin layers of sweet pastry; also called a **dead fly biscuit** or a **fly cemetery**.

squat absolutely nothing or none. A shortening of **diddly-squat**.

squatter **1.** a person who settled on crown land to run stock, especially sheep, initially without government permission but later with a lease or licence. **2.** one of a group of rich and influential rural landowners. Hence, **squattocracy**, the long-established and wealthy landowners who regard themselves as an aristocracy.

squeal to turn informer; to disclose or reveal something secret.

squealie a loutish car manoeuvre in which the tyres are made to squeal.

squeeze a boyfriend or girlfriend; a lover.

squib **1.** a racehorse or greyhound that starts well but finishes terribly. Also called a **damp squib**. From *squib* for a type of firecracker – a damp one doesn't go off. **2.** a coward. Aussie slang since the 1900s. Hence, to **squib it** is to act in a cowardly fashion; to pike out.

squid ring a calamari ring, as called in WA, SA and Tas.

squillion an extremely large amount. Also called a **squintillion**. A person with a squillion dollars is, of course, a **squillionaire** or a **squintillionaire**. Similar sums are **gillion**, **jillion** and **zillion**.

squirrel to subject someone to a squirrel grip.

squirrel grip a handful of nuts – that is, the grabbing and squeezing of someone's testicles. Similar to the **Christmas hold** (see entry).

squirt **1.** a small or insignificant fellow. **2.** a little child or kid. **3.** an act of male urination.

squitters diarrhoea.

squiz a quick but close look. Aussie slang since the 1910s. Perhaps a blend of *squint* and *quiz*. Hence, to look at quickly but closely.

stack a crash or accident involving a motor vehicle, bicycle, or the like; a fall in skating, skiing or snowboarding. Hence, as a verb, to crash. *He's stacked his new car.*

stacked of a woman, having large breasts. Originally 1940s US slang.

stack on to produce or put something on. *They really stack on a great party.* Aussie slang since the 1940s. Commonly in the phrases **stack on an act** or **stack on a turn** meaning to make an appalling big fuss over nothing, and **stack on a blue** meaning to start a fight.

stacks a great amount; tons. *There's stacks of room for everyone.*

stack up zeds to sleep. Originally 1950s US slang – but Aussified by changing 'zees' to 'zeds'. In origin referring to the cartoonist's convention of representing snoring with a long, flowing line of zeds.

staffies after-work drinks put on for the staff.

stag film a pornographic film. Also called a **stag movie**.

stag party a party, exclusively for men, with entertainment such as strippers, prostitutes, pornographic films, and the like.

stalk the erect penis. Venerable slang dating back to the 1600s.

stallion a very sexually active man, especially a well-endowed one. This one dates back to the 1500s.

stand out like dogs balls to be prominent or conspicuous.

stand over to intimidate someone, generally with the threat of violence. *I was sick of being stood over by his goons.* Aussie slang since the 1930s.

standover merchant one who bullies or intimidates; one who threatens violence to gain a desired result; a hoodlum. Also called a **standover man**.

starfish trooper a gay man. Punning on the movie *Starship Troopers* (1997) and *starfish* = anus.

star fucker a person who engages in sexual intercourse with celebrities. US slang from the 1970s.

starkers **1.** totally naked. Short for 'stark naked'. **2.** absolutely insane. Short for 'stark raving mad'. Both originally British slang.

Starlight Hotel sleeping out under the stars.

starting stalls in Kalgoorlie, street stalls at which prostitutes sit on stools advertising their services.

starver a saveloy. Aussie slang since the 1940s.

starve the lizards! Heavens above! Good lord! Great Aussie exclamation of surprise or exasperation. Occasionally in the form **stiffen the lizards!** First recorded back in the 1920s. Little heard these days, especially not used by city folk. See the similar expression **stone the crows!**

stash a cache of drugs for personal use.

statie a student at a state school.

Steak and Kidney rhyming slang for 'Sydney'. First recorded way back in 1905.

steam out-moded slang for booze or grog. A popular term from the 1940s to the 1970s.

steamer a lightweight one-piece wetsuit with long sleeves and legs.

stemmy a schoolkid's term for the penis. Hence, a dickhead. *Don't give the ball to that stemmy!* Also, simply, a **stem**.

-ster used with a colloquialising force to create nicknames (often prefaced by 'the'): *the Magster* (Margaret); *the Gregster* (Greg); *Goughster* (Gough Whitlam); *the Igster* (Iggy Pop). See **-meister**.

sterling back in colonial days, British-born. As opposed to **currency** (see entry).

St Georges Terrace cocky in WA, a person who owns a country property, often for purposes of tax avoidance, but who lives and works in Perth.

stick **1.** a very thin person. **2.** a surfboard. **3.** the penis. Hence the phrases **up the stick** meaning pregnant, and **had the stick** meaning ruined, wrecked, fucked. **4.** an injection of an illegal drug.

stick book a pornographic magazine – used as an masturbatory aid by men. Aussie slang since the 1960s. Also called a **stick mag**.

sticker licker in SA, a parking inspector. See **brown bomber** for the full set of regionalisms.

stickjaw an especially sticky toffee.

stick like shit to a blanket to adhere strongly; to cling to or follow tenaciously; to shadow.

stick out like dogs balls to be prominent or conspicuous.

the sticks **1.** any remote region far from civilisation; the outback. **2.** in Aussie Rules, the goal posts.

stick sister a woman who knowingly shares a man with another woman. Aussie slang since the 1980s.

stickybeak **1.** an inquisitive, prying person. An Australian original this, dating from the 1920s. Hence, as a verb, to pry or meddle, to stick your nose in where it isn't wanted. **2.** a look merely to satisfy your own inquisitiveness. *We went to the inspection just to have a stickybeak.* Since the 1970s commonly shortened to **sticky**. *Have a sticky at this.* **3.** a type of black seed which sticks to clothing.

stiff **1.** a dead body or corpse. **2.** unlucky. *How stiff can a bloke be?* Old Aussie slang, originally meaning broke or penniless. **3.** an erect penis. Also called a **stiffy**. **4.** a letter sent in or out of jail illicitly.

stiff cheese! Tough luck! Sucked in! Also commonly as **stiff cheddar!** Aussie slang dating from the 1970s – a variant of British slang *Hard cheese!* which dates back to the 19th century. An older Australian expression was **stiff luck!** which dates back to the 1910s. All of these can be simply shortened to the direct and unforgiving retort **stiff!** or cruelly enhanced by the word 'shit' – *Ha ha, stiff shit! You got everything you deserved!*

stiffener an alcoholic drink.

stiffen the crows! Heavens above! Good lord! A variant of **stone the crows!** First recorded in the 1930s. Similar is **stiffen the lizards!** and the uncommon **stiffen the wombats!**

stiffo! Tough luck!

stiffy an erect penis.

sting **1.** a confidence trick or scam; a police undercover operation. Originally US slang. **2.** a drug given to a racehorse to make it run faster. Aussie slang dating from the 1940s. **3.** strong drink. Aussie slang since the 1920s.

stinger net in Qld, a net for keeping out box jellyfish.

stink bomb the seed of some species of acacia which give off a foul smell.

stinker **1.** a black eye. **2.** an unpleasant person or thing. **3.** a very hot and humid day. **4.** a western grey kangaroo.

stink finger fondling the vagina. *They were having a game of stink finger.*

stinko drunk. Originally British slang of the 1920s, but used in Oz at least since the 1950s.

stipe a stipendiary steward at a racecourse. Laconic Aussie slang since the 1900s.

stir **1.** to taunt, tease or needle, especially just for the fun of it. Aussie slang dating from the 1960s. Probably a shortening of 'stir the possum', which is recorded much earlier. **2.** prison. Originally 19th century British slang – origin unknown.

stir-crazy crazy as a result of being institutionalised in jail. Hence, suffering from being cooped up anywhere.

stir the possum to create a disturbance or uproar. A sleeping possum does not take well to being stirred up. Aussie slang since the 1900s.

stoked amazed, thrilled, delighted, blown away.

stoned **1.** under the influence of drugs, especially marijuana. **2.** completely drunk. Both originally 1950s US slang – adopted in Australia by the 1960s.

stoner a heavy user of marijuana; a total cone head.

stone the crows! Heavens above! Good lord! Great Aussie exclamation of surprise or exasperation. Dates back to the 1920s. One classic saying that is sadly dying out. Similar phrases, also on the verge of extinction, are **stiffen the crows!** and **starve the lizards!**

stonk a child's clay playing marble. Dating back to the 1950s. Always an inferior type of marble. The word comes the English dialects of Lancashire and Cheshire. Also called a **stonkey**.

stonker **1.** in World War I, to kill. *Bill got stonkered by a whizzbang.* Hence, to stop someone in their tracks; to defeat or overcome, as in a competition. Aussie slang, probably from *stonker* 'a type of marble' – perhaps a big one that was used to knock away smaller ones. **2.** to make stone drunk. *This rum'll stonker you good and proper.*

stonkered **1.** defeated or outdone; stopped dead in your tracks; exhausted; unable to go on. **2.** totally drunk. **3.** satisfied after a large meal; full up to pussy's bow.

store jack a store security officer.

storm and strife Aussie rhyming slang for 'wife'. A less common form of **trouble and strife**.

stoush **1.** a fight or brawl; hence, an argument or altercation. Aussie slang since the 1890s. Perhaps originating from Scottish dialect *stash* 'a commotion or quarrel'. Used by soldiers to refer to war or a battle. World War I was commonly known as **the Big Stoush**. **2.** as a verb, to fight with someone; to hit or bash someone.

Strad local shortening of Stradbroke Island, Qld. Also known as **Straddie**.

straightie an extremely conservative person; one who conforms to orthodox forms of behaviour. Also called a **straightie 180**.

strain the potatoes to urinate. Also, alternatively, **strain the spuds**. Aussie slang since the 1960s.

strap-on a dildo which can be worn strapped around the waist and hence moved by pelvic thrusts.

strawb laconic Aussie way of saying 'strawberry'. *Get us a punnet of strawbs.*

strawberry fete in SA, a country concert with strawberries and cream for supper.

street cred credibility or status among people of the urban counterculture or the trendy, fashionable set.

streetie **1.** a street prostitute. **2.** a street kid.

the strength of the important facts about something. *I didn't get the strength of it.* If you ask *What's the strength of this bloke?* it means 'What's he up to?'

stress head an extremely stressy person; a person easily stressed.

stretch a term of imprisonment. Originally 19th century British slang.

Stretch a jocular form of address to a tall person. *G'day Stretch.*

strewth! My God! Good lord! Heavens above! Hell's bells! Actually originally British, but recorded in Australia since the beginning of the 1900s, and iconically Australian. In origin a shortened form of the exclamation *God's truth!* Also commonly spelt **struth!**

strides trousers. Originally 19th century British slang, but now used chiefly in Australia.

strike a light! an exclamation of surprise. First recorded in the 1920s. Australians have been particularly adept at coining variations on this theme in which you call on God to visit increasingly ridiculous punishments on you. Aussie originals – with their earliest known dates include **strike me blue** (1902), **dead** (1932), **fat** (1895), **handsome** (1955), **pink** (1892), **purple** (1904), and **roan** (1917). The British form **strike me lucky** is also used here. These can all be shortened to simply **strike me!** Or, with even greater brevity, to the simple **strike!**

Strine characteristic spoken Australian English – what linguists call 'broad Australian' – that is, the type spoken by country folk and ockers, not university professors, politicians and the well-to-do. *He wouldn't know what a dunny is, he doesn't talk Strine!* Coined by Alastair Morrison and made popular in 1965 through his book *Let Stalk Strine* (=let's talk 'Stralian). Posing as 'Afferbeck Lauder' (=alphabetical order), Professor of Strine Studies at Ezz Rock, Morrison set about respelling perfectly ordinary words and phrases into seemingly meaningless gobbledegook that was only understood once you read it out loud. Examples include **Gloria Soame** for *glorious home*; **laze and gem** for *ladies and gentlemen*; **muncer go** for *months ago*; **sly drool** for *slide rule*; and (the most renowned and oft quoted example) **Emma Chisit** for *How much is it?* Now used affectionately for Australian English generally.

stroke mag a pornographic magazine for wanking to.

strong of the same as the **strength of** (see entry).

struth! a variant spelling of **strewth!** (see entry).

strut your stuff to proudly display your skills or favourable attributes.

Stuart Diver rhyming slang for 'survivor'. After the famous survivor of the tragic Thredbo landslide disaster in 1997.

stubby a small, squat beer bottle. An Australian original this – dating back to the 1960s.

stubby holder a great Aussie invention. Essentially a receptacle for a stubby or beer can which keeps the cold beer insulated from both the hand and the harsh Australian heat. Also called a **stubby cooler**.

stud an attractive virile man; a sexually successful man; a ladies' man or Don Juan. Originally US slang.

stud magnet a woman whom many men find sexually attractive.

stud muffin a charming and physically attractive man.

stuff **1.** a euphemism for the verb 'fuck'. *Go stuff yourself!* Hence, to ruin or wreck. *You've stuffed it now.* Also, used in exclamations and phrases where it can be replaced with 'damn' – such as **stuff it!** meaning damn it! fuck it! To **not give a stuff** meaning to not give a damn/fuck. **2.** drugs. *He's been on and off the stuff for some time now.*

stuff about/around a euphemism for *fuck about/around.*

stuff-all a euphemism for *fuck-all.*

stuffed **1.** a euphemism for *fucked* – both for its literal and metaphorical meanings – that is, exhausted; ruined or wrecked; astounded; bothered; in an impossible position; heavily pissed or stoned; deplorable. **2.** replete with food.

stuff up a euphemism for *fuck up.* Hence, the noun, **stuff-up**. *This is a complete and utter stuff-up.*

stuvac in NSW, vacation from school, college, university, or the like, in the period before exams, to allow students to study for the exams. Called **swot vac** in the rest of the country.

subbie **1.** a subcontractor, especially a truckie or builder. **2.** a dull or stupid person. So called because they have 'sub-normal' intellect. Not very PC!

submarine ball in cricket, a delivery that stays very low.

submarine races a non-existent event used as an excuse to go somewhere quiet. *Let's go watch the submarine races down at the river.*

Such is life! an exclamation of resignation to the harsh facts of life. Reputed to be the last words of that great Australian existential philospher – Ned Kelly.

suck **1.** to perform oral sex. Old sexual slang, dating back to the 19th century in Britain. **2.** to be utterly dreadful. *Westies suck badly! Homework really sucks!* Commonly also spelt **sux**, especially when used in graffiti. This was originally US slang from the 1960s and made its way into Australia in the 1980s. It owes its origins to the fellatio sense – which has been around much longer, and certainly many people are conscious of this. To **suck the big one** is a variant that makes the metaphor inescapable. However, despite its etymology it is not actually a rude word since it is generally used without thought of its origins, and is quite common among kids who are too young to even know what oral sex is.

sucked in! Serves you right! Aussie kids' slang since the 1970s expressing gleeful enjoyment when someone else has justly failed or received their come-uppance. There are many variations on this theme, such as **sucko!** or **suck eggs!** or **suck a rat!** and the highly offensive forms **suck shit!** and **suck fuck!** Other crude phrases which express a gloating over another's downfall are **suck my arse!** and **suck on that!** or **suck it harder!** – these last two referring to the act of fellatio.

sucker a person easily deceived or imposed upon; a dupe; a victim of a swindle or con job; someone who has been sucked in. Originally 19th century US slang.

suck face to French kiss; to swap spit. Originally US slang.

suckhole an obsequious or ingratiating person; a sycophant or toady. Aussie slang since the 1940s. Hence, to crawl to someone. *He's been suckholing the boss.*

suck off to bring to orgasm by oral sex.

sucky **1.** fawning and servile; crawling. **2.** no good, dreadful crap. *Love songs are sucky, insipid crap.* **3.** of the surf, having a strong backwash at the base of a wave.

suds beer. Originally US slang from the 1900s, but used in Oz since at least the 1920s.

suds artist an inveterate beer drinker.

suffer! a gleeful respose to another's justly deserved misfortune. Common in the playground – kids can be so cruel!

suffer a recovery to endure a hangover after a big night on the booze. Aussie slang since the 1880s.

sugar and spice Aussie rhyming slang for 'nice'.

suicidal **1.** quite dangerous and outrageously gutsy. *Taking that wave was suicidal.* **2.** absolutely excellent. *That skater dood's got suicidal gear.*

suicide blonde a woman who has dyed her own hair blonde rather than have it done by a hairdresser, with predictable results. So called because she *died* (*dyed*) *by her own hand.*

suicide season in the tropical north, the approach of the Wet. Causes extreme tension and irritability.

suit a derogatory term for a businessman or businesswoman who has to wear a suit as part of daily work.

sunbeam a plate or utensil which was laid out but not used at a meal and hence does not need to be washed up. Compare **moonbeam**.

Sunday session in WA, the hours on Sunday at which a particular pub is open – of shorter duration than during the rest of the week. Usually begins after lunch and goes to late afternoon.

sundowner a swagman who arrives at a homestead at nightfall, too late for work, but obtains shelter for the night and hopefully a food handout.

sunnies sunglasses. Aussie slang since the 1980s.

Sunshine stilettos Melbourne slang for daggy suede moccasins – named after the suburb where they are common.

'sup a greeting used by cool, with-it youth. It is an abbreviated form of **whassup**.

super full-strength beer, as opposed to **unleaded**. Also used for other 'full-strength' items, such as cola containing caffeine.

sure as shit absolutely; without a doubt.

sure beats shovelling shit said of a job that is bad, but not *that* bad.

sure thing **1.** a certainty; something assured beyond any doubt. **2.** a racehorse or greyhound tipped to win. **3.** a woman who is a definite prospect for sexual intercourse.

surfboard women's slang for a large sanitary napkin.

surfie a devotee of surfboard riding; one who lives the life of a surfer – sun-bleached hair, tanned hide, waxed feet. Aussie slang since the 1960s. The Americans use the term **surfer** – but actually this is originally Australian as well, dating back to the 1910s. Of course, back then it didn't refer to surfboard riding, but rather to what used to be called 'surf-bathing' – that is, swimming in the surf and bodysurfing.

surfie chick a female who is part of the surfie subculture.

surf rat a surfing enthusiast.

suss **1.** unreliable; needing confirmation. *Her story sounded very suss to me.* Short for 'suspicious'. **2.** to imagine or surmise. *I sussed that I was no longer welcome.* Hence, to understand or comprehend. *She's got you sussed.* Originally short for 'suspect'.

susso government unemployment benefits, especially provided during the Depression. Known as 'sustenance' – the current term is, of course, 'the dole'. *I spent a year on the susso.* Hence also, an unemployed person receiving government handouts.

suss out to work out.

sux the same as **suck** – but this spelling is generally reserved for graffiti. *School sux! Britney sux!* or *You sux!* Originally a respelling of *sucks*, the third person present singular of *suck*, but also used for first and second person and the plural, where, despite its spelling, it is pronounced 'suck'. Thus *Teachers sux* is said as 'teachers suck', not 'teachers sucks'.

swag **1.** a bundle or a blanket-roll containing personal belongings and useful items carried by a traveller through the bush or by an itinerant looking for work. The defining feature of the **swagman**. Also commonly called a **bluey** or, less commonly, a **Matilda** or **shiralee**. First recorded in the 1840s in Australia and the 1850s in New Zealand. **2.** a bedroll, without belongings; hence, a traveller's bedding unrolled for sleeping in. *We hopped into our swags right away as the night was already cold.* **3.** an unspecified but large number or quantity. *There was a swag of people at the meeting.*

swagman a man who travels about the country on foot, carrying his possessions in a swag and living on his earnings from occasional jobs, or gifts of money or food. First recorded in the 1860s and since the 1890s commonly shortened to **swaggie**. The term was also in common use in New Zealand, but there it was generally shortened to *swagger* rather than *swaggie*. The era of swagmen, at its height during the Great Depression, came to an end with World War II, but the swagman has lived on in Australian cultural history, and is the central figure of Australia's national song, *Waltzing Matilda*. A female itinerant was, of course, known as a **swagwoman** – but these were always rare.

swallower a person who swallows down the proceeds of fellatio – as opposed to a **spitter**.

swamp donkey an imbecile.

swamp hog an ugly woman.

swampy **1.** a surfer. **2.** in Tassie, a person from Invermay, a suburb of Launceston.

swanger the penis.

swap spit to French kiss; to suck face.

swat vac a variant spelling of **swot vac** (see entry).

swear like a trooper to swear strongly and often.

sweet all right, okay, in order. *Don't worry mate – everything's sweet.* Aussie slang since the 1890s.

sweet cop an easy job or task. Aussie slang since the 1910s.

sweetener **1.** a bribe. **2.** a financial or other benefit added to something on offer.

Sweet Fanny Adams a euphemism for *sweet fuck-all.* First recorded in a glossary of Australian World War I digger slang in 1918. Also in the form **sweet FA**.

sweet fuck-all very little; next to nothing. *He's done sweet fuck-all about it.*

swiftie a con job or swindle. Aussie slang since the 1940s.

swing the bag to work as a bookmaker.

swing the lead to be idle when there is work to be done.

switch hitter a bisexual person.

swot vac vacation from school, college, university, or the like, in the period before exams, to allow students to study for the exams. Called **stuvac** in NSW.

swy **1.** the game of two-up. This alternative name for Australia's national gambling game dates back to the 1910s, and is an Anglicisation of the German word *zwei* 'two'. Also called the **swy game**. **2.** old slang for a two-shilling coin or the sum of two shillings. Now obsolete. **3.** in prison it has two meanings, two ounces of tobacco, or a two-year jail sentence.

Sydders a colloquial form of Sydney.

Sydney Harbour Aussie rhyming slang for 'barber'.

Sydney or the bush! all or nothing, as in making a do or die attempt, gambling against the odds, or the like.

sypho Aussie slang version of 'syphilis'. Been around since the 1940s.

syphon the python of a male, to urinate.

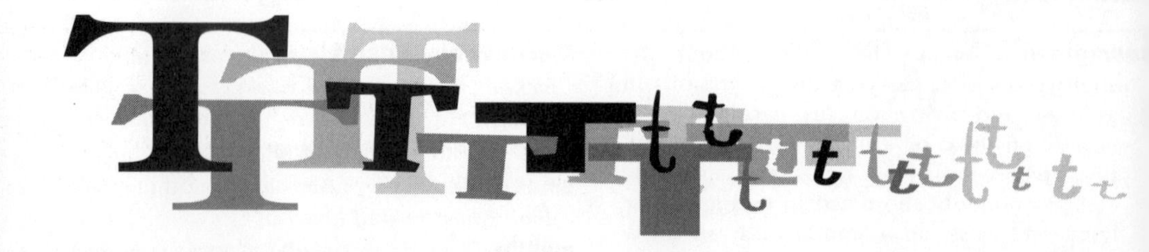

tacker a young kid. Originally from the British dialects of Devon and Cornwall and used in Oz since at least the 1940s.

tack-o-rama completely tacky.

tad a little bit. *Sorry, I'll be a tad late.* Originally US slang of the 1940s, and in the 19th century meaning a small boy. Some have suggested it is a shortening of *tadpole*.

taddie a tadpole.

tadpoling catching tadpoles and keeping them in a jar or the like – a common children's pastime.

Taffy a Welshman. This is actually the Welsh form of *Davy*, a shortened form of *David*, a common proper name in Wales and name of the Welsh patron saint.

tag **1.** a graffiti artist's signature. **2.** a name for the schoolyard game chasey, used the country wide, but the favoured term in ACT. See **chasey** for the full set of regionalisms. **3.** in Aussie Rules, to continuously follow or mark an opponent closely.

tag dag someone with their shirt tag sticking out of their collar.

tagger **1.** a graffiti writer, especially one who repetitively scrawls their graffiti name or 'tag' over and over again, establishing some notion of 'turf'. Or merely for the sake of 'recognition' by which their egos are somehow boosted. **2.** in Aussie Rules, a player who tags an opponent.

tail **1.** the backside, rump or arse. An old term dating back to the 1300s. **2.** hence, a dismissive term for a woman considered as a sex object. *There's a nice bit of tail.* Originally British slang of the 19th century. **3.** a person who follows another, such as a private detective. *The cops put a tail on him.* Hence, as a verb, to follow someone secretly.

tail 'em in two-up, to make the coins land with tails upwards. The opposite of **head 'em**.

tailie in two-up, a person who consistently bets on tails. As opposed to a **headie**.

take a chill pill Calm down! Relax!

take away the toys but leave the playground to have a hysterectomy.

take down to defraud, cheat or swindle someone. Aussie slang since the 1890s.

take-down a swindle.

take out to win a prize, trophy, or the like. *She took out the Gold Logie for the second year in a row.* Aussie slang since the 1970s.

take the knock in horseracing, to admit that you are unable to settle your debts.

take the micky out of to make someone seem foolish; to tease someone.

take your picture to see a flash of a woman's underpants up her skirt.

talent **1.** women or men viewed as possible sexual partners. Originally used by men of women. **2.** the members of the underworld. Old Aussie slang dating back to the 1870s. Now rare or used in historical writings.

talk out of your arse to talk nonsense.

talk the leg off an iron pot said of someone who won't shut up.

talk underwater People who won't shut up are said to be able to talk underwater. If they never, ever shut up, then they can **talk ten feet underwater with a snorkel in their mouth**.

tallie in Qld, a 750 ml bottle of beer. Generally called a **long neck** elsewhere, except WA, where the term **king brown** is favoured.

tall poppy a person who is pre-eminent in a particular field; a person with great status. Australians in general have a bit of a negative view of tall poppies, especially if they seem to get above themselves. When this happens they need to be cut down to size. The Aussie penchant for such pruning is known as the **tall poppy syndrome**.

tall timber very tall AFL footballers.

tally-hos cigarette papers. After the most common brand. Also called **papers** or, in Tasmania, **tissues**.

tank **1.** underworld slang for a safe. **2.** to deliberately lose a match or a contest.

tanked drunk – or, more properly, fully drunk, as opposed to **half-tanked**.

tank loaf a loaf of bread, usually white, baked in a cylindrical tin with corrugated sides resembling a water tank. This is the common term in Qld, NSW, ACT and WA. The other states call it a **pipe loaf**.

tank man underworld slang for a crim who specialises in stealing from safes.

tanner old slang for a sixpence. Origin unknown. Died out with the introduction of decimal currency.

tantie a temper tantrum. Aussie slang since the 1980s. A diminutive form highlighting the childishness of the behaviour.

tan track the rectum; hence, to **ride the tan track** is to practise anal sex. A real tan track is a horseracing track with tanbark on it.

tap dancer Aussie rhyming slang for 'cancer'.

tappet a car nut or petrolhead. Also, a hoon. Common term in Qld. Also called a **tappet head**.

Tarjey a Target department store. Pronounced *tar-zhay* with an affected, high-falutin' tone. *I bought my new jacket at Tarjey.* A jocular mispronunciation as though it was the name of an haute couture fashion house. Also spelt **Tarjay**.

arn in Tasmania, the common term for a small mountain lake.

arnies a child's word for sultanas.

art **1.** a promiscuous woman; a slut. **2.** a prostitute. **3.** in a weakened sense, any woman. Formerly common, but now obsolete, as the negative senses now predominate. Unbeknown to most people is the fact that this strongly derogatory word was originally used in a very positive sense to refer to a girlfriend or sweetheart. In fact, in the early years of the 20th century a charming compliment was to call a woman a **bonzer tart** – though this was only among the slangy working class. C.J. Dennis conjectured that in origin **tart** was a contraction of *sweetheart*, but this is a little hard to believe. It was first recorded in print in Hotten's English *Slang Dictionary* of 1864, where Hotten states it is used 'by the London lower orders', and only of women dressed in their best clothes 'like the jam tarts in the swell bakers' shops'. Hence, it could be that it is a shortening of rhyming slang *jam tart* 'sweetheart'.

tart up to adorn or make attractive, especially with cheap ornaments and cosmetics.

Tasmaniac an inhabitant of Tasmania.

Tassie colloquial rendering of Tasmania. Aussie slang since the 1890s.

taw **1.** a playing marble, especially a highly prized one. **2.** a marker used in hopscotch. Also spelt **tor**.

tax **1.** to steal. *He taxed my ruler.* **2.** among schoolkids, a levy imposed by a friend on some item you probably won't mind sharing. *She took some of my hot chips as a chip tax.*

taxi! a cry used when someone exhibits obvious drunkenness. This joke is not new. In Victorian England they had a similar cry of 'Coach!'

teacher arms the arms of an overweight or matronly woman, having flabby triceps.

tea leaf rhyming slang for 'thief'. Originally British slang from the 1900s.

team cream an occasion on which a number of males have sexual intercourse with one female; a gang bang.

tear-arse to run or drive at manic speed.

teasy of a baby, irritable.

tea-towel head a racist term for an Arabic person. Hence, the **tea-towel brigade**, that is, Arabic people as a whole.

tech head a derogatory term for a technically minded person, especially a computer geek.

techie a technical services employee. Also called a **techo**.

technicolour yawn the act of vomiting. Aussie slang since the 1960s. A term dear to and principally spread by Barry Humphries.

teddy bear rhyming slang for 'lair'. Aussie slang since the 1940s.

teev a newish way of shortening the term 'TV', which is itself a shortening of 'television', which is a shortening of 'television set'.

tell it to Ricki (Lake) Stop complaining! Referring to Ricki Lake, US talk-show host, on whose show people air their trivial personal problems.

temporary Australian a motorcycle rider who does not wear proper protective gear.

ten a ten fluid ounce glass of beer. Formerly a term in common use, but now found chiefly in Tasmania and Queensland. See the entry for **middy** for synonyms.

Tennant Creek Aussie rhyming slang for 'Greek'.

tenner an obsolete term for a ten pound note or the sum of ten pounds. Transferred to ten dollars after the introduction of decimal currency in 1966.

teno tenosynovitis; inflammation of the tendon sheath, especially in the wrists, resulting from RSI. It was all the rage in the 1980s when every man and his dog seemed to be getting it. The mania has died down somewhat now.

Territory confetti ring pulls from beer cans.

Territory rig formal attire in the Top End. See **Darwin rig** for an explanation.

terrorist a derisive term for a 'tourist' – used by the local inhabitants of an area.

Terry toon a pimp. From Aussie rhyming slang for '**hoon**' (see entry).

thang the southern US way of saying 'thing'. Used in stock phrases such as *the latest thang*, *a happenin' thang*, and *do your thang*.

thank you Deanna That was bloody obvious! Referring to Deanna Troy from *Star Trek – The Next Generation* who was forever giving startlingly obvious 'insights' for which she was kindly thanked by captain and first mate.

thank your mother for the rabbits an old jocular expression of farewell.

thatch **1.** the hair covering the head. **2.** the pubic hair, especially of a woman.

that's the shot! That's the right way to go about it! Encouraging Aussie slang since the 1960s.

that's the way the cookie crumbles That's the way of things. Such is life.

them's fightin' words a jocular expression of disagreement or mild anger. Borrowed from US movies. In the US there is a legal category of words called *fighting words*, defined as 'those which by their very utterance inflict injury or tend to incite an immediate breach of the peace'.

them's the breaks Such are the vicissitudes of life.

thickhead a stupid or slow person.

thingo Aussie way of saying 'thingummy' or 'thingamyjigget' or 'thingamabob' or even 'thingy'. It has been in common use since the 1960s.

things are crook in Tallarook The situation is not good. Wonderful rhyming phrase, dating back to the 1960s at least. This is more common in Victoria, the home state of Tallarook. In NSW things tend to be crook in either **Muswellbrook** or **Coolongolook**.

think the sun shines out of your arse to have a very high opinion of oneself. An even harsher expression is **think your shit doesn't stink**.

third leg the penis.

threads clothes. Originally US slang from the 1920s.

three-corner jack a vicious spiky seed of a nasty introduced weed of South African origin. See **doublegee** for the complete set of regionalisms.

three-dog night a very cold night, colder than a two-dog night, but not as cold as a four-dog night. See **dog**, def. 7.

threepenny bits rhyming slang for 'the shits'. Originally British. In Australia and New Zealand it was converted to **trey bits** (see entry).

throne the toilet.

throttling pit the toilet. A Bazza McKenzie-ism.

throw another shrimp on the barbie a phrase supposed by Americans to be indicative of the Australian idiom. This misconception stems from an advertising campaign run in the 1980s by the Australian Tourist Commission featuring Paul Hogan, from whose lips the faux ocker phrase dropped. Of course 'real' Aussies would only ever say 'throw another prawn on the barbie' – and they would hardly ever say that anyhow because what kind of dinkum Aussie bloke cooks prawns on the barbie? The barbie is for great bloody bits of steak and fatty snags that spit everywhere and piles of onions.

throw a Reggie to have a temper tantrum. This phrase is especially common in Tassie.

throwdown **1.** a small firework which explodes when thrown onto a surface. **2.** a small bottle of beer, smaller than a stubby.

throw in your marbles to die.

thrummer an obsolete term for a threepence. An extension of older British slang *thrum*.

thugby a derogatory term used by AFL folk for Rugby Union or Rugby League.

thump in WA, to steal.

thunder bags underpants.

thunderbox a toilet. Originally British slang of the 1930s.

thunder thighs a person with large, fat legs.

tick **1.** credit or trust. *We bought the groceries on tick.* Venerable slang dating from the 16th century. **2.** in Tasmania, a mattress. Shortened form of *ticking*, the cotton fabric used.

ticker **1.** a watch. **2.** the heart. *He's got a dicky ticker.* **3.** courage, bravery, guts. *You don't have the ticker to face him.*

tickle the ivories to play the piano.

tickle the peter to rob the till. Aussie slang since the 1940s.

tick-tack **1.** a type of manual semaphore once popularly used at racetracks between bookmakers and their touts. Hence as a verb, to communicate via this code. Tick-tacking was commonly used to signal to people outside the course, and was highly illegal. Sadly this deft art has now fallen into disuse. **2.** a type of skateboard manoeuvre, originating in the 1970s, in which the front wheels are made to hit the ground to the right and left alternatively.

tick tock a small black and orange cicada found in WA.

tick up to obtain something on credit.

tiddly slightly drunk; tipsy. Originally 19th century British slang. Perhaps ultimately from rhyming slang *tiddlywink* 'drink'.

tier in Tasmania, a mountain range.

Tiersman in SA, a timber-getter who works in the Tiers (the Mount Lofty Ranges).

tiggy a Qld and Vic name for the schoolyard game chasey. In Qld also shortened to **tig**. See **chasey** for the full set of regionalisms.

tiggy tiggy touchwood a derisive term for an AFL game in which free kicks keep on being awarded for minor infringements.

tight **1.** drunk. **2.** stingy. Both originally 19th century British slang. Often exemplified by analogy, especially for the second meaning, as **tight as a bull's arse in fly-time**, **tight as a fish's arse** (that is, watertight), and **tight as a mouse's ear**.

tight-arsed **1.** miserly or stingy. **2.** inhibited or repressed; rigid and unrelaxed.

tightwad a close-fisted or stingy person. Originally US slang of the 1900s.

TI handbag Top End slang for a cask of wine. Standing for Thursday Island. A racist slur referring to Indigenous problem drinking.

tike a variant spelling of **tyke**.

tilly in Qld and rural northern NSW, a ute. Using the middle bit of the word *utility*, rather than the front end.

timothy old slang for a brothel. Now obsolete. Perhaps from rhyming slang *Timothy Titmouse* 'house'.

a Tim Tam short of a packet not having full intelligence; stupid; moronic. For similar comparisons see the entry for **short of**.

Tim Tam suck a culinary treat in which two diagonally opposite corners of an Arnott's Tim Tam biscuit are bitten off and hot coffee is then sucked through the biscuit via these openings. At a certain critical point the whole biscuit must be deftly tossed into the mouth, otherwise it disintegrates in your hands. Also called the **Tim Tam slam** or a **Tim Tam straw**.

tin old slang for money or dosh. Originally British slang of the 1830s.

tin arse a lucky person. Hence, **tin-arsed**, lucky. Aussie slang since the 1940s.

tingle a telephone call.

tin hares the greyhounds; greyhound racing.

tin kettling a noisy ritual in which tins, pots, and the like, are banged by a crowd of people, as at weddings and similar occasions.

tinkle to urinate. Hence, an act of urination. Imitative of the sound of a stream of urine in a toilet bowl.

tin lid Aussie rhyming slang for 'kid'. This dates way back to 1905.

tinned dog canned meat. Old Aussie slang dating back to the 1890s.

tinnie **1.** a can of beer. Aussie slang since the 1960s. **2.** a light, aluminium-hulled boat.

tinny lucky. From **tin arse** (see entry).

tin tank rhyming slang for the 'bank'.

tin teeth dental braces.

tip **1.** the tips of the marijuana plant dried and prepared for smoking. **2.** a NSW name for the schoolyard game chasey. Also called **tips**. See **chasey** for the full set of regionalisms.

tip-and-run a variant name for the kids' cricket game in which you have to run every time you hit the ball. This is the most common term in WA. In SA it is more commonly known as **tippy go** or **tippy-go-run**, and in Queensland you find the terms **tipsy** and **tipsy run**. See **hit-and-run** for more information.

tip slinger a racecourse tout who makes tips to many different punters with the hope of getting some gratuity if a horse gets up.

tip the bucket on someone to denigrate someone. Referring to a sanitary can full of shit, and thus the same as 'to heap shit on someone'. Aussie slang since the 1950s.

tired and emotional a euphemistic description of a person who is drunk, especially applied to fat lazy politicians who contribute to the country by coming to parliament half-pissed and falling asleep. The phrase originated in Britain in the 1960s in *Private Eye* magazine, but is quite common in the lofty halls of Australian parliament.

tissues in Tas, cigarette papers. Elsewhere called **papers** or **tally-hos**.

tit a female breast. Mildly rude or impolite, but commonly used leeringly by men. Originally a dialect pronunciation of *teat*. If a baby is **on the tit**, then it is suckling. If something **gets on your tits** then it really annoys you, man or woman.

titfer a hat. British slang from the 1930s. Short for rhyming slang *tit for tat*, which in the full form dates back to the late 19th century.

tit fuck a rubbing of the erect penis on and between the breasts of a sexual partner. Hence, as a verb, to engage in a tit fuck.

titless **1.** literally, without breasts, but commonly used disparagingly of flat-chested women. A crude male term. *Shut up you titless mole.* **2.** to **scare someone titless** is to really frighten them.

tit-off to grope or fondle the breasts of a female.

tits and bums denoting a type of low-grade entertainment featuring much exposed female flesh.

titty a female breast. Originally used in British dialect, it is now puerile slang.

titty hard-ons erect nipples of a woman's breasts, especially when showing through clothing.

tizz up to dress up in glamorous fashion. Aussie slang dating from the 1960s. Also in the form **tizzy up**.

tizzy a state of somewhat hysterical confusion and anxiety, often expressed in frantic but ineffectual activity. *Don't get in a tizzy.* Originally US slang of the 1930s. Also known as a **tizz**.

tjuzs another spelling of **zhuzh** (see entry).

to-and-from rhyming slang for 'Pom', that is, an English person. Aussie slang since the 1940s.

the Toaster a derisive nickname for the apartment and retail building running along East Circular Quay, Sydney.

toastie a toasted sandwich. Also called a **toastie-toastie**.

tockley the penis. A term invented by *Picture* magazine, Sydney.

todge nonsense; rubbish.

todger the penis. Originally British slang of the 1950s. Hence, **todger dodger**, a lesbian.

toecutter **1.** a criminal thug who intimidates and brutalises people for a crime boss. **2.** a particularly ruthless person, especially in politics.

toe jam black gunk under the toe nails or between the toes.

toe rag a contemptible person.

toey **1.** of a racehorse, eager to run. Aussie slang since the 1930s. **2.** anxious, apprehensive, edgy. Aussie slang since the 1950s. If you are really toey then you could be described as **toey as a Roman sandal**. **3.** fast, speedy. This meaning first appears in the 1970s.

togged up dressed up.

togs **1.** clothes. *Shove your work togs in a bag.* **2.** a swimming costume. *I'll need some new togs this summer.* Especially common in Qld, NSW and Victoria.

Tojo **1.** during World War II, a hated Japanese soldier. So called after Hideki Tojo the Japanese military commander and figurehead. On cracker night effigies of Tojo were burnt by children the country over. **2.** a Toyota Landcruiser 4WD.

toke a puff of a cigarette or joint. Originally US slang of the 1950s. Hence, a **toker** is a dope smoker.

tomato a cricket ball.

tombowler a large marble. Also spelt **tomboller** or **tombola**.

tombstone a wheelie-bin.

tomfoolery rhyming slang for 'jewellery'. Originally British, from the 1930s.

Tommy in World War I, a British soldier. A shortening of **Tommy Atkins**, which was originally a name used for a private in specimen forms of the British cavalry and infantry from 1815.

Tom Thumb rhyming slang for 'rum'. Recorded in Australia since 1905.

tomtits rhyming slang for 'the shits', either diarrhoea or a bad mood. British and Australian since the 1940s.

ton **1.** in cricket, the score of one hundred runs. **2.** in Aussie Rules, one hundred goals scored by a player in a season. **3.** the speed of one hundred miles an hour, especially on a motorcycle. Fell out of use with the move to kilometres, for which 100 is no special speed.

tongue-pash to French kiss.

tonguey a French kiss; a kiss in which the tongue is used.

tonguing dying for a drink.

tonk **1.** in cricket, a powerful slog of the ball. Hence, to give the ball a tonk. *He tonked it over mid-wicket.* **2.** a homosexual man. From rhyming slang *tonka bean* 'queen'. **3.** the penis.

Tonka tough extremely tough. From the Tonka brand of heavy-duty toy trucks, back-hoes, and other heavy equipment.

tonsil hockey French kissing; tongue kissing.

too cool for school extremely sophisticated, fashionable, smart, and the like. Cooler than cool and hence disdainful of just about everything.

toodle-em-buck a spinning device used by children back in the 1920s for gambling on horse races, especially the Melbourne Cup. It consisted of a circular board divided into sectors with the names and odds of horses in each one, the whole being spun like a roulette wheel.

too easy, Campese That is extremely easy! Rhyming expression, after Rugby Union legend David Campese.

tool **1.** the penis. Venerable slang dating back to the 16th century. Hence, as a verb, to fuck. **2.** an idiot, jerk or dickhead.

tool around **1.** of a man, to have casual sex with many partners. **2.** to fool about or spend time idly. *They've been tooling about all arvo and haven't done anything.* Also, commonly used to refer to driving about for amusement's sake when you've got nothing to do.

toolies speedos. For a full set of synonyms see **sluggos**.

too much information a recent phrase commonly used to rebuke someone for saying something unsavoury.

Toorak tractor a city-only 4WD that never sees off-road conditions, principally used for shopping and shuttling kids to and from school. Also called a **Toorak taxi**. Originally Melbourne slang, this term has spread throughout the entire country and is the most common of all the variants, all based on the names of affluent suburbs. Perth has the **Dalkeith tractor**, Adelaide the **Burnside warrior**, and Brisbane the **Kenmore tractor**. In Sydney the terms are legion, including **Balmain bulldozer**, **Balmoral bulldozer**, **Double Bay tractor**, **Mosman tractor**, **North Shore tank** and **Turramurra tractor**. Commonly also called a **wanker tank**.

tooshie angry or upset. *Don't get tooshie with me.*

toot a toilet or dunny. Aussie slang since the 1960s. In origin perhaps an alteration of *toilet*.

toot sweet immediately. A humorous alteration of French *tout de suite*.

tootsy **1.** a foot. Originally 19th century British slang. Hence, to **play tootsy** is to touch feet secretly under a table. **2.** a belittling term for a woman. Originally US slang from the 1890s.

top **1.** the best; excellent. *He's a top bloke. That was top fun.* Top Aussie slang since the 1970s. **2.** the active partner in homosexual anal sex. As opposed to the **bottom**. Also called a **top man**.

the Top the northern part of Australia. *We travelled across the Top.*

top brass high ranking military officers.

Top End the northern part of the Northern Territory. Hence, a **Top Ender** is a person living in the Top End.

top-heavy of a woman, having large breasts.

top notcher **1.** a first-rate person. **2.** a sawyer who works on top of the log.

top off to inform on someone or dob them in. Aussie slang since the 1930s. Hence, as a noun, **top-off**, a police informer.

top of the wozza **1.** at the top; in the prime position. *He's top of the wozza in some big oil company.* Probably derived from *The Wazzir*, the Anzacs' nickname for *Haret el Wasser* the red-light district of Cairo, and scene of the **Battle of the Wazzir** (see entry). Apparently the best and most expensive brothels were at the top of the Wazzir. **2.** terrific; the best. *It has a top of the wozza stereo system.*

toppie in cricket, a delivery with top spin, or a top spin bowler.

tops wonderful, great, terrific. *We had a tops time. The party was tops.* Also used as an adverb. *The Swans played tops this arvo.* Generally used by kids and adolescents. Aussie slang since the 1950s.

top yourself to commit suicide.

tor another spelling of **taw** (see entry).

torpedo **1.** in Aussie Rules, a kick in which the ball spins around its axis. Also called a **torp**

or **torpie**. **2.** in SA, a long bun loaf with icing on top, usually cut into slices and buttered.

Torri a Torana car.

toss an act of masturbation. Hence, to **not give a toss** is to not care a damn.

tosser a stupid or annoying person; a jerk; literally, a wanker. Occasionally termed a **toss head**.

toss it in to abandon or give up on something.

tossle the penis. Coarse Aussie slang since the 1940s. Also spelt **tossel**.

toss off to masturbate. Originally 19th century British sexual slang.

tosspot a drunkard; a pisspot. Venerable slang dating back to the 1500s.

toss-up an even chance. *The election is a toss-up.*

toss your hat in to make a preliminary assessment of a situation.

total **1.** to thoroughly wreck a vehicle by crashing it. **2.** to completely ruin anything.

tote the totalisator. Aussie slang since the 1890s.

t'othersider in WA, a person living on the other side of the Nullarbor Plain.

totty a young, attractive woman. British slang since the 1890s, but only adopted in Australia in the 1990s.

tottymungous of a woman, extremely attractive.

touch **1.** to borrow money from someone, especially with scant respect for returning the same. **2.** a person from whom money can be borrowed. Generally referred to as an **easy touch** or **soft touch**.

touchie a footy touch umpire.

tough shit! a crude way of saying 'tough luck!' Also found in the form **tough titties!** And in a typically laconic Aussie way, commonly just shortened to **tough!**

touse a euphemistic way of referring to the **shithouse** or toilet. Polite Aussie slang since the 1940s.

tout **1.** a racecourse tipster; an urger; specifically one who tips many different horses in a race to different people in the hope of receiving a gratuity from one of the winning punters. **2.** a person who watches and times practising racehorses in order to gain information for giving tips. **3.** a spy or informer. **4.** to work as a tout at a racecourse.

towie a tow truck, or tow truck driver.

town bike a derogatory term for a woman who has sex with many different men in her local area; a woman with a reputation for sleeping around. Aussie slang since the 1940s.

townie one who comes from a town and is ignorant of country ways. Aussie slang since the 1820s.

toy boy the young male partner of an older woman or homosexual male, especially one who receives financial favours in return for services rendered.

toy town **1.** a derisive term for any neat and new housing development. **2.** a derogatory term for the ACT local government and parliament, which was instituted in 1987. Used by people who considered that the territory's small size and lack of industry didn't warrant a parliament.

trac in prison, a stubborn, unmanageable prisoner. Aussie slang since the 1960s. Extracted from the word 'intractable'.

track **1.** the open road; hence, to be **on the track** meant to be travelling as a swagman. Aussie slang since the 1860s. Also known as the **wallaby track**. **2.** a warder who will carry contraband messages or goods out of or into a prison for an inmate. Aussie prison slang since the 1950s.

the Track the Stuart Highway running between Darwin and Alice Springs. To go **down the track** is to go south from Darwin, and naturally, to go **up the track** is to go north from the Alice.

trackie tracksuit, as in **trackie pants** or **trackie top**, and, of course, **trackie daks** are tracksuit pants. Hence, **trackies**, a tracksuit. *I spent all morning in me trackies.*

Trackie Valley a derisive name for Tuggeranong in the ACT.

tracks scars or marks on the arms or legs caused by habitual use of a hypodermic needle. Also called **track marks**.

trade among homosexuals, a pick-up for casual sex. See **rough trade**.

Tradies a tradesmen's club.

traino a train station.

train smash **1.** a savoury dish hastily concocted from such ingredients as eggs, sausages, tomatoes, onions, tomato sauce, beans, and the like. **2.** tomato sauce.

train surfing the practice of riding on top of a moving railway carriage.

trammie a tram conductor or driver.

tramp in WA, to sack someone from a job. *I got tramped last week.*

trannie **1.** a transistor radio. **2.** a transformer. **3.** a transparency. **4.** a transvestite. **5.** a transsexual.

trap **1.** the mouth. *Shut your trap!* Originally British slang of the 18th century. **2.** a colonial police officer or trooper. Originally recorded in Australia in 1812 in a glossary of convict slang. So called because they 'trapped' offenders. Now only used in historical texts.

the traps any place you frequent. *I've seen him around the traps.* Aussie slang since the 1930s. Originally referring to a route along which a person had laid traps which they then habitually visited to collect the game that had been caught.

trash **1.** an abusive term for people viewed as worthless or inferior types, especially if from another race or social stratum. *I don't associate with that trash.* Now most common in the compound **white trash** (see entry). **2.** verbal abuse designed to hassle the opposition and put them off their game; sledging. Also known as **trash talk**. **3.** to speak unfavourably of; to rubbish. **4.** to utterly wreck. *They totally trashed the joint.* **5.** to mess up a person's room, as in a college, as a prank. **6.** to hassle or abuse someone verbally, especially in order to put them off their game.

trashed **1.** completely drunk. **2.** out of it on some drug or other.

traveller a can or bottle of beer consumed while driving; a roadie.

trawl to search for a sexual partner.

treadly a bicycle. Aussie slang. A kid's word since the 1960s. Also called a **deadly treadly** (see entry).

tree hugger a disparaging term for an environmentalist – used by people who care more for their right to keep on burning petrochemicals than they do for the environment.

Trekkie an avid fan of the television series *Star Trek*. Also sometimes called a **Trekker**.

trendoid a trendy person.

trey bit a threepenny piece; threepence. Also simply called a **trey**. Disappeared with the advent of decimal currency in 1966. From old British slang *trey* 'three', from Old French.

trey bits **1.** rhyming slang for 'the shits', either diarrhoea or a bad mood. **2.** rhyming slang for 'tits'. Dating from the 1960s.

triantelope a huntsman spider. Venerable Aussie slang dating back to the 1840s. Also called a **trantylope**.

triantiwontigongolope a mythical insect or beastie. Sometimes portrayed as a dreadfully dangerous bunyip-like creature in order to frighten children or naive city folk visiting the bush. Coined by CJ Dennis in his *A Book For Kids*, 1921. Commonly bastardised into forms having less syllables, as *triantiwontygong, triantiwontigog, triantimontygoggle* and *trianiwonigong*.

trick **1.** a prostitute's customer. **2.** superb, classy. *It had a really trick engine.*

trike **1.** a child's tricycle. **2.** a railway fettler's three-wheeled hand-operated flatcar. In WA called a **kalamazoo**.

trip **1.** a period under the influence of LSD or a similar drug; a quantity of a hallucinogen prepared for taking. Hence, as a verb, to experience the effects of LSD or another hallucinogen. **2.** something that amazes; a spin-out.

trippy **1.** of a drug, tending more towards the hallucinogenic. *This new stuff I got is really trippy.* **2.** of an experience, strange, weird, bordering on the surreal.

triss an effeminate male homosexual. Aussie slang since the 1950s. Occasionally in the form **trizz**. Origin unknown.

trissy **1.** in the manner of an effeminate homosexual male. **2.** frilly and girly.

trizzie an obsolete term for a threepenny coin.

troll **1.** to go about looking for a casual sexual partner; to cruise. **2.** an old derogatory term for a prostitute or promiscuous woman. A shortening of 'trollop'. It is Aussie slang from the 1880s, but is no longer heard.

trolleyed out of it from taking too many drugs. Also known as being **off your trolley**.

Trono the township of Toronto, NSW.

troopie a Toyota Landcruiser Troop Carrier 4WD.

troppo **1.** mentally disturbed. Originally World War II Aussie slang, referring to mental illness resulting from long military service in the tropics. Especially common in the phrase **go troppo**. **2.** of a building, designed for tropical weather.

the trots **1.** diarrhoea. From British slang of the 1900s. **2.** harness racing. Aussie slang since the 1890s.

trouble and strife rhyming slang for 'wife'. Recorded in Australia since 1905. Occasionally heard in the variant form **storm and strife**.

trough in WA, SA, Vic and Tas, a laundry tub. In Tas, also called a **trove**.

trough lolly a urinal disinfectant lozenge.

trove in Tas, a laundry tub. Also called a **trow**. See **trough**.

truckie a truck or semi-trailer driver. Aussie slang since the 1910s.

true blue **1.** genuine; fair dinkum. *They were true blue bushies from the outback.* **2.** fair dinkum Aussie. *She's true blue.* **3.** as a noun, an Australian. *You're a true blue now.*

true dinks Fair dinkum! Not heard much any more, but lingers on in Victoria more than anywhere else.

Trumpy a Triumph motorcycle.

trundler in cricket, a bowler, particularly one who bowls slow medium pace.

tryhard **1.** one who tries, and fails, to gain social acceptance or to be cool. **2.** one who attempts to be like someone else. *She's a Britney tryhard.*

T-shirts in pool, bigs. As opposed to **singlets**.

tube **1.** a can of beer. *Let's sink a few tubes.* **2.** a bottle of beer. **3.** the barrel of a breaking wave. **4.** the television. *Just veging out in front of the tube.*

tube time the amount of time a surfer has spent riding tubes of waves, used as a measure of experience.

tubs among musicians, the drums.

tucker great Aussie slang for food. *It's time for tucker.* Has been in constant use since the 1850s. Originally meaning a meal, that is, something to be tucked away (in the stomach).

tucker bag a bag used for carrying food, as by a swagman.

tucker box a box for carrying a food supply. The most famous of all such boxes is the one at Five Mile, just outside Gundagai, NSW. The story goes that a drover left his trusty dog to guard his tucker box while he went off on an errand, but, through some fatal misadventure, he never returned and the faithful dog remained on guard until its own death. Since 1932 the dog on the tucker box has been commemorated in the form of a statue at Five Mile. Interestingly, this legend only arose to explain a bowdlerised form of an old folk song. In the original song the dog 'shat in the tucker box', to the chagrin of the owner and the amusement of his fellows. This was a little too rude for decent ears, and so 'sat on' was substituted for 'shat in'.

tucker fucker **1.** a microwave oven. **2.** a bad cook. **3.** tomato sauce.

tucker out to weary, tire, exhaust. Aussie slang dating from the 1910s.

tuckshop arms the arms of an overweight or matronly woman with flabby triceps.

tug of a male, to masturbate. Hence, an act of male masturbation.

Tuggers the suburb of Tuggeranong, ACT. A resident of this suburb is called a **Tugger**.

tullawong in Byron Bay, a name of the currawong, a large black and white native bird.

tummy banana the penis. Aussie slang since the 1960s. A term championed by Barry Humphries.

tune to successfully gain another's sexual favours; to crack on to someone.

tune-up a belting. *Dad gave me a tune-up for breaking the window.*

tunnel rat in the Vietnam War, soldiers, usually of small stature, who volunteered for operations inside the Viet Cong's extensive tunnel system.

turd **1.** a piece of excrement. One of the original Anglo-Saxon four-letter words. **2.** a despicable person. Venerable slang, it has been used as an insult since the 1400s.

turd burglar a male homosexual from the homophobic perspective. See **dung puncher** for a swag of synonyms, including **turd packer**, **turd trapper** and **turd surfer**.

turdicle in the Australian Antarctic Territory, a frozen dog turd.

turd strangler a plumber.

turf **1.** the territory belonging to a street gang. **2.** the world of horseracing. Often also spelt with a capital T. *He makes his living from the Turf.*

turkey **1.** a foolish person; an absolute goose. **2.** something which is unsuccessful; a flop.

turkey's nest in rural areas, a small watering hole for stock.

turn **1.** a party. Aussie slang since the 1950s. **2.** a fuss or commotion; a display of bad temper. *He's stacked on another turn.* Also Aussie slang since the 1950s.

turn dog to turn traitor or to display cowardice. Also known as **turning dingo**.

turning Japanese vigorously engaged in masturbating. Referring to closing the eyes until they are like slits.

turn it on **1.** to start a fight or argument; to kick up a fuss. **2.** to go all out; to strive to the best of your abilities. **3.** to engage in sexual activity without restraint. *She really turns it on.* Aussie sexual slang since the 1940s. **4.** to provide a bang-up feast for a party.

turn it up! Stop it! Give it a break!

turn off to disgust, especially sexually. Hence, a **turn-off** is something less than appealing.

turn on to arouse or excite, especially sexually. Hence, a **turn-on** is that which gets you going.

turn on the waterworks to begin to cry, often for the sake of gaining sympathy or getting your own way.

turn-up a surprise; an unexpected reversal of fortune. Also known as a **turn-up for the books**. This latter was originally horseracing slang, where book = bookmaker. When a long-shot wins a race it is a turn-up for the books because they do not have to pay out big as there will have been little money bet on it. Aussie slang since the 1950s.

turps booze or grog. Hence, to be **on the turps** is to be on a drinking binge.

Turramurra tractor Sydney slang, a derogatory term for a city-only 4WD. See **Toorak tractor** for a host of synonyms.

tush the arse or backside. Originally US slang of the 1960s – an alteration of the earlier *tochis*, from Yiddish.

twat **1.** the vagina or vulva. Venerable slang dating back to the 1600s, and possibly an original Anglo-Saxon four-letter word. The language Old Norse had *thveit* 'a slit, a forest clearing', which could metaphorically do for a vagina, and could have been borrowed in Anglo-Saxon times after the Viking invasions brought many Old Norse terms into English. **2.** a stupid person. Occasionally spelt **twot**.

tweak **1.** in cricket, extra spin imparted to a bowl. *He gives the ball a good tweak.* **2.** in surfing, to find good waves; to fluke some good surf.

tweaker a finger-spinner in cricket.

the Tweed Tweed Heads at the mouth of the Tweed River in north-eastern NSW.

tweeds trousers. Aussie slang since the 1950s.

tweenie a beer bought between shouts; a wedge. *Youse blokes are drinking too slow, I'm going to have a tweenie.*

twenty-eight a subspecies of the ringneck parrot found in forested areas of south-western WA. So called in imitation of its call.

24/7 twenty-four hours a day, seven days a week.

twerp an insignificant or stupid person. Also spelt **twirp**. Originally British slang of the 1920s, but used in Australia since at least the 1940s. One story, supported by no less a scholar than J.R.R. Tolkien, states that it originally referred to one *T.W. Earp* of Exeter College, Oxford – who it seemed was generally disliked. A lovely tale, if it is true.

twinkle to urinate. Hence, an act of urination. Imitative of the sound of a stream of urine in a toilet bowl.

twistie a twist-top bottle of beer.

twit a fool or twerp. Originally British slang of the 1920s. Origin unknown. There is an urban legend that twit is a technical term for 'pregnant goldfish', used by fish breeders. This is utter nonsense. Female goldfish lay eggs which are then inseminated by the male – they don't actually get pregnant, though they do get 'egg-laden' or 'ripe'. Even so, an egg-laden goldfish isn't called a twit either. The story probably arose with someone trying to see just what kind of twit would believe such a story.

two bob **1.** old slang term for a florin or two shilling coin. Transferred to twenty cents after the introduction of decimal currency in 1966. Used in many colloquial expressions. To **have two bob each way** is to hedge your bets. If you're **not the full two bob**, then you're a bit slow. Something of little worth is **not worth two bob**. And your **two bob's worth** is an old Aussie version of the usual 'two cents worth'. **2.** a round mark left by a hammer in wood, as from mis-hitting a nail. **3.** a circular pattern made on the ground by driving a car in a tight circle at high speed and causing the rear wheels to skid; a doughnut.

two-bob lair a cheap, flashy lair.

two-bob watch a cheap and crappy watch, literally, one that only cost two bob. Commonly used as a metaphor for dysfunctional people or things. You can be **silly as a two-bob watch**, or **mad as a two-bob watch**, or **bent as a two-bob watch**. If your car doesn't run well, then it **goes like a two-bob watch**. And, if someone is stacking on a turn, then they are **carrying on like a two-bob watch**.

two-dog night a pretty cold night, colder than a one-dog night, but not as cold as a three-dog night. See **dog**, def. 7.

two-fifths of five-eighths of fuck-all an even smaller amount than fuck-all.

two for the Valley in Qld, a polite way of saying 'Up yours!' Comes from the signal of holding up two fingers to indicate to the tram conductor that you want 'Two tickets to Fortitude Valley'.

two ones in two-up, a throw of a head and a tail, requiring the coins to be tossed again. Also simply called **ones**.

two pot screamer someone who gets drunk after consuming very little alcohol.

twosies a childish term for defecation. Compare **onesies**.

2SM Sydney slang for a cup of coffee or tea made with two sugars and milk. Originally punning on the name of a Sydney radio station. Sweeter than the **1SM**.

twot a variant spelling of **twat**.

two-up the classic Australian gambling game in which two coins are thrown off a kip into the air so that they spin. Bets are laid on whether they fall heads or tails – a fall of one head and one tail requiring the coins to be tossed again. Also called **swy** or the **national game**. The term is first recorded back in 1884, and for most of its life the game has been illegal. It was popular with soldiers in World War I and thus became an Anzac Day staple, generally tolerated by the law, and finally made legal for that day alone. Two-up is now also legal in casinos and a few two-up schools in country towns where it is sanctioned as a tourist attraction.

two-up king a leading organiser of two-up schools.

two-up school an organised game of two-up. The most famous of these was Thommo's two-up school in Sydney which was founded by Joe Thomas around about 1910 and flourished up to the 1960s. Joe Thomas died in 1954. In the boom years following World War II it apparently cleared £5000 a week, and had a permanent staff of about 40 – including cockatoos, ring keepers, chuckers out, clerks, and so on. Police raided it often, but it continued nevertheless.

tyke **1.** a Roman Catholic. Aussie slang since the 1900s. Probably an alteration of *Teague* a nickname for an Irishman. **2.** a small kid. Also spelt **tike**.

tyre kicker a person who checks out cars on sale, but has no intention of buying one.

Super

Concepts.

Forest
Hills.

Hi Ben,

Mace Red,

Staying @ ____.

Cheers,

P.

U

uber- the latest cool prefix added to words to make intensive forms. Thus if someone is cooler than cool, they are *uber-cool*. A fan who is more fanatic than the run-of-the-mill fanatical fan is an *uber-fan*. It comes from the German word meaning over or above. A deadset spunk is an *uber-babe* or an *uber-hunk*.

uc dai loi in the Vietnam War, an Australian soldier.

uey a U-turn. Aussie slang since the 1970s. To take a U-turn you either **chuck a uey** or **hang a uey**. While everyone says it, no one is really sure how to spell this great Aussie word. Other efforts have been **u-ie**, **uee**, and even **youee**.

ugari another spelling of **eugari** (see entry).

uggies colloquial shortening of **ugg boots** – which is now a term trademarked by an American company. The origin of the term is not clear. One suggestion is that it is short for *ugly boot*.

ugly as a bagful of arseholes really, really unattractive; very ugly. Even worse is to be **as ugly as a bagful of arseholes tied with a string of farts**.

ugly stick a mythical stick with which a person has been hit in order to make them ugly.

ugly tree a mythical tree from which an ugly person is said to have fallen. *Crikey! He looks like he's fallen out of the ugly tree and hit every branch on the way down.*

uh-oh, spaghetti-os an exclamation indicating that something has gone wrong.

u-ie a variant spelling of **uey** (see entry).

umpie an umpire. Laconic Aussie slang since the 1960s.

umpteen an indefinite number, especially a very large or immeasurable number. Hence, **umpteenth**, as in *This is the umpteenth time I've told you this!*

Uncle Bob Everything is fine! *Okay, that's great. Uncle Bob!* From the phrase **Bob's your uncle**.

Uncle David in Aboriginal English, a fifty dollar note. So called as it has a picture of David Unaipon on it.

uncle from Fiji an imaginary wealthy uncle or financial backer.

Uncle Willy rhyming slang for 'silly'. Originally British from the 19th century.

unco awkward or clumsy. Short for 'unco-ordinated'. Hence, a clumsy person. A common insult used by schoolkids.

uncooked crustacean see the entry for **don't come the raw prawn**.

uncool unfashionable or unsophisticated; totally lacking in cool; daggy. *Paisley is way uncool.*

uncut of a man, uncircumcised.

underdaks underpants. From **daks** meaning pants. Also called **underchunders** or **underdungers**.

underground mutton rabbit meat used as food. Aussie slang since the 1910s.

undergunned among surfies, riding with a surfboard that is too small for the conditions.

unfuckable too ugly to crack it for a root.

unhip not cool; daggy.

unhung of a person, despicable or contemptible – that is, having committed some crime for which they should be hanged.

uni typical Aussie way of shortening 'university'. Since the 1890s.

unleaded low-alcohol beer, as opposed to **super**. Also applied to caffeine-free cola, and the like.

unna isn't it? (in Aboriginal English).

unreal excellent; unbelievably wonderful. *It's been so unreal seeing you again.* Aussie youth slang since the 1970s. Exactly the same as **untold**. *We had untold fun.*

up 1. in kids' games, the player who must catch the other players. Common in Qld, but also used in Tas. See **it** for the full set of regional variations. **2.** of a male, fully lodged in sexual embrace with a partner. *He's probably up her right now.* Hence the classic Australian question regarding the sexual and monetary relationships of a set of people: **Who's up who, and who's paying the rent?** Metaphorically if two people are **up one another** they are crawling to one another. Also, to be **up yourself** is to be fabulously conceited. **3.** furious with someone. *She was up him for being late.*

up a gumtree in all sorts of strife. Aussie slang dating from the 1850s.

upper a stimulant drug like amphetamine. Originally US slang from the 1960s.

upter no good, broken down, worthless. Recorded first during World War I and originally short for **up to putty**, but now interpreted as a euphemism for **up to shit**.

up the creek in a dire predicament; in trouble. If you are in even more trouble then you are **up the creek without a paddle**. These are of course just euphemisms for the full form, used when you are in really, really, really bad trouble, which is **up shit creek without a paddle in a barbed wire canoe**.

up the duff pregnant. Aussie slang since the 1940s. Probably from old slang *duff*=pudding, as in 'in the pudding club'.

up the pole in dire straits; facing difficulties. Aussie slang dating from the 1900s.

up there Cazaly a cry of encouragement, especially at the AFL. Originally a cry directed at Aussie Rules legend Roy Cazaly.

up the spout **1.** ruined; lost. **2.** pawned. **3.** pregnant.

up the stick pregnant. Aussie slang since the 1940s. From *stick* 'penis'.

up the track in Alice Springs, to travel north up the Stuart Highway towards Darwin.

up to putty worthless; no good. Aussie World War I slang. Probably from the inherent worthlessness of putty. This has now been superseded by the coarser expression **up to shit**.

up you Damn you! Fuck you! Aussie slang since the 1940s. Commonly written **upya**, and in the plural, **upyas**.

up your arse! short for 'shove it up your arse'. In other words, to hell with it! Commonly shortened to **up yours**.

up yourself completely conceited. The metaphor behind this is that you are so in love with yourself that you are actually rooting yourself.

urger a racecourse tipster; a petty trickster who cajoles others out of their money. Aussie slang since the 1910s.

us a common Aussie pronoun meaning 'me'. Thus *Give us a look* means 'Give me a look'.

use to take narcotics: *He's been using for about three years now.*

useful as... Australians have been diligent in coining ironic phrases to denote the completely useless. Firstly, there are those with a rural flavour. Such as **useful as a bucket under a bull**, **a dead dingo's donger**, **a dry thunderstorm**, **a sore arse to a boundary rider**, **a wether at a ram sale**, **tits on a bull**, or **two knobs of billy-goat poop**. Then there are anatomical similes, including **useful as a witch's tit**, **a wart on the hip**, **a cunt full of cold water** (or **boiled snow**) or **a third armpit**. Other phrases tend to associate objects that functionally don't go together, such as **useful as a glass door on a dunny**, **a pocket on a singlet**, **a roo-bar on a skateboard**, **a submarine with screen doors**, **an arsehole on a broom**, **a glass eye at a key hole**, and **an ashtray on a motorbike**. Finally, there are those that refer to things out of place, to wit: **useful as a nun at a buck's night**, **a pork chop at a Jewish barbecue**, **a spare dick at a wedding**, or **a tart at a christening**.

user **1.** a drug addict. **2.** a derogatory term for a person who exploits other people in interpersonal relationships with complete disregard for the emotional damage caused.

ute a utility truck or utility van. Economic Aussie slang since the 1940s. In Qld and northern NSW, it is more commonly termed a **tilly**.

uterus a silly term for a utility truck or 'ute'. *I'll have to move the uterus before you can get out.*

vadge the vagina. Also spelt **vag**.

vag **1.** vagrancy. Originally US slang, but used in Oz since the 1870s up until 1979, when the Vagrancy Act was abolished. Hence, **on the vag**, charged with vagrancy. **2.** to arrest on a vagrancy charge.

the Valley the Brisbane suburb of Fortitude Valley. See also **two for the Valley**.

Valspeak that subset of American slang used by Valley girls, that is, teenage girls residing in The Valley, that is, the San Fernando Valley, the northern part of the city of Los Angeles. This particular style of slang exploded onto the world stage in the 1980s and popularised many terms that now are standard slang the world over. Examples include, *airhead, awesome, gnarly, gross, rad, to the max* and the ubiquitous use of *like*.

vamoose to make off or decamp. Commonly used as a command. Chiefly US slang, but used here since the 1920s.

vasso **1.** vaseline. **2.** a vasectomy.

Vatican roulette the rhythm method of contraception.

VB shoulder a sore shoulder resulting from habitual carrying of cases of Victoria Bitter beer.

veeb Victoria Bitter beer; a glass, can or bottle of this. Also **veebers**.

Vee Dub a Volkswagen car. Aussie slang since the 1970s.

veg to relax and become mentally inactive. Short for 'vegetate'. Also known as **veging out**.

vegaquarian a 'vegetarian' who deigns to eat seafood.

Vegas a shortening of **Bris-Vegas** – that is, Brisbane.

Vegemite a thick, black paste, a yeast extract with tons of salt, beloved by all true blue Aussies. In the early 1920s American Dr Cyril P. Callister, working for the Fred Walker Company, later bought by Kraft Foods Limited, invented this iconic Australian food. In 1923 a national contest was held in Australia to find the spread a name, and Fred Walker's daughter chose Vegemite from hundreds of entries. As initial sales were sluggish, due in part to the popularity of the similar British product Marmite, Walker tried to rename Vegemite to 'Parwill' – that is, 'Marmite, but Parwill' (Ma might, but Pa will!). This marketing ploy was tried out in Qld only, but it failed and Vegemite returned to its original name. Of course, Kraft is an American company, but – ah-hem – it's un-Australian to think about that fact when eating Vegemite! In terms of slang, Vegemite is used in the phrase **happy little Vegemite**, used to refer to someone in a good mood. This stems from a Vegemite radio advertising jingle that first hit Australian airwaves in 1954. Also, **little Vegemite** has come to mean a child. Thus you can have a *clever little Vegemite* or a *top little Vegemite* or a *good little Vegemite*. It's always a positive thing to be a little Vegemite. However, there is a 'darker' side to Vegemite slang, for since the 1980s to **drill for vegemite** has meant to practise anal sex. And thus we have the **Vegemite driller**, a disparaging term for a homosexual man, and the **Vegemite valley**, the rectum as used for anal sex.

vegie **1.** vegetable. *He's dug a little vegie patch.* Aussie slang since the 1950s. Hence, **vegies**, vegetables. *No ice-cream till you eat all your vegies.* **2.** of school subjects, of the lowest academic standard. *I'm only doing vegie maths.*

vego a vegetarian. Hence, as a adjective, vegetarian. *I know some great vego dishes.*

veranda bum a large bum.

veranda over the toy shop a kind way of referring to a beer gut.

verbal diarrhoea nonsense spoken at length.

verse among kids, to play against. *We're versing the Catholic school tomorrow.* This word comes about from a misunderstanding of the word 'versus', treating it as though it was 'verses'. Thus to conjugate, if you have

Joey's versus Marist, then *Joey's are versing Marist*, or *Joey's have versed Marist*.

vertically challenged short.

Very Bad beer a derogatory name for Victoria Bitter beer, used by that small percentage of the populace that actually doesn't like it.

vet **1.** a veterinary surgeon. **2.** a war veteran. A borrowing from US English which became especially common only after the Vietnam War. Before this, servicemen who had returned home were normally known as *returned soldiers, returned servicemen* or *ex-servicemen*.

VI of a dead body, putrefied and infested with maggots. Standing for *Vermin Infested*.

Victor Bravo Victoria Bitter beer; a glass, can or bottle of this.

Vic-wit a NSW derogatory term for a Victorian driver, modelled on *dimwit*.

vid a video.

Vietnamatta the Sydney suburb of Cabramatta, noted for its large Vietnamese community.

vinegar stroke the final masturbatory tug at the point of ejaculation. So called from the squinched-up face. Aussie slang since the 1960s.

Vinnie's an opportunity shop run by the St Vincent de Paul Society. *I got this great bargain at Vinnie's today*. Also in the fuller form **St Vinnie's**.

vino wine. *Will I open a bottle of vino?* From the Italian.

vino collapso cask wine – as opposed to **vino vitrio**, wine in a bottle.

vinyl music recorded on vinyl, as opposed to CDs.

Violent Beer Victoria Bitter beer; a glass, can or bottle of this.

the Violet Crumbles a nickname for the Sydney Kings basketball team – so called from their purple and gold colours.

the virus the HIV virus. *He's got the virus*.

visually challenged ugly.

vitamin B Victoria Bitter beer.

vitamin E the drug ecstasy.

voice like a... Someone with an unpleasant, rasping voice is said to have a **voice like a chain being dragged through gravel**. An even harsher voice is described as being **like a chainsaw hitting granite**. Other poetic descriptions of vocal cacophony are a **voice like a strangled fowl**, a **voice like a billygoat sitting on tin** and a **voice like a knife that has been left stuck in a lemon too long**. Compare **head like a...**

Volksie a Volkswagen car.

Vomit Bomb a can of Victoria Bitter – a term used by haters of the said amber fluid.

VPL the edge of underwear seen through an overgarment. Standing for *Visible Panty Line*.

Vuh Buh a drink of Victoria Bitter beer – jocularly pronounced as the initials in baby talk.

wack a variant spelling of **whack**. This variation also occurs in other forms such as **whacker**, which is sometimes spelt **wacker**.

Wacko Jacko an international press nickname for Michael Jackson. Little do they know that this name was coined by an Australian journalist working for Brisbane's *Courier-Mail*. Of course, in Australia, the same nickname was applied to former AFL player and personality Mark Jackson.

wad **1.** a large sum of money. **2.** a stupid or annoying person; a jerk. Chiefly used in the military. **3.** for a man to **shoot his wad** is to ejaculate.

waddy a hefty club. Named after the traditional Aboriginal weapon, the name for which comes from Dharug, the extinct Aboriginal language of the Sydney region.

wag to deliberately stay away from school without permission; to play truant. Originally 19th century British slang. See **wop** for an original Aussie variant.

Wagga Beach local name for a strip of sand on the bend of the Murrumbidgee River at Wagga.

wagga rug a rough improvised blanket made of wheat bags. Also called a **wagga blanket** or simply a **wagga**. Aussie slang since the 1900s. Named after the township of Wagga Wagga in central NSW.

walkabout **1.** a journey taken on foot by an Aboriginal in which they live by traditional methods. Recorded since the 1910s and originally Aboriginal pidgin. See **go walkabout**. **2.** a short walk or inspection, often to see what is going on. *I'll just take a walkabout and see what I can find.*

Wallaby Bob's cousin ruined, wrecked, rooted (get it? *Roo Ted* is Wallaby Bob's cousin). *Man I am feeling like Wallaby Bob's cousin.* Aussie slang since the 1970s. Also heard in the form **Wallaby Bobbed**, as in *I'm a bit Wallaby Bobbed at the moment.*

wallaby jack a type of sturdy jack commonly used on four-wheel drives. It has a long handle which in use looks a bit like a wallaby's tail bouncing up and down. Technically known as a hi-lift jack.

wallaby track the open road as formerly used by swagmen. Also simply called **the wallaby**. Hence, **on the wallaby**, living as a swagman looking for work.

wallie a wallet.

wallop booze. From its poleaxing effect.

walloper a police officer – as viewed by those on the receiving end. Aussie slang since the 1940s.

wally a fool; a stupid person. Originally British slang of the 1960s.

Walter Mitty a person who poses as a returned war veteran. Named after *Walter Mitty*, the title character of James Thurber's short story *The Secret Life of Walter Mitty* (1939) and successful movie of the same title starring Danny Kaye (1947), who is given to self-aggrandising daydreams especially involving heroic war scenarios.

waltzing Matilda travelling on foot with a swag to look for work. See **Matilda** for more information.

wandering hands the hands of a man who 'can't keep his hands to himself'.

wang **1.** the **whanger** (see entry). **2.** to hit. *I wanged him on the head.*

wank **1.** to masturbate. Hence, an act of masturbation. *I was caught having a wank.* Originally British slang of the 1940s. Origin uncertain – perhaps from Scottish and northern English dialect *whank, whang* 'to beat or flog', but perhaps a nasalised variant of **whack** (see entry). **2.** a load of self-indulgent crap. *A three thousand dollar weekend to get in touch with yourself – what a wank!* **3.** a person exhibiting self-indulgent behaviour; a wanker.

wankasaurus a very egotistical, self-important or obnoxious person; a really, really big wanker.

wanker **1.** literally, a masturbator. **2.** a contemptible person; a self-indulgent or egotistical person; someone who is up themselves. A very common insult in Australia.

wanker tank a city-only 4WD that never sees off-road conditions. See **Toorak tractor** for a host of synonyms.

wankery conceited rubbish; wanky behaviour. Also called **wankerism**.

wankfest what happens when a bunch of self-satisfied wankers get together.

wank off **1.** to masturbate. **2.** Go away! Piss off!

wank on to go on at length; to rabbit on, especially with self-indulgent talk.

wanky pretentious, conceited, self-indulgent.

wank yourself to delude yourself with visions of grandeur.

wannabe **1.** a person who aspires to be like someone else. *He's a Rambo wannabe.* **2.** a person who aspires to a particular role in life but has not achieved it. *She's an Olympic wannabe.* **3.** a person who poses as a returned war veteran. Also called a **Walter Mitty** (see entry).

warby shabby, grotty, unkempt; disgusting or unappealing. Aussie slang since the 1920s. Hence, a **warb** is a grotty person or a derelict. Perhaps from Scottish *warbie* 'a type of maggot which infests cattle'.

war paint make-up, cosmetics. Originally US slang dating from the 1860s.

warp speed an exceedingly fast speed. Originally from the nomenclature of science fiction.

warrigal **1.** a dingo. This term comes from Dharug, the extinct Aboriginal language of the Sydney region, in which it meant 'wild dingo', as opposed to a domesticated one (see **dingo**). **2.** an Aborigine living in the traditional manner as opposed to one who has become assimilated into the white community; a myall. **3.** a wild horse or brumby.

Warwick Farms Aussie rhyming slang for 'arms'. After the name of a Sydney racecourse. Commonly shortened to **warwicks**.

washboard stomach a stomach with well-defined, well-toned, rippling muscles.

washer-upperer a kids' term for one who washes the dishes.

waste to murder or kill, especially by shooting. Originally US slang.

wasted **1.** completely exhausted. **2.** totally pissed or zonked out on drugs – or both.

waste of space a stupid or useless person.

water burner a poor cook.

water fountain a drinking fountain, especially in Qld, Tas, SA and WA. See **bubbler** for the full set of regionalisms.

watering hole a pub or bar. Also called a **waterhole**.

water sports sexual activities involving urination.

waterworks **1.** the bladder and urinary system. **2.** to **turn on the waterworks** is to begin to cry, often for the sake of gaining sympathy or getting your own way.

wax in kids' games, to form a team with another player; to take alternate turns at batting, kicking, and the like; to partner someone. *Jonno and Tez are waxing* means they are partnering one another. A great bit of Aussie kids' slang. Probably from the verb *whack* 'to share or divvy up'.

waxhead a derogatory term for a surfie. So called in reference to the wax used on surfboards. Also shortened to **waxie**.

way extremely, totally, fully. Used as an intensifier. *She's way cool. It's open 'til way late.* Originally US slang, picked up by Aussie kids in the 1980s.

the Wazzir Anzac slang for the red-light district in Cairo. From the Arabic *Haret el Wasser.* Scene of the legendary **Battle of the Wazzir**.

wedding tackle the male genitalia.

wedge a beer bought between shouts; a tweenie. *Gibbo couldn't wait for the next round, so he had a wedge.*

wedgie **1.** a prank in which someone's pants are grabbed and pulled up sharply in order to wedge the clothing uncomfortably into the anal cleft. Originally US, but happily adopted by Aussie kids. **2.** a wedge-tailed eagle.

wee urine; an act of urination. *I'm just going for a wee.* Originally British slang of the 1930s, and imitative of the sound of a stream of urine onto the side of a chamber pot. Hence, as a verb, to urinate. Commonly used with children. Also in the duplicated form **wee-wee**.

weed **1.** a weak, puny person, especially a male; a weakling. **2.** a surfer. **3.** marijuana. *Where can I score some weed?* Also called the **evil weed**. **4.** tobacco; hence, a cigarette. Now rare, if used at all.

wee juggler a Major Mitchell cockatoo. A beautiful example of the 'Law of Hobson-Jobson' at work in Australia. The Law of

Hobson-Jobson is the linguistic process whereby a word borrowed from one language is changed so that it resembles words in another language. Of course Major Mitchell cockatoos are not small birds that can juggle. The word is a corruption of the word *wijugula*, the name of the bird in the Aboriginal language Wiradjuri, from central NSW.

weener the penis, especially a small one. Hence, a man with a small penis. Also called a **weenie**.

weero in WA, the cockatiel. From the south-west WA Aboriginal language Nyungar.

weirdo one who behaves in a strange, abnormal, or eccentric way.

weirdometer a mythical machine that measures weirdness.

well-endowed **1.** of a man, with large genitalia. Also known as **well-hung**. **2.** of a woman, with large breasts. Also known as **well-stacked**.

wellington an act of sexual intercourse. Short for *wellington boot*, rhyming slang for 'root'. Australian slang since the 1970s.

well-oiled drunk.

Wenty the Sydney suburb of Wentworthville.

were you born in a tent? a phrase used to reprimand a person who has forgotten to close a door.

Werribee trout Melbourne slang for a floating piece of human excrement in the ocean. See **blind mullet** for a swag of synonyms.

Werris Creek **1.** Aussie rhyming slang for 'Greek'. **2.** rhyming slang for 'leak', that is, an act of urination.

Werro the Sydney suburb of Werrington.

westie your typical Aussie yobbo type – mullet haircut, flannos and jeans, from the low socio-economic stratum. Originally a derogatory term for a person from the western suburbs of Sydney. In Sydney, **westie** is applied disparagingly to any person living west of your own suburb – thus a Bondi inhabitant may call a person from Ryde a westie, but Ryde inhabitants would not consider themselves as such, and instead apply the term to people from Parramatta, who in turn apply it to people from Penrith, and so on. Only inner city trendies and residents of beachy suburbs are not ever labelled westies. As a general rule of thumb, the typical westie features become more prominent the further you move west from Sydney's centre – though, that is also true the further you go north and south. First recorded in the 1970s, **westie** has now spread to most of NSW, and is even used in Ballarat where the less affluent part of town is to the west.

the Wet the wet season in Australia's tropical north.

wet fart a fart in which some liquid waste is also ejected.

wet patch a wet area left on bedding after sexual intercourse.

wet sock an insipid, characterless person; a drip; a killjoy.

wettie among surfers, a wetsuit. Hence, **wettie rash**, a rash caused by the wearing of wetsuits.

whack **1.** to place in a rough or slap-dash manner. *Just whack it down in the corner. She whacked a dirty big line through it.* **2.** a go or attempt. *I'll take a whack at any job.* **3.** a portion or share. *He still has to pay his whack.* A share of booty. *Give me my whack now.* **4.** an act of male masturbation; a wank.

whacked **1.** exhausted. *I am whacked from all that work.* **2.** out of it on drugs. Also known as **whacked out**.

whacker a stupid person; an eccentric or weirdo. Literally, one who masturbates (see **whack off**). Aussie slang since the 1960s.

whacko **1.** eccentric, crazy; bizarre. **2.** an expression of surprise, pleasure, delight, and the like. Aussie slang since the 1930s. Also, since the 1940s, in the extended forms **whacko the chook, whacko the diddle oh** and **whacko the did**.

whack off of a male, to masturbate.

whack off with to steal. *Who whacked off with my ciggies?*

whack the illy an obsolete phrase meaning to perform a confidence trick or to be a con artist. The origin of the term **illywhacker**. No one quite knows what an 'illy' is – but it may be a variant of the term **eelie** (see entry).

whack up to divide up; to share out.

whacky baccy marijuana.

whale a big-time gambler. As opposed to a **minnow**.

wham bam thank you ma'am descriptive of the act of sexual intercourse, especially when quick and unromantic. Also used in relation to anything done quickly and without care.

whammy a supernatural spell or curse directed at a person. A **double whammy** is a stroke of amazing bad luck, or two strokes of bad luck coming together. Even worse are the **triple whammy** and the **quadruple whammy**. Originally 1940s US slang, and popularised by *Li'l Abner* (created by Al Capp in the 1950s) in which a character named Evil-Eye Fleegle would paralyse people with either a *single whammy* 'a look with one evil eye' or a *double whammy* 'a look with both evil eyes'.

whanger the penis. Also called a **whang**.

wharfie a dock worker. Aussie slang since the 1910s.

whassup a form of greeting used among cool adolescents. *Whassup, bro?* A 1990s borrowing from the US.

what can I do you for? a humorous way of asking 'What can I do for you?'

whatever 'It doesn't matter' or 'As you wish'. *You can come if you like. Whatever.* Often used as a dismissive rejoinder. *Oh, whatever! Let's just get on with it.* A recent adoption of US usage.

what price...? What do you think of... ? *What price the old man now?* Generally a rhetorical question. Originally 19th century British slang, from horseracing parlance, where it is a question asking what odds are currently being offered on a horse.

whatsit a thingummyjig. *Where's the whatsit gone?* Also called a **whosey-whatsit**.

what's that got to do with the price of fish? What's the relevance of what you just said? Sometimes this is expressed as **what's that got to do with the price of potatoes?** Note, the sarcasm implied by these phrases will be lost if you are actually discussing the price of fish or potatoes, so please be careful.

what's the deal? What is going on? An Americanism from the 1940s, made its way Down Under in the 1990s.

what's the go? What is going on? Why is that so?

what's-their-face a term for someone whose name you cannot remember. If you haven't forgotten their sex you can say either **what's-her-face** or **what's-his-face**, as the case may be.

what's your poison? what would you like to drink?

what the fuck! a harsh and impolite way of saying 'What the Hell!'

wheelie 1. driving on the back wheel of a bicycle or motorbike with the front wheel held in the air. 2. a skidding of the driving wheels of a motor car while accelerating. 3. a person in a wheelchair. Not very PC, this one.

wheel man the driver of a getaway car.

wheels a motor vehicle. *I need to get some wheels quick.* Originally British slang of the 1950s.

when the shit hits the fan when the trouble really begins.

whiffy smelly, especially used of a person in dire need of a wash or some deodorant, or both.

while your arsehole points to the ground while one is alive and kicking. *I'll never come at it, not while my arsehole points to the ground.* Aussie slang since the 1950s.

whim-wham for a goose's bridle a fanciful, non-existent object, used as an answer to an unwanted question. *'What's that hole in the backyard?' 'It's a whim-wham for a goose's bridle.'* Originally used in British dialect. Also called a **wigwam** or a **wing-wong for a goose's bridle**. A *whim-wham* is a trinket. The idea of a goose's bridle is totally fanciful so the whole phrase is an elaborate put-down.

whinge to complain or grizzle. An ancient word that goes right back to the original Anglo-Saxon. In Australia it appears in the 1930s, but only became popular after World War II where, presumably, it was picked up from the Brits by men and women serving overseas. Occasionally spelt **winge**.

whingeing Pom an English person who is always criticising and complaining about life in Australia. Aussies have been whingeing about whingeing Poms since the 1960s.

whinger an inveterate complainer; a bloody nark who's always got something to grumble about.

whip-around an impromptu collection of money for a present, farewell, good cause, etc.

whippy 1. the finishing post in children's games. A slang term peculiar to NSW and Qld. 2. a hiding place for money. 3. money stashed away. 4. in gambling, the pot or kitty. 5. money found and then kept by police when executing a warrant.

whip the cat to vent frustration over something that can't be changed; to cry over spilt milk. An Aussie slang expression since the 1840s.

whirly-whirly a miniature whirlwind that picks up dust and rubbish – common in the outback. Also called a **whirly-wind**, especially in Qld.

white-ant to undermine a person, organisation or enterprise. Aussie slang since the 1920s.

white can **1.** a can of Carlton Draught beer. **2.** a can of Swan Light beer. As opposed to a **blue**, **green**, **red** or **yellow can** (see entries).

whitefellow a European Australian, as opposed to an Aboriginal. So called since the 1820s. Originally a word from Aboriginal pidgin English, formed as a counterpart to **blackfellow** (see entry). Commonly used as an adjective to refer to non-Aboriginal concerns or activities. *That's whitefellow business.* Also spelt **whitefella** and **whitefeller**, to capture the usual pronunciation.

white leghorn a woman dressed to play lawn bowls.

white maggot a derogatory term for an Aussie Rules umpire.

white mouse in the Vietnam War, a local Vietnamese police officer. So called from their uniforms.

white pointer an Anglo female lying on her back sunbathing topless.

white rabbits among kids, a phrase to invoke immunity from being punched. Especially used on the first day of any month with the letter 'r' in its name – failure to say it can result in your being punched repeatedly until you do. This is an old British folk tradition brought to Australia. It can also be used in the game of **punch buggy** to make yourself safe from being hit. Another use is when sitting around a camp fire – if the smoke is blowing in your face you say 'I hate white rabbits' to make the smoke change direction.

white trash originally, the poor white population in the southern states of the US. Later, used of poor white people anywhere. In the US, the term dates back to the 1830s, and it has been used in Australia since the early 1900s, but has only become common in the last few decades.

whitey a racist designation for a person of European stock. In Australia equivalent to **whitefellow**, but used pejoratively.

whizz **1.** amphetamine. **2.** used among car salesmen, to illegally wind back the odometer on a car prior to reselling it.

whizzer a variant spelling of **wyssa**.

whoa-boy a drain and embankment dug diagonally across a steep farm track.

the whole box and dice everything; the whole kit and caboodle. Fair dinkum Aussie expression used since the 1880s.

a whole nother completely different. Created by the insertion of 'whole' into the word 'another'. *That's a whole nother story.*

whole shebang everything; the works; the lot. Originally 19th century US slang. The origin of 'shebang' is unknown.

whoo an exclamation of pleasure and excitement. *Whoo yeah!* Also extended to **whoo-ee**.

whoopee **1.** an exclamation of joy and elation – equivalent to 'Hooray!' However, commonly spoken with extreme sarcasm to express just the opposite – equivalent to 'So what!' In this second sense often in the form **whoopee-do**. **2.** to **make whoopee** is to engage in uproarious merrymaking or to engage in sexual merrymaking.

whooshka a recent expression imitating the sound of something happening suddenly. *I opened the box and whooshka, out raced the cat.*

whopper **1.** something uncommonly large for its kind. **2.** a big lie.

whosie-whatsit a thingummyjig. Also simply called a **whosie** or a **whatsit**.

who's robbing this coach? Who is in charge here? A rhetorical question meaning 'Stay out of it!' The story goes that Ned Kelly was bailing up a coach one day and proclaimed 'I'm going to rob all the men and fuck all the women'. To which one of the male passengers said, 'You can't do that, you dreadful man', only to be shouted down by a female passenger saying, 'Who's robbing this coach, you or Mister Kelly?' Clearly apocryphal, but why ruin a good story with the truth?

who's up who and who's paying the rent? a question regarding the sexual and monetary relationships of a group of people. Aussie slang dating back to World War II.

WHS the Wandering Hands Society – that is, men who can't keep their hands to themselves.

wicked used as an intensifier: extremely good, cool, excellent. *That's a wicked coat.* Also, as an adverb, well, brilliantly. *I hope you do wicked in your exams.* In common use by adolescents and schoolkids. Borrowed in the 1980s from US slang.

widdle **1.** baby talk for 'little'. *I just want a widdle bit.* **2.** urine; an act of urination. *I'm just going for a widdle.* Originally British slang of the 1950s. Hence, as a verb, to urinate. Commonly used with children.

wide boy a swindler, petty crim or spiv. Originally British slang of the 1930s.

wide brown land Australia. After the 1908 poem by Dorothea Mackellar.

wide-on sexual arousal in a woman. A counterpart to the male **hard-on**.

widgie in the 1950s and 60s, a teenage female delinquent; the counterpart of the **bodgie**. Widgies were especially noted for wild behaviour and free sexuality, and for dressing in tight, revealing skirts and sweaters, and having short, duck-tailed haircuts. The origin of the term is a bit of a mystery. One theory is that it is a blend of the words *women* and *bodgie*, but this doesn't have the ring of truth about it. Another more charming solution is that it referred to the hairstyle which had a vee or *wedge* at the back – it is but a small step from *wedgie* to *widgie*.

widgie talk a type of pig Latin used by widgies.

widow-maker **1.** a dead tree branch which is likely to snap off and kill a person below. One of the much-touted dangers of the Australian landscape which put fear into the hearts of overseas visitors. **2.** in Aussie Rules, a very high kick which, as it descends, puts the marker in danger of injury; a hospital kick.

widow's curtains the flabby triceps of an overweight or matronly woman.

wife beater **1.** a long thin loaf of bread. In the spirit of egalitarianism, also called a **husband beater**. **2.** a workman's blue singlet. A dreadful slur on the working class male.

wife's best friend the penis.

wife starver a prisoner serving time for defaulting on maintenance payments. Aussie slang since the 1910s. More forcefully called a **cunt starver**.

wigga a disparaging term for a white person who emulates African-American style and culture, specifically hip-hop or rap culture. A blend of *white* and *nigger*. Also spelt **wigger**.

wigged out stoned on dope.

wigwam for a goose's bridle an Aussie variant of **whim-wham for a goose's bridle** (see entry). An attempt to make a recognisable word out of *whim-wham* even if it doesn't make sense.

wild colonial boy a bushranger. So called after the eponymous hero of the famous folk song, dating from about 1880. Hence, a young, spirited, Aussie bloke of fierce independence and having a true blue disregard for authority; a larrikin.

wild man of Bungaree a wild-looking, unkempt fellow. *Where have you been? You look like the wild man of Bungaree.* From Bungaree near Ballarat, Victoria.

William the third a piece of excrement. Also the act of defecation. Rhyming slang for 'turd'. Right royally related to **Henry the third** and **Richard the third**. The **William** variation on the theme is an Australian invention, the other two being borrowed from British slang.

willing gutsy and eager; willing to fight; willing to take on any challenge. Aussie slang since the 1890s.

willy **1.** a wallet. **2.** an amount of money for gambling. **3.** the penis. **4.** to **chuck a willy** or **throw a willy** is to throw a tantrum.

willy-willy a miniature whirlwind that picks up dust and rubbish, common in the outback. Recorded from the 1890s. From the Aboriginal language Yindjibarndi of the Fortescue River district of WA. Compare **cockeyed bob**.

wimp a meek, spineless person, especially a man. Originally US slang dating back to the 1920s, but only reaching Australian shores in the 1980s. Probably after J. Wellington Wimpy, feeble uncle of Popeye the Sailor Man.

wimpish of the nature of a wimp; gutless, cowardly. Also, **wimpy**.

wimp out to renege in a cowardly manner.

the Windies the West Indian international cricket team. Aussie slang since the 1960s.

window-licker an intellectually disabled person. Not very PC this one!

Windoze a derogatory term for the Microsoft Windows PC operating system – the joke being that one is liable to *doze* while waiting for it to do something.

wind wanker a contemptuous term for a windsurfer, especially used by surfies.

wine-dot a habitual drinker of wine; a plonk artist. Punning on *Wyandotte*, a breed of chicken. Aussie slang since the 1940s.

winge a variant spelling of **whinge**.

wing nut a person with large, protruding ears. From the nut (as in nuts and bolts) of the same name which has two protruding wings.

wing-wong for a goose's bridle an Aussie variant of **whim-wham for a goose's bridle** (see entry).

Winnies Winfield brand cigarettes. Coming in two colours, **Winnie Blues** and **Winnie Reds**.

wino one addicted to drinking wine. Originally US slang from the 1910s.

win on to successfully flirt with someone.

wipe to dismiss or reject a person; to refuse to have anything to do with them. Aussie slang since the 1940s.

wish the fluffy airborne seed of various plants, such as the moth vine or Scotch thistle. If you catch one, you can make a wish on it. See **Santa Claus** for synonyms.

wizz **1.** amphetamine; speed. **2.** an act of urinating; urine. Also spelt **wiss**. **3.** the female genitals. Also called a **wizzer**.

wobbly a tantrum; hence to **chuck a wobbly** is to throw a tantrum. If an engine or machine has chucked a wobbly, then it has broken down.

wobigong something that does not go with other things. The odd one out.

wodge a large lump, pile or mass.

wof a fool or idiot. An acronym from *Waste Of Flesh*.

wog **1.** a person of Mediterranean or Middle Eastern extraction, or of similar complexion and appearance. This is the peculiarly Australian usage of the word. Originally it was British nautical slang dating back to the 1920s and referring to Indians. In Britain it then came to include Arab peoples, and eventually the Spanish, French, and so on. Hence the English xenophobic catchphrase 'Wogs begin at Calais'. Australian soldiers stationed in the Middle East in World War II picked the word up and brought it back home, where it was subsequently applied to post-war migrants from southern Europe, otherwise known as New Australians. These were largely Italians, Greeks, Maltese, Yugoslavians, Poles and Lebanese. Unlike the British use, Indians and Pakistanis are not generally classed as 'wogs' in Australia. For most of its life 'wog' was used in an out-and-out racist way, but since the 1980s the word began to be used by those very people at whom it had been directed to refer to themselves, and is now firmly established as a word of pride within the ethnic population. However, it is still offensive when used by Anglos. As to the origin, well, there is an unsubstantiated theory that it is an acronym from *Worthy Oriental Gentleman*. This is one of those after-the-fact explanations that is not worth wasting half a brain cell on. The other prevailing theory is that it is a shortening of *golliwog*, referring to the frizzy hair of wogs – which doesn't really make much sense either since Indians (to whom it was first applied) aren't frizzy-haired. In the final analysis all we can positively say is 'origin unknown'. **2.** any language spoken by 'wogs'. *They spent half the evening speaking in wog.* **3.** in World War II, to trade with the local inhabitants of a foreign country where a soldier was stationed. *He's been making a lot of money wogging army boots.* **4.** a germ, especially a germ leading to a minor ailment such as a cold or a stomach upset. Hence, a cold or other illness caused by a germ. *He's been off work all week with a bad wog.* Aussie slang since the 1930s. In fact, this meaning is not known outside Australia and can be the cause of confusion, such as the time an Australian woman working in England rang her boss and told him she couldn't come to work because she was *in bed with a wog!* Formerly, the term was also applied to any grub, beetle, or the like, that caused damage to crops. In origin this is a completely different word to the ethnic *wog*, but nevertheless just where it comes from is a mystery.

wogball soccer – which is especially popular with Australians of Mediterranean descent.

wog boy a young adult male 'wog'. The feminine counterpart is the **wog girl** or the **wog chick**.

wog chariot a derisive word for a type of car favoured by young ethnic boys – in the 1970s these were invariably Valiants, but now are more likely to be some flashy, tricked-up, muscle car with subwoofers from hell. This term was popularised by Ted Bullpit in the TV comedy *Kingswood Country*.

woggify **1.** to imbue with 'wog' style or culture. **2.** to hot a car up.

woggy **1.** stereotypically ethnic. As *woggy food*, a *woggy dress*, or a *woggy car*. **2.** suffering from a cold or other minor illness.

wog mansion a large, two-storeyed, extravaganza of a domestic home, as commonly built by Southern European immigrants – often complete with Corinthian columns and a three-tiered fountain.

wombat **1.** your typical, chauvinistic Aussie bloke – so called because he 'eats, roots and leaves'. This joke has been around since the 1960s. **2.** someone who is slow-moving or slow-witted. Aussie slang since the 1900s. So called after the well-known nocturnal, burrowing marsupial. The word itself comes from the extinct Aboriginal language of the Sydney region, Dharug.

wombat-headed dull, stupid, block-headed. A great Aussie insult originated by Ned Kelly in his famous Jerilderie letter of 1879. Ned asked: 'Is my brothers and sisters and my mother not to be pitied also who has no alternative only to put up with the brutal and cowardly conduct of a parcel of big ugly fat-necked wombat-headed big-bellied magpie-legged narrow-hipped splaw-footed sons of Irish Bailiffs or English landlords which is better known as Officers of Justice or Victorian Police?'

womb broom a crass term for a large penis.

womble of a wombat, to walk with the characteristic gait of a wombat. *He was just wombling along.* Nothing to do with the cute furry characters which inhabit Wimbledon.

womp to bodysurf.

wongi a yarn or chat among friends. Also, as a verb, to talk or chat. Originally Aboriginal pidgin English.

wood butcher a rough carpenter.

wood duck a person who is easily duped. Also called a **woodie**.

wooden to job someone on the head with a great big club.

woody an erect penis. Originally US slang of the 1990s.

woofering an initiation punishment in the Australian Army in which the nozzle of a vacuum cleaner is applied to the genitals of a male cadet.

woolly nose in SA, a railway fettler. See also **hairy leg** and **snake charmer**.

woolly pullie Royal Australian Navy slang for a pullover.

woolly woofter Aussie rhyming slang for 'poofter'.

Woop Woop an imaginary town or district that is extremely remote. First recorded back in 1918 and formed by duplicating a sound, like many Aussie placenames of Aboriginal origin. Back in the 1920s there was a sawmill named Woop Woop about 10 km north west of Wilga. It was established in 1925, and it is believed the name is derived from the sound made by frogs common in the area. The New Zealand version of this is **the wop wops**, which has been around since the 1950s.

wooza **1.** a derogatory term for a young woman. Also called a **wooz** or **woozie**. **2.** the female genitals.

wop **1.** a racist term for an Italian. Originally US slang of the 1910s. Perhaps from Italian *guappo* 'bold' or 'showy'. **2.** to take a day off school illegally; to wag. Dating back to the 1940s, and perhaps originating in the frequency with which migrant children took time off school to help in their family businesses.

wopcacker a stunning example of something. Aussie slang around from the 1940s, but not heard any longer. Still common in NZ though.

worker's crack bum cleavage showing above a worker's low-slung stubbies.

work like a drover's pup to work your heart out.

work your guts out to work as hard as is possible; to slave.

worms thin worm-like extrusions created by spreading Vegemite and butter or margarine on two Arnott's Vita-Weat biscuits and squeezing them together. A favourite pastime of Aussie kids.

worrywart a chronic worrier. Originally US slang.

wouldn't be dead for quids an Aussie expression of lust for life.

wouldn't feed it to a Jap on Anzac Day said of food, absolutely disgusting.

wouldn't it! an exclamation indicating dismay or disgust. Aussie slang since the 1940s. It is actually a euphemistic shortening of **wouldn't it root you!** Other forms of the phrase are also euphemistic, such as **wouldn't it rip you**, **wouldn't it rotate you**, or **wouldn't it rot your socks**.

wouldn't know if a tram was up him until it rang its bell a phrase descriptive of a particularly unaware fellow. There are a lot of similar phrases, dating back to the 1960s, including **wouldn't know if his arse was on fire** and the delightful **wouldn't know if a band was up him until he got the drum.**

wouldn't work in an iron lung a phrase describing a completely lazy person. The notion is that even if something else was doing the breathing for them, they wouldn't work. Great Aussie slang since the 1970s.

wowser a killjoy, spoilsport or nark; a person who doesn't know how to have fun and wishes to prevent others from doing so; a puritanical prude who publicly complains about other people's behaviour; a no-good do-gooder. It first appears in the 1890s in the Sydney *Truth* newspaper and was later claimed by the editor John Norton to be of his own coinage – from the slogan *We Only Want Social Evils Remedied*. However, some correspondents to that paper at the time denied Norton's claim.

wowserish prudish. Also, **wowseristic**.

wowserism puritanical behaviour.

wrapped enthralled; stoked. *He was wrapped with his new promotion.*

wrap-up an enthusiastic approval or recommendation. *He gave the new product a good wrap-up.* Also, simply a **wrap**. *It got a good wrap.* Aussie slang since the 1930s.

wrap yourself around to eat. *Here, wrap yourself around these sangers.*

wrinklie an elderly person.

write yourself off to do something that totally incapacitates you – such as getting totally pissed or tearing your cruciate ligament.

wrong'un **1.** in cricket, a delivery bowled by a wrist-spinner which looks as if it will break one way but in fact goes the other; a bosie or googly. **2.** a horse that has not been run on its merits. Also known as a **dead'un**. **3.** a criminal.

wrote the book on to be an expert at, especially a self-proclaimed expert. *Do I know anything about picture-hanging? I wrote the book on it!*

wuss an overly timid or ineffectual person; weakling or wimp. Originally US slang of the 1970s and borrowed into Oz in the 1990s.

wuss bag an exceedingly pathetic wuss.

wussy feeble, cowardly, wimpish.

wyssa in the Australian Antarctic Territory, a telex message. So called after the arbitrarily devised telex code *wyssa* which stood for 'All my love darling'. Also spelt **wyzza** or **whizzer**.

X-phile a fan of the television show *The X-Files*.

XYZ a polite aside informing someone that their fly is undone. Standing for 'eXamine Your Zipper'.

-y a variant spelling of the suffix **-ie** (see entry).

the Y the YMCA or YWCA.

yabber to talk or chat; to chatter or rabbit on. *Stop yabbering will ya?* Aussie slang since the 1840s, from an Aboriginal language. Hence, a conversation. *We had a bit of a yabber about it.*

yabby a freshwater crayfish native to central and eastern mainland Australia, and introduced into Western Australia and Tasmania. The name comes from the Aboriginal language Wembawemba of central Victoria. Yabbies are also known throughout the country as **crayfish** or simply **cray**, but should not be confused with lobsters or rock lobsters which are marine creatures, and do not live in fresh water (the confusion arises from the fact that rock lobsters are called crayfish in Tasmania, and parts of SA and NSW). But, getting back to the well-known freshwater crayfish, these are known around the country by a number of interesting regionalisms. Alphabetically, **crawbob** is found in NSW and Qld; **crawchie** in coastal Qld and north-east NSW; **craybob** in NSW and south Qld; and **craydab** in NSW and ACT. To add another level of confusion, these tasty little beggars are also known colloquially as **lobsters**. This has been reported from all states, but is most common in Qld, where the word is shortened to **lobby**. Clear as mud? Well, I haven't finished yet. In WA, where the yabby is a recent import, there are a bunch of other native freshwater crayfish which go by the names of **gilgie** (pronounced with an initial soft 'g', and thus also spelt **jilgie**, and colloquialised as **joogie**), **koonac** and **marron**. These three look quite different to the trained eye, but to the neophyte they are often confused with the yabby, and vice versa, and so the names are often used loosely. Apart from this, there are also the terms **blackie**, **bluey** and **greenie**, which all refer to different stages of yabby development.

yabbying fishing for yabbies. Generally done with a piece of rotting meat attached to a line – you wait until the yabby has its nipper on the meat and then you fling it out onto the land.

yacca a South Australianism for the xanthorrhoea or grass tree. From an Aboriginal language.

yack **1.** to talk or chatter. Originally British slang. Hence, a chat. *We were having a yack about it only yesterday.* **2.** to vomit. Hence, an instance of vomiting.

yacker talk or chatter. *There was a lot of yacker going on.* Hence, as a verb, to chat. Aussie slang since the 1880s. Not to be confused with **yakka**.

yada yada yada and so on and so forth; blah blah blah. Recently adopted from US television shows. Also spelt **yadda yadda yadda**.

yaffle to waffle on. A term especially common in Tasmania.

yahoo a rough, coarse or uncouth person. From the *Yahoos*, a race of brutes having the form of human beings and embodying all the degrading passions of humanity, invented by Jonathan Swift in his book *Gulliver's Travels*, 1726.

yahoo around to act in a rough, loutish manner.

yakka hard work, especially manual labour. Aussie slang since the 1880s and coming from the Aboriginal language Yagara, from the Brisbane region. Now most commonly found in the collocation **hard yakka**, or in the phrase **all yack and no yakka**, used to describe someone who's always talking about what they're going to do instead of doing it.

Yank a mildly derisive term for an American. Shortened from **Yankee**, which is also used, but not as commonly. Originally an American word for New Englanders, and during the Civil War applied to the soldiers of the Federal army. Origin uncertain.

Yankeeland a derisive nickname for the United States.

Yankee shout a social outing where each person pays their own way. Aussie slang since the 1940s.

Yank tank a large car of American manufacture.

yardie **1.** a general assistant in a hotel; a yardman. **2.** a person employed to do the running around in a car yard; the yard gopher.

yard pet among used car salesmen, a car which doesn't sell.

yarn **1.** a talk or chat. *We were just having a quiet yarn about old times.* Amazing as it may seem, this meaning is peculiar to Australia and New Zealand. The verb use, to chat or gossip, is also common in Oz and NZ, but is also used elsewhere. **2.** an exaggerated story or tale, especially a long one about extraordinary events. Hence, to tell stories or tall tales.

Yarra banker a soapbox orator on the banks of the Yarra.

the Yartz the Strine pronunciation of 'the Arts'.

yea (accompanied by a hand gesture to indicate size) this much. *She's a little girl, only about yea high.* Originally US slang of the 1960s. Origin unknown.

yeah, no a very recent expression used to show agreement, despite its literal ambiguity. *Yeah, no, you're right about that.*

yeah, right! yeah, sure! Used with a sarcastic tone to express disagreement.

yee-haa **1.** an exclamation of abandonment when commencing some exciting activity. Originally the clichéd, exultant cry of the US cowboy. **2.** used ironically to denote that one is not excited. *I've got to mow the lawn today – yee-haa.*

yello a humorous variant of the word 'hello', commonly used when answering the phone.

yellow **1.** cowardly. Originally US slang from the 1850s. **2.** a racist designation for people of Asian background. **3.** a racist designation for people of mixed Aboriginal and white blood.

yellow can a can of Castlemaine XXXX beer. As opposed to a **blue**, **green**, **red** or **white can** (see entries).

yellow Monday a type of yellow cicada.

yellow sticker a yellow defect notice stuck to a car window. In Victoria it is also called a **canary**.

yellow velvet **1.** women of Asian background viewed as sex objects. **2.** sexual relations with a woman of Asian background.

yike a brawl or argument. Aussie slang since the 1940s. Origin unknown.

yips **1.** nervousness which causes a golfer to miss an easy putt. *She's got a bad case of the yips.* **2.** a similar complaint affecting any person playing a sport.

yip stick in golf, a broomstick putter.

YMCA dinner a meal made from leftovers. Standing for *Yesterday's Muck Cooked Again.*

yo **1.** an exclamation used to call someone's attention. **2.** an expression of agreement; also used to indicate presence at a roll call. Very American in flavour, but used humorously in Oz. **3.** an exclamation used to show approval or pleasure. Adopted by Australian adolescents in the 1980s from US usage.

yobbo a hooligan or lout. *I was hassled by a bunch of drunken yobbos on their way home from the football.* Also, an unrefined or uncultured person. *I gotta change out of me stubbies, I don't wanna look like a yobbo.* Originally British slang of the 1920s, and in origin an extension of **yob**, which is also used here. Yob itself was originally backslang for *boy*, and in 19th century English referred to a young male.

yobby befitting a yobbo. *I'm sick of his yobby behaviour.* Also in the form **yobbish**.

yodel to vomit. Aussie slang since the 1960s.

yoe a ewe. A British dialect variant of the Standard English word. No longer current except in the well-known song lyrics 'The ringer looks around and he's beaten by a blow / And he curses the old snagger with the bare-bellied yoe'. What all this means is that the fastest shearer in the shed (the ringer), was beaten by the slowest shearer (the snagger) whose ewe (yoe) is bare-bellied, that is, has already lost its belly wool and so is quicker to shear. This song was first published in 1946, having been collected from one Mrs Sloane of Lithgow, NSW, who was 60 at the time, and who had learnt all of her songs from her mother in the early part of the 20th century. Also spelt **yeo**.

Yogie a derogatory term for a resident of Canberra. So called because ACT number plates begin with the letter Y. Especially common on the NSW south coast.

yonks ages; a long time. *We haven't seen them for absolutely yonks.* Originally British slang of the 1960s. Common in Australia since the 1980s. Origin unknown.

yonnie a stone or pebble. A stone suitable for throwing. Known quite widely, but especially common in Victoria. There are a number of similar words from all over the country for this same item, all of which probably come from Aboriginal languages and seem phonetically related to one another. In Victoria there is also the **brinnie**, Queensland has the **gonnie**, SA has the **ronnie**. Along the east coast of the mainland you also can find the **connie**. In WA there is the **boondie**, which, however, can also be used to mean a large rock, or a type of sand bomb used by kids to throw at one another, and the **coondie**. There are two other words for a throwing stone, both of which are found all over the country: **goolie**, which is probably related to the previous words, and **gibber**, the only one for which a definite origin is known. It is from Dharug, the extinct Aboriginal language of the Sydney region.

you beaut! a cry of joyful praise. Aussie slang since the 1940s. Also common in the form **you little beaut!** or **you little beauty!**

you get that Life's like that. A catchphrase of doleful resignation. *The toilet's blocked again! Oh well, you get that.*

you'll do a great Aussie compliment. *He had muscles on his muscles and thighs like tree trunks. I looked at him and said 'You'll do'.*

young'un a young person; a youngster.

your blood is worth bottling you are a fantastic person; you're a legend.

youse 1. a common Aussie plural form of the second person pronoun 'you'. *Where are youse two going?* Sometimes spelt **yous**, and also **yers** or **yas**. First recorded back in the 1890s, this is a borrowing from Irish English, where it is usually spelt *yez*. It is interesting to note that Irish Gaelic did have a separate plural for the form of the second person pronoun, and thus it is only sensible that they created one in their own variety of English. **2.** also used as a singular form of 'you'. *I ain't afraid of youse.* This seems to appear in the 1910s.

you wish! an expression denoting that someone has unrealistic expectations or ideas. *Beat me in a race? Yeah right, you wish!*

you wouldn't read about it! What bad luck!

yow 1. a cry of pain. **2.** used as a warning cry that the police are coming. Hence, to **keep yow** is to act as a lookout. Compare **nit**.

yowie a mythical Aboriginal beast, something akin to the sasquatch or yeti. The word comes from the Aboriginal language Yuwaalarraay, from up Lightning Ridge way. Not to be confused with the **bunyip**.

yucko disgusting, unpleasant, repulsive. The opposite of **yummo**.

yummo 1. having a very nice taste. **2.** beautiful; gorgeous.

yummy mummy a delectably beautiful young mother.

yum, yum, pig's bum a gleeful exclamation used of delicious food.

yuppie a young urban professional person, typified as having a high disposable income to spend on luxury consumer goods and generally being a self-important prat. A 1980s acronym from *Young Urban Professional* or *Young Upwardly-mobile Professional.* Originally British, but quickly spreading throughout the English-speaking world. Also shortened to **yup**.

zack a former slang term for a sixpence. When decimal currency came in, this term was transferred to a five cent piece. You don't hear it much these days, except in the phrase **to not have a zack**, to be penniless. First recorded back in the 1890s, and possibly derived from Scottish *saxpence* 'sixpence'.

zambuck a St John Ambulance officer. Old slang dating back to the 1910s. So called after the proprietary name of an antiseptic ointment they commonly used.

zap **1.** to cook in a microwave oven. **2.** to change TV stations with a remote control.

zapper a remote control for a video, television, or the like.

Z-car a federal government vehicle. Because they had number plates which began with the letter 'Z'.

zebbie among birdos, a zebra finch.

zhuzh to plump or fluff up; to primp; to invest with flair and pizazz. A recent arrival via the TV show *Queer Eye for the Straight Guy*. There has been much debate about just how to spell this cute little neologism. Apart from **zhuzh** the most common spelling is **tjuzs** – which has the unfortunate problem of using different consonant groups (*tj* and then *zs*) to spell the same sound. Some people have claimed this is the 'official' spelling, but since the term has passed into general slang, it is now up to common usage to decide on the best spelling – and so only time will tell.

ziff a beard. A classic Aussie slang word that has sadly died out now. First recorded back in 1917. Origin unknown.

zilch nothing. Originally 1960s US slang. Origin unknown.

zillion an unimaginably large amount. A person with a zillion dollars is, of course, a **zillionaire**. Similar sums are **gillion**, **jillion**, **squillion** and **squintillion**.

zip nothing; zero. *I scored zip.* Also in the extended form **zippo**. Recently it has become commonly used in the phrase **zip, zero, nada**, in other words, nothing at all.

zit a pimple. Originally US slang of the 1960s. Perhaps imitative of the eruption of pus caused by squeezing a pimple.

zizz a nap or sleep. From the cartoonist's *zzz*, representing of the sound of snoring. See **stack up zeds**.

zombie **1.** a dull, brainless person. **2.** marijuana.

zoned out spaced out, as from taking drugs.

zonked **1.** exhausted. **2.** really drunk or stoned. Also in the form **zonked-out**.

zonkerpede any unknown creepy-crawlie insect.

zonks a long, long time. An alternative to the more usual **yonks**. *I haven't visited him for zonks.*

zooter in cricket, a deceptive type of wrist-spin delivery, a variation of a leg-break bowl similar to a flipper. Also spelt **zoota**.

zot a pimple. An Aussie variant of the (originally) US **zit**.